Self-Concept, Motivation, and Identity

Underpinning Success With Research and Practice

A volume in
International Advances in Self Research
Herbert W. Marsh, Rhonda G. Craven, Dennis M McInerney, *Series Editors*

Self-Concept, Motivation, and Identity

Underpinning Success With Research and Practice

edited by

Frédéric Guay
Université Laval

Herbert Marsh
Australian Catholic University

Dennis M. McInerney
The Hong Kong Institute of Education

Rhonda G. Craven
Australian Catholic University

IAP
INFORMATION AGE PUBLISHING, INC.
Charlotte, NC • www.infoagepub.com

Library of Congress Cataloging-in-Publication Data

A CIP record for this book is available from the Library of Congress
http://www.loc.gov

ISBN: 978-1-68123-167-9 (Paperback)
978-1-68123-168-6 (Hardcover)
978-1-68123-169-3 (ebook)

Printed in the United States of America

CONTENTS

PREFACE

In many life situations our SELF helps us to act. From achieving a complex course of actions to doing homework, from moral judgments to choosing a career, we consistently solicit our SELF. Although the SELF is sometimes helpful in guiding these behaviors, at other times it could put us in difficult situations leading to irrational thinking and decision making. The concept of the SELF has a long history that dates back from the ancient Greeks to more contemporary thinkers. Research on the SELF relates to a range of phenomena including self-esteem, self-concept, self-protection, self-verification, self-awareness, identity, self-efficacy, self-determination etc. that could be sharply different or very similar. Despite this long tradition of thinkers and the numerous studies conducted on the SELF, this concept still needs a definition because it is not a singular construct, but rather a collection of related constructs. In the philosophical literature, the legitimacy of the concept of "SELF" has been brought into question. Some authors have argued that the self is not a psychological entity per se, but rather an illusion created by the complex interplay between cognitive and neurological subsystems. Although no definitive consensus has been reached regarding the SELF, we emphasize in this volume that aspects of the SELF including self-concept, motivation, and identity are crucial for understanding and driving human behavior.

Self-concept, motivation and identity: Underpinning success with research and practice provides a unique insight into self-concept and its relations to motivation and identity from varied theoretical and empirical perspectives. This volume is the fifth of a monograph series entitled "*International advances in self research*" that Herbert W. Marsh, Dennis M. McInerney, and Rhonda

Self-Concept, Motivation, and Identity, pages vii–viii

G. Craven started in 2000. In each edition, we have noted how this field of research is in a state of flux with numerous theoretical, methodological, and practical innovations. The aim of this fifth volume is therefore to propose both theoretical and methodological ideas and to present empirical evidence demonstrating the importance of SELF theory and research to guide effective practice. The scope of the volume is thus broad, and includes chapters covering different life contexts (interpersonal relationships, politics, education, vocational interests and choices, and health) and developmental periods (childhood, adolescence, adulthood). This volume will take the reader on a groundbreaking tour of various SELF components and explain why these components are important for behavioral health changes, academic achievement and learning, positive self-beliefs, moral convictions of politicians, identity development, career choices, relational difficulties, and self-regulated learning.

—Frédéric Guay
Herbert W. Marsh
Dennis McInerney
Rhonda G. Craven

CHAPTER 1

INTENTIONAL-SELF REGULATION AND IDENTITY PROCESSES IN ADOLESCENCE

Perspectives on Research and Application

Sara K. Johnson
Tufts University

Richard M. Lerner
Tufts University

I'm eighteen and I don't know what I want
Eighteen I just don't know what I want
Eighteen I gotta get away
I gotta get out of this place
I'll go runnin' in outer space oh yeah

I got a baby's brain and an old man's heart took eighteen years to get this far
Don't always know what I'm talkin' about feels like I'm livin' in the middle of doubt

—*I'm Eighteen*, Alice Cooper (Cooper et al., 1970)

Self-Concept, Motivation, and Identity, pages 1–27

Adolescence is a period of major change in both the individual and his/her social context. Indeed, adolescence may be the major period of change in the life span; in this regard, it may surpass even infancy, in that adolescents (individuals in the second decade of life; Lerner & Steinberg, 2009) have the cognitive and behavioral skills to contribute intentionally to the course of their physical, psychological, and social changes (Lerner, Freund, DeStefanis, & Habermas, 2001). Therefore, in the context of determining for himself or herself what the changes he/she is experiencing means for who he/she is (in other words, engaging in the self-definitional processes integral to identity development; Côté, 2009)—the adolescent can use self-determined goals (aims, aspirations, hopes, or purposes) to navigate through these changes, and he or she can therefore be an active agent in his/her own development (Lerner, 1982; Lerner & Busch-Rossnagel, 1981; Lerner et al., 2001; Lerner & Walls, 1999).

As depicted in the above epigram from the song by Alice Cooper (1970), this navigation, although fraught with uncertainty, involves two fundamental sets of processes integral to the development of self—intentional self-regulation and identity. The purpose of this chapter is to discuss the linkage in adolescence between these two sets of processes and to present a conception of their connection that may be used to advance research and to frame applications aimed at promoting positive development among youth.

The links between identity and self-regulatory processes may be the fundamental theoretical and practical issues in the study of adolescent development. Lerner et al. (2001) have noted that identity development is "arguably the central construct of adolescence" (p. 33; see also Côté, 2009) and that, as well, the "regulation by individuals of their relations with their complex and changing context is the key problem for successful development" (p. 30) in adolescence and, in addition, across life (Baltes, Lindenberger, & Staudinger, 2006; Brandtstädter, 1998; Gestsdóttir & Lerner, 2007, 2008). Given the theoretical salience of self-regulatory processes in positive development in general, and in successful identity development in particular, it is useful to describe the nature of these agentic processes, and we do so in the following section.

ON THE NATURE AND ROLE OF INDIVIDUAL AGENCY

When I was younger, so much younger than today
I never needed anybody's help in any way
But now these days are gone I'm not so self-assured
Now I find I've changed my life and opened up the doors

Help me if you can, I'm feeling down
And I do appreciate you being 'round
Help me get my feet back on the ground
Won't you please, please help me?

—*Help*, The Beatles (Lennon & McCartney, 1965)

Perhaps paradoxically, individual agency involves bidirectional relations with the ecology of human development; this ecology may be either the cultural/institutional world, the physical environment, or, as illustrated by the Beatles' song noted above, other people. The fundamental process of life involves mutually influential relations between the developing person and his or her context. These relations enable the person to survive across his or her life, and they also support and maintain the context, which itself enables the individual's survival and development (Brandtstädter, 1998, 1999, 2006; Darwin, 1859, 1872; Gould, 1977; Johanson & Edey, 1981). These processes involve the individual person (including his or her genetic and epigenetic processes and behavioral propensities) and the social, physical, ecological, and cultural facets of the context (Jablonka & Lamb, 2005). Brandtstädter (1998) noted that these bidirectional processes govern, or "regulate," the course of both individual and contextual change, and accordingly, he termed these relations "developmental regulations" (represented using double-headed arrows: individual ←→ context relations). When these relations benefit both the individual and the context, Brandtstädter (1998) termed them *adaptive developmental regulations*.

Developmental regulations are systemically integrated links between individuals and settings (Overton, 2013, in press; Overton & Müller, 2013; Tobach & Greenberg, 1984); in other words, in theory the components of the regulations cannot be separate from each other. For discussion purposes, however, it is useful to recognize that these regulations have both individual and contextual components. For instance, among humans, ecological processes of familial care, education, and socialization support the individual and at the same time instill in him or her an orientation to support the institutions of society (e.g., Jablonka & Lamb, 2005; Johanson & Edey, 1981; Lewontin, 2000). In turn, within the individual, processes of self-regulation enable the person to contribute to individual ←→ context relations (Gestsdóttir & Lerner, 2008; Lerner et al., 2001); these processes may be organismic or intentional. Organismic processes of self-regulation may involve hypothalamic functioning, circadian rhythms, or in some cases, features of temperament (e.g., thresholds of responsivity, intensity of reactions, or latency to adjustment to new stimulation; Chess & Thomas, 1999; Thomas, Chess, Birch, Hertzig, & Korn, 1963). Intentional self-regulation processes involve agentic actions. These actions can include the individual acting directly on the context as well as the individual responding to actions of the context; however, even these responses are moderated by the purposes or goals of the individual (Brandtstädter, 1998, 1999, 2006; Geldhof, Little, & Colombo, 2010; Gestsdottir & Lerner, 2008; McClelland et al., in press, 2010), a point to which we return later in this chapter. Thus, self-regulation is an agentic process.

There are several models of intentional self-regulation processes that have been used to understand the role of individual purposes or goals across the life span (e.g., Baltes & Baltes, 1990; Baltes et al., 2006; Brandtstädter, 1998, 1999, 2006; Freud & Baltes, 2002; Freund, Li, & Baltes, 1999; Heckhausen, 1999; Heckhausen, Wrosch, & Schulz, 2010; McClelland et al., in press). All of these models seek to understand the integration of actions of the individual and the actions of the context within adaptive individual ←→ context relations. Research associated with these models has sought to describe, explain, and, in the service of promoting mutually beneficial exchanges between people and their settings, optimize the cognitive, emotional, and behavioral facets of the individual (e.g., his or her purposes, sense of agency, attentional skills, or executive functions; McClelland et al., 2010; Müller & Kerns, in press; Sokol, Hammond, Kuebli, & Sweetman, in press).

Most research in this area has used age-specific models and methods to study intentional self-regulation within childhood, adolescence, or the adult years (for a review, see McClelland et al., in press). Some models of intentional self-regulation, however, are intended to be useful across the life span. One instance of such a life-span conception is the model of Selection, Optimization, and Compensation presented by Baltes, Freund, and colleagues (e.g., Baltes et al., 2006; Freund & Baltes, 2002). Although the Selection (S), Optimization (O), and Compensation (C; SOC) model was primarily used by its originators to study adult development (among primarily German samples), in recent years the model has been used increasingly to assess intentional self-regulation among individuals from middle/late childhood through adolescence and young adulthood (Lerner, Lerner, Bowers, & Geldhof, in press). In the following section, we describe this model in more detail.

THE SELECTION, OPTIMIZATION, AND COMPENSATION MODEL OF INTENTIONAL SELF-REGULATION

Dream on, dream on, dream on.
Dream until your dream comes true.

—*Dream On*, Aerosmith (Tyler, 1973)

Self-regulation is a cognitive, behavioral, and emotional skill that enables individuals to select and execute behaviors that are in pursuit of a particular goal (Brandtstädter, 1998). In other words, intentional self-regulation depicts how people make choices, plan actions that are appropriate to reach their goals, and regulate the execution of their actions; this conception of self-regulation makes it a central process of human functioning (Bandura, 2001; Brandtstädter, 1998; Demetriou, 2000; Lerner et al., 2001; McClelland et al., 2010). Conceptualizing self-regulation in this way also implicates a person's sense of self—his or her self-definition or identity—as the organizing attribute of the individual. This organizing attribute guides the person in making the selections, or setting the goals, from which subsequent actions pertinent to intentional self-regulation derive. Examples of these pertinent subsequent actions include taking steps to optimize one's chances to attain one's goals or acting to compensate when one's means for attaining a goal are blocked or when one fails.

The SOC model (Baltes, 1997; Baltes & Baltes, 1990; Freund & Baltes, 2002) is an action-theoretical approach to self-regulation. Action theories, such as SOC, are based on the assumption that human behavior is goal-directed. The SOC approach emphasizes four self-regulatory processes: elective selection, optimization, compensation, and loss-based selection. *Elective selection* (ES) refers to an individual's ability to commit to a set of meaningful goals and entails organizing selected goals into a hierarchy that accounts for personal and environmental needs (Freund & Baltes, 2002).

Once an individual selects a goal, or a hierarchy of goals, he or she must next follow through with actually achieving the goal(s). In the terminology of the SOC model, self-regulated actions that move an individual closer to attaining his or her selected goal(s) are called *optimization*. Optimization includes the acquisition and development of the means, resources, skills, and cognitive abilities (such as attentional focus and inhibitory control) (Freund & Baltes, 2002) that enhance the probability of attaining one's goals. Optimization applies to an individual's initial attempt to reach a goal, but researchers using the SOC model note that individuals must also adaptively navigate setbacks, losses, and failures by implementing alternative means to reach a goal. In the SOC model, these latter processes are termed *compensation* (Freund & Baltes, 2002).

The final component specified in the SOC model, *loss-based selection* (LBS), lies at the intersection of Selection and Compensation. Baltes and colleagues define LBS as a form of selection, but differentiate LBS from ES by specifying LBS as pertaining to events in which an individual responds to an obstacle (Freund & Baltes, 2002). LBS might entail selecting new goals, reconsidering the importance of previously selected goals, rearranging one's goal hierarchy, or replacing one goal by dedicating additional energy toward another goal (i.e., an act of deselection).

Some researchers have questioned whether LBS is relevant to self-regulation during normative adolescent development (e.g., Gestsdóttir & Lerner, 2007), given that LBS was originally conceived of as a construct pertinent to self regulation in the face of age-related losses in functioning. Other researchers, however (e.g., Gestsdóttir, Bowers, von Eye, Napolitano, & Lerner, 2010), have noted that, although adolescents do not typically face aging-related declines, they nonetheless may find their goals blocked or unattainable for a variety of other reasons. We agree with this second set of researchers and maintain that LBS is a necessary part of any discussion of the relation between the SOC model of intentional self-regulation and identity development during adolescence.

SOC AND IDENTITY DEVELOPMENT IN ADOLESCENCE

In a soldier's stance, I aimed my hand
At the mongrel dogs who teach
Fearing not that I'd become my enemy
In the instant that I preach
My existence led by confusion boats
Mutiny from stern to bow
Ah, but I was so much older then
I'm younger than that now

—*My Back Pages,* Bob Dylan (Dylan, 1964)

The application of the SOC model to adolescence is based on the idea that the second decade of life is a natural laboratory for studying self-regulation processes due to the fundamental changes in self-definition that are happening during this period and the fact that these changes are intimately linked to the identity processes prototypic of the period (Côté, 2009; Lerner et al., 2001). Moreover, and as illustrated by the opening epigram from the song by Alice Cooper (1970), there are multiple dimensions of change involved in adolescence, involving physical and physiological functioning (Susman & Dorn, 2009, 2013), emotional changes (e.g., Compas & Reeslund, 2009; McElhaney, Allen, Stephenson, & Hare, 2009), and cognitive changes (Kuhn, 2009), all of which are involved in the identity processes occurring during this time (Côté, 2009). The confluence of these developments enable researchers to assess the impact of changes in the person's actual and self-defined self on the adaptive developmental regulations integral to healthy, positive development in adolescence and in subsequent portions of the life span. In essence, then, the SOC model assesses (a) the individual's selection of goals, which are based on his/her self-defined goal hierarchy; (b) the attempts the individual makes to optimize his/her chances of attaining his/her preferred goals, based on the means he/she finds acceptable or available, given his/her sense of self and contextual environment; and (c) how the person acts to compensate when strategies for or actions aimed at optimization are not successful, again based on his/her view of available alternatives that are deemed acceptable.

Accordingly, individuals' enactment of the processes involved in the SOC model (as well as other models of intentional self-regulation) depends on them having a sense of self that frames the goals one selects, the evaluation of what optimization means are appropriate for one's self, and what compensatory actions and/or loss-based selections are similarly consonant with one's sense of self. Hence, self-regulatory processes and identity processes of self-definition are intimately interconnected in adolescence (Lerner et al., 2001). In fact, and as in the above-noted epigram from Bob Dylan (1964), the interrelation of these two processes is clear when one considers the problems of successful self-regulation that exist among youth who are confused about their self-definition (e.g., Côté, 2009; Marcia, 1980).

Indeed, focusing on bidirectional relations between individuals and their contexts leads to the conclusion that "it is through transaction with their social and cultural environment that individuals form personal conceptions of possible and desired developmental courses, as well as acquire the knowledge and means to implement them" (Brandtstädter & Lerner, 1999, p. xvi). In other words, bidirectional relations between individuals and contexts form the basis for identity-development processes. This theoretical proposition has been widely accepted among identity-development researchers for a long time (see, for example, Josselson, 1994), but the process of practically implementing this idea within research designs has been considerably slower (Bosma & Kunnen, 2008). Nevertheless, it is important to understand the centrality of individual ←→ context relations in attempting to depict the links between intentional self-regulation and identity development.

CONCEPTUALIZING IDENTITY DEVELOPMENT WITHIN THE FRAME OF INDIVIDUAL ←→ CONTEXT RELATIONS

Who is that girl I see staring straight back at me?
Why is my reflection someone I don't know?

Somehow I cannot hide who I am, though I've tried.
When will my reflection show who I am inside?

—*Reflection*, Christina Aguilera (Palmer, Fukai, & Singleton, 1998)

We conceptualize identity as "the sameness and continuity of the person's psychological functioning, interpersonal behavior, and commitments to roles, values, and beliefs" (Côté, 2009, p. 267); put another way, the idea of identity refers to "a cognitive structure that incorporates all of a person's answers to the question, 'who am I?'" (Gollwitzer, Bayer, Scherer, & Seifert,

1999, p. 283). Social psychological scholars classify answers, or components of identity, into (a) physical attributes (e.g., "I am tall"); (b) social categories, either chosen (e.g., "I am a husband") or ascribed (e.g., "I am African American); and (c) dispositions, skills, values, aptitudes, and/or interests (e.g., "I am kind" or "I am an athlete"). Developmental scientists often use the domains of ego, personal, and social identity (Schwartz & Pantin, 2006).

In terms of studying how identity *develops*, considerable work has focused on the concepts of exploration and commitment. Original work in this area, such as the identity status model (e.g., Marcia, 1980), viewed exploration as the process through which individuals sorted through identity-relevant options, and commitment as the endpoint of that process. In other words, exploration was thought to end once commitments were made, and commitments were viewed as stable and relatively unchanging. These ideas were exemplified through the identity-achievement status, which individuals were classified into if they reported having made commitments after a period of exploration. More recently, however, researchers have recognized that commitment itself also represents an ongoing process (e.g., Gollwitzer et al., 1999; Luyckx, Goossens, Soenens, & Beyers, 2006); identity choices must be accompanied by implementation efforts, and even once identity elements have been attained (e.g., becoming a physician), they require ongoing work to maintain. Furthermore, because identity represents the intersection between self and society (Bosma & Kunnen, 2001; Josselson, 1994), changes in either the individual (e.g., an adolescent experiencing an injury that prohibits athletic participation) or his or her environment (e.g., an adolescent's parents deciding to move across the country) may lead to the reevaluation or consideration of commitments.

Luyckx and colleagues (Luyckx et al., 2006; Luyckx et al., 2008) have developed a model of identity development that incorporates this explicit focus on both exploration and commitment as processes. They have proposed "unpacking" exploration and commitment into four elements (Luyckx et al., 2006): Exploration in Breadth, Exploration in Depth, Commitment Making, and Identification with Commitment. They conceptualize these elements as forming a process of identity development as follows. During Exploration in Breadth, which corresponds to Marcia's (1980) definition of exploration, individuals survey potential identity elements. This exploration may lead to making commitments to certain identity aspects, which corresponds to Marcia's (1980) definition of commitment. After making commitments, individuals explore them in depth (i.e., found out more about them or try them out) to decide whether the initial commitment is appropriate. This process may lead individuals to identify with their commitments (e.g., believe strongly that they are appropriate) or return to exploration in breadth if the commitment is deemed unsuitable. Luyckx et al. (2008) have added a ruminative component to exploration; individuals who score highly on this dimension are "stuck" in continued contemplation of identity issues and are unable to eventually make commitments, perhaps because they are overwhelmed by the choices (Schwartz, Côté, & Arnett, 2005) or lack the self-regulatory skills to successfully enact processes of identity development.

During the adolescent period, the increasing prominence of identity processes and young people's developing self-regulation skills may intersect in potentially important ways. Identity-related goals may provide rich motives for using ISR skills; these skills, in turn, may promote adolescents' successful navigation of identity-related challenges. As such, we believe that connecting the ISR and identity development literatures is productive, because SOC processes of individual ←→ context relations extend "the study of identity by depicting the changing relations youth have with their contexts as they act to define themselves during this period" (Lerner et al., 2001, p. 34). How, then, may SOC and identity-related processes interrelate? We address this question in the following section. We organize our discussion using the SOC components for the sake of presentation, but we note that, consistent with the RDS-based model framing our approach to youth development, identity development and SOC processes are systemically fused or integrated.

Selection

One way or another I'm gonna find ya,
I'm gonna getcha getcha getcha getcha.

—*One Way or Another*, Blondie (Harry & Harrison, 1978)

As described above, within the SOC model (e.g., Freund & Baltes, 2002), selection refers to how people develop, elaborate, structure, and commit themselves to goals. Selection is divided into two components: Elective selection (ES) and loss-based selection (LBS). These two aspects of selection are of course related within the SOC model. However, they may operate at different points in the SOC process, and we discuss them separately to illustrate how they each may relate to identity development.

Elective Selection

Could I have been a parking lot attendant?
Could I have been a millionaire in Bel Air?
Could I have been lost somewhere in Paris?
Could I have been your little brother?
Could I have been anyone other than me?
Could I have been anyone?

—*Dancing Nancies*, Dave Matthews Band (Matthews, 1994)

Elective selection refers to how people choose goals from among a variety of alternatives. As people choose goals, they must also integrate these goals into a hierarchically ordered system (i.e., some goals must necessarily be given higher priority than others). This focus on choosing goals gives a clear connection to identity development. Many goals are, directly or indirectly, identity related (e.g., Gollwitzer et al., 1999); for example, identity-relevant goals may include what type of person the adolescent wants to become (particular characteristics such as being caring or friendly) as well as roles and identifications that the adolescent wants to acquire (e.g., career aspirations). Indeed, adolescents' identity-related goals are often the topic of conversation; adults frequently ask adolescents about their life and career goals.

When choosing the number and nature of goals to pursue, adolescents must balance their desires or interests with their assessment of whether they and their context have the resources to attain these goals. In the SOC model, potential challenges of this balance include either under- or overselection of goals. Underselection, in this context, refers to having too many goals, or not engaging in enough "selection," whereas overselection refers to having too few goals, or "selecting" too much. In the SOC model, both over- and underselection are viewed as potentially problematic (Baltes & Baltes, 1990; Baltes et al., 2006; Freund & Baltes, 2002). Overselection (i.e., too few goals) may be an indication of an unwillingness (or inability) to engage in exploration and entertain possibilities for one's life. In contrast, underselection (i.e., too many goals), especially if it is sustained over a long period of time, may represent an unwillingness to make commitments to specific goals.

The relation between ES and identity development, however, may be more complex during adolescence. Using data from the 4-H Study of Positive Youth Development, Napolitano Bowers, Gestdóttir, Depping et al. (2011) showed that consistently low levels of ES (e.g., underselection or having many goals) were related to consistently high levels of positive youth development. The authors suggest that not engaging in too much selection during this time can be beneficial because it is developmentally appropriate for adolescents to be entertaining many (potentially identity-related) goals. However, Napolitano Bowers, Gestdóttir, Depping et al. also found that consistently high levels of ES—focusing exclusively on just a few goals—were also associated with consistently high levels of positive youth development. This pattern of results suggests that the same ES strategy may not work equally well for all adolescents, especially depending on the extent of exploration that is taking place and the context in which the adolescent is situated.

At the beginning of a phase of exploration, entertaining many goals may be entirely appropriate. For example, adolescents may hold several goals about the same domain at the same time, such as considering multiple college or career options, as illustrated by the above-noted epigram by the

Dave Matthews Band (1994). As the exploration phase proceeds, however, it is expected that adolescents will begin to whittle down their list of goals and focus on the most desirable and attainable ones (e.g., choosing a college to attend or a career option to pursue, at least for the time being). An extended period of underselection may, at some point, transition from a beneficial moratorium to a state of rumination (Luyckx, Schwartz, Goossens, Beyers, & Missotten, 2011), from which it may be difficult to recover. It may also be the case that the amount of selection that is adaptive may depend on the number and nature of resources in the adolescents' environment. For adolescents in low-resource environments, overselection (i.e., having very few goals) may enable them to marshal resources most effectively (in the service of only a few goals). Certain contexts, or individuals, may not contain enough resources to enable productive work toward a large number of goals.

Finally, we believe that exploration can, in and of itself, constitute a goal to be selected. For example, adolescents may set as a goal for themselves to "figure out what career I want to have" or something similar. This type of goal is not typically how the SOC model is used. That is, goals are usually thought of as being based on decisions having already been made rather than as having the decision-making process itself (or the resolution of it) be the goal that is selected. However, in the adolescent portion of ontogeny, it may be uniquely important to explore one's options. The potential importance of exploration itself as a goal will be addressed again in a later section, when we describe the prominence of the skills that adolescents use to work toward their goals (i.e., optimization and compensation).

Loss-Based Selection

> *And if you can't be with the one you love, honey, love the one you're with.*
>
> —*Love the One You're With,* Stephen Stills (Stills, 1970)

In contrast to ES, which refers to goals that are aimed at desired states and indicate growth, LBS refers to how individuals react to a decline in resources (e.g., means to attain a goal; Freund & Baltes, 2002). Effective LBS strategies may include reconstructing the nature of a goal to increase the chance of attaining it, or selecting a different goal. The difference between selection of goals in LBS, as compared to ES, is that goals in LBS are chosen based on original goals being blocked or unattainable, whereas ES goals are chosen based on their inherent desirability.

As the SOC model originated in the study of adult development and aging, LBS was originally used to describe how individuals dealt with age-related declines in functioning, but, as we noted above, it is nonetheless an important component of adolescents' intentional self-regulation skills. Many goals that adolescents have (either in the short or long term) may be blocked, or adolescents may fail repeatedly to attain them. LBS skills may also be particularly relevant for youth from low-resource backgrounds, as these youth may be more likely to experience contextual barriers to their goals.

Optimization

Tomorrow's getting harder make no mistake.
Luck ain't even lucky, got to make your own breaks.

—*It's My Life*, Bon Jovi (Bon Jovi, Sambora, & Martin, 2000)

In the SOC model, optimization involves choosing, and using, strategies and resources that help individuals pursue the goals they have selected. Commonly noted optimization processes focus on qualities such as diligence, grit, and perseverance, and these attributes are certainly important optimization avenues. However, optimization skills are broader and can include marshaling support and resources from others to attain goals.

We believe that optimization abilities connect with the identity-development process because these skills can be used in the service of attaining (and maintaining) identity-related goals. As we noted above, these goals can also explicitly include ones related to processes of exploration themselves. Accordingly, we propose that optimization skills may be a key factor in productive identity development; in particular, these skills may be very important as adolescents engage in the process of exploration. For example, adolescents may be in the process of deciding on a career goal or choosing which type or kind of career may be best for them. As they are making this selection, they may have several ideas in mind for what kind of career they want. Effective optimization skills, used in the service of this exploration, can enable adolescents to find opportunities and gather information about these possibilities. Adolescents without effective optimization skills, however, may entertain these career options without any way of effectively exploring them. This unproductive exploration may lead to adolescents being "stuck" in a ruminative state (Luyckx et al., 2011).

The presence of effective optimization skills may, in part, explain the positive and negative relations that contemporary identity research has found with exploration. In a positive way, exploration is associated with curiosity and openness to experience (e.g., Luyckx et al., 2006), but from the negative perspective, it is also associated with depressive symptoms and lowered self-esteem (e.g., Schwartz, Zamboanga, Weisskirch, & Rodriguez, 2009). As Luyckx et al. (2008) note, "the extent to which exploration is associated with self-discovery or with distress likely depends partially on the quality and coherence of the exploration process itself" (p. 86). This potential connection further suggests that improving intentional self-regulation skills could reduce the distress that is associated with identity exploration for some adolescents and young adults. We return to this idea in the subsequent section on applications.

Optimization skills remain relevant even after commitments have been made. As suggested by the Luyckx et al. (2008) model, and echoed by other researchers (e.g., Gollwitzer et al., 1999), making commitments does not, for most individuals, end the identity-development process. Individuals must engage with their newly chosen commitments and decide whether the commitments are a "good fit." Given the information gleaned during this process, termed *exploration in depth* in the Luyckx et al. (2008) model, or from other life changes (e.g., a decrease in family economic resources), adolescents may reevaluate their commitments in the light of new information. Indeed, some research has shown that this process of reconsideration of commitment happens, to at least a small extent, on a day-to-day basis (Klimstra et al., 2010).

To add complexity to the challenge of optimization, the strategies and resources that adolescents choose to use must also themselves be compatible with personal and social goals and values. In other words, there may be multiple ways to attain a particular goal, but using optimization skills means that the adolescent chooses to use strategies and acquire resources that align with his or her personal values (also an identity component) as well as the values of important others (e.g., parents). Accordingly, we believe that learning and developing effective optimization strategies may also represent an instantiation of identity work for adolescents, as adolescents may explore or try different optimization strategies in order to find the ones that work best for them and are consistent with other aspects of their identity. In other words, adolescents must learn about themselves, their goals, and skills and abilities in order to figure out the best way to work toward particular goals. Of course, such understanding on the part of an adolescent may create potential conflicts for him or her. For instance, a choice one makes about how to attain a particular goal (such as becoming popular or becoming a varsity athlete) may conflict with other facets of identity he or she may hold (such as not using drugs or focusing on one's academic achievements).

Compensation

You can't always get what you want,
But if you try sometimes,
Well you might find,
You get what you need.

—*You Can't Always Get What You Want,*
Rolling Stones (Jagger & Richards, 1969)

Compensation is closely tied to, but distinct from, LBS (as described above). Within the SOC model, compensation refers to actions aimed at counteracting or avoiding losses in the face of a loss of goal-relevant means. In other words, compensation represents the strategies that people devise when they encounter obstacles to attaining (and maintaining) their goals. Faced with such difficulties, individuals may choose another goal (i.e., give up); this strategy would be classified as LBS. In contrast, individuals may retain the same goal but adjust the strategies they are using, and that strategy is termed *compensation.* Both compensation and LBS can be effective and healthy strategies (e.g., Gestdóttir et al., 2010), but may be appropriate in different situations. Individuals with strong intentional self-regulation skills have the ability to appraise the situation and judge the appropriate course of action.

Compensation skills also show a clear connection to identity development; as anyone who has been an adolescent (i.e., everyone) may recall, not every identity-related goal that adolescents choose will work out in the way that they want. Compensation skills may also come into play when adolescents are engaging in exploration in depth (i.e., finding out about a particular goal that they have chosen); it is likely that adolescents may determine, through the process of exploration in depth, that some commitments they have chosen are no longer appropriate, for a variety of reasons. Although these types of setbacks are extremely common within the normative process of adolescent identity development (e.g., Compas & Reesland, 2009), very little research from the identity development perspective has focused on what happens when adolescents' identity-related goals and processes do not go the way that they intended. We believe that high levels of compensation skills can help adolescents navigate these challenges effectively and may also reduce the distress associated with identity work (which may, at least in part, be related to difficulties that adolescents encounter along the way of working toward identity-related goals).

Summary

In sum, there may be numerous and nuanced links between the individual ←→ context-relational processes involved in intentional self-regulation, as operationalized in the present discussion by reference to the SOC model, and the set of individual ←→ context relations involved in identity development. The ideas we have presented about these interrelations remain in large part conceptions that require new research. Indeed, we have noted that the study of individual ←→ context relations have not been a prominent feature of research on adolescent identity development, despite repeated calls for such study (e.g., Bosma & Kunne, 2008). As such, there are few datasets that enable some of the specific research ideas that we have suggested as particular fruitful areas for assessment (e.g., regarding links between, for instance, LBS or compensation and identity development in adolescence) to even be illustrated.

However, we have been able to draw some examples of the potential usefulness of exploring links between intentional self-regulation and identity development by reference to research conducted as part of the 4-H Study of Positive Youth Development (e.g., Napolitano, Bowers, Gestdóttir, Depping et al., 2011; and see Bowers, Wang, Tirrell, & Lerner, in press; Lerner, von Eye, Lerner, & Lewin-Bizan, 2009; Lerner, von Eye, Lerner, Lewin-Bizan, & Bowers, 2010; Lerner, Lerner, von Eye, Bowers, & Lewin-Bizan 2011). We turn briefly to a discussion of this dataset in order to illustrate how the research ideas we have forwarded may be pursued. In addition, this illustration will also enable us to briefly discuss the ways in which the research we have suggested may be used in evidence-based programs designed to enhance adolescent development by strengthening the links between intentional self-regulation and identity development.

TESTING THE LINKS BETWEEN INTENTIONAL SELF-REGULATION AND IDENTITY PROCESSES: A POSITIVE YOUTH DEVELOPMENT MODEL

I'm starting with the man in the mirror.
I'm asking him to change his ways.
And no message could have been any clearer.
If you want to make the world a better place,
Take a look at yourself and then
Make a change.

—*Man in the Mirror*, Michael Jackson (Garrett & Ballard, 1988)

We have suggested that the links between intentional self-regulatory processes—as operationalized through the use of the SOC model—and identity-development processes should enhance the likelihood of adolescents being involved in adaptive developmental regulations (i.e., mutually beneficial individual ←→ context relations). If so, then youth should thrive, as individuals, and the context that supports youth also should benefit, for instance, through young people finding purpose and meaning in contributing effectively to the institutions and people of their communities and to civil society (Lerner, 2004; Sherrod, Torney-Purta, & Flanagan, 2010; Zaff, Boyd, Li, Lerner, & Lerner, 2010). A means to test this idea has been presented in the articulation of what has been termed the Positive Youth Development (PYD) perspective (e.g., Bowers et al., 2010; Lerner et al., 2005, 2011, in press). The PYD perspective is a conception of youth thriving that has explicitly used as its foundational idea the individual ←→ context relations of focal concern in adaptive developmental regulations (and, more broadly, in what have been termed relational developmental systems models of human development; Overton, in press; Overton & Müller, 2013). The PYD perspective has been elaborated in the context of a longitudinal study conducted by Lerner and colleagues; the 4-H Study of PYD (e.g., Bowers et al., 2010; Lerner et al., 2005). This research has sought to identify the individual and ecological relations that may promote thriving and, as well, that may have a preventive effect with regard to risk/problem behaviors. Within the 4-H Study, thriving is understood as the growth of attributes that mark a flourishing, healthy young person (e.g., the characteristics termed the "Five Cs" of PYD—*competence, confidence, character, connection, and caring*) (Eccles & Gootman, 2002; Lerner et al., 2005; Roth & Brooks-Gunn, 2003a, 2003b).

The key hypothesis tested in this PYD conception is that, if (a) the strengths of youth (e.g., a young person's SOC skills) can (b) be aligned with the resources for positive growth found in families, schools, and communities (e.g., the capacities of adults to provide for young people a nurturing, positive milieu in which their strengths may be enhanced and positively directed) (Benson, Scales, & Syvertsen, 2011; DuBois & Rhodes, 2006; Karcher, Davis, & Powell, 2002; Lewin-Bizan, Bowers, & Lerner, 2010; Rhodes & Lowe, 2009); then (c) young people's healthy development will be optimized (Lerner, 2004). A secondary hypothesis is that, given that positively developing youth should be involved in adaptive developmental regulations, then a thriving young person should act to contribute to the context that is benefiting him or her; there should be contributions to self, family, community, and civil society (Jelicic, Bobek, Phelps, Lerner, & Lerner, 2007; Lerner et al., 2005). In other words, if positive development rests on mutually beneficial relations between the adolescent and his/her ecology, then thriving youth should be positively engaged with and act to enhance their world. Further, the adolescent should be less prone to engage in risk/problem behaviors.

As summarized in numerous publications emanating from the 4-H Study (e.g., Bowers et al., 2014; and for a review, see Lerner et al., in press), SOC skills are the major predictors within and across grades 5 to 12 (approximately ages 10 to 18 years) of the indicators of PYD and, as well, of youth contributions to their families, schools, and communities. Indeed, high SOC scores are linked to active and engaged citizenship in youth (e.g., Zaff, Kawashima-Ginsberg, & Lin, 2011). These findings may be interpreted as supporting the idea that SOC skills are linked to both youth thriving and to finding meaning in being active agents of positive events/changes in their social ecology, of the presence therefore of adaptive developmental regulations between youth and their contexts.

Moreover, there is evidence that, when youth have goals directed to allocating their out-of-school time (OST) to extracurricular activities, SOC enables such purposes to be actualized. For example, Urban, Lewin-Bizan, and Lerner (2010) assessed 4-H Study participants from grades 5 to 7 in order to explore if youth intentional self-regulation abilities moderated the effect of participation in OST activities on PYD among adolescents living in neighborhoods with relatively low levels of ecological assets. Overall, Urban et al. found that youth in these settings who had the greatest capacity to self-regulate (i.e., youth with the highest SOC scores) benefited the most from involvement in OST activities, in terms of PYD, depressive symptoms, and risk behaviors. These relations were particularly strong for girls. In turn, Mueller et al. (2011) used data from grades 8, 9, and 10 of the 4-H Study to examine the relations between adolescents' SOC abilities and their participation in youth development (YD) programs across grades 8 and 9 in predicting grade-10 PYD and Contribution. Results indicated that although self-regulation skills alone predicted PYD, self-regulation and YD program participation both predicted Contribution. In addition, grade-8 YD participation positively predicted grade-9 SOC, which in turn predicted grade-10 PYD and Contribution.

In sum, although not designed to test directly the ideas we have forwarded about the links between intentional self-regulation and identity development, some research from the 4-H Study of PYD illustrates the potential fruitfulness of such empirical work. In addition, the 4-H Study has provided an evidence base for applications aimed at enhancing intentional self-regulatory processes among adolescents. This applied work suggests ways in which practitioners can enact evidence-based programs that promote thriving among youth by enhancing their intentional self-regulatory abilities.

OPPORTUNITIES FOR EVIDENCE-BASED APPLICATIONS TO ENHANCE THE LINKS BETWEEN INTENTIONAL SELF-REGULATION AND IDENTITY DEVELOPMENT

You're the first one when things turn out bad.
You know I'll never be lonely.
You're my only one, and I love the things I really love the things that you do.
You're my best friend.

—*You're My Best Friend,* Queen (Deacon, 1976)

One avenue for enhancing young people's self-regulatory skills is through their relationships with important nonparental adults, such as mentors. To capitalize on this potentiality, Bowers and colleagues (Bowers, Napolitano et al., 2013; Napolitano et al., 2014; Napolitano, Bowers, Gestdóttir, & Chase, 2011) used research derived from the 4-H Study of PYD to design what they term the *GPS to Success* intervention materials. The materials are intended to help mentors in youth-serving organizations discuss, assess, and build within youth intentional self-regulation skills (again, operationalized through use of the SOC model). The core tools of *GPS to Success* are a set of rubric-based measures for mentors and youth to assess youth ISR skills—the *GPS to Success* growth grids.

The *GPS to Success* growth grids use the metaphor of a car's GPS navigation system—you "choose your destination" and your GPS (your SOC skills) provides "strategies" that lead you to your destination (achieving a goal). In the GPS framework, "G" stands for "Goal Selection," and reflects Selection skills; "P" stands for "Pursuit of Strategies," and reflects Optimization skills; and "S" stands for "Shifting Gears" and reflects Compensation skills.

The items used in the GPS grids were derived from the specific skills represented in the SOC model, and they also incorporated concepts from PYD literature (e.g., Benson, 2008; Damon, 2008; Dweck, 2006; Larson, 2000, 2006). There is evidence for the reliability of the GPS scales, convergent validity between mentee's self-reported ratings on the growth grids and their scores on a short form of the SOC questionnaire, predictive validity between GPS growth grid scores and scores for PYD, and significant correlations between mentee's self-reported ratings and mentor's ratings on the GPS growth grids (Bowers, Napolitano et al., 2013).

Bowers et al. (in press) examined the longitudinal relations between mentor-mentee relationships and SOC skills using data from 415 mentor-mentee dyads from mentoring programs around the United States. The 415 ethnically and socioeconomically diverse youth and their mentors had used the GPS growth grids within their mentoring relationships. A cross-lagged structural equation model indicated that a latent factor of mentor-mentee relationship quality predicted growth in a latent factor of youth intentional self-regulation skills. These findings supported the role of mentors in promoting the development of youth ISR. Earlier in this chapter, we suggested that intentional self-regulation skills could be used to decrease the stress that is often involved when youth are engaged in identity exploration, and accordingly, it may be that programs designed specifically to enhance these types of skills, such as mentoring programs that use the *GPS to Success* tools, may facilitate less stressful identity explorations among youth.

Clearly, however, the data that support the use of the *GPS to Success* tools do not speak also to their specific relevance in programs explicitly directed to enhancing the identity development of youth. A small amount of research has been conducted specifically in this area, however, and interest in the idea of interventions for identity development is growing (e.g., Archer, 2008; Montgomery, Hernandez, & Ferrer-Wreder, 2008). Several researchers have piloted interventions specifically designed to promote positive identity development of adolescents and young adults. These interventions have typically involved assessment of identity development through indices of exploration and/or related skills (e.g., problem-solving), or commitment and/or related skills (e.g., group affilitations). These two indices (exploration and commitment) are useful operationalizations of theory-predicated identity processes. For instance, Ferrer-Wreder and colleagues (2002) tested a school-based intervention with urban minority youth; specifically, they focused on helping young people "begin to transform their lives through the development of a critical understanding of their life context, a sense of control and responsibility over their lives, and an increasingly proactive participation in defining for themselves who they are and what they believe in" (p. 180). Quantitative results showed a general pattern of increases in the skills and attitudes associated with identity development (e.g., problem-solving skills) as well as some positive findings regarding the promotion of exploration. Similar pilot programs have been described by Berman, Kennerley, and Kennerley (2008), as well as by Schwartz, Kurtines, and Montgomery (2005). Although these authors did not explicitly use the terminology of intentional self-regulation when describing the targets of these interventions, all three programs included some manner of focus on skills that are related to intentional self-regulation. For example, Ferrer-Wreder and colleagues' (2002) intervention focused on problem-solving skills, which are broadly related to all aspects of intentional self-regulation, especially as operationalized through the SOC model.

The intimate links we have drawn between intentional self-regulation processes and identity-development processes suggest that combining facets of these two processes within an intervention context may be especially useful. As the above examples illustrate, work that has already been done in these areas (e.g., interventions targeted at either intentional self-regulation skills or identity development) is compatible with our perspective on the relation between these two processes. We propose that interventions that focus on either intentional self-regulation skills or identity development may be strengthened by also incorporating aspects of the other process. For example, adding an explicit focus on SOC skills to an identity-development intervention may result in more "productive" exploration for participants and conversely, incorporating discussions of identity issues into an intervention such as GPS may promote especially rich targets toward which youth can focus their developing skills. Such possibilities are worthy of testing in applied research and serve as an illustration of how applied developmental scientists may work to enhance the healthy and positive development of youth through focusing on the integrative relations between processes of intentional self-regulation and of identity among youth.

CONCLUSIONS

Who are you, I really want to know.

—*Who Are You?* The Who (Townshend, 1978)

Within developmental science, increasing attention is being paid to models that take integrative, relational approaches to understanding how processes within the individual and between the individual and his/her context that interrelate to constitute the fundamental changes of human life (e.g., Lerner, in press). *In other words, these relational developmental systems conceptions direct theory and research to consider mutually influential relations between an individual and his or her context. As we have explained in this chapter, these relations, which we have termed developmental regulations, constitute the basic processes of human development* (Overton, in press; Overton & Müller, 2013). In this chapter, we have argued that in adolescence, the links between this regulatory process and the central developmental task of this period of life—identity development—are intricately and intimately related.

In 2001, Lerner et al. called for developmental research to focus on the interrelations between processes of intentional self-regulation and of identity development, to be undertaken in the service of describing, explaining, and optimizing the key facets of human development during the second decade of life. We believe the present chapter has underscored and extended this appeal. Out hope is that the ideas we have presented will stimulate new, basic, and applied developmental science aimed at better understanding and promoting thriving within the adolescent years and as such, helping young people navigate their transitions to the ensuing decades of the life course.

ACKNOWLEDGMENT

The preparation of this chapter was supported in part by grants from the John Templeton Foundation. The authors thank the undergraduate and graduate students in the Institute for Applied Research in Youth Development at Tufts University for their help in selecting the song excerpts used in this chapter.

REFERENCES

Archer, S. (2008). Identity and interventions: An introduction. *Identity: International Journal of Theory and Research, 8*(2), 89–94.

Baltes, P. B. (1997). On the incomplete architecture of human ontogeny: Selection, optimization, and compensation as foundations of developmental theory. *American Psychologist, 52,* 366–380.

Baltes, P. B., & Baltes, M. M. (1990). Psychological perspectives on successful aging: The model of selective optimization with compensation. In P. B. Baltes & M. M. Baltes (Eds.), Successful aging: Perspectives from the behavioral sciences (pp. 1–34). New York, NY: Cambridge University Press.

Baltes, P. B., Lindenberger, U., & Staudinger, U. M. (2006). Lifespan theory in developmental psychology. In W. Damon & R. M. Lerner (Eds.), & R. M. Lerner (Vol. Ed.), Handbook of child psychology: Vol. 1. Theoretical models of human development (6th ed., pp. 569–664). Hoboken, NJ: Wiley.

Bandura, A. (2001). The changing face of psychology at the dawning of a globalization era. *Canadian Psychology, 42*(1), 12–24.

Benson, P. L. (2008). *Sparks: How parents can help ignite the hidden strengths of teenagers.* San Francisco, CA: Jossey-Bass.

Benson, P. L., Scales, P. C., & Syvertsen, A. K. (2011). The contribution of the developmental assets framework to positive youth development theory and practice. In R. M. Lerner, J. V. Lerner, & J. B. Benson (Eds.), *Advances in Child Development and Behavior, 41,* 195–228.

Berman, S. L., Kennerley, R. J., & Kennerley, M. A. (2008). Promoting adult identity development: A feasibility study of a university-based identity intervention program. *Identity: An International Journal of Theory and Research, 8,* 139–150.

Bon Jovi, J., Sambora, R., & Martin, M. (2000). It's my life [recorded by Bon Jovi]. On *Crush* [record]. New York, NY: Island.

Bosma, H. A., & Kunnen, E. S. (2001). Determinants and mechanisms in ego identity development: A review and synthesis. *Developmental Review, 21,* 39–66.

Bosma, H. A., & Kunnen, E. S. (2008). Identity-in-context is not yet identity development-in-context. *Journal of Adolescence, 31,* 281–289.

Bowers, E. P., Li, Y., Kiely, M. K., Brittian, A., Lerner, J. V., & Lerner, R. M. (2010). The Five Cs model of positive youth development: A longitudinal analysis of confirmatory factor structure and measurement invariance. *Journal of Youth and Adolescence, 39,* 720–735.

Bowers, E. P., Napolitano, C. M., Arbeit, M. R., Chase, P., Glickman, S. A., Lerner, R. M., & Lerner, J. V. (2013). On a pathway toward thriving: Evaluating the effectiveness of tools to promote positive development and intentional self regulation in youth. *Journal of Youth Development, 8*(3), 4–31.

Bowers, E. P., Wang, J., Tirrell, J. M., & Lerner, R. M. (in press). The role of mentor–mentee relationships in the development of intentional self regulation among adolescents. *Journal of Community Psychology.*

Brandtstädter, J. (1998). Action perspectives on human development. In W. Damon & R. M. Lerner (Eds.) & R. M. Lerner (Vol. Ed.), *Handbook of child psychology: Vol. 1. Theoretical models of human development* (5th ed., pp. 807–863). New York, NY: Wiley.

Brandtstädter, J. (1999). The self in action and development: Cultural, biosocial, and ontogenetic bases of intentional self-development. In J. Brandtstädter & R. M. Lerner (Eds.), *Action and self-development: Theory and research through the life-span* (pp. 37–65). Thousand Oaks, CA: Sage.

Brandtstädter, J. (2006). Action perspectives on human development. In W. Damon & R. M. Lerner (Eds.) & R. M. Lerner (Vol. Ed.), Handbook of child psychology: Vol. 1. C. Molenaar (Ed.), *Theory and Method. Volume 1 of the Handbook of Child Psychology and Developmental Science* (7th ed.). Editor-in-chief: R. M. Lerner. Hoboken, NJ: Wiley.

Brandtstädter, J., & Lerner, R. M. (1999). Development, action, and intentionality: A view of the issues. In J. Brandtstädter & R. M. Lerner (Eds.), *Action and self-development: Theory and research through the life-span* (pp. ix–xx). Thousand Oaks, CA: Sage.

Chess, S., & Thomas, A. (1999). *Goodness-of-fit: Clinical applications from infancy through adult life.* Philadelphia, PA: Brunner/Mazel.

Compas, B. E., & Reeslund, K. L. (2009). Processes of risk and resilience during adolescence. In. R. M. Lerner & L. Steinberg (Eds.), *Handbook of adolescent psychology* (3rd ed., pp. 561–588). Hoboken, NJ: Wiley.

Cooper, A., Bruce, M., Buxton, G., Dunaway, D., & Smith, N. (1970). I'm eighteen [recorded by Alice Cooper]. *On Love It to Death* [record]. Los Angeles: Straight Records.

Côté, J. M. (2009). Identity formation and self-development in adolescence. In R. M. Lerner & L. Steinberg (Eds.), *Handbook of adolescent psychology. Vol 1. Individual bases of adolescent development* (3rd ed., pp. 266–304). New York, NY: Wiley.

Damon, W. (2008). *The path to purpose: Helping our children find their calling in life.* New York, NY: Simon & Schuster.

Darwin, C. (1859). *The origin of species by means of natural selection or the preservation of favoured races in the struggle for life.* London, England: Murray.

Darwin, C. (1872). *The expression of emotions in man and animals.* London, England: Murray.

Deacon, J. (1976). You're my best friend [recorded by Queen]. On *A night at the opera* [record]. New York, NY: Elektra.

Demetriou, A. (2000). Organization and development of self-understanding and self regulation: Toward a general theory. In M. Boekaerts, P. R., Pintrich, & M. Zeidner (Eds.), *Handbook of self-regulation* (pp. 209–251). San Diego, CA: Academic.

DuBois, D. L., & Rhodes, J. E. (2006). Youth mentoring: Bridging science with practice. *Journal of Community Psychology, 34,* 547–565.

Dweck, C. (2006). *Mindset: The new psychology of success.* New York, NY: Ballantine.

Dylan, B. (1964). My back pages. On *Another Side of Bob Dylan* [record]. New York, NY: Columbia Records.

Eccles, J., & Gootman, J. (Eds). (2002). *Community programs to promote youth development.* Washington, DC: National Academies Press.

Ferrer-Wreder, L., Lorente, C. C., Kurtines, W., Briones, E., Bussell, J., Berman, S., & Arrufat, O. (2002). Promoting identity development in marginalized youth. *Journal of Adolescent Research, 17*(2), 168–187.

Freund, A. M., & Baltes, P. B. (2002). Life-management strategies of selection, optimization and compensation: Measurement by self-report and construct validity. *Journal of Personality and Social Psychology, 82,* 642–662.

Freund, A. M., Li, Z. H., & Baltes, P. B. (1999). The role of selection, optimization, and compensation in successful aging. In J. Brandtstädter & R. M. Lerner (Eds.), *Action and development: Origins and functions of intentional self-development* (pp. 401–434). Thousand Oaks, CA: Sage.

Garrett, S., & Ballard, G. (1988). Man in the mirror [recorded by Michael Jackson]. On *Bad* [record]. New York, NY: Epic.

Geldhof, G. J., Little, T. D., & Colombo, J. (2010). Self-regulation across the lifespan. In M. E. Lamb, A. Freund (Vol. Eds.), & R. M. Lerner (Ed.), *The handbook of life-span development. Vol 2: Social and emotional development* (pp. 116–157). Hoboken, NJ: Wiley.

Gestsdóttir, S., Bowers, E. P., von Eye, A., Napolitano, C. M., & Lerner, R. M. (2010). Intentional self-regulation in middle adolescence: The emerging role of loss-based selection in positive youth development. *Journal of Youth and Adolescence, 39,* 764–782.

Gestsdóttir, S., & Lerner, R. M. (2007). Intentional self-regulation and positive youth development in early adolescence: Findings from the 4-H Study of Positive Youth Development. *Developmental Psychology, 43*(2), 508–521.

Gestsdóttir, G., & Lerner, R. M. (2008). Positive development in adolescence: The development and role of intentional self regulation. *Human Development, 51,* 202–224.

Gollwitzer, P. M., Bayer, U., Scherer, M., & Seifert, A. E. (1999). A motivational-volitional perspective on identity development. In J. Brandtstädter & R. M. Lerner (Eds.), *Action and self-development: Theory and research through the life-span* (pp. 283–314). Thousand Oaks, CA: Sage.

Gould, S. J. (1977). *Ontogeny and phylogeny.* Cambridge, MA: Belknap Press of Harvard University Press.

Harry, D., & Harrison, N. (1978). One way or another [recorded by Blondie]. On *Parallel Lines* [record]. London, England: Chrysalis Records.

Heckhausen, J. (1999). *Developmental regulation in adulthood: Age-normative and socio-cultural constraints as adaptive challenges.* New York, NY: Cambridge University Press.

Heckhausen, J., Wrosch, C., & Schulz, R. (2010). A motivational theory of life-span development. *Psychological Review, 117*(1), 32–60.

Jablonka, E., & Lamb, M. (2005). *Evolution in four dimensions: Genetic, epigenetic, behavioral, and symbolic variation in the history of life.* Cambridge, MA: MIT Press

Jagger, M., & Richards, K. (1969). You can't always get what you want [recorded by the Rolling Stones]. On *Let it bleed* [record]. London, England: Decca.

Jelicic, H., Bobek, D., Phelps, E. D., Lerner, J. V., & Lerner, R. M. (2007). Using positive youth development to predict contribution and risk behaviors in early adolescence: Findings from the first two waves of the 4-H Study of Positive Youth Development. *International Journal of Behavioral Development, 31*(3), 263–273.

Johanson, D. C., & Edey, M. A. (1981). *Lucy: The beginnings of humankind.* New York, NY: Simon & Schuster.

Josselson, R. (1994). The theory of identity development and the question of intervention. In S. L. Archer (Ed.), Interventions for adolescent identity development (pp. 12–25). Thousand Oaks, CA: Sage.

Karcher, M. J., Davis, C., & Powell, B. (2002). The effects of developmental mentoring on connectedness and academic achievement. *School Community Journal, 12*(2), 35–50.

Klimstra, T. A., Luyckx, K., Hale, W. A., Frijns, T., van Lier, P. A., & Meeus, W. H. J. (2010). Short-term fluctuations in identity: Introducing a micro-level approach to identity formation. *Journal of Personality and Social Psychology, 99*(1), 191–202.

Kuhn, D. (2009). Adolescent thinking. In. R. M. Lerner & L. Steinberg (Eds.), *Handbook of adolescent psychology* (3rd ed., pp. 152–186). Hoboken, NJ: Wiley.

Larson, R. W. (2000). Toward a psychology of positive youth development. *American Psychologist, 55*(1), 170–183.

Larson, R. (2006). Positive youth development, willful adolescents, and mentoring. *Journal of Community Psychology, 34*(6), 677–689.

Lennon, J., & McCartney, P. (1965). Help! [recorded by The Beatles]. On *Help!* [record]. London: Parlophone.

Lerner, R. M. (1982). Children and adolescents as producers of their own development. *Developmental Review, 2,* 342–370.

Lerner, R. M. (2004). *Liberty: Thriving and civic engagement among America's youth.* Thousand Oaks, CA: Sage.

Lerner, R. M. (in press). Preface. In R. M. Lerner (Editor-in-chief), *Handbook of Child Psychology and Developmental Science* (7th ed.). Hoboken, NJ: Wiley.

Lerner, R. M., & Busch-Rossnagel, N. A. (Eds.). (1981). *Individuals as producers of their development: A life-span perspective.* New York, NY: Academic.

Lerner, R. M., Freund, A. M., De Stefanis, I., & Habermas, T. (2001). Understanding developmental regulation in adolescence: The use of the selection, optimization, and compensation model. *Human Development, 44,* 29–50.

Lerner, R. M., Lerner, J. V., Almerigi, J., Theokas, C., Phelps, E., Gestsdottir, S., . . . von Eye, A. (2005). Positive youth development, participation in community youth development programs, and community contributions of fifth-grade adolescents: Findings from the first wave of the 4-H Study of Positive Youth Development. *Journal of Early Adolescence, 25*(1), 17–71.

Lerner, R. M., Lerner, J. V., Bowers, E., & Geldhof, G. J. (in press) Positive youth development: A relational developmental systems model. In W. F. Overton & P. C. Molenaar (Eds.), *Theory and method.* Volume 1 of the *Handbook of child psychology and developmental science* (7th ed.). Editor-in-chief: R. M. Lerner. Hoboken, NJ: Wiley.

Lerner, R. M., Lerner, J. V., von Eye, A., Bowers, E. P., & Lewin-Bizan, S. (2011). Individual and contextual bases of thriving in adolescence: A view of the issues. *Journal of Adolescence, 34*(6), 1107–1114.

Lerner, R. M., & Steinberg, L. (2009). The scientific study of adolescent development. In R. M. Lerner & L. Steinberg (Eds.). *Handbook of adolescent psychology* (3rd ed., pp. 3–14). Hoboken, NJ: Wiley.

Lerner, R. M., von Eye, A., Lerner, J. V., & Lewin-Bizan, S. (2009). Exploring the foundations and functions of adolescent thriving within the 4-H Study of Positive Youth Development: A view of the issues. *Journal of Applied Developmental Psychology, 30*(5), 567–570.

Lerner, R. M., von Eye, A., Lerner, J. V., Lewin-Bizan, S., & Bowers, E. P. (2010). Special issue introduction: The meaning and measurement of thriving: A view of the issues. *Journal of Youth and Adolescence, 39*(7), 707–719.

Lerner, R. M., & Walls, T. (1999). Revisiting individuals as producers of their development: From dynamic interactionism to developmental systems. In J. Brandtstädter & R. M. Lerner (Eds.), *Action and self-development: Theory and research through the life-span* (pp. 3–36). Thousand Oaks, CA: Sage.

Lewin-Bizan, S., Bowers, E. P., & Lerner, R. M. (2010). One good thing leads to another: Cascades of positive youth development among American adolescents. *Development and Psychopathology, 22*(4), 759–770.

Lewontin, R. C. (2000). *The triple helix.* Cambridge, MA: Harvard University Press.

Luyckx, K., Goossens, L., Soenens, B., & Beyers, W. (2006). Unpacking commitment and exploration: Preliminary validation of an integrative model of late adolescent identity formation. *Journal of Adolescence, 29,* 361–378.

Luyckx, K., Schwartz, S. J., Berzonsky, M. D., Soenens, B., Vansteenkiste, M., Smits, I., & Goossens, L. (2008). Capturing ruminative exploration: Extending the four-dimensional model of identity formation in late adolescence. *Journal of Research in Personality, 42,* 58–82.

Luyckx, K., Schwartz, S. J., Goossens, L., Beyers, W., & Missotten, L. (2011). Processes of personal identity formation and evaluation. In S. J. Schwartz, K. Luyckx, & V. Vignoles (Eds.), *Handbook of identity theory and research* (pp. 77–98). New York, NY: Springer.

Luyckx, K., Soenens, B., & Goossens, L. (2006). The personality-identity interplay in emerging adult women: Convergent findings from complementary analyses. *European Journal of Personality, 20,* 195–215.

Marcia, J. M. (1980). Ego identity development. In J. Adelson (Ed.), *Handbook of adolescence psychology* (pp. 109–137). New York, NY: Wiley.

Matthews, D. J. (1994). Dancing nancies [recorded by Dave Matthews Band]. On *Under the table and dreaming* [record]. New York, NY: RCA.

McClelland, M. M., Geldhof, G. J., Cameron, C. E., & Wanless, S. B. (in press). Development and self-regulation. In W. F. Overton & P. C. Molenaar (Eds.), *Theory and method.* Volume 1 of the *Handbook of child psychology and developmental science* (7th ed.). Editor-in-chief: R. M. Lerner. Hoboken, NJ: Wiley.

McClleland, M. M., Ponitz, C. C., Messersmith, E., & Tominey, S. (2010). Self-regulation: The integration of cognition and emotion. In W. Overton & R. M. Lerner (Eds.), *The handbook of lifespan development. Vol 1. Cognition, neuroscience, methods* (pp. 509–553). Hoboken, NJ: Wiley.

McElhaney, K. B., Allen, J. P., Stephenson, J. C., & Hare, A. L. (2009). Attachment and autonomy during adolescence. In R. M. Lerner & L. Steinberg (Eds.), *Handbook of adolescent psychology* (3rd ed., pp. 358–403). Hoboken, NJ: Wiley.

Montgomery, M. J., Hernandez, L., & Ferrer-Wreder, L. (2008). Identity development and intervention studies: The right time for a marriage? *Identity: An International Journal of Theory and Research, 8*(2), 173–182.

Mueller, M. K., Phelps, E., Bowers, E. P., Agans, J., Urban, J. B., & Lerner, R. M. (2011). Youth development program participation and intentional self-regulation skills: Contextual and individual bases of pathways to positive youth development. *Journal of Adolescence, 34*(6), 1115–1126.

Müller, U., & Kerns, K. (in press). The development of executive function. In L. S. Liben & U.

Müller (Eds.), *Cognitive processes,* Volume 2 of the *Handbook of child psychology and developmental science* (7th ed.). Editor-in-chief: R. M. Lerner. Hoboken, NJ: Wiley.

Napolitano, C. M., Bowers, E. P., Arbeit, M. R., Chase, P., Geldhof, G. J., Lerner, J. V., & Lerner, R. M. (2014). The *GPS to Success* Growth Grids: Measurement properties of a tool to promote intentional self-regulation in mentoring programs. *Applied Developmental Science, 18*(1), 46–58.

Napolitano, C. M., Bowers, E. P., Gestdóttir, S., & Chase, P. (2011). The development of intentional self-regulation in adolescence: Describing, explaining, and optimizing its link to positive youth development. *Advances in Child Development and Behavior, 41,* 19–38.

Napolitano, C. M., Bowers, E. P., Gestsdóttir, S., Depping, M., von Eye, A., Chase, P., & Lerner, J. V. (2011). The role of parenting and goal selection in positive youth development: A person-centered approach. *Journal of Adolescence, 34*(6),1137–1149.

Overton, W. F. (2013). Relationism and relational-developmental-systems: A paradigm for developmental science in the post-Cartesian era. In R. M. Lerner & J. B. Benson (Eds.), Embodiment and epigenesis: Theoretical and methodological issues in understanding the role of biology within the relational developmental system. *Advances in Child Development and Behavior, 44,* 21–94.

Overton, W. F. (in press). Process and relational developmental systems. In W. F. Overton & P. C. Molenaar (Eds.), *Theory and method.* Volume 1 of the *Handbook of child psychology and developmental science* (7th ed.). Editor-in-chief: R. M. Lerner. Hoboken, NJ: Wiley.

Overton, W. F., & Müller, U. (2013). Development across the life span: Philosophy, concepts, theory. In R. M. Lerner, M. A. Easterbrooks, & J. Mistry (Eds.), *Handbook of psychology: Developmental psychology* (Vol . 6, pp. 19–58). Editor-in-chief: I. B. Weiner. New York, NY: Wiley.

Palmer, K., Fukai, J., & Singleton, J. (1998). Reflection [recorded by Christina Aguilera]. On *Christina Aguilera* [CD]. New York, NY: RCA Records.

Rhodes, J. E., & Lowe, S. R. (2009). Mentoring in adolescence. In R. M. Lerner & L. Steinberg (Eds.), *Handbook of adolescent psychology: Vol. 2. Contextual influences on adolescent development* (3rd ed., pp. 152–190). Hoboken, NJ: Wiley.

Roth, J. L., & Brooks-Gunn, J. (2003a). What is a youth development program? Identification and defining principles. In. F. Jacobs, D. Wertlieb, & R. M. Lerner (Eds.), *Enhancing the life chances of youth and families: Public service systems and public policy perspectives: Vol. 2, Handbook of applied developmental science: Promoting positive child, adolescent, and family development through research, policies, and programs* (pp. 197–223). Thousand Oaks, CA: Sage.

Roth, J. L., & Brooks-Gunn, J. (2003b). What exactly is a youth development program? Answers from research and practice. *Applied Developmental Science, 7,* 94–111.

Schwartz, S. J., Côté, J. E., & Arnett, J. J. (2005). Identity and agency in emerging adulthood: Two developmental routes in the individualization process. *Youth and Society, 37*(2), 201–229.

Schwartz, S. J., Kurtines, W. M., & Montgomery, M. J. (2005). A comparison of two approaches for facilitating identity exploration processes in emerging adults: An exploratory study. *Journal of Adolescent Research, 20*(3), 309–345.

Schwartz, S. J., & Pantin, H. (2006). Identity development in adolescence and emerging adulthood: The interface of self, context, and culture. In A. P. Prescott (Ed.), *The concept of self in psychology* (pp. 45–85). Hauppauge, NY: Nova Science.

Schwartz, S. J., Zamboanga, B. L., Weisskirch, R. S., & Rodriguez, L. (2009). The relationships of personal and ethnic identity exploration to indices of adaptative and maladaptive psychosocial functioning. *International Journal of Behavioral Development, 33,* 131–144.

Sherrod, L. R., Torney-Purta, J., & Flanagan, C. A. (Eds.). (2010). *Handbook of research on civic engagement in youth.* New York, NY: Wiley.

Sokol, B. W., Hammond, S., Kuebli, J., & Sweetman, L. (in press). The development of agency. In W. F. Overton & P. C. Molenaar (Eds.), *Theory and method.* Volume 1 of the *Handbook of child psychology and developmental science* (7th ed.). Editor-in-chief: R. M. Lerner. Hoboken, NJ: Wiley.

Stills, S. (1970). Love the one you're with. On *Stephen Stills* [record]. New York, NY: Atlantic Records.

Susman, E. J., & Dorn, L. D. (2009). Puberty: Its role in development. In. R. M. Lerner & L. Steinberg (Eds.), *Handbook of adolescent psychology* (3rd ed., pp. 116–151). Hoboken, NJ: Wiley.

Susman, E. J., & Dorn, L. D. (2013). Puberty: Its role in development. In R. M. Lerner, M. A. Easterbrooks, & J. Mistry (Eds.), *Handbook of psychology, Volume 6: Developmental psychology* (2nd ed., pp. 289–320). Editor-in-chief: I. B. Weiner. Hoboken, NJ: Wiley.

Thomas, A., Chess, S., Birch, H. G., Hertzig, M. E., & Korn, S. (1963). *Behavioral individuality in early childhood.* New York, NY: New York University Press.

Tobach, E., & Greenberg, G. (1984). The significance of T. C. Schneirla's contribution to the concept of levels of integration. In G. Greenberg & E. Tobach (Eds.), *Behavioral evolution and integrative levels* (pp. 1–7). Hillsdale, NJ: Erlbaum.

Townshend, P. (1978). Who are you? [recorded by the Who]. On *Who are you?* [record]. Universal City, CA: MCA.

Tyler, S. (1973). Dream on [recorded by Aerosmith]. On *Aerosmith* [record]. New York, NY: Columbia Records.

Urban, J. B., Lewin-Bizan, S. & Lerner, R. M. (2010). The role of intentional self regulation, lower neighborhood ecological assets, and activity involvement in youth developmental outcomes. *Journal of Youth and Adolescence, 39*(7), 783–800.

Zaff, J., Boyd, M., Li, Y., Lerner, J. V., & Lerner R. M. (2010). Active and engaged citizenship: Multi-group and longitudinal factorial analysis of an integrated construct of civic engagement. *Journal of Youth and Adolescence, 39*(7), 736–750.

Zaff, J. F., Kawashima-Ginsberg, K., & Lin, E. S. (2011). Advances in civic engagement research: Issues of civic measures and civic context. In R. M. Lerner, J. V. Lerner, & J. B. Benson (Eds.), *Advances in Child Development and Behavior, 41,* 271–306.

CHAPTER 2

SELF-ENHANCING SELF-PRESENTATION

Interpersonal, Relational, and Organizational Implications

Constantine Sedikides
University of Southampton

Vera Hoorens
KU Leuven

Michael Dufner
Universität Leipzig

Most individuals have an unduly high estimation of themselves. They privately believe in their intrinsic merit: they are competent, likeable, moral, attractive. In short, they are "worth it" (as a certain *L'Oreal* commercial would put it). And they are worth it a bit more than their doppelgänger. This is indeed the essence of self-enhancement. People regard themselves more favorably than they view others, than others view them, or than objective criteria ascertain (Alicke & Sedikides, 2011).

Self-Concept, Motivation, and Identity, pages 29–55

Privately holding self-enhancing beliefs is associated with higher levels of psychological health (Alicke & Sedikides, 2009; Dufner et al., 2012; Dufner, Reitz, & Zander, in press; O'Mara, Gaertner, Sedikides, Zhou, & Liu, 2012). But what happens when these beliefs are expressed in public or when an audience infers them? Is the self-enhancer better off or in trouble? And what are the consequences for others? We are concerned with *self-enhancing self-presentation* (SESP) and its social (i.e., interpersonal, relational, organizational) benefits and costs. As an exemplar of one form of SESP with complex relationships to benefits and costs, we deal with narcissism in depth in the latter part of the chapter.

SELF-ENHANCING SELF-PRESENTATION

Self-presentation is an inherent quality of social interaction (Goffman, 1959). Indeed, self-presentation in the form of biographical narratives, social anecdotes, gossip, or social media posts may constitute over 70% of conversational content (Dayter, 2014; Dunbar, Duncan, & Marriott, 1997; Emler, 1994). Clearly, social behavior is, to a great degree, self-presentation.

Individuals are often motivated to present themselves in a way that maximizes desirable outcomes for them (e.g., material compensations, social approval, friendship, career advancement, status, self-esteem; Leary & Kowalski 1990). They may pursue this goal through an array of tactics (Gibson & Sachau, 2000; Hewitt & Stokes, 1975; Jones & Pittman, 1982; Lee, Quigley, Nesler, Corbett, & Tedeschi, 1999). Examples include *ingratiation* (trying to make oneself liked), *intimidation* (projecting the potential to be powerful or dangerous), *supplication* (displaying weakness to gain compassion or assistance), *sandbagging* (creating low performance expectations though false claims of inability), *self-handicapping* (preparing the ground for external attributions for failure by obstructing one's own performance), *excuse-making* (denying responsibility for wrongdoings), and *disclaimers* (explaining problems before they are expected to occur). We focus on a more general tactic: presenting a positive self-image to others. This tactic, which we call *SESP*, has also been labeled enhancement (Schlenker, 1980), entitlement (claiming responsibility for desirable outcomes; Tedeschi & Lindskold, 1976), self-promotion (displaying one's abilities; Jones & Pittman, 1982), and self-exemplification (presenting oneself as morally good).

We would like to highlight a crucial difference between actual self-enhancement and SESP. The former describes the tendency to privately maintain a positive self-view, whereas the latter describes a tendency to create the impression that one exceeds their actual ability. An example of SESP would be a person who is moderately intelligent, but nevertheless presents himself as highly intelligent. SESP is often a consequence of actual self-enhancement in the sense that positive self-views can be conveyed to observers (von Hippel & Trivers, 2011). In this case, our fictional person would truly believe in his intelligence and broadcast this positive self-view to others. Yet SESP is not necessarily rooted in actual self-enhancement. It is possible that individuals present a favorable image of themselves without actually believing in it (Sedikides & Gregg, 2008).

THE DOUBLE-EDGED SWORD OF SESP

How effective is SESP? Specifically, to what extent are self-enhancers viewed favorably or unfavorably by their intended audience and under what circumstances? Moreover, what are the aftermaths of observer impressions for the self-enhancer? The relevant literature is intricate and sometimes contradictory (Hoorens, 2011; Leary, 1995; Schlenker, 2012; Schlenker & Leary, 1982; Sedikides, Gregg, & Hart, 2008). We turn to a review of it, with the aim to clarify it and derive practical implications.

We address the issue of SESP effectiveness largely from the perspective of the basic dimensions of warmth/likeability or communion and competence or agency (Abele & Wojciszke, 2014; Paulhus & Trapnell, 2008). We discuss whether individuals who present themselves as warm/likeable are liked particularly well and whether those who present themselves as competent are viewed as such. Are SESPers met with favorable or unfavorable audience reactions?

SESP and Favorable Feedback

A sizeable part of the literature indicates that SESPers are often viewed favorably. Miller, Cooke, Tsang, and Morgan (1992, Study 1) found that actors who engaged in SESP were viewed as more competent, but not necessarily as more likeable, than those who self-deprecated. Carver, Kus, and Scheier (1994) reported that observers were more willing to interact with a person who, in an interview, self-enhanced (i.e., presented an optimistic outlook) rather than self-deprecated (i.e., presented a pessimistic outlook) or was neutral (i.e., presented a balanced outlook) about their future. Helweg-Larsen, Sadeghian, and Webb (2002) replicated this pattern. Participants were more willing to interact with someone who claimed that he was less (vs. more) likely than others to experience negative events, but were equally willing to interact with someone who claimed that he was as likely as others to experience such events. In the same vein, Le Barbenchon, Milhabet, Steiner, and Priolo (2008) showed that participants were more willing to interact with a person who displayed moderate or strong (compared to weak) personal optimism.

SESP appears to be effective in job interviews. Participants who took the role of a recruiter and judged applicants on the basis of videotaped selection interviews rated a self-enhancing (vs. non-self-enhancing) applicant more positively, stated that they would be more likely to hire him, and were more willing to invite him for a follow-up interview (Proost, Schreurs, De Witte, & Derous, 2010). SESPers in this case may have appeared overconfident (i.e., conveying the impression that they ranked high in the group). Indeed, overconfident actors are perceived as more competent than they truly are (Kennedy, Anderson, & Moore, 2013). More generally, SESPers at job interviews are seen as more competent but not as more likeable than non-SESPers (Dipboye & Wiley, 1977; Higgins & Judge, 2004).

The apparent effectiveness of SESP may be partially due to the correspondence bias (Gilbert & Malone, 1995). Observers routinely, if not spontaneously, draw inferences about presenters' traits (Vonk, 1999) and often conclude that the presenters' claims reflect their true personality dispositions (Gurevitch, 1984). Consistent with this proposition, participants judged a person (i.e., actor) who proclaimed expectations for above-average performance in a tennis tournament or on an exam as both more competent and more likable compared to a person who expressed average or below-average expectations (Schlenker & Leary, 1982). Similarly, participants judged an actor who pronounced above-average problem-solving ability as more intelligent than an actor who admitted below-average ability (Vonk, 1999).

SESP and Unfavorable Feedback

A portion of the literature indicates that SESP may elicit unfavorable reactions. Gordon (1996) reported in a meta-analysis that individuals who present themselves as likable are liked better when they engage in other-enhancement, opinion conformity, or self-deprecating displays. They are disliked, however, when they engage in promotion of their competence.

Godfrey, Jones, and Lord (1986) clarified these findings. Pairs of participants conversed twice for 20 minutes each on a topic of their own choosing. In the first conversation, participants got to know each other. In the second conversation, which occurred a week later, one member of each pair was randomly assigned to the role of "presenter," the other to the role of "target." One third of presenters were instructed to make themselves as likeable to the target as possible, and another third to appear to the target as competent as possible. The remaining presenters received no instructions. Following both the first and second conversation, pair members rated each other on likability and competence. Targets judged presenters who strove to make a likeable impression as more likable, but not as more competent, after the second conversation than after the first one. Targets judged presenters who strove to make a competent impression as no more competent, but as less likable, after the second conversation than after the first one.

Subsequent videotape analyses revealed that presenters who received "liking" instructions spent more time listening than talking, agreed more often with targets' opinions, and used a great deal more ingratiation strategies (e.g., paying the partner an occasional compliment, showing interest by smiling and nodding, identifying similarities, pointing to common acquaintances) during the second than during the first conversation. Presenters who received "competence" instructions controlled the conversation by being more talkative and less agreeable, touted their achievements, evaded topics relevant to the targets' areas of expertise, and strove verbally and nonverbally to appear confident (e.g., by sitting up straight). Such self-oriented and noningratiating behaviors explain why these presenters were judged as relatively dislikable. However, even when self-enhancing presenters succeed in coming across as competent, they may be seen as socially unappealing (Powers & Zuroff, 1988) or undesirable dating partners (Van Tongeren, Davis, & Hook, 2014).

SESP may involve internal attributions for success. In research by Wosinska, Dabul, Whetstone-Dion, and Cialdini (1996), participants read a vignette describing the way a company employee reacted to the news of a productivity award and congratulatory remarks. The employee's reaction was *self-enhancing* ("Thanks...I just knew I would win"), suggesting entitlement, *neutral* ("Thanks, I heard about it unofficially this morning"), or *modest* ("Thanks, but I think I was mostly lucky"), suggesting the contribution of external factors. Participants were least favorable to the self-enhancing employee.

SESP may also involve avoidance of personal responsibility for failure. Observers dislike actors who eschew (compared to those who endorse) responsibility for their failures (Carlston & Shovar, 1983). Forsyth, Berger, and Mitchell (1981) tested the generalizability of this finding by examining how group members respond to another member's claim about his personal responsibility for failed group performance. The other member claimed strong responsibility (he contributed more than other members), equal responsibility (he contributed as much as others), or weak responsibility (he contributed minimally). Members who claimed weak (vs. equal or strong) responsibility for failure were evaluated less favorably.

RECONCILING THE DIVERGENT EFFECTS OF SESP

Our review so far suggests a resolution to the paradox of mixed SESP perceptions: SESP is viewed favorably in the domain of competence, but unfavorably in the domain of likeability. Yet this is not the whole story. Beliefs about the desirability of SESP, and accompanying observer reactions to it, depend on the conversational context in which SESP occurs, the verifiability and intentionality of SESP, cultural norms prescribing how people in general and members of social groups in particular ought to present themselves, how SESP is expressed, and whether SESP reflects true versus perceived self-enhancement. We address these issues in turn.

Conversational Context of SESP

Contextual cues affect the nature, extent, and likelihood of SESP. For example, actors scale their self-aggrandizing statements to match those of another person (Vorauer & Miller, 1997) and describe themselves more favorably when they know that observes have evaluated them as above average than as average or below average (Gergen & Wishnov, 1965). They also engage in more SESP when they receive (bogus) feedback that they are likely to outperform others than being outperformed by others (Schlenker, 1975). Furthermore, reality constraints curb the positivity of self-presentations. For example, actors make more positive self-presentations to strangers than to friends (Tice, Butler, Muraven, & Stillwell, 1995).

Context also influences the reception of SESP by an audience. For example, observers form favorable impressions of an actor who, over the course of a conversation with a partner, extols his intellectual prowess in response to specific (rather than general) questions from his partner or in an effort to match (rather than surpass) his partner's favorable self-descriptions (Holtgraves & Srull, 1989). Similarly, actors are evaluated favorably when SESP occurs as a retort to the presence (rather than the absence) of an audience question (Tal-Or, 2010). Finally, whether the context is competitive or cooperative makes a difference. For example, SESP elicits a more favorable reaction in a competitive setting (e.g., job interview) than a cooperative setting (e.g., conversation with friend) (Kruger & Gilovich, 1999, Studies 3–4). Such contextual shifts may be due to norm docility (i.e., obedience) versus violation (i.e., resistance). Self-aggrandizing in response to questions upholds social norms, whereas self-aggrandizing willy-nilly violates social norms.

Cultural Norms Surrounding SESP

Cultural norms may partially determine whether self-enhancing presenters are likely to reap more benefits or endure more costs than their modest counterparts. Schmid, Frauendorfer, and Popovic (2011) examined how the cultural background of job recruiters influenced their evaluation of a job applicant's self-presentational style. The job recruiters originated from cultures whose norms endorsed the acceptability of SESP (i.e., Canada) or the acceptability of modesty (i.e., Switzerland), and the applicant's style during a job interview was either self-enhancing or modest. Canadian job recruiters were more favorable toward hiring self-enhancing presenters, whereas Swiss job recruiters were more favorable toward hiring modest presenters.

The Schmid et al. (2011) findings suggest that SESP is associated with favorable hiring decisions in cultures that value self-enhancement but not necessarily in cultures that value modesty. Yet SESP may occur in abundance even in cultures that value modesty. Wu (2011) examined incidences of self-praise in everyday social exchanges in China. On the basis of audiotaped and videotaped conversations, Wu identified three common practices that conversants used when engaging in SESP. Specifically, they disguised their self-praise as a complaint (i.e., complaining about the many duties that a highly prestigious position brings along), modified their self-praise (i.e., by retracting it after first having engaged in it), or disclaimed the possession of a desirable characteristic i.e., by stating that they have done something good but adding that it was not really exceptional). Another demonstration of SESP capitalized on the principle that collectivism (i.e., putting the interests of the group above those of the individual), but not individualism (i.e., putting the interests of the individual above those of the group), is an East Asian cultural ideal (Markus & Kitayama, 1991). East Asians presented themselves as superior to other group members on collectivistic attributes (e.g., loyal, agreeable, compromising) and behaviors (e.g., follow the rules according to which your group operates, follow confrontation with your group), but not on individualistic attributes (e.g., leader, original, unique) and behaviors (e.g., trust your own instinct rather than the group's instinct, disagree with your group when you believe your group is wrong") (Sedikides, Gaertner, & Toguchi, 2003; Sedikides, Gaertner, & Vevea, 2005).

Within a given culture, different social norms may dictate the appropriateness of SESP for social groups. Gender is an example: SESP is more acceptable in men than women. A boastful self-disclosure is rated as more masculine than a feminine one (Miller et al., 1992, Study 2). Also, men report using SESP (e.g., self-promotion, boasting of their association with high-status others) more frequently than women (Guadagno & Cialdini, 2007). Moreover, self-promoting women may come across as more competent than self-effacing women do, but they are also seen as more socially unattractive than self-effacing women or than self-promoting men are (Rudman, 1998). Intriguingly, these views are expressed only by female observers, a results pattern that needs to be replicated before firm inferences are drawn. Regardless, gender differences in SESP may be more pronounced in cultures characterized by larger gender inequality.

Verifiability and Intentionality of SESP

Observers typically do not possess information about the truthfulness of SESP. When they do, though, they are influenced by it. In general, observers lean favorably toward presenters who can match their publicly stated (and positive) expectations with performance (Brickman & Seligman, 1974) and presenters who can put to test their claims of competence (Bond, Kwan, & Li, 2000). If observers have reason to believe that an actor is competent and likeable (e.g., on the basis of her grade-point average or scores on a personality test), they evaluate her more favorably when she self-enhances than when she self-derogates. If, on the other hand, observers have reason to believe that an actor is incompetent and unlikeable, they evaluate her more favorably when she self-derogates than when she self-enhances (Jones & Shrauger, 1970). This pattern is qualified, though. If an actor performs outstandingly, observers evaluate her more favorably when her self-presentation is somewhat self-deprecating (i.e., downplaying her performance) than when it is accurate (Brickman & Seligman, 1974; Schlenker & Leary, 1982). Accuracy does not always help the acceptability of SESP.

It matters whether observers consider SESP intentional or unintentional. In Lafrenière, Sedikides, Van Tongeren, and Davis (2014, Experiments 1–2), observers read vignettes of an actor who self-enhanced either intentionally (i.e., in a planful or foreseeable manner; Bratman, 1987) or unintentionally. Observers' impressions of the actor differed as a function of her self-enhancement intentionality. They judged the actor as more immoral, unintelligent, and unfriendly when she engaged in SESP (no matter intentionally or unintentionally) rather than accurately (cf. Robinson, Johnson, & Shields, 1995; Tice et al., 1995; Wosinska et al., 1996). However, they judged the actor as more immoral and unintelligent, but as equally unfriendly, when she self-enhanced intentionally rather than unintentionally. Observers disapproved of intentional self-enhancement.

Expression of SESP

Robinson et al. (1995) compared the impressions elicited by highly self-enhancing claims with those elicited by self-deprecating and moderately self-enhancing claims. Observers looked more favorably upon moderately self-enhancing claims than either highly self-enhancing or self-depreciating claims, and they regarded moderately self-enhancing claimants as more likeable, honest, and authentic than their counterparts. These findings suggest that SESP is more effective when subtle than when blatant. Anderson, Brion, Moore, and Kennedy (2012, Study 4) reinforced this conclusion. Following completion of group tasks that involved cooperative responding to questions, observers judged fellow group members as more competent when these group members expressed more (than less) certainty in their answers.

SESP may also differ in linguistic form, such as level of abstraction. Presenters may boast concretely (e.g., performance level) or abstractly (e.g., ability level). A performance claim, due to its here-and-now character, may be more socially acceptable in the eyes of someone who needs to make a proximal decision about the claimant; however, an ability claim, due to its future implications, may be more socially acceptable in the context of a distal decision (Trope & Liberman, 2010). This is what Proost, Germeys, and Schreurs (2012, Study 2) found. Participants assigned to a recruiter role judged an applicant for a job opening that needed to be filled in the proximal or distal future. Recruiters judged a proximal-future applicant more favorably when he described specific than abstract achievements, but judged a distal-future applicant more favorably when he talked about abstract than specific achievements.

Hoorens, Pandelaere, Oldersma, and Sedikides (2012, Experiments 1–7) also examined how the expression of SESP influences observer reactions. Observers read vignettes of actors who self-enhanced either in the communion (i.e., friendship) or agency (i.e., student ability) domain. Specifically, actors made socially comparative self-enhancing claims ("I am a better person to be friends with than others"), socially comparative self-enhancing claims accompanied by a disclaimer ("I don't mean to say that I am a better person to be friends with than others, but..."), or temporally comparative self-superiority claims ("I am a better person now to be friends with than I was in the past"). Hoorens et al. contrasted observers' reactions to these claims and claimants against observers' reactions to noncomparative self-enhancing claims ("I am a good person to be friends with"), self-equality claims ("I am as good a person to be friends with as others are"), or other-enhancing claims ("She is a better person to be friends with than others"). Finally, Hoorens et al. assessed the inferences that observers made about the claimants' self-view, the claimants' view of others, and the claimants' view of the observer.

Observers disapproved of socially comparative self-enhancing claims and claimants more so than of any other type of claims or claimants. Such disapproval cut across the domains of communion (i.e., friendship) and agency (i.e., student ability) and across settings in which the claim was made (i.e., public vs. private). Observers' condemnation of socially comparative self-enhancing claims was driven by their inference that the claimant viewed other people in general and the observer in particular in an unfavorable light. The inference, then, that the claimant held the observer in contempt accounted for the rejection of the claim (Hoorens et al., 2012, Experiment 7). According to this account, observers rebuffed the socially comparative self-enhancer as a way to protect themselves from the threat that this comparison posed to their self-esteem or mood (Alicke, 2000; Sedikides, 2012). Such a self-protective rejection may have instigated an antagonistic or hostile response toward the claimant (Kowalski, 1997).

Perceived Versus Actual Self-Enhancement and SESP

Conflicting findings may be due, at least in part, to the discrepancy between perceived and actual self-enhancement. Dufner, Denissen, and colleagues (2013) defined *perceived self-enhancement* in terms of inferences that an observer makes about actors, their claims, or their performance. These are inferences about actors' private (and positive) views of themselves. As a reminder, *actual self-enhancement* refers to private (and positive) self-views. It is possible that observers are favorably inclined toward actual self-enhancement, which is not necessarily observable by others, but unfavorably inclined toward perceived self-enhancement.

Do actual and perceived self-enhancement elicit differing impressions? Dufner, Denissen et al. (2013) assessed separately perceived and actual self-enhancement. To assess actual self-enhancement, they instructed participants (i.e., actors) to take an aptitude test and rate themselves on that aptitude. They derived the actual self-enhancement score by partialing the actual aptitude from the self-rated aptitude. Subsequently, they asked observers to indicate their impressions of actors. Dufner, Denissen et al. assessed perceived self-enhancement through observer inferences about actors' self-views. If self-views were judged as inflated, perceived self-enhancement was high. We will describe these studies below on the basis of actual versus perceived self-enhancement.

In an online survey (Dufner, Denissen et al., 2013, Study 1), actors completed a verbal intelligence (i.e., vocabulary) test and proceeded to rate themselves on verbal knowledge. Observers (i.e., friends) rated actors on perceived self-enhancement and likability. The more actors engaged in actual self-enhancement, the more they were liked. However, the results for perceived self-enhancement were different. Actors with moderate levels of perceived self-enhancement (i.e., those who were perceived as neither self-enhancing nor self-derogating) were liked better. A follow-up investigation involving a round-robin design replicated these findings (Dufner, Denissen et al., Study 3). Acquainted participants were randomly assigned to groups and interacted regularly over 8 months. Participants rated each other several times on intelligence and likability. They all took an IQ test and provided subjective ratings of their intelligence. The higher actual self-enhancement was, the more favorable observers' impressions were over time. However, moderate, compared to high, perceived self-enhancement evoked more favorable reactions.

Dufner, Denissen et al. (2013, Study 1) also focused on perceived emotional stability as an outcome variable. Friends judged actual self-enhancers as emotionally stable: the more actors engaged in actual self-enhancement, the more emotionally stable they were deemed. However, friends' judgments of perceived self-enhancers were mixed. They regarded slightly-to-moderately perceived self-enhancers as emotionally stable, but highly perceived self-enhancers as emotionally unstable. These effects were replicated in the round-robin study (Dufner, Denissen et al., 2013, Study 3). Observers again judged actual self-enhancers as emotionally stable. In addition, they judged moderate perceived self-enhancers as emotionally stable, but high perceived self-enhancers as emotionally unstable. Finally, Dufner, Denissen et al. (Study 3) looked into perceived social influence as an outcome variable. Observers judged high actual self-enhancers as socially influential. However, they judged perceived self-enhancers as socially influential as well, even at extreme levels of perceived self-enhancement. Interestingly, actual and perceived self-enhancement interacted such that actors with high actual self-enhancement paired with high perceived self-enhancement were deemed as most socially influential.

In all, research by Dufner, Denissen, and colleagues (2013) illustrates that actual and perceived self-enhancement are linked to discrepant social consequences. Actual self-enhancement is linearly related to observer favorability. However, only moderate perceived self-enhancement is linked with favorable observer impressions. High perceived self-enhancement is met with disapproval, although it is seen as influential.

ON THE RELATIONAL AND ORGANIZATIONAL IMPLICATIONS OF SESP

It is often difficult to know whether the results of SESP studies reflect actual versus perceived self-enhancement. We will assume that most such studies reflect perceived self-enhancement for sure, and may or may not reflect actual self-enhancement. We will consequently assume that high levels of SESP (including high levels of narcissism, a personality trait with a strong proclivity to SESP) elicit unfavorable impressions, although they may buy social influence. We discuss interpersonal costs and benefits of SESP in the relational and organizational domains.

Relational Implications

Is SESP associated with, or does it promote, long-term relational liabilities? SESP may be linked with relationship deterioration. For example, some findings suggest that the disruptive behavior of SESPers may contribute to longer-term relational difficulties (Paulhus, 1998). At the same time, there are indications that self-enhancers are capable of maintaining friendships and intimate relationships. For example, intellectual and academic self-enhancement are longitudinal predictors of peer-rated likability in university work groups and classes (Dufner et al., 2012, in press). Also, self-enhancers may form long-term relationships through complementarity processes, that is, by attracting friends or partners who both admire them and care for them (Campbell, 1999). Self-enhancers may use their relationships for their own gain, such as to maintain or enhance their self-conceptions (Sedikides, Campbell, Reeder, Elliot, & Gregg, 2002).

Narcissists are a case in point. Narcissism reflects an egocentric, self-aggrandizing, dominant, and manipulative interpersonal orientation or self-presentational style (Morf, Horvath, & Torchetti, 2011; Paulhus, Westlake, Calvez, & Harms, 2013). Narcissists continuously seek admiration from their social environment in order to elevate the positivity of their self-views (Back et al., 2013; Campbell & Campbell, 2009), and SESP seems an appropriate means for this goal. So, what are the relational implications of narcissism? Narcissists report decreased relationship dysfunction in the short term (Campbell, 1999), and report relatively high dyadic adjustment, relationship commitment, and relationship satisfaction in long-term relationships. Are these self-reports reciprocated by partner reports? It would appear that this is the case. For example, narcissists are viewed as physically attractive (Holtzman & Strube, 2010) and are ascribed relatively high mate value, due not only to their perceived physical attractiveness but also to their perceived social boldness (Dufner, Rauthmann, Czarna, & Denissen, 2013). Narcissists, upon acquaintance, come across as interesting, energetic, competent, well-adjusted, and entertaining (Back, Schmukle, & Egloff, 2010; Paulhus, 1998). Also, they create excitement and bring satisfaction in the early stages of the relationship (Foster, Shrira, & Campbell, 2006).

Yet the weight of the evidence points to a damaging influence of narcissism on long-term relationships. Narcissists are disagreeable and high in need for power (Horton & Sedikides, 2009), are low on empathy or perspective-taking (Hepper, Hart, & Sedikides, 2014), and respond with aggression to criticism (Bushman & Baumeister, 1998). Indeed, with increased familiarity, narcissists come to be disliked by their acquaintances (Paulhus, 1998) due to their arrogant and antagonistic behavior (Küfner, Nestler, & Back, 2013). Narcissists regard themselves as superior to their partners (Campbell, Rudich, & Sedikides, 2002), make downward social comparisons toward important others (Krizan & Bushman, 2011), and occasionally denigrate their partners to preserve their own self-esteem (John & Robins, 1994). Narcissism is associated with low levels of emotional closeness, a game-playing love style, stronger perceptions of romantic alternatives, higher flirting, lower accommodation of relational conflict, and infidelity (Buss & Shackelford, 1997; Campbell & Foster, 2002; Foster et al., 2006). In addition, narcissism is related to stronger endorsement of myths and enjoyment of films depicting rape (Bushman, Bonacci, Van Dijk, & Baumeister, 2003), to sexual assault (Bushman et al., 2003), and to serving longer time in prison (Bushman & Baumeister, 2002).

Based on the above-reviewed research, one would expect for the partners of narcissists to be dissatisfied by the relationship. Indeed, evidence indicates so among dating university students (Lam, 2012). Facets of narcissism in the sexual domain exhibit a similar pattern. In particular, three facets (sexual exploitation, sexual entitlement, and low sexual empathy) were negatively linked to marital satisfaction, whereas another facet (sexual skill) was positively linked to marital satisfaction (McNulty & Widman, 2013). Additional research suggests that narcissism is linked to courtship violence (Ryan, Weikel, & Sprechini, 2008), domestic violence (Simmons, Lehmann, Conn, & Fowler, 2005), and spouse-abuse recidivism (Hamberger & Hastings, 1990). On the other hand, narcissism is unrelated to marital satisfaction over the first 5 years of marriage (McNulty & Widman, 2013). Perhaps some aspects of narcissism (e.g., an overly positive self-view) have beneficial influences on relationship outcomes, whereas other aspects (e.g., tendency to derogate other) have detrimental influences, and in marriages beneficial and detrimental influences cancel each other out (Back et al., 2013).

Organizational Implications

Workplace incivility may hinder the tendency to self-enhance at work and may thus lead to employee disengagement (Chen et al., 2013). Yet, although low and moderate levels of SESP may have functional implications for the workplace (Grijalva, Harms, Newman, Gaddis, & Fraley, 2013), high levels of it may complicate matters. Narcissistic self-presentation on the part of the employee or the manager provides a fitting example. Given its rising societal levels (Cai, Kwan, & Sedikides, 2012; Twenge & Campbell, 2008), narcissism in organizational or political settings has been emerging as a critical issue (Campbell, Hoffman, Campbell, & Marchisio, 2011). In the following sections, we discuss the organizational implications of narcissistic employees and managers.

Employee or Subordinate Self-Enhancement

As we discussed, at first, narcissists give off positive impressions (Back et al., 2010; Paulhus, 1998). However, impression positivity wanes and gives rise to active disliking as observers get to know the narcissist better (Czarna, Dufner, & Clifton, 2014; Paulhus, 1998). It follows that the narcissistic employee may come to be seen as a threat to the team (Tannen, 1994). In particular, the employee may be seen as hampering group harmony and obstructing project completion (Sheldon & Bettencourt, 2002) through the display of poor interpersonal skills (e.g., excessive self-praise, condescension, antagonism, hostility; Morf & Rhodewalt, 1993).

As a result of organizational distraction, managers may become frustrated at the failure of the narcissistic employee to benefit from constructive or improving feedback (Campbell, Goodie, & Foster, 2004, Study 3). Managers may also become frustrated at the narcissistic employee's persistence in putting self-interest above organizational interest. For example, narcissism is positively associated with higher anger at work (Penney & Spector, 2002), increased workplace counterproductive behavior (O'Boyle, Forsyth, Banks, & McDaniel, 2012; Penney & Spector, 2002), and tendencies to endorse more unethical practices in sales contexts (Soyer, Rovenpor, & Kopelman, 1999). Such a set of self-defeating behaviors may culminate in workplace ostracism (Smart Richman, & Leary, 2009) and negative career implications (McCall & Lombardo, 1983).

Narcissists can be charming, friendly, and warm (Back et al., 2010; Paulhus, 1998), but not indiscriminately so. Instead, they pursue the formation and consolidation of social alliances with persons that they regard as high status (Campbell, 1999; Horton & Sedikides, 2009). Narcissists, then, may be keen to conceal their indifference or hostility toward managers through a veneer of approach behavior and flattery. For example, narcissists may ingratiate themselves to their manager in an attempt to profit from managerial approval. Consistent with this possibility, high (compared to low) narcissists mimic to a greater degree high-status rather than low-status others despite, not liking better the former than the latter (Ashton-James & Levordashka, 2013). However, such an ingratiation strategy may backfire. Narcissistic employees may be seen as sycophantic (the "slime effect;" Vonk, 1998), thus making their position in the organization even more untenable. It is possible, of course, that managers value being ingratiated upon by employees. In this case, the narcissists' ingratiation strategy may gain traction with the manager (at least in the short term) but may be alienating to their colleagues (Ralston, 1985).

Manager or Leader Self-Enhancement

Narcissists may be particularly attracted to leadership positions, given that such positions enable them to achieve the goals of power, admiration, self-esteem, material gains, and access to desirable mates. In a study by Deluga (1997), raters completed the Narcissistic Personality Inventory (NPI; Raskin & Terry, 1988) on behalf of U.S. presidents, based on relevant biographical descriptions (i.e., content analyses of presidential speeches). U.S. presidents came off as far more narcissistic than the average U.S.

student (who is also not short on narcissism; Twenge & Campbell, 2008). This study suggests that narcissists are attracted to, and likely to reach, leadership positions.

Indeed, it would appear that subordinates are likely to perceive narcissistic attributes (e.g., extraversion, self-confidence, success in public performance; Grijalva et al., 2013; Wallace & Baumeister, 2002) as well-suited for leadership positions and may even be prone to elect narcissists to leadership positions. Three studies by Brunell and her colleagues (2008) illustrate this point. Participants (university students in Studies 1–2, business executives in Study 3) responded to the NPI and then became involved in four-person group discussions. Narcissists emerged (i.e., were seen by other group members) as leaders (see also Grijalva et al., 2013).

Follow-up research qualified the Brunell et al. (2008) findings. Pittinsky and Rosenthal (2008) also had small groups engage in discussion, but on repeated occasions. Narcissists emerged as leaders in the initial group interactions, but not in later interactions (cf. Paulhus, 1998). Moreover, Hogan and Hogan (2001) found that narcissistic (i.e., bold or arrogant) leaders were seen as high on self-promotion, sociability, and limit testing, but were seen also as high on likelihood of holding strong opinions, expecting special treatment, and taking advantage of others. Finally, Nevicka, De Hoogh, Van Vianen, and Ten Velden (2013) showed that narcissists were chosen more often as leaders, and narcissistic leaders were seen as more desirable, regardless of whether their liabilities (e.g., arrogance, exploitativeness) were salient or not, but only under conditions of uncertainty (i.e., when the company ostensibly underwent a period of financial instability and losses). This research suggests that narcissists may emerge as leaders, especially under conditions of uncertainty, but will likely be met in the long run with mixed impressions by followers or objective observers.

Researchers have distinguished between leader emergence and leader effectiveness (Hogan, Curphy, & Hogan, 1994; Grijalva et al., 2013). The above-described evidence indicates that, at least in the short run, narcissists are likely to emerge as leaders. But do narcissists make effective leaders? Campbell, Bush, Brunell, and Shelton (2005) addressed this question in a commons dilemma paradigm. This entails pitting the individual's short-term interests against the group's long-term interest over the sharing of common resource (e.g., timber). When participants make decisions that serve their short-term interests, the results can be detrimental to the broader community (Hardin, 1968). In the Campbell et al. (2005) research, undergraduate students assumed the role of a forestry company CEO. Their job was to harvest forests in competition with other forestry companies represented by students in adjacent rooms. Narcissistic CEOs harvested more timber at Time 1 in relation to their competitors. The more those narcissistic CEOs harvested, the more rapidly the forests got depleted and the less timber could be harvested overall. Taken together, narcissistic leadership was effective in the short run and for the self, but ineffective in the long run or for the broader society. These findings were corroborated by a recent meta-analysis (Grijalva et al., 2013).

Do narcissists make effective transformational leaders (Campbell et al., 2011)? Transformational leadership is gauged by its impact on followers. It entails the clear communication of a vision encompassing organizational goals, and it aims to inspire followers to alter perceptions, expectations, and motivations toward accomplishing these goals (Bass, 1985). Transformational leadership has four components: (a) idealized influence (i.e., provision of a role model that instills pride while gaining trust and respect), (b) inspirational motivation (i.e., articulation of an inspiring vision), (c) intellectual stimulation (i.e., challenge of assumptions, stimulation of creativity, encouragement of problem-solving), and (d) individualized consideration (i.e., attention to the needs of the followers, mentoring followers).

Deluga (1997) reported that narcissistic U.S. presidents are deemed more charismatic, which can be considered a component of transformational leadership (i.e., idealized influence). Also, Judge, LePine, and Rich (2006) found a positive association between narcissism and self-ratings of global transformational leadership. Khoo and Burch (2008) did not replicate this pattern. However, fine-grained analyses of their data revealed a positive relation between narcissism and idealized influence, but a negative relation between narcissism and individual consideration. These results suggest that narcissists score high on the charismatic component of transformational leadership, but low on its other-oriented component. Consistent with this finding, narcissistic managers are rated by their superiors as lacking on the interpersonal side of management and on integrity (but as no worse on competence) compared to nonnarcissistic managers (Blair, Hoffman, & Helland, 2008).

Watts and colleagues (2013) addressed the issue of narcissistic transformational leadership effectiveness based on the histories of 42 U.S. presidents. Narcissistic presidents were more effective in crisis management, agenda setting, and legislative initiatives. However, they were also more frequently the subject of congressional impeachment resolutions and behaved in a more unethical manner. In a similar vein, narcissism is linked to acceptance of workplace deviance (Judge et al., 2006) and to proneness to white-collar crime (Blickle, Schlegel, Fassbender, & Klein, 2006). Stein (2013) used the example of Richard "Dick" Fuld, CEO and chairman of Lehman Brothers from 1994 to 2008 to illustrate the ups and downs of narcissistic leadership. Under Fuld's headship, this highly fractured company was re-united and throve with regard to market capitalization and net revenue. Fuld was also praised for his decisive response to the 9/11 attacks, which impacted directly upon Lehman Brothers' global headquarters. These may have been the reasons why Fuld's autocratic leadership style, which showed zero tolerance for dissent, was consented to by his subordinates. His boldness, arrogance, and risk-proneness, however, led to ruinous financial investments and decisions, resulting in Lehman Brothers' bankruptcy and triggering a global financial crisis.

The Richard "Dick" Fuld case suggests that the effectiveness of narcissistic leadership may be contingent on contextual factors (Campbell & Campbell, 2009). As Rosenthal and Pittinsky (2006) put it, it is possible that narcissistic leaders are effective in domains that require charisma and extraversion (e.g., sales), but ineffective in domains that require the formation and maintenance of relationships and trust (e.g., community projects). Yet, even when charisma is required, narcissistic leadership has the potential to result in follower exploitation and societal calamity, as it might have been with several notorious narcissistic leaders (e.g., Charles Manson, Hitler, Mao Tse-tung, Stalin; Conger, 1989; House & Howell, 1992). In all, although narcissists are likely to evoke disarray when they need to maintain a functional order, they may do an acceptable job at establishing a new order (Rosenthal & Pittinsky, 2006).

Let us examine the above-described possibility more closely. Is narcissistic leadership typically effective when the times call for the establishment of a new order? Transformational or visionary leadership may entail public risks (e.g., large-scale acquisitions or corporate strategy changes). Chatterjee and Hambrick (2007) obtained an estimate of CEOs' narcissism based on a number of indicators (e.g., use of first-person pronouns at interviews, photograph size in corporate reports) and then linked narcissism with corporate performance. CEO narcissism was unrelated to level of corporate performance. However, narcissism was positively linked to corporate performance volatility. Narcissistic CEOs were indulging in huge public risks. Sometimes these risks paid off, other times they did not. However, in financial terms, performance variability is a liability, as it diminishes corporate value; that is, stable performance is considered as more valuable than fluctuating performance, controlling for outcomes. As such, narcissistic leadership had a net negative impact on the corporation. Narcissists may temporarily infuse the organization with energy or purpose, but they do not seem to be particularly effective in establishing a new order.

In all, high levels of SESP, as manifested by narcissists, are associated with organizational upheaval. Narcissistic employees are seen as impeding group harmony and productivity. Narcissistic managers may infuse the organization with excitement in the short run, but inflict relational and financial damage in the long run.

CONCLUDING REMARKS

Self-presentation is an integral part of social behavior. One type of self-presentation is SESP. Research indicates that individuals are capable of SESP, especially in the communion domain. Yet SESP has interpersonal, relational, and organizational implications.

Actual self-enhancement entails mostly favorable consequences. Perceived self-enhancement is met with disapproval, and those perceived to self-enhance highly are regarded as emotionally unstable and socially unappealing albeit socially influential. Perceived self-enhancers are disliked partly because they are deemed to show contempt for others and predominantly because they are deemed to show contempt for the observer. Context, however, moderates observer disapproval of SESP. For example, SESP is looked upon favorably when it occurs in response to a question, is accompanied by evidence, or is part of a job interview (especially in Western culture). Still, at the interpersonal level, actual self-enhancement (i.e., possession of unwarrantedly positive self-views) entails mostly favorable consequences. Actual self-enhancers are liked and are deemed as emotionally stable as well as socially attractive.

An intriguing case of SESP is narcissism. Narcissists are judged physically attractive and, in the initial stages of acquaintance, as interpersonally appealing. Also, in the initial stages of dating relationships, they are rated as exciting and satisfying partners. However, in later stages of acquaintance or relationships, they are judged as interpersonally unappealing and relationally troublesome.

At the organizational level, narcissism follows similar temporal patterns. Although an employee may be seen as contributing energetically to the organization early on, he or she will likely be seen as undermining morale and productivity in the long run. Negative consequences may ensue both for the organization and the employee. Narcissistic leaders are also a mixed bag. Because they are seen as socially influential, if not dominant, narcissists are preferred as leaders, especially under conditions of uncertainty. Their effectiveness, though, leaves a lot to be desired. Despite occasional early successes, they do not seem to reap viable organizational benefits and instead are liable to generate organizational turmoil.

REFERENCES

Abele, A. E., & Wojciszke, B. (2014). Communal and agentic content. A dual perspective model. *Advances in Experimental Social Psychology 50,* 195—255. doi:10.1016/B978-0-12-800284-1.00004-7

Alicke, M. D. (2000). Evaluating social comparison targets. In J. Suls & L. Wheeler (Eds.), *Handbook of social comparison: Theory and research* (pp. 271–294). New York, NY: Plenum.

Alicke, M. D., & Sedikides, C. (2009). Self-enhancement and self-protection: What they are and what they do. *European Review of Social Psychology, 20,* 1–48. doi:10.1080/10463280802613866

Alicke, M. D., & Sedikides, C. (2011). *Handbook of self-enhancement and self-protection.* New York, NY: Guilford.

Anderson, C., Brion, S., Moore, D. A., & Kennedy, J. A. (2012). A status-enhancement account of overconfidence. *Journal of Personality and Social Psychology, 103,* 718–735. doi:10.1037/a0029395

Ashton-James, C. E., & Levordashka, A. (2013). When the wolf wears sheep's clothing: Individual differences in the desire to be liked influence nonconscious behavioral mimicry. *Social Psychological and Personality Science, 4,* 643–648. doi:10.1177/1948550613476097

Back, M. D., Küfner, A. C., Dufner, M., Gerlach, T. M., Rauthmann, J. F., & Denissen, J. J. (2013). Narcissistic admiration and rivalry: Disentangling the bright and dark sides of narcissism. *Journal of Personality and Social Psychology, 10,* 1013–1037. doi:10.1037/a0034431

Back, M. D., Schmukle, S. C., & Egloff, B. (2010). Why are narcissists so charming at first sight? Decoding the narcissism-popularity link at zero acquaintance. *Journal of Personality and Social Psychology, 98,* 132–145. doi:10.1037/a0016338

Bass, B. M. (1985). *Leadership and performance.* New York, NY: Free Press.

Blair, C. A., Hoffman, B. J., & Helland, K. A. (2008). Narcissism in organizations: An empirical look at managerial integrity and effectiveness. *Human Performance, 21,* 254–276.

Blickle, G., Schlegel, A., Fassbender, P., & Klein, U. (2006). Some personality correlates of business white-collar crime. *Applied Psychology, 55,* 220–233. doi:10.1111/j.1464-0597.2006.00226

Bond, M. H., Kwan, S. Y., & Li, C. (2000). Decomposing a sense of superiority: The differential social impact of self-regard and regard for others. *Journal of Research in Personality, 34,* 537–553. doi:10.1006/jrpe.2000.2297

Bratman, M. E. (1987). *Intentions, plans, and practical reason.* Cambridge, MA: Harvard University Press.

Brickman, P., & Seligman, C. (1974). Effects of public and private expectancies on attributions of competence and interpersonal attraction. *Journal of Social Psychology, 42,* 559–568.

Brunell, A. B., Gentry, W. A., Campbell, W. K., Hoffman, B. J., Kuhnert, K. W., & DeMarree, K. G. (2008). Leader emergence: The case of the narcissistic leader. *Personality and Social Psychology Bulletin, 34,* 1663–1676. doi:10.1177/0146167208324101

Bushman, B. J., & Baumeister, R. F. (1998). Threatened egotism, narcissism, self-esteem, and direct and displaced aggression: Does self-love or self-hate lead to violence? *Journal of Personality and Social Psychology, 75,* 219–229. doi:10.1037/0022-3514.75.1.219

Bushman, B. J., & Baumeister, R. F. (2002). Does self-love or self-hate lead to violence. *Journal of Research in Personality, 36,* 543–545. doi:10.1016/S0092-6566(02)00502-0

Bushman, B. J., Bonacci, A. M., Van Dijk, M., & Baumeister, R. F. (2003). Narcissism, sexual refusal, and aggression: Testing a narcissistic reactance model of sexual coercion. *Journal of Personality and Social Psychology, 84,* 1027–1040. doi:10.1037/0022-3514.84.5.1027

Buss, D. M., & Shackelford, T. K. (1997). Susceptibility to infidelity in the first year of marriage. *Journal of Research in Personality, 31,* 193–221. doi:10.13072/midss.640

Cai, H., Kwan, V., & Sedikides, C. (2012). A sociocultural approach to narcissism: The case of modern China. *European Journal of Personality, 26,* 529–535. doi:10.1002/per.852

Campbell, W. K. (1999). Narcissism and romantic attraction. *Journal of Personality and Social Psychology, 77,* 1254–1270. doi:10.1037/0022-3514.77.6.1254

Campbell, W. K., Bush, C. P., Brunell, A. B., & Shelton, J. (2005). Understanding the social costs of narcissism: The case of the tragedy of the commons. *Personality and Social Psychology Bulletin, 31,* 1358–1368. doi:10.1177/0146167205274855

Campbell, W. K., & Campbell, S. M. (2009). On the self-regulatory dynamics created by the peculiar benefits and costs of narcissism: A contextual reinforcement model and examination of leadership. *Self and Identity, 8,* 214–232. doi:10.1080/15298860802505129

Campbell, W. K., & Foster, C. A. (2002). Narcissism and commitment in romantic relationship: An investment model analysis. *Personality and Social Psychology Bulletin, 28,* 484–495. doi:10.1177/0146167202287006

Campbell, W. K., Goodie, A. S., & Foster, J. D. (2004). Narcissism, overconfidence, and risk attitude. *Journal of Behavioral Decision Making, 17,* 297–311. doi:10.1002/bdm.475

Campbell, W. K., Hoffman, B. J., Campbell, S. M., & Marchisio, G. (2011). Narcissism in organizational contexts. *Human Resource Management Review, 21,* 268–284. doi:10.1016/j.hrmr.2010.10.007

Campbell, W. K., Rudich, E., & Sedikides, C. (2002). Narcissism, self-esteem, and the positivity of self-views: Two portraits of self-love. *Personality and Social Psychology Bulletin, 28,* 358–368. doi:10.1177/0146167202286007

Carlston, D. E., & Shovar, N. (1983). Effects of performance attributions on others' perceptions of the attributor. *Journal of Personality and Social Psychology, 44,* 515–525.

Carver, C. S., Kus, L. A., & Scheier, M. F. (1994). Effects of good versus bad mood and optimistic versus pessimistic outlook on social acceptance versus rejection. *Journal of Social and Clinical Psychology, 13,* 138–151. doi:10.1521/jscp.1994.13.2.138

Chatterjee, A., & Hambrick, D. C. (2007). It's all about me: Narcissistic chief executive officers and their effects on company strategy and performance. *Administrative Science Quarterly, 52,* 351–386. doi:10.2189/asqu.52.3.351

Chen, Y., Ferris, L., Kwan, H. K., Yan, M., Zhou, M., & Hong, Y. (2013). Self-love's lost labor: A self-enhancement model of workplace incivility. *Academy of Management Journal, 56,* 1199–1219. doi:10.5465/amj.2010.0906

Conger, J. A. (1989). *The charismatic leader. Behind the mystique of exceptional leadership.* San Francisco, CA: Jossey-Bass.

Czarna, A. Z., Dufner, M., & Clifton, A. D. (2014). The effects of vulnerable and grandiose narcissism on liking-based and disliking-based centrality in social networks. *Journal of Research in Personality, 50,* 42–45. doi:10.1016/j.jrp.2014.02.004

Dayter, D. (2014). Self-praise in microblogging. *Journal of Pragmatics, 61,* 91–102. doi:10.1016/j.pragma.2013.11.021

Deluga, R. J. (1997). Relationship among American presidential charismatic leadership, narcissism, and rated performance. *Leadership Quarterly, 8,* 4965. doi:10.1016/S1048-9843(97)90030-8.

Dipboye, R. L., & Wiley, J. W. (1977). Reactions of college recruiters to interviewee sex and self-presentation style. *Journal of Vocational Behavior, 10,* 1–12.

Dufner, M., Denissen, J. A., Sedikides, C., Van Zalk, M., Meeus, W. H. J., & Van Aken, M. A. G. (2013). Are actual and perceived intellectual self-enhancers evaluated differently by social perceivers? *European Journal of Personality, 27,* 621–633. doi:10.1002/per.1934

Dufner, M., Denissen, J. A., Van Zalk, M., Matthes, B., Meeus, W. H. J., Van Aken, M. A. G., & Sedikides, C. (2012). Positive intelligence illusions: On the relation between intellectual self-enhancement and psychological adjustment. *Journal of Personality, 80,* 537–571. doi:10.1111/j.1467-6494.2011.00742.x

Dufner, M., Rauthmann, J. F., Czarna, A. Z., & Denissen, J. J. A. (2013). Are narcissists sexy? Zeroing in on the effect of narcissism on short-term mate appeal. *Personality and Social Psychology Bulletin, 39,* 870–882. doi: 10.1177/0146167213483580

Dufner, M., Reitz, A. K., & Zander, L. (in press). Antecedents, consequences, and mechanisms: On the longitudinal interplay between academic self-enhancement and psychological adjustment. *Journal of Personality.*

Dunbar, R. I. M., Duncan, N. D. C., & Marriott, A. (1997). Human conversational behavior. *Human Nature, 8,* 231–246. doi:10.1007/BF02912493

Emler, N. (1994). Gossip, reputation, and social adaptation. In R. F. Goodman & A. Ben-Zeíev (Eds.), *Good gossip* (pp. 117–138). Lawrence: University of Kansas Press.

Forsyth, D. R., Berger, R. E., & Mitchell, T. (1981). The effect of self-serving versus other-serving claims of responsibility on attraction and attribution in groups. *Social Psychology Quarterly, 44,* 59–64.

Foster, J. D., Shrira, I., & Campbell, W. K. (2006). Theoretical models of narcissism, sexuality, and relationship commitment. *Journal of Social and Personal Relationships, 23,* 367–386. doi:10.1177/0265407506064204

Gergen, K. G., & Wishnov, B. (1965). Others' self-evaluations and interaction anticipation as determinants of self-presentation. *Journal of Personality and Social Psychology, 2,* 348–358.

Gibson, B., & Sachau, D. (2000). Sandbagging as a self-presentation strategy: Claiming to be less than you are. *Personality and Social Psychology Bulletin, 26,* 56–70. doi:10.1177/0146167200261006

Gilbert, D. T., & Malone, P. S. (1995). The correspondence bias. *Psychological Bulletin, 117,* 21–38. doi:10.1037/0033-2909.117.1.21

Godfrey, D., Jones, E. E., & Lord, C. (1986). Self-promotion is not ingratiating. *Journal of Personality and Social Psychology, 50,* 106–115. doi:10.1037/0022-3514.50.1.106

Goffman, E. (1959). *The presentation of self in everyday life.* New York, NY: Doubleday.

Gordon, R. A. (1996). Impact of ingratiation on judgments and evaluations: A meta-analytic investigation. *Journal of Personality and Social Psychology, 71*, 54–70. doi:10.1037/0022-3514.71.1.54

Grijalva, E., Harms, P. E., Newman, D. A., Gaddis, B. H., & Fraley, R. C. (2013). Narcissism and leadership: A meta-analytic review of linear and non-linear relationships. *Personnel Psychology*. Advance online publication. doi:10.1111/peps.12072

Guadagno, R. E., & Cialdini, R. B. (2007). Gender differences in impression management in organizations: A qualitative review. *Sex Roles, 56*, 483–494. doi:10.1007/s11199-007-9187-3

Gurevitch, Z. D. (1984). Impression formation during tactical self-presentation. *Social Psychology Quarterly, 47*, 262–270. doi:10.2307/3033823

Hamberger, L. K., & Hastings, J. (1990). Recidivism following spouse abuse abatement counseling: Treatment program implications. *Violence and Victims, 5*, 157–179.

Hardin, G. (1968). The tragedy of the commons. *Science, 162*, 1243–1248.

Helweg-Larsen, M., Sadeghian, P., & Webb, M. S. (2002). The stigma of being pessimistically biased. *Journal of Social and Clinical Psychology, 21*, 92–107.

Hepper, E. G., Hart, C. M., & Sedikides, C. (2014). Moving Narcissus: Can narcissists be empathic? *Personality and Social Psychology Bulletin, 40*, 1079–1091. doi:10.1177/0146167214535812

Hewitt, J. P., & Stokes, R. (1975). Disclaimers. *American Sociological Review, 40*, 1–11.

Higgins, C. A., & Judge, T. A. (2004). The effect of applicant influence tactics on recruiter perceptions of fit and hiring recommendations: A field study. *The Journal of Applied Psychology, 89*, 622–632. doi:10.1037/0021-9010.89.4.622622

Hogan, R., Curphy, G. J., & Hogan, J. (1994). What we know about leadership: Effectiveness and personality. *American Psychologist, 49*, 493–504.

Hogan, R., & Hogan, J. (2001). Assessing leadership: A view from the dark side. *International Journal of Selection and Assessment, 9*, 40–51.

Holtgraves, T., & Srull, T. K. (1989). The effects of positive self-descriptions on impressions: General principles and individual differences. *Personality and Social Psychology Bulletin, 15*, 452–462. doi:10.1177/0146167289153014

Holtzman, N. S., & Strube, M. J. (2010). Narcissism and attractiveness. *Journal of Research in Personality, 44*, 133–136. doi:10.1016/j.jrp.2009.10.004

Hoorens, V. (2011). The social consequences of self-enhancement and self-protection. In M. D. Alicke & C. Sedikides (Eds.), *Handbook of self-enhancement and self-protection* (pp. 235–257). New York, NY: Guildford.

Hoorens, V., Pandelaere, M., Oldersma, F., & Sedikides, C. (2012). The hubris hypothesis: You can self-enhance but you'd better not show it. *Journal of Personality, 5*, 1237–1274. doi:10.1111/j.1467-6494.2011.00759.

Horton, R. S., & Sedikides, C. (2009). Narcissistic responding to ego threat: When the status of the evaluator matters. *Journal of Personality, 77*, 1493–1525. doi:10.1111/j.1467-6494.2009.00590.

House, R., & Howell, J. M. (1992). Personality and charismatic leadership. *Leadership Quarterly, 3*, 81–108.

John, O. P., & Robins, R. W. (1994). Accuracy and bias in self-perception: Individual differences in self-enhancement and the role of narcissism. *Journal of Personality and Social Psychology, 66,* 206–219. doi:10.1037/0022-3514.66.1.206

Jones, E. E., & Pittman, T. S. (1982). Toward a general theory of strategic self-presentation. In J. Suls (Ed.), *Psychological perspectives on the self* (pp. 231–261). Hillsdale, NJ: Erlbaum.

Jones, S. C., & Shrauger, J. S. (1970). Reputation and self-evaluation as determinants of attractiveness. *Sociometry, 33,* 276–286. doi:10.1037/0022-3514.73.4.747

Judge, T. A., LePine, J. A., & Rich, B. L. (2006). Loving yourself abundantly: Relationship of the narcissistic personality to self-and other perceptions of workplace deviance, leadership, and task and contextual performance. *Journal of Applied Psychology, 91,* 762–776.

Kennedy, J. A., Anderson, C., & Moore, D. A. (2013). When overconfidence is revealed to others: Testing the status-enhancement theory of overconfidence. *Organizational Behavior and Human Decision Processes, 122,* 266–279. doi:10.1016/j.obhdp.2013.08.005

Khoo, H. S., & Burch, G. S. J. (2008). The 'dark side' of leadership personality and transformational leadership: An exploratory study. *Personality and Individual Differences, 44,* 86–97.

Kowalski, R. M. (1997). Aversive interpersonal behaviors: An overarching framework. In R. M. Kowalski (Ed.), *Aversive interpersonal behaviors* (pp. 215–233). New York, NY: Plenum.

Krizan, Z., & Bushman, B. J. (2011). Better than my loved ones: Social comparison tendencies among narcissists. *Personality and Individual Differences, 50,* 212–216. doi:10.1016/j.paid.2010.09.031

Kruger, J., & Gilovich, T. (1999). "Naïve cynicism" in everyday theories of responsibility assessment: On biased assumption of bias. *Journal of Personality and Social Psychology, 76,* 743–753.

Küfner, A. C. P., Nestler, S., & Back, M. D. (2013). The two pathways to being an (un)popular narcissist. *Journal of Personality, 81,* 184–195. doi:10.1111/j.1467-6494.2012.00795.x

Lafrenière, M.-A., K., Sedikides, C., Van Tongeren, D. R., & Davis, J. L. (2014). *On the perceived intentionality of self-enhancement.* Manuscript under review, University of Southampton.

Lam, Z. K. W. (2012). Narcissism and romantic relationship: The mediating role of perception discrepancy. *Discovery—SS Student E-Journal, 1,* 1–20.

Leary, M. R. (1995). *Self-presentation: Impression management and interpersonal behavior.* Boulder, CO: Westview.

Leary, M. R., & Kowalski, R. M. (1990). Impression management: A literature review and two component model. *Psychological Bulletin, 107,* 34–47. doi:10.1037/0033-2909.107.1.34.

Le Barbenchon, E., Milhabet, I., Steiner, D. D., & Priolo, D. (2008). Social acceptance of exhibiting optimism. *Current Research in Social Psychology, 14,* 52–63.

Lee, S., Quigley, B. M., Nesler, M. S., Corbett, A. B., & Tedeschi, J. T. (1999). Development of a self-presentation tactics scale. *Personality and Individual Differences, 26,* 701–722. doi:10.1016/S0191-8869(98)00178-0

Markus, H., & Kitayama, S. (1991). Culture and the self: Implications for cognition, emotion, and motivation. *Psychological Review, 98,* 224–253. doi:10.1037/0033-295X.98.2.224

McCall, M., & Lombardo, M. (1983). *Off the track: Why and how successful executives get derailed* (Technical Rep. No. 2 1). Greensboro, NC: Center for Creative Leadership.

McNulty, J. K., & Widman, L. (2013). The implications of sexual narcissism for sexual and marital satisfaction. *Archives of Sexual Behavior, 42,* 1021–1032. doi:10.1007/s10508-012-0041-5

Miller, L. C., Cooke, L. L., Tsang, J., & Morgan, F. (1992). Should I brag? Nature and impact of positive and boastful disclosures for women and men. *Human Communications Research, 18,* 364–399. doi:10.1111/j.1468-2958.1992.tb00557.x

Morf, C. C., Horvath, S., & Torchetti, L. (2011). Narcissistic self-enhancement: Tales of (successful?) self-portrayal. In M. D. Alicke & C. Sedikides (Eds.), *Handbook of self-enhancement and self-protection* (pp. 399–424). New York, NY: Guilford.

Morf, C. C., & Rhodewalt, F. (1993). Narcissism and self-evaluation maintenance: Explorations in object relations. *Personality and Social Psychology Bulletin, 19,* 668–676. doi:10.1177/0146167293196001

Nevicka, B., De Hoogh, A. H. B., Van Vianen, A. E. M., & Ten Velden, F. S. (2013). Uncertainty enhances the preference for narcissistic leaders. *European Journal of Social Psychology, 43,* 370–380. doi:10.1002/ejsp.1943

O'Boyle, E. H., Jr., Forsyth, D. R., Banks, G. C., & McDaniel, M. A. (2012). A meta-analysis of the Dark Triad and work behavior: A social exchange perspective. *Journal of Applied Psychology, 97,* 557–579. doi:10.1037/a0025679

O'Mara, E. M., Gaertner, L., Sedikides, C., Zhou, X., & Liu, Y. (2012). A longitudinal-experimental test of the panculturality of self-enhancement: Self-enhancement promotes psychological well-being both in the West and the East. *Journal of Research in Personality, 46,* 157–163. doi:10.1016/j.jrp.2012.01.001

Paulhus, D. L. (1998). Interpersonal and intrapsychic adaptiveness of trait self-enhancement: A mixed blessing? *Journal of Personality and Social Psychology, 74,* 1197–1208. doi:10.1037/0022-3514.74.5.1197

Paulhus, D. L., & Trapnell, P. D. (2008). Self-presentation of personality: An agency-communion approach. In O. P. John, R. W. Robins, & L. A. Pervin (Eds.), *Handbook of personality psychology: Theory and research* (pp. 492–517). New York, NY: Guilford.

Paulhus, D. L., Westlake, B. G., Calvez, S. S., & Harms, P. D. (2013). Self-presentation style in job interviews: The role of personality and culture. *Journal of Applied Social Psychology, 43,* 2042–2059. doi:10.1111/jasp.12157

Penney, L. M., & Spector, P. (2002). Narcissism and counterproductive behavior: Do bigger egos mean bigger problems? *International Journal of Selection and Assessment, 10,* 126–134. doi:10.1111/1468-2389.00199

Pittinsky, T. L., & Rosenthal, S. A. (2008). *From selection to rejection: The trajectory of narcissistic leaders.* Unpublished Manuscript, Harvard University.

Powers, T. A., & Zuroff, D. C. (1988). Interpersonal consequences of overt self-criticism: A comparison with neutral and self-enhancing presentations of self. *Journal of Personality and Social Psychology, 54,* 1054–1062. doi:10.1037/0022-3514.54.6.1054

Proost, K., Germeys, F., & Schreurs, B. (2012). When does self-promotion work? The influence of temporal distance on interviewer evaluations. *Journal of Personnel Psychology, 11,* 109–117. doi:10.1027/1866-5888/a000062

Proost, K., Schreurs, B., De Witte, K., & Derous, E. (2010). Ingratiation and self-promotion in the selection interview: The effects of using single tactics or a combination of tactics on interviewer judgments. *Journal of Applied Social Psychology, 40,* 2155–2169. doi:10.1111/j.1559-1816.2010.00654.x

Ralston, D. A. (1985). Employee ingratiation: The role of management. *The Academy of Management Review, 10,* 477–487. doi:10.2307/258129

Raskin, R. N., & Terry, H. (1988). A principal-components analysis of the narcissistic personality inventory and further evidence of its construct validity. *Journal of Personality and Social Psychology, 54,* 890–902. doi:10.1037/0022-3514.54.5.890

Robinson, M. D., Johnson, J. T., & Shields, S. A. (1995). On the advantages of modesty: The benefits of a balanced self-presentation. *Communication Research, 22,* 575–591. doi:10.1177/009365095022005003

Rosenthal, S. A., & Pittinsky, T. L. (2006). Narcissistic leadership. *The Leadership Quarterly, 17,* 617–633.

Rudman, L. A. (1998). Self-promotion as a risk factor for women: The costs and benefits of counterstereotypical impression management. *Journal of Personality and Social Psychology, 74,* 629. doi:10.1037/0022-3514.74.3.629

Ryan, K. M., Weikel, K., & Sprechini, G. (2008). Gender differences and narcissism in courtship violence in dating couples. *Sex Roles, 58,* 802–813. doi:10.1007/s11199-008-9403-9

Schlenker, B. R. (1975). Self-presentation: Managing the impression of consistency when reality interferes with self-enhancement. *Journal of Personality and Social Psychology, 32,* 1030–1037. doi:10.1037/0022-3514.32.6.1030

Schlenker, B. R. (1980). *Impression management: The self-concept social identity and interpersonal relations.* Monterey, CA: Brooks/Cole.

Schlenker, B. R. (2012). Self-presentation. In M. R. Leary & J. P. Tangney (Eds.), *Handbook of self and identity* (2nd ed., pp. 542–570). New York, NY: Guilford.

Schlenker, B. R., & Leary, M. R. (1982). Social anxiety and self-presentation: A conceptualization and model. *Psychological Bulletin, 92,* 641–669. doi:10.1037/0033-2909.92.3.641

Schmid, M. M., Frauendorfer, D., & Popovic, L. (2011). Self-promoting and modest job applicants in different cultures. *Journal of Personnel Psychology, 10,* 70–77. doi:10.1027/1866-5888/a000034

Sedikides, C. (2012). Self-protection. In M. R. Leary & J. P. Tangney (Eds.), *Handbook of self and identity* (2nd ed., pp. 327–353). New York, NY: Guilford.

Sedikides, C., Campbell, W. K., Reeder, G., Elliot, A. J., & Gregg, A. P. (2002). Do others bring out the worst in narcissists? The "Others Exist for Me" illusion. In Y. Kashima, M. Foddy, & M. Platow (Eds.), *Self and identity: Personal, social, and symbolic* (pp. 103–123). Mahwah, NJ: Erlbaum.

Sedikides, C., Gaertner, L., & Toguchi, Y. (2003). Pancultural self-enhancement. *Journal of Personality and Social Psychology, 84,* 60–70. doi:10.1037/0022-3514.84.1.60

Sedikides, C., Gaertner, L., & Vevea, J. L. (2005). Pancultural self-enhancement reloaded: A meta-analytic reply to Heine (2005). *Journal of Personality and Social Psychology, 89,* 539–551. doi:10.1037/0022-3514.89.4.539

Sedikides, C., & Gregg, A. P. (2008). Self-enhancement: Food for thought. *Perspectives on Psychological Science, 3,* 102–116. doi:10.1111/j.1745-6916.2008.00068.x

Sedikides, C., Gregg, A. P., & Hart, C. M. (2008). The importance of being modest. In C. Sedikides & S. J. Spencer (Eds.), *The self* (pp. 163–184). New York, NY: Psychology.

Sheldon, K. M., & Bettencourt, B. A. (2002). Psychological need-satisfaction and subjective well-being within social groups. *British Journal of Social Psychology, 41,* 25–38. doi:10.1348/014466602165036

Simmons, C. A., Lehmann, P., Cobb, N., & Fowler, C. R. (2005). Personality profiles of women and men arrested for domestic violence: An analysis of similarities and differences. *Journal of Offender Rehabilitation, 41,* 63–81.

Smart Richman, L., & Leary, M. R. (2009). Reactions to discrimination, stigmatization, ostracism, and other forms of interpersonal rejection: A multimotive model. *Psychological Review, 116,* 365–383. doi:10.1037/a0015250.

Soyer, R. B., Rovenpor, J. L., & Kopelman, R. E. (1999). Narcissism and achievement motivation as related to three facets of the sales role: Attraction, satisfaction and performance. *Journal of Business and Psychology, 14,* 285–304. doi:10.1037/1076-8998.10.4.330

Stein, M. (2013). When does narcissistic leadership become problematic? Dick Fuld at Lehman Brothers. *Journal of Management Inquiry, 22,* 282–293.

Tal-Or, N. (2010). Bragging in the right context: Impressions formed of self-promoters who create a context for their boasts. *Social Influence, 1,* 23–29. doi:10.1080/15534510903160480

Tannen, D. (1994). *Talking from 9 to 5.* New York, NY: Morrow.

Tedeschi, J. T, & Lindskold, S. (1976). *Social psychology: Interdependence, interaction, and influence.* New York, NY: Wiley.

Tice, D. M., Butler, J. L., Muraven, M. B., & Stillwell, A. M. (1995). When modesty prevails: Differential favorability of self-presentation to friends and strangers. *Journal of Personality and Social Psychology, 69,* 1120–1138. doi:10.1037/0022-3514.69.6.1120

Trope, Y., & Liberman, N. (2010). Construal level theory of psychological distance. *Psychological Review, 117,* 440–463. doi:10.1037/a0018963

Twenge, J. M., & Campbell, S. M. (2008). Generational differences in psychological traits and their impact on the workplace. *Journal of Managerial Psychology, 23,* 862–877. doi:10.1108/02683940810904367

Van Tongeren, D. R., Davis, D. E., & Hook, J. N. (2014). Social benefits of humility: Initiating and maintaining romantic relationships. *The Journal of Positive Psychology, 9,* 313–321. doi:10.1080/17439760.2014.898317

von Hippel, W., & Trivers, R. (2011). The evolution and psychology of self-deception. *Behavioral and Brain Sciences, 34,* 1–16. doi:10.1017/S0140525X10001354

Vonk, R. (1998). The slime effect: Suspicions and dislike of likeable behavior toward superiors. *Journal of Personality and Social Psychology, 74,* 849–864. doi:10.1037/0022-3514.74.4.849

Vonk, R. (1999). Impression formation and impression management: Motives, traits, and likeability inferred from self-promoting and self-deprecating behavior. *Social Cognition, 17,* 390–412. doi:10.1521/soco.1999.17.4.390

Vorauer, J. D., & Miller, D. T. (1997). Failure to recognize the effect of implicit social influence on the presentation of self. *Journal of Personality and Social Psychology, 73,* 281–295. doi:10.1037/0022-3514.73.2.281

Wallace, H. M., & Baumeister, R. F. (2002). The performance of narcissists rises and falls with perceived opportunity for glory. *Journal of Personality and Social Psychology, 82,* 819–834. doi:10.1037/0022-3514.82.5.819

Watts, A. L., Lilienfeld, S. O., Smith, S. F., Miller, J. D., Campbell, W. K., Waldman, I. D., . . . Faschingbauer, T. J. (2013). The double-edged sword of grandiose narcissism: Implications for successful and unsuccessful leadership among U.S. presidents. *Psychological Science, 24,* 2379–2389. doi:10.1177/0956797613491970

Wosinska, W., Dabul, A. J., Whetstone-Dion, R., & Cialdini, R. B. (1996). Self-presentational responses to success in the organization: The costs and benefits of modesty. *Basic and Applied Social Psychology, 18,* 229–242.

Wu, R.-J. R. (2011). A conversation analysis of self-praising in everyday Mandarin interaction. *Journal of Pragmatics, 43,* 3152–3176. doi:10.1016/j.pragma.2011.05.016

CHAPTER 3

THE POLITICAL SELF

Sean T. Stevens
Rutgers University

Stephanie M. Anglin
Rutgers University

Lee Jussim
Rutgers University

Politics exists in some form in most, if not all, human societies. Political behavior has even been observed in some nonhuman primates (de Waal, 2013). Intense attitudes and beliefs often form the basis for activism and collective action (Simon & Klandermans, 2001). Indeed, activism has made events such as the abolishment of slavery and outright segregation in some societies possible. Yet because activists tend to organize around a shared grievance, it appears to also possess a dark side—a need for a rival or "enemy" to spur collective action in pursuit of a political goal (Martin, Scully, & Levitt, 1990; Simon & Klandermans, 2001). In the political domain, the "enemy" appears to take at least two potential forms: an obstacle to achieving desired ends or, groups attempting to undo already achieved programs, policies, institutions, or practices. What is it about politics that generates such intensity and animosity? How can a social domain trigger such intense

Self-Concept, Motivation, and Identity, pages 57–81

positive feelings and reactions while at the same time rely on what appears to be a foundation of negative feelings and reactions?

In this chapter we present a perspective that suggests that, at least for some people, politics is a central component of their identity. For others, politics may remain a more peripheral concern but temporarily become a central component of their identity due to situational factors. Regardless of its permanence, when politics is a central component of the self, it appears that the protection of one's political self becomes paramount. We suggest this is because many political attitudes and beliefs are, in part, reflections of one's moral intuitions. Moralized issues help people define themselves and identify like-minded others (Graham & Haidt, 2010), yet they also make compromise with those who hold different views difficult (Skitka, 2010).

We first connect the political domain to issues of self and identity and then provide a brief theoretical overview of our approach. Next, we explore how the political domain provides people with opportunity to satisfy their need for affiliation and inclusion with others. Finally, we explore how the political domain also offers opportunity for people to satisfy their need for differentiation and distinctiveness from others.

POLITICS AND THE SELF

People simultaneously seek inclusion with and differentiation from others (Brewer, 1999). These two opposing needs are part of a psychological mechanism that attempts to balance this tension and obtain a state of optimal distinctiveness (Brewer, 1991). Thus, large-scale societies spur the formation of smaller subgroups that can balance these competing needs more effectively. The political domain represents a social context in which the inclusion-differentiation dynamic constitutes an almost ever-present tension. In this chapter, we propose the construct of the *political self*, a subdivision of the self that helps an individual navigate the tension between the competing needs for assimilation and differentiation within the political domain.

In general, the self serves organizational and motivational functions. It organizes self-relevant information, such as one's identities, roles, groups, attitudes, values, and goals (Sherman & Cohen, 2006), into self-schemas that allow people to hold cognitive generalizations about the self. These self-schemas are based on their prior experiences and make it easier to process, evaluate, retrieve, and respond to self-relevant information (Markus, 1977). Most people also strive to maintain a positive self-image leading them to interpret and evaluate information in a self-serving manner. Self-defining traits, values, beliefs, attitudes, goals, groups, and relationships are looked upon favorably, whereas alternative characteristics, views, and affiliations are evaluated less favorably or, at times, even denigrated and denounced (Brewer, 1999). This logic can be extended to the collective self (Ellemers, Spears, & Doosje, 2002; Tajfel & Turner, 1986). That is, people often strive to maintain a positive group image, make favorable social comparisons that differentiate their group from others, and resist incompatible and/or negative information about their group (Doosje, Branscombe, Spears, & Manstead, 1998;).

Thus, the political self organizes one's beliefs, attitudes, and affiliations and aids in the processing of politically relevant information. People use their value and belief systems to define themselves as unique individuals and to affiliate with others who share their views (Sherman & Cohen, 2006). Moreover, as we show later, people often display self-serving political biases when evaluating people based on their ideological views and ideologically relevant information. These biases function to enhance one's self-image and social identity within the political domain through favoring the in-group *and* derogating political out-groups.

We have limited our analysis of the political self to two ideological identifications within the political domain, liberal and conservative. Although there are a number of other potential political identifications, the bulk of psychological research has focused primarily on these two groups. We further propose that although liberals and conservatives have different values underlying their political views (Graham, Haidt, & Nosek, 2009) both groups are committed to maintaining their beliefs and promoting their group interests. In this way, the political self is similar across ideological lines. Indeed, we suspect that the political self serves similar functions across the political spectrum.

Furthermore, we do not define these ideologies by the specific policies, parties, or organizations they support. Rather we consider them general patterns of thought and behavior that have largely remained consistent across time and place (Jost, Glaser, Kruglanski, & Sulloway, 2003). Specifically, those who self-identify as conservative have demonstrated a heightened desire for social conformity and a respect for cultural tradition (Altemeyer, 1996; Feldman, 2003). Those who self-identify as liberals on the other hand have demonstrated a heightened desire for uniqueness and a tendency to challenge long-standing norms and traditions (Haidt, 2012; Stern, West, & Schmidt, 2014). Thus, these patterns of thought appear to produce a psychological affinity for attitudes, beliefs, values, and, potentially, social policies available within one's social context that match one's underlying psychological intuitions, motives, and needs (Jost, Federico, & Napier, 2009; Jost et al., 2003). To further clarify, this chapter focuses on the psychological characteristics of those who identify as liberal and conservative. We acknowledge that there is a robust debate over whether ideology is ideally conceptualized in a unidimensional (e.g., left-right, liberal-conservative) or multidimensional fashion (Feldman & Johnston, 2014; Jost, 2006; Stenner, 2009) but believe such a discussion is beyond the scope of this chapter.

THEORETICAL OVERVIEW

The necessity of interdependence has led humans to develop psychological adaptations for group living (Brewer, 1997; Haidt, 2012). It also introduces bedrock social organization dilemmas[1] (BSODs; Hibbing, Smith, & Alford, 2013; Smith, Oxley, Hibbing, Alford, & Hibbing, 2011) that are universal to most, if not all, human societies. A BSOD is a social problem that arises from living within a large-scale interdependent human society. It is a general descriptive category that can be used to group more specific cases that arise in different human societies and thus provide a way to understand cross-cultural commonalities within the political domain. For instance, BSODs include how to share resources, how to punish free-riders, exploiters, and social deviants; how to manage intergroup relations; and how to distribute scarce resources (Hibbing et al., 2013).

Although considered universal, the specific form BSODs take within a given society is context dependent. For instance, debates over interracial marriage or same-sex marriage constitute peripheral issues organized around stable definitional cores (Jost et al., 2003) concerned with in-group identification, inequality, and access to intangible resources such as status, opportunity, and rights. The peripheral issues, such as which aggrieved group is challenging an oppressive law, can change over time, but within a society, the core of the debate, who is worthy of certain status, opportunities, and rights, persists.

The persistence of BSODs implies that different preferred solutions emerge among members of the same society. If everyone agreed on a solution there would not be a dilemma. In this way, BSODs can be considered *essentially contested concepts*, which do not and cannot have an agreed-upon meaning (MacKenzie, 2003). That there are fundamental ideas, concepts, or dimensions along which humans disagree, and appear to almost always disagree, is psychologically interesting and important, in part, because these disagreements provide opportunity for the political self to satisfy the competing needs of assimilation and differentiation.

THE POLITICAL SELF AND THE NEED FOR ASSIMILATION

One theme that underlies many BSODs concerns balancing the rights and needs of the individual against those of the larger community (Brewer, 1991; Feldman, 2003; Haidt, 2012). Within large-scale human societies, a broad national identity often exists. Optimal-distinctiveness theory (Brewer, 1991) suggests this national identity would have difficulty achieving optimal distinctiveness because increased identification with a national social identity will result in feelings of depersonalization and trigger a desire to express individuality.

Yet the needs for assimilation and differentiation are dynamic and hold each other in check. The need for differentiation spurred by immersion into a larger social group ultimately prompts a need for assimilation into smaller social groups that better satisfy both needs simultaneously (Brewer, 1999). These subgroups, and especially political subgroups, can be organized around a shared grievance (or a collection of shared grievances)—the lack of a solution for a BSOD or the presence of an inadequate one. This is often a prerequisite for the development of a politicized group identity and collective action (Simon & Klandermans, 2001).

Ideological identification implies a psychological affinity for an ideological narrative that details how social reality *should* and *ought* to be like, why current reality diverges from this ideal, and how to solve this predicament (Martin et al., 1990). Thus, the shared narrative that helps bind people together into a political group (Graham & Haidt, 2010) capable of taking action (Simon & Klandermans, 2001) is a reflection of individual group members being psychologically similar.

Foundations of Similarity: Psychological Characteristics of Liberals

Psychological research indicates consistent associations between liberalism and cognitive flexibility[2] (Jost et al., 2003; Onraet, Van Hiel, Dhont, & Pattyn, 2013; Stevens, 2013; Van Hiel, Onraet, & De Pauw, 2010), openness to experience (Jost et al., 2003), a desire to for uniqueness (Stern et al., 2014), and a greater tendency to experience collective (or group-based) guilt (Klandermans, Werner, & van Doorn, 2008; Roccas, Klar, & Liviatan, 2004). Liberals' intuitive moral concerns generally focus on care and fairness, and give less weight to moral concerns associated with issues of sanctity, authority, or loyalty (Graham et al., 2009; Haidt & Graham, 2009).

Consistent with the association between liberalism and cognitive flexibility (Jost et al., 2003), liberals display a greater tendency to adopt situational explanations for people's behavior (e.g., Skitka, 1999; for an exception, see Morgan, Mullen, & Skitka, 2010). Compared to conservatives, liberals tend to rely less on stereotypes in person perception (Altemeyer, 1996; Stern, West, Jost, & Rule, 2013). Additionally and consistent with the association between liberalism and a need for uniqueness, liberals do not identify as strongly with national and ethnic in-groups as conservatives (Altemeyer,

1996; Klandermans et al., 2008; Roccas et al., 2004). Finally, the experience of collective guilt appears to motivate greater acceptance of policies typically associated with liberalism (in the United States) such as affirmative action (Branscombe, Slugoski, & Kappen, 2004), increased environmental regulations (Ferguson & Branscombe, 2010), and the withdrawal of American and British troops from Iraq (Iyer, Schmader, & Lickell, 2007).

Foundations of Similarity: Psychological Characteristics of Conservatives

Extensive research on the psychological foundations of political conservatism (e.g., Altemeyer, 1996; Jost et al., 2003) has found consistent associations between conservatism and cognitive rigidity (e.g., needs for order, structure, and closure; intolerance of ambiguity; Jost et al., 2003; Onraet et al., 2013; Van Hiel et al., 2010), threat sensitivity (Onraet et al., 2013; Van Hiel et al., 2010), and disgust sensitivity (Horberg, Oveis, Keltner, & Cohen, 2009; Inbar, Pizarro, Iyer, & Haidt, 2012;). Conservatism is also consistently associated with intuitive moral concerns about loyalty, authority, and sanctity (Haidt, 2012).

These psychological characteristics, in part, produce an affinity for conservative ideologies or social movements (Haidt, 2012; Jost et al., 2009, 2003). For instance, conservatives' heightened threat sensitivity (Onraet et al., 2013; Van Hiel et al., 2010) often manifests as conservatives perceiving the world as a more dangerous place than do liberals (Altemeyer, 1996). Compared to liberals, conservatives are more likely to employ stereotypes across a wide range of behavioral domains (e.g., unemployment, AIDS infection, being impacted by a natural disaster) and possess a tendency to make dispositional attributions over situational ones (Altemeyer, 1996; Skitka, 1999). The replicability of these findings has led to widespread acceptance of the view that conservatism is a form of motivated social cognition adopted in response to social threat and uncertainty (Jost et al., 2003).

Political Ideology as Motivated Social Cognition

The psychological literature has focused almost exclusively on conservatism (e.g., Altemeyer, 1996; Jost et al., 2003). Despite this, we agree with Jost et al. (2003) "that conservative ideologies—*like virtually all other belief systems*—are adopted in part because they satisfy some psychological needs" (p. 340, emphasis added). Indeed, in the conclusion of their meta-analysis on conservatism as motivated social cognition, Jost et al. encouraged investigations into the psychological motives underlying liberalism. In this spirit, Stern et al. (2014) assessed beliefs and preferences on political (e.g., "America should strive to strengthen its military") and nonpolitical (e.g., "I like poetry") stimuli and then measured perceived in-group consensus among liberals, conservatives, and moderates. In student and nonstudent samples, liberals underestimated their similarity to other liberals while conservatives and moderates overestimated their similarity to other conservatives and moderates. This underestimation of similarity was driven by liberals' stronger need for uniqueness compared to conservatives and moderates.

Consistent with Stern et al.'s (2014) findings, compared to conservatives, liberals are more likely to experience collective guilt and criticize their national or ethnic in-group for harmful actions, such as excessive acts of warfare (Roccas et al., 2004), damage to the environment (Ferguson & Branscombe, 2010), and slavery and apartheid (Branscombe et al., 2004; Klandermans et al., 2008). Supporting the notion that liberalism, too, may be a form of motivated social cognition, political values can drive attributions. For instance, even though conservatives tend to reach dispositional explanations for behavior more easily than do liberals (Skitka, 1999) this effect can be reversed. Three different studies showed that liberals were more likely to reach dispositional conclusions and blame U.S. Marines who killed civilians in Iraq and police officers in Chicago who killed an escaped cougar from the zoo for their actions (Morgan et al., 2010). This reversal was driven primarily by a desire to maintain value consistency. In other words, people's attributions were shaped by whether or not the attributions were consistent with their values.

The term *motivated social cognition* probably characterizes political ideologies generally, and we consider ideological identification a reflection of one's moral social identity (Parker & Janoff-Bulman, 2013). Moral social identities emerge when widespread societal consensus on a BSOD does not exist. For instance, the legality of abortion remains a contentious issue in some democracies (e.g., United States, Ireland) with divisions between prochoice and prolife camps. Thus, moral social identities are, to a degree, based on the existence of an oppositional out-group. Identification with the moral in-group is, in part, driven by perceived threat from the moral out-group and a desire to distance (or differentiate) one's self from them (Parker & Janoff-Bulman, 2013). In other words, ideological in-groups are often sustained by ideological out-groups that threaten the in-group's ideals. Those competing ideals are often anchored in nonrational moral intuitions. To understand such processes, we turn to research on the moral foundations of politics.

The Moral Foundations of Politics

Morality may, in part, underlie political attitudes, beliefs, and affiliations (e.g., Haidt, 2012; Skitka & Bauman, 2008). The process of moralization (Rozin, 1999) imbues attitudes and beliefs with moral conviction (Skitka,

2010; Tetlock, Kristel, Elson, Green, & Lerner, 2000), the strong and absolute belief that something is right or wrong without the need for proof or evidence (Skitka, Bauman, & Sargis, 2005; Skitka & Mullen, 2002). A moral conviction requires little cognitive effort to maintain, is driven primarily by affect, is experienced more intensely than other attitudes and beliefs, and is considered objectively and universally true (Skitka, 2010).

Effron and Miller (2012) further suggest the moralization of a political issue, and thus the development of moral convictions concerned with it provides people with the social legitimacy to express their attitudes and beliefs and to advocate for positions in which they do not possess a strong material stake. Examples of this phenomenon may include males who support pro-choice policies or heterosexuals who support same-sex marriage. Additionally, it may provide legitimacy for supporting policies that are against one's own material interests, such as people of lower socioeconomic status who support tax cuts for the wealthy and people of high socioeconomic status who support strong social safety nets even at the expense of tax increases on the wealthy. Consistent with this analysis, moral convictions predicted voting during the 2000 and 2004 U.S. presidential elections, even when controlling for factors such as party affiliation and attitude strength (Skitka & Bauman, 2008). Likewise, attitudes over a 7-year period in a representative sample of American adolescents revealed that political disengagement was highest among males who did not possess moral convictions about social and political issues (Snell, 2010).

The potential consequences of moralization at the group and societal levels of behavior include government action (e.g., regulation; prohibition); increased institutional support (e.g., from schools or foundations) for reform; scientific investigation into processes and relationships that ultimately confirm the moral qualities of the issue; and a license to express strong public disapproval (e.g., irritation; outrage) of those perceived as transgressing the new moral value (Rozin, 1999). These behavioral consequences can provide the political self with further opportunities for assimilation. Specifically, government action, increased institutional support, and scientific confirmation may create opportunity for social validation and ideological cohesion among psychologically similar individuals that further reinforce their moral conviction. In other words, moral convictions provide a foundation for the development of value- and belief-based systems that allow people to both define themselves as unique individuals within the political domain, satisfying the need for differentiation (explored in more detail below), and to affiliate with others who hold similar views (Sherman & Cohen, 2006), thereby satisfying the need for assimilation. This affiliation helps people create a shared sociopolitical reality (Jost et al., 2009) and further reinforces social bonds (Graham & Haidt, 2010).

In sum, the process of moralization (Rozin, 1999) and the development of moral convictions (Skitka, 2010) can motivate political behavior. For instance, moral convictions about discrimination motivated group-based anger (e.g., "I feel angry because of what happened to the Dutch Muslim woman"), group efficacy (e.g., "I think together we can successfully fight against discrimination of Dutch Muslims"), and collective action tendencies (e.g., "I would like to participate in a demonstration against discrimination toward Dutch Muslims") in Dutch non-Muslims following discrimination against a Dutch Muslim woman (van Zomeren, Postmes, Spears, & Bettache, 2011). Additionally, moral outrage—a reaction to a moral transgression consisting of affective, cognitive, and behavioral components (Tetlock et al., 2000)—mediated the impact of the system justifying attitudes on support for redistributive socioeconomic policies (Jost et al., 2012; Wakslak, Jost, Tyler, & Chen, 2007). Such findings are consistent with the idea that moral outrage over a shared grievance can be a prerequisite for collective action (Martin et al., 1990; Simon & Klandermans, 2001).

Moral Foundations Theory

Because moral convictions are affectively driven, require little cognitive effort to maintain, are experienced more intensely than other attitudes and beliefs, and are assumed to be objective and universally true (Goodwin & Darley, 2012), they are fairly resistant to change (Skitka, 2010). Where, then, do these moralized political convictions come from? This is precisely one of the questions at the heart of Moral Foundations Theory (MFT; Haidt, 2012; Haidt & Graham, 2009), a social intuitionist model (Haidt, 2001) that proposes a specific set of intuitions, or foundations, that shape our moral judgments.

MFT rests on four main claims: (a) Nativism—the human mind is prepared, via natural selection, to respond to certain sets of patterns in the social environment; (b) Cultural learning/socialization revises this foundation through development and experience within a culture and society; (c) Intuitionism—intuitive moral judgments precede moral reasoning, which is often employed for socially strategic purposes (Haidt, 2001); and, (d) Moral pluralism—there are many foundations of morality because each helped humans face many different types of recurrent BSODs (Graham et al., 2013; Haidt, 2012).

Briefly, MFT proposes a set of innate psychological adaptations, universal to most if not all human societies. These psychological adaptations, or moral foundations, developed in response to adaptive problems posed by particular recurring BSODs such as how to care for the sick and elderly, how to distribute scarce resources, and how to navigate social hierarchy

(Haidt, 2012). Specifically, five moral foundations are proposed: Care/harm, Fairness/cheating, Loyalty/betrayal, Authority/subversion, and Sanctity/degradation (Haidt 2012).[3] The addition of a sixth foundation, Liberty/oppression, has also been provisionally proposed (Iyer, Koleva, Graham, Ditto, & Haidt, 2012).

The moral foundations can be further categorized into the *individualizing* foundations of Care, Fairness, and Liberty and the *binding* foundations of Loyalty, Authority, and Sanctity. The individualizing foundations are primarily based on the ethic of autonomy, where the individual is the primary unit of value while the binding foundations are based primarily on the ethics of community and divinity, where group cohesion and stability and the belief that it is morally necessary to live in a pure, dignified way are, respectively, prioritized (Shweder, Much, Mahapatra, & Park, 1997). Modernization increases the emphasis a society places on the individualizing foundations relative to the binding foundations promoting increased individualism (Haidt & Graham, 2009). Decreased emphasis on the binding foundations can potentially weaken social cohesion and stability as individual expression, or uniqueness, is promoted over social conformity (Haidt & Graham, 2009). Thus, in many modern Western democracies, the individualizing and binding foundations may frequently find themselves in conflict with one another.

Moral Foundations Theory and the Political Self

The distinction between the individualizing and binding foundations roughly parallels the tension between needs for distinctiveness and assimilation (Brewer, 1991). Indeed, we suggest that the moral foundations constitute some of the psychological adaptations for group living suggested by Brewer (1997) and others (Haidt, 2012). According to MFT, each foundation developed because of a particular adaptive challenge within the social environment (Haidt, 2012; Haidt & Graham, 2009). Care developed as a means to protect one's children, Fairness developed in response to concerns over how to reap the benefits of cooperation with non-kin, and Liberty developed in response to the challenge of living in small groups with individuals who may attempt to dominate, constrain, and oppress others. Loyalty developed in response to a need to form cohesive coalitions with non-kin, Authority developed in response to a need to forge beneficial relationships within social hierarchies, and Sanctity developed to avoid contaminants in order to maintain body and spiritual purity (Graham et al., 2013; Haidt, 2012).

MFT contends that cultural variation in morality can, in part, be explained by how different cultures emphasize the moral foundations (Haidt,

2012). Indeed, it is theorized that cultures can expand or reduce the set of triggers for each moral foundation through socialization and the development of shared social reality. In other words, personal experience (e.g., specific events such as 9/11) and socialization (e.g., demographic differences, exposure to cultural narratives) within a culture can shape how the moral foundations are emphasized, and as a result, how they guide intuitions and judgments, at both the individual and cultural levels. For example, intuitions associated with the Sanctity foundation can be triggered by exposure to taboo ideas such as communism, fascism, or racism (Graham & Haidt, 2012; Haidt & Graham, 2009). What a given individual considers taboo however is presumed to depend on how this individual emphasizes the moral foundations *and* his or her cultural experience (Haidt, 2012).

Applying MFT to the political domain within a culture or society provides a connection between BSODs and the differences that can develop over how to solve them. Moral foundations research has found that self-identified liberals place greater emphasis on the individualizing foundations of Care, Fairness, and Liberty, compared to the binding foundations of Loyalty, Authority, and Sanctity. They also place a greater emphasis on the individualizing foundations compared to self-identified conservatives (Haidt, 2012). Consistent with this, self-identified liberals tend to view issues such as stem cell research and climate change as moral issues about providing care and preventing harm (Clifford & Jerrit, 2013; Feinberg & Willer, 2013). In contrast, self-identified conservatives, who place equal emphasis on the individualizing and binding foundations (Haidt, 2012), view stem cell research as a moral issue about maintaining sanctity (Clifford & Jerrit, 2013). They do not view climate change as a moral issue about preventing harm, although when the issue is recast as one concerning sanctity, by focusing on pollution levels and the need to purify the air, the differences in attitudes about climate change between liberals and conservatives are reduced (Feinberg & Willer, 2013).

How people emphasize the moral foundations also impacts political behavior. For example, religious leaders' sermons emphasize different moral foundations depending on their congregation's political leanings, with more liberal congregations emphasizing concerns associated with Care and Fairness and more conservative congregations emphasizing concerns associated with Loyalty, Authority, and Sanctity (Graham et al., 2009). Consistent with this, supporters of stem cell research tend to rely on rhetoric which appeals to the Care foundation while opponents rely on rhetoric which appeals to the Sanctity foundation (Clifford & Jerrit, 2013). Finally, on a number of "culture war" issues within the United States (e.g., abortion rights, gay rights, gun control, enhanced interrogation tactics), attitudes were better predicted by the moral foundations than self-reported political ideology (Koleva, Graham, Iyer, Ditto, & Haidt, 2012; Stevens, 2013).

Moral Convictions, Moral Outrage, and the Political Self

The moral foundations therefore provide a stable definitional core around which people can organize their attitudes, beliefs, and preferences about BSODs. The liberal moral domain is primarily concerned with how the individual is treated, while the conservative moral domain also includes concerns about how individual behavior impacts the social cohesion within a society (Haidt, 2012; Haidt & Graham, 2009). These different moral concerns produce different and often opposing interpretations of political events and issues (Clifford & Jerrit, 2013; Feinberg & Willer, 2013).

Tetlock et al. (2000) proposed that a series of moral outrage and moral cleansing processes occur in response to perceived moral transgressions. Moral outrage consists of affective (e.g., anger, disgust, shame), cognitive (e.g., negative dispositional attributions), and behavioral (e.g., derogation or ostracism of transgressors, physical aggression toward deviants) components. The experience of moral outrage triggers a need for moral cleansing—attitudes, beliefs, and behaviors that attempt to restore or establish the preferred moral order. For instance, liberals appear morally outraged by how historically disadvantaged groups continue to face discrimination and oppression. Thus, as a way to reduce moral outrage, liberals often advocate policies that take such historical disadvantages into consideration to promote diversity and inclusiveness (Haidt, 2012).

The moral outrage and moral cleansing processes suggested by Tetlock et al. (2000) are grounded in a model of psychological equilibrium. They come online when social reality diverges from an ideal and promotes actions (moral cleansing) that reduce negative affect (moral outrage). In other words, a good deal of political behavior, particularly when an issue has become moralized, may reflect moral outrage and moral cleansing processes. This is similar to the view of Simon and Klandermans (2001), who proposed that a shared grievance is a prerequisite for collective action in the political realm. Thus, an integration of these literatures with research on moral conviction (Rozin, 1999; Skitka, 2010), the moral foundations (Graham et al., 2009; Haidt, 2012), and broader issues of self and identity (Brewer 1991; Sherman & Cohen, 2006) offers a novel way to understand political behavior.

Conclusions: The Political Self, the Need for Affiliation, and Morality

Many political attitudes appear to reflect deeper moral concerns (Koleva et al., 2012; Stevens, 2013). The certainty and rigidity with which these attitudes are held are a result of their moral tinge—moral attitudes and beliefs are considered facts about the world that are objectively and universally true (Goodwin & Darley, 2012). Once moral convictions become central to the self (Leach, Ellemers, & Barreto, 2007), they require little cognitive effort to maintain, are driven primarily by affect (Haidt, 2001), are experienced more intensely than other attitudes and beliefs (Skitka, 2010), and are considered facts about the world (Goodwin & Darley, 2012).

We therefore suspect that in the political domain, rigidity is associated with moral conviction regardless of whether an individual identifies as a liberal or a conservative. We further suggest that the consistent association between cognitive rigidity and conservatism reported in the social psychological literature (Jost et al., 2003) is, in part, driven by how the conservatives emphasize the moral foundations. Because conservatives emphasize both the individualizing and binding foundations, they may possess a greater number of moral convictions compared to liberals. Thus, the set of stimuli within the political domain that can trigger the moral outrage-moral cleansing process proposed by Tetlock et al. (2000) in conservatives is larger than the set of stimuli that can trigger the same process in liberals, which may result in conservatives demonstrating more rigidity in their beliefs.

In sum, shared moral convictions allow people to satisfy their need for affiliation through agreement on a shared sociopolitical reality. This shared reality is replete with a narrative that describes how current social reality came to be, how this reality diverges from its ideal form, and what should be done to restore or establish this ideal. An ideological narrative also defines heroes attempting to restore or establish the ideal moral order and villains who stand in their way (Graham & Haidt, 2012; Martin et al., 1990). Thus, the political self is, in part, defined by an individual's attitudes toward their political in-group as well as attitudes toward rival political out-groups (Parker & Janoff-Bulman, 2013). We now turn to an exploration of how the political self helps people define villains in an ideological narrative, because we suspect this is one way for people to satisfy a need for differentiation within a large-scale society.

THE POLITICAL SELF AND THE NEED FOR DIFFERENTIATION

Social identity theory has long held that people derive their identity in part from their social groups (Tajfel & Turner, 1986). Because people are motivated to maintain a positive self-concept (and their group memberships are important to their self-definitions), people often evaluate in-groups more favorably than out-groups. This in-group favoritism is not always linked to out-group derogation (Brewer, 1999). The political domain within a large-scale society however, complicates these matters. Individuals share a broad social identity (e.g., national identity) that likely triggers feelings of immersion and thus a need for differentiation. Disagreement over how to solve BSODs allows political subgroups to develop and provide an opportunity for differentiation in the political domain.

Self-Serving Political Biases

The social cognition literature indicates that people also express positive attitudes toward *ideas* shared by members of their in-group and negative attitudes toward ideas held by the out-group. Morality is often central to the self-concept (Leach et al., 2007), and self-enhancement motives can drive people to process, interpret, and evaluate social reality in a self-serving manner. People are often more accepting of evidence consistent with their preexisting beliefs and are critical of evidence that challenges their views (Edwards & Smith, 1996; Klacsynski, 2000). This phenomenon has been referred to as confirmation bias (Lord, Ross, & Lepper, 1979) or motivated reasoning (Kunda, 1990).

Individuals' preexisting political beliefs can bias their evaluation of ideologically relevant evidence and arguments concerning a wide range of topics. For instance, confirmation biases have occurred when people have assessed information about capital punishment (Edwards & Smith, 1996; Liu & Ditto, 2013; Lord et al., 1979), gun control (Taber & Lodge, 2006), affirmative action (Crawford, 2012; Crawford, Jussim, Cain, & Cohen, 2013), gay rights (Crawford et al., 2013; Munro & Ditto, 1997), and abortion (Edwards & Smith, 1996). It appears that such socially strategic reasoning is triggered by individuals' automatic affective response to belief-relevant information (Haidt, 2001; Zajonc, 1980). That is, people can be largely unaware of the fact that their reasoning is emotionally driven and biased because post hoc rationalization processes provide illusions of objectivity and conscious deliberation (Haidt, 2001).

Indeed, exposure to political stimuli automatically triggers an initial affective response (Lodge & Taber, 2005). Thus, when political information is consistent with individuals' political attitudes and beliefs, they experience a positive affective response, which leads them to process the information heuristically and assimilate it into their existing ideological views (Munro & Ditto, 1997; Klaczynski, 2000). However, when political views are challenged, people experience negative arousal, which induces effortful processing aimed at disconfirming the evidence (Munro & Ditto, 1997). For instance, people analyze counterattitudinal evidence longer, generate more and stronger counterarguments in response to it, and list more flaws with the research than they do in response to confirmatory evidence (Lord et al., 1979; Taber & Lodge, 2006).

These self-serving political biases serve to further differentiate individuals and the political groups they identify with from political rivals. The upshot of such biased processes is to create positive illusions that "We, and our views, are objective, logical, and evidence-based, whereas they, and their views, are not." Thus, "we" are intellectually superior (because of our greater use of logic and evidence) and "our" positions are anchored in "our objective" assessments of "reality," whereas "their" positions are irrational and unjustified. In other words, people often enhance the image of their political in-group, and by extension their self-image, through the derogation of a rival political out-group.

Political Conflicts are Often Moral Conflicts

Political differences are disagreements over positions and policy, but they are often not *merely* such disagreements. Because liberals and conservatives emphasize different moral foundations (Graham et al., 2009; Haidt, 2012) and hold different moral convictions (Morgan et al., 2010), political disagreement often reflects fundamental and sometimes even *nonnegotiable* moral differences. Differences, therefore, are not mere disagreements; they can become (or at least perceived as) *moral transgressions*, violations of fundamental principles of morality. That is, to someone who is prochoice, a prolife position may not be perceived as a mere disagreement; it may be perceived as violating the fundamental rights of individual women. To someone who is prolife however, a prochoice position may similarly not be perceived as a mere disagreement; instead, it reflects a violation of the sanctity of human life.

We therefore propose that once a political issue, such as abortion rights, becomes moralized, several psychological and political consequences likely follow: (a) Individual positions on the issue can serve as expressions of ideological identity (Kahan, 2014); (b) Such positions serve the differentiation need by distinguishing people from their political opponents; (c) Conflicts that appear political but which are primarily moral are not readily resolved by negotiating and compromising on issues of policy; (d) Political involvement is further energized because of perceived or feared moral transgressions by political rivals; and, (e) In some extreme cases, politically motivated violence may even occur (Graham & Haidt, 2012; Skitka, 2012). For instance, some anti-abortion activists have bombed abortion clinics and murdered doctors who are willing to perform abortions, and some environmentalists have committed arson and bombed property owned by people who are perceived to have damaged the environment.

In other words, moral differences can trigger a moral outrage-moral cleansing process whereby people are driven to restore their preferred moral order (Tetlock et al., 2000) through collective action (van Zomeren et al., 2011; Wakslak et al., 2007). Because many people think about their moral convictions as objective facts about the world (Goodwin & Darley, 2012; Skitka 2010), those who hold different moral convictions tend to trigger negative affect and are often perceived as immoral (Haidt, Rosenberg, & Hom, 2003; Tetlock et al., 2000). Once people are categorized as immoral, the perception generalizes across situations and contexts and becomes difficult to change (Trafimow, 2001). Subsequent moral behavior by the same target(s) is often met with suspicion and typically explained with reference to situational factors (Wojciszke & Szymkow, 2003).

In line with this view, Parker and Janoff-Bulman (2013) have proposed that moral social identities are oppositional. In three studies, people's positive and negative feelings toward morality-based in-groups and out-groups (e.g., prolife or prochoice) or nonmorality-based in-groups and out-groups (e.g., Yankees or Red Sox fans) were assessed. Moral in-groups, compared to nonmoral in-groups, generated fewer positive emotions, while moral out-groups, compared to nonmoral out-groups, generated more negative emotions. People's moral social identities were based on in-group positivity and out-group negativity. Moral social identities may therefore result from a desire to affiliate and belong *and* a desire to distance the self from undesirable others (Parker & Janoff-Bulman, 2013).

Political Intolerance as Moral Intolerance

We thus propose that political conflicts can become imbued with the types of moral outrage and moral cleansing processes discussed earlier in this chapter. These processes may in turn further serve to differentiate the political self from political rivals and potentially perpetuate ideological conflict. Political intolerance may, in other words, often be a reflection of moral intolerance where one's political rivals are cast as the villains. Interestingly, Haidt et al. (2003) reported that people were less tolerant of moral differences, such as stances on abortion rights and gun control, than racial, gender, or class differences. People also reported less desire for moral diversity at their university, within a lecture, and from a potential roommate. Finally, when assessed on one's desire to date, and thus interact closely with an individual, moral diversity had a negative impact while demographic differences did not.

Consistent with these findings, recent research indicates that ideological differences often inspire hostility and intolerance directed toward one's ideological opponents. Three independent research groups have converged on an *ideological conflict hypothesis* (ICH; Brandt, Reyna, Chambers, Crawford, & Wetherell, 2014). The ICH suggests that people on the left and right express similarly high levels of prejudice toward out-groups perceived as ideologically opposed, including demographic groups. For example,

Chambers, Schlenker, and Collisson (2013) tested two competing hypotheses: Conservatives are more racially prejudiced than liberals vs. Liberals and conservatives are equally prejudiced against groups perceived as their ideological opponents. Both perspectives predict that conservatives will dislike African Americans more than liberals (either because conservatives are more prejudiced or because African Americans are overwhelmingly left of center in their politics). The hypotheses differ, however, in predicting differences in reactions to *ideologically opposed and ideologically similar African Americans*. If conservatives are more racially prejudiced, they should dislike a liberal African American more than liberals dislike a conservative African American. This would occur because conservatives have two bases for hostility (prejudice and ideology), whereas liberals only have one (ideology). Similarly, if conservatives are more racially prejudiced, then liberals should like a liberal African American more than conservatives like a conservative African American.

If, however, ideology drives much of what appears to be racial prejudice, then liberals should dislike a conservative African American as much as conservatives dislike a liberal African American; and conservatives should like a conservative African American as much as liberals like liberal African Americans. Chambers et al. (2013) confirmed these latter ideological conflict predictions. In integrating these and other results (Crawford & Pilanski, 2013; Wetherell, Brandt, & Renya, 2013), Brandt et al. (2014) show high levels of intolerance to ideological opponents among *both* liberals and conservatives, including not just dislike but willingness to deprive one's opponents of basic rights guaranteed by the U.S. Constitution.

Such ideological prejudice is readily understood from the perspective developed in the present chapter. It is likely rooted in moral conviction and justified through the sorts of political-serving motivational biases reviewed earlier. Such processes psychologically bolster perceptions of the superiority of one's beliefs and one's moral-political groups. As such, they also enable people to differentiate themselves from others within their society by categorizing political out-groups and their members as bad and immoral.

Exaggeration of Political Differences

Finally, there is good evidence that political (Chambers, Baron, & Inman, 2006; Chambers & Melnyk, 2006) or moral (Graham, Nosek, & Haidt, 2012) stereotypes are typically exaggerations of real differences. That is, people correctly identify issues where an ideological or moral divide exists in the issue positions of the rival groups (Chambers et al., 2006; Graham et al., 2012). Yet they also tend to exaggerate the extent of these differences so that their rivals appear more extreme and unwilling to compromise. For instance, prochoice activists greatly exaggerated the difference between their attitude positions concerning women's reproductive rights (a core value issue for prochoice proponents) and those of their prolife rivals. Prolife activists, on the other hand, greatly exaggerated the difference between both group's attitude positions on the value of human life (a core value issue for prolife proponents; Chambers et al., 2006). Typically, the extent of exaggeration was greatest among those identified more strongly with a political group and/or whose attitudes were more extreme (Chambers et al., 2006; Chambers & Melnyk 2006).

Like the ideological-prejudice research reviewed above, our perspective on the political self offers a way to explain these exaggeration effects (Chambers et al., 2006; Chambers & Melnyk, 2006). Simply put, the political self may drive one to exaggerate the extremity of a political rival's position in order to further differentiate the self from a moral out-group. This exaggeration can then further license intolerance and derogation of political rivals and thus possibly perpetuate political conflict.

Conclusions: The Political Self, the Need for Differentiation, and Morality

We contend that morality is pluralistic (see also Graham et al., 2013; Haidt, 2012). Additionally, positive moral behavior is, to an extent, expected from in-group members and thus appears to have less impact on person perception than immoral behavior (Trafimow, 2001; Wojciszke & Szymkow, 2003). In other words, immoral behavior is more diagnostic and is presumed to provide more information about a person than moral behavior. The belief that one is good and moral, and by extension the belief that the groups one belongs to are good and moral, can become central to the self (Leach et al., 2007). We suspect this belief is partially maintained through the self-serving political biases reviewed above and through the derogation of one's political rivals. Indeed, Simon and Klandermans (2001) suggest that a politicized collective identity requires the recognition of a shared grievance and an opposition or enemy to mobilize against.

Psychological research supports these claims. People have immediate affective reactions to most, if not all, stimuli they encounter and these reactions can color their subsequent reasoning and judgment (Zajonc, 1980). This is particularly true of stimuli in the moral (Haidt, 2001) and political (Lodge & Taber, 2005) domains, which we contend often constitute the same thing. Blame is often assigned to the target who elicits the most negative affect in a given situation (Alicke, 2000). Moral/political social identities can be based on in-group favoritism and out-group negativity (Parker & Janoff-Bulman, 2013), and there is greater opposition to moral diversity than racial, gender, or class diversity at a variety of levels of interpersonal interaction (Haidt et al., 2003).

In other words, in the political domain, derogating political rivals by declaring one's own political group, and thus oneself, morally superior and above reproach enhances one's personal and social identities. This is one of the political self's primary functions—self-enhancement. That is, when one maintains that their beliefs, and by extension the political in-group's beliefs, are grounded in objective facts and are therefore good and moral while one's political rivals are cast as evil, immoral, and stubbornly resistant to acknowledging facts about the world, they are simultaneously engaging in self-enhancement processes and satisfying the need for differentiation in the political domain.

THE POLITICAL SELF: CONCLUSIONS

Large-scale human societies introduce a psychological tension between needs for affiliation and differentiation (Brewer, 1991). Psychologically, individuals strive to achieve a state of psychological equilibrium or optimal distinctiveness. In this chapter, we have suggested that the political domain offers people an opportunity to balance these competing needs. This appears particularly true of Western democracies where individual autonomy is actively promoted (Haidt, 2012; Shweder et al., 1997). In such societies, people are encouraged to develop individual autonomy and differentiate themselves, yet often simultaneously, are also encouraged to participate in self-governance through collective action and cooperation.

We have reviewed psychological evidence that, taken together, suggests many political conflicts constitute moral conflicts (Haidt, 2012; Parker & Janoff-Bulman, 2013). The process of moralization (Rozin, 1999) can turn political preferences into moral convictions (Skitka, 2010). Moral convictions become central to the self (Ellemers et al., 2007), appear primarily driven by affect (Haidt, 2001), and require little effort to maintain (Skitka, 2010). New information consistent with the moral conviction is accepted as objectively true without a need for evidence or critical analysis (Rozin, 1999; Skitka, 2010).

Moral convictions provide perceivers with a way to identify people within one's society who are "like me" and are therefore considered trustworthy and reliable in social interaction. They also provide people with a way to identify others who are "not like me" and thus seen as suspicious, or worse, as the enemy (Parker & Janoff-Bulman, 2013). In other words, unlike most social identities (Brewer, 1999), the political self is, in part, based on positive feelings toward one's political comrades *and* negative feelings about one's political rivals (Parker & Janoff-Bulman, 2013). Thus, one of the primary psychological functions of the political self is to engage in self-enhancement processes that paint the self and one's in-group in an extremely positive light *and* depict one's rivals in a way that justifies derogation and intolerance.

The negative affect often directed toward political opponents may actually motivate collective action and political participation. The acknowledgment of a shared grievance and the identification of an external opponent or enemy who is considered responsible and blamed for current social reality diverging from a preferred ideal is a prerequisite for collective action (Simon & Klandermans, 2001). Moral convictions help people define who is to blame for deviations from this preferred ideal. Thus, when it comes to politics, people appear more often motivated by what they oppose, and possibly even fear, than by what they support.

Our view of the psychology underlying political behavior is therefore broadly consistent with the idea that decision-making processes are typically more averse to losses than driven by possible gains, one of the main conclusions of prospect theory (Kahneman & Tversky, 1979; see also Haselton & Nettle, 2006). Indeed, despite the hopes of those credited with the founding of democratic governance, most political reasoning appears to operate in a similar fashion to their reasoning in other domains. Political reasoning is often a cloak for moral reasoning. As such, it often reflects socially strategic self-enhancement processes that satisfy the dual psychological needs for affiliation and differentiation.

NOTES

1. Smith et al. (2011) used the term bedrock issues of social organization. Hibbing et al. (2013) referred to bedrock social dilemmas. We adopt the term bedrock social organization dilemmas because as we elaborate on further below we consider a number of political attitudes and beliefs manifestations of underlying moral intuitions concerned with how to solve moral dilemmas that inevitably arise from human interdependence (see also Haidt, 2012).
2. We use the term "cognitive flexibility" to refer to lower needs for order, structure, and closure and/or a higher need for cognition.
3. Prior to 2012, different terms were used: Care/harm; Fairness/reciprocity, In-group/loyalty, Authority/respect, Purity/sanctity.

REFERENCES

Alicke, M. D. (2000). Culpable control and the psychology of blame. *Psychological Bulletin, 126,* 556–574.

Altemeyer, R. A. (1996). *The authoritarian specter.* Cambridge, MA: Harvard University Press.

Brandt, M. J., Reyna, C., Chambers, J. R., Crawford, J. T., & Wetherell, G. (2014). The ideological-conflict hypothesis: Intolerance among both liberals and conservatives. *Current Directions in Psychological Science, 23,* 27–34.

Branscombe, N. R., Slugoski, B., & Kappen, D. M. (2004). The measurement of collective guilt: What it is and what it is not. In N. R. Branscombe & B. Doosje (Eds.), *Collective guilt: International perspectives* (pp. 16–34). New York, NY: Cambridge University Press.

Brewer, M. B. (1991). The social self: On being the same and different at the same time. *Personality and Social Psychology Bulletin, 17*(5), 475–482.

Brewer, M. B. (1997). On the social origins of human nature. In C. McGarty & S. A. Haslam (Eds.), *The message of social psychology: Perspectives on mind in society* (pp. 54–62). Malden, UK: Blackwell.

Brewer, M. B. (1999). The psychology of prejudice: In-group love or out-group hate? *Journal of Social Issues, 55,* 429–444.

Chambers, J. R., Baron, R. S., & Inman, M. L. (2006). Misperceptions in intergroup conflict. *Psychological Science, 17,* 38–45.

Chambers, J. R., & Melnyk, D. (2006). Why do I hate thee? Conflict misperceptions and intergroup mistrust. *Personality and Social Psychology Bulletin, 32,* 1295–1311.

Chambers, J. R., Schlenker, B. R., & Collisson, B. (2013). Ideology and prejudice: The role of value conflicts. *Psychological Science, 24,* 140–149.

Clifford, S., & Jerit, J. (2013). How words do the work of politics: Moral Foundations Theory and the debate over stem-cell research. *Journal of Politics, 75,* 659–671

Crawford, J. T. (2012). The ideologically objectionable premise model: Predicting biased political judgments on the left and right. *Journal of Experimental Social Psychology, 48,* 138–151.

Crawford, J. T., Jussim, L., Cain, T. R., & Cohen, F. (2013). Right-wing authoritarianism and social dominance orientation differentially predict biased evaluations of media reports. *Journal of Applied Social Psychology, 43,* 163–174.

Crawford, J. T., & Pilanski, J. M. (2013). Political intolerance, right *and* left. *Political Psychology.* doi:10.1111/j.1467-9221.2012.00926.x

de Waal, F. B. M. (2013). *The bonobo and the atheist: In search of humanism among the primates.* New York, NY: Norton.

Doosje, B., Branscombe, N. R., Spears, R., & Manstead, A. S. R. (1998). Guilty by association: When one's group has a negative history. *Journal of Personality and Social Psychology, 75,* 872–886.

Edwards, K., & Smith, E. E. (1996). A disconfirmation bias in the evaluation of arguments. *Journal of Personality and Social Psychology, 71,* 5–24.

Effron, D. A., & Miller, D. T. (2012). How the moralization of issues grants social legitimacy to act on one's attitudes. *Personality and Social Psychology Bulletin, 38,* 690–701.

Ellemers, N., Spears, R., & Doosje, B. (2002). Self and social identity. *Annual Review of Psychology, 53,* 161–186.

Feinberg, M., & Willer, R. (2013). The moral roots of environmental attitudes. *Psychological Science, 24,* 56–62.

Feldman, S. (2003). Enforcing social conformity: A theory of authoritarianism. *Political Psychology, 24,* 41–74.

Feldman, S., & Johnston, C. (2014). Understanding the determinants of political ideology: Implications of structural complexity. *Political Psychology, 35,* 337–358.

Ferguson, M. A., & Branscombe, N. R. (2010). Collective guilt mediates the effect of beliefs about global warming on willingness to engage in mitigation behavior. *Journal of Environmental Psychology, 30,* 135–142.

Goodwin, G. P., & Darley, J. M. (2012). Why are some moral beliefs perceived to be more objective than others? *Journal of Experimental Social Psychology, 48,* 250–256.

Graham, J., & Haidt, J. (2010). Beyond beliefs: Religion binds individuals into moral communities. *Personality and Social Psychology Review, 14,* 140–150.

Graham, J., & Haidt, J. (2012). Sacred values and evil adversaries: A moral foundations approach. In M. Mikulincer & P. R. Shaver (Eds.), *The social psychology of morality: Exploring the causes of good and evil,* (pp. 11–31). Washington, DC: American Psychological Association.

Graham, J., Haidt, J., Koleva, S., Motyl, M., Iyer, R., Wojcik, S. P., & Ditto, P. H. (2013). Moral Foundations Theory: The pragmatic validity of moral pluralism. *Advances in Experimental Social Psychology, 47,* 55–130.

Graham, J., Haidt, J., & Nosek, B. A. (2009). Liberals and conservatives rely on different sets of moral foundations. *Journal of Personality and Social Psychology, 96,* 1029.

Graham, J., Nosek, B. A., & Haidt, J. (2012). The moral stereotypes of liberals and conservatives: Exaggeration of differences across the political spectrum. *PloS ONE, 7*(12), e50092.

Haidt, J. (2001). The emotional dog and its rational tail: A social intuitionist approach to moral judgment. *Psychological Review, 108,* 814–834.

Haidt, J. (2012). *The righteous mind: Why good people are divided by politics and religion.* New York, NY: Pantheon.

Haidt, J., & Graham, J. (2009). Planet of the Durkheimians, where community, authority, and sacredness are foundations of morality. In J. T. Jost, A. C. Kay, & H. Thorisdottir (Eds.), *Social and psychological bases of ideology and system justification* (pp. 371–401). New York, NY: Oxford University Press.

Haidt, J., Rosenberg, E., & Hom, H. (2003). Differentiating diversities: Moral diversity is not like other kinds. *Journal of Applied Social Psychology, 33,* 1–36.

Haselton, M. G., & Nettle, D. (2006). The paranoid optimist: An integrative evolutionary model of cognitive biases. *Personality and Social Psychology Review, 10,* 47–66.

Hibbing, J. R., Smith, K. B., & Alford, J. R. (2013). *Predisposed: Liberals, conservatives, and the biology of political differences.* New York, NY: Routledge.

Horberg, E. J., Oveis, C., Keltner, D., & Cohen, A. B. (2009). Disgust and the moralization of purity. *Journal of Personality and Social Psychology, 97,* 963–976.

Inbar, Y., Pizarro, D. A., Iyer, R., & Haidt, J. (2012). Disgust sensitivity, political conservatism, and voting. *Social Psychological and Personality Science, 3,* 537–544.

Iyer, R., Koleva, S., Graham, J., Ditto, P., & Haidt, J. (2012). Understanding libertarian morality: The psychological dispositions of self-identified libertarians. *PLoS ONE, 7*e42366. doi:10.1371/journal.pone.0042366

Iyer, A., Schmader, T., & Lickell, B. (2007). Why individuals protest the perceived transgressions of their country: The role of anger, shame, and guilt. *Personality and Social Psychology Bulletin, 33*, 572–587.

Jost, J. T. (2006). The end of the end of ideology. *American Psychologist, 61*, 651–670.

Jost, J. T., Chaikalis-Petritsis, V., Abrams, D., Sidanius, J., van der Toorn, J., & Bratt, C. (2012). Why men (and women) do and don't rebel effects of system justification on willingness to protest. *Personality and Social Psychology Bulletin, 38*, 197–208.

Jost, J. T., Ferderico, C. M., & Napier, J. L. (2009). Political ideology: Its structure, functions, and elective affinities. *Annual Review of Psychology, 60*, 307–337.

Jost, J. T., Glaser, J., Kruglanski, A. W., & Sulloway, F. J. (2003). Political conservatism as motivated social cognition. *Psychological Bulletin, 129*, 339–375.

Kahan, D. M. (2014, June 25). Climate science communication and the measurement problem. *SSRN*. Retrieved from http://ssrn.com/abstract=2459057

Kahneman, D., & Tversky, A. (1979). Intuitive prediction: Biases and corrective procedures. *TIMS Studies in Management Science, 12*, 313–327.

Klaczynski, P. A. (2000). Motivated scientific reasoning biases, epistemological beliefs, and theory polarization: A two-process approach to adolescent cognition. *Child Development, 71*, 1347–1366.

Klandermans, B., Wener, M., & van Doorn, M. (2008). Redeeming apartheid's legacy: Collective guilt, political ideology, and compensation. *Political Psychology, 29*, 331– 349.

Koleva, S. P., Graham, J., Iyer, R., Ditto, P. H., & Haidt, J. (2012). Tracing the threads: How five moral concerns (especially purity) help explain culture war attitudes. *Journal of Research in Personality, 46*, 184–194.

Kunda, Z. (1990). The case for motivated reasoning. *Psychological Bulletin, 108*, 480–498.

Leach, C. W., Ellemers, N., & Barreto, M. (2007). Group virtue: The importance of morality (vs. competence and sociability) in the positive evaluation of ingroups. *Journal of Personality and Social Psychology, 93*, 234–249.

Liu, B. S., & Ditto, P. H. (2013). What dilemma? Moral evaluation shapes factual belief. *Social Psychological and Personality Science, 4*, 316–323.

Lodge, M., & Taber, C. S. (2005). The automaticity of affect for political leaders, groups, and issues: An experimental test of the hot cognition hypothesis. *Political Psychology, 26*, 455–482.

Lord, C. G., Ross, L., & Lepper, M. (1979). Biased assimilation and attitude polarization: The effects of prior theories on subsequently considered evidence. *Journal of Personality and Social Psychology, 37*, 2098–2109.

MacKenzie, I. (2003). The idea of ideology. In R. Eccleshall, A. Finlayson, V. Geoghegan, M. Kenny, M. Lloyd, I. MacKenzie, & R. Wilford (Eds.) *Political ideologies: An introduction* (3rd ed, pp. 1–16). New York, NY: Taylor & Francis.

Markus, H. (1977). Self-schemata and processing information about the self. *Journal of Personality and Social Psychology, 35*, 63–78.

Martin, J., Scully, M., & Levitt, B. (1990). Injustice and the legitimation of revolution: Damning the past, excusing the present, and neglecting the future. *Journal of Personality and Social Psychology, 59*, 281–290.

Morgan, G. S., Mullen, E., & Skitka, L. J. (2010). When values and attributions collide: Liberals' and conservatives' values motivate attributions for alleged misdeeds. *Personality and Social Psychology Bulletin, 36,* 1241–1254.

Munro, G. D., & Ditto, P. H. (1997). Biased assimilation, attitude polarization, and affect in reactions to stereotype-relevant scientific information. *Personality and Social Psychology Bulletin, 23,* 636–653.

Onraet, E., Van Hiel, A., Dhont, K., & Pattyn, S. (2013). Internal and external threat in relationship with right-wing attitudes. *Journal of Personality, 81,* 233–248.

Parker, M. T., & Janoff-Bulman, R. J. (2013). Lessons from morality-based social identity: The power of out-group "hate," not just in-group "love." *Social Justice Research, 26,* 81–96.

Roccas, S., Klar, Y., & Liviatan, I. (2004). Exonerating cognitions, group, identification, and personal values as predictors of collective guilt among Jewish-Israelis. In N. R. Branscombe & B. Doosje (Eds.), *Collective guilt: International perspectives* (pp. 130– 147). New York, NY: Cambridge University Press.

Rozin, P. (1999). The process of moralization. *Psychological Science, 10,* 218–221.

Sherman, D. K., & Cohen, G. L. (2006). The psychology of self-defense: Self-affirmation theory. *Advances in Experimental Social Psychology, 38,* 184–242.

Shweder, R., Much, N., Mahapatra, M., & Park, L. (1997). The "big three" of morality (autonomy, community, divinity) and the "big three" explanations of suffering. In A. Brandt & P. Rozin (Eds.), *Health and morality* (pp. 119–169). New York, NY: Routledge.

Simon, B., & Klandermans, B. (2001). Politicized collective identity: A social psychological analysis. *American Psychologist, 56,* 319–331.

Skitka, L. J. (1999). Ideological and attributional boundaries on public compassion: Reactions to individuals and communities affected by a natural disaster. *Personality and Social Psychology Bulletin, 25,* 793–808.

Skitka, L. J. (2010). The psychology of moral conviction. *Personality and Social Psychology Compass, 4,* 267–281.

Skitka, L. J. (2012). Moral convictions and moral courage: Common denominators of good and evil. In M. Mikulincer, & P. R. Shaver (Eds.), *The social psychology of morality: Exploring the causes of good and evil* (pp. 349–365). Washington, DC: American Psychological Association.

Skitka, L. J., & Bauman, C. W. (2008). Moral conviction and political engagement. *Political Psychology, 29,* 29–54.

Skitka, L. J., Bauman, C. W., & Sargis, E. G. (2005). Moral conviction: Another contributor to attitude strength or something more? *Journal of Personality and Social Psychology, 88,* 895–917.

Skitka, L. J., & Mullen, E. (2002). Understanding judgments of fairness in a real-world political context: A test of the value protection model of justice reasoning. *Personality and Social Psychology Bulletin, 28,* 1419–1429.

Smith, K. B., Oxley, D. R., Hibbing, M. V., Alford, J. R., & Hibbing, J. R. (2011). Linking genetics and political attitudes: Reconceptualizing political ideology. *Political Psychology, 32,* 369–397.

Snell, P. (2010). Emerging adult civic and political disengagement: A longitudinal analysis of lack of involvement with politics. *Journal of Adolescent Research, 25,* 258–287.

Stenner, K. (2009). Three kinds of conservatism. *Psychological Inquiry, 20,* 142–159.

Stern, C., West, T. V., Jost, J. T., & Rule, N. O. (2013). The politics of gaydar: Ideological differences in the use of gendered cues in categorizing sexual orientation. *Journal of Personality and Social Psychology, 104,* 520–541.

Stern, C., West, T., & Schmidt, P. G. (2014, January). The liberal illusion of uniqueness. *Psychological Science,25*(1), 137–144. Retrieved from http://pss.sagepub.com/content/suppl/2014/01/17/25.1.DC1/PSYS_25_1_Full_Issue.pdf

Stevens, S. T. (2013). *Political ideology as moral vigilance.* Unpublished doctoral dissertation, Rutgers University, New Brunswick, NJ.

Taber, C. S., & Lodge, M. (2006). Motivated skepticism in the evaluation of political beliefs. *American Journal of Political Science, 50,* 755–769.

Tajfel, H. & Turner, J. C. (1986). The social identity theory of inter-group behavior. In S. Worchel & L. W. Austin (Eds.), *Psychology of intergroup relations* (2nd ed., pp. 7–24). Chicago, IL: Nelson Hall.

Tetlock, P. E., Kristel, O. V., Elson, K. S., Green, M. C., & Lerner, J. (2000). The psychology of the unthinkable: Taboo trade-offs, forbidden base rates, and heretical counterfactuals. *Journal of Personality and Social Psychology, 78,* 853–870.

Trafimow, D. (2001). The effects of trait type and situation type on the generalization of trait expectancies across situations. *Personality and Social Psychology Bulletin, 27,* 1463–1468.

van Hiel, A., Onraet, E., & De Pauw, S. (2010). The relationship between social cultural attitudes and behavioral measures of cognitive style: A meta-analytic integration of studies. *Journal of Personality, 78,* 1765–1800.

van Zomeren, M., Postmes, T., Spears, R., & Bettache, K. (2011). Can moral convictions motivate the advantaged to challenge social inequality?: Extending the social identity model of collective action. *Group Processes and Intergroup Relations, 14,* 735–753.

Wakslak, C. J., Jost, J. T., Tyler, T. R., & Chen, E. S. (2007). Moral outrage mediates the dampening effect of system justification on support for redistributive social policies. *Psychological Science, 18,* 267–274.

Wetherell, G., Brandt, M. J., & Reyna, C. (2013). Discrimination across the ideological divide: The role of perceptions of value violations and abstract values in discrimination by liberals and conservatives. *Social Psychology and Personality Science, 4,* 658–667.

Wojciszke, B., & Szymkow, A. (2003). Emotions related to others' competence and morality. *Polish Psychological Bulletin, 34,* 135–142.

Zajonc, R. B. (1980). Feeling and thinking: Preferences need no inferences. *American Psychologist, 35,* 151.

CHAPTER 4

A PERSONAL AGENCY VIEW OF SELF-REGULATED LEARNING

The Role of Goal Setting

Barry J. Zimmerman
City University of New York

Dale H. Schunk
The University of North Carolina at Greensboro

Maria K. DiBenedetto
Bishop McGuinness Catholic High School

Current theories of human learning, motivation, and self-regulation view individuals not as passive recipients of environmental inputs but rather as active creators of their thoughts, behaviors, and outcomes (Ryan, 2012; Zimmerman & Schunk, 2011). Our sense of personal agency defines us as intentional, proactive, and striving beings. But how do we become agents in shaping our lives? Much progress has been made in recent years in iden-

Self-Concept, Motivation, and Identity, pages 83–114

tifying key self-regulatory processes and sources of motivation of agents. This chapter recounts the development and application of a social cognitive cyclical model of self-regulated learning, with particular attention to the central role of goal setting.

A *goal* is the behavior or outcome that one is consciously attempting to perform or attain. *Goal setting* refers to the process of establishing a standard or objective to serve as the aim of one's actions. Goal setting can affect students' learning, motivation, and self-regulation in multiple ways (Zimmerman, 2008a). By setting goals, students are more apt to choose to engage in goal-relevant tasks and sustain their attention on them and less likely to become distracted by nongoal-relevant activities. Goals also can promote effort and persistence directed toward goal attainment. Further, goals can increase one's affective reactions (e.g., satisfaction) as one observes progress toward goal attainment and goal completion. Collectively these activities sustain motivation and self-regulatory activities and promote learning.

The purpose of this chapter is to discuss the theoretical and empirical evidence relevant to the role that goal setting plays in individuals' motivation and self-regulated learning. In particular, our aim is to show how goal setting allows persons to exert a large degree of control over their actions and the outcomes of those actions.

We initially discuss a social cognitive perspective on self-regulated learning that highlights the role of goal setting. We explain the characteristics of goals and the types of goals that individuals may set, as well as their relation to other self-regulatory processes. We conclude the chapter by describing two interventions using goal setting to help students become better self-regulated learners.

SOCIAL COGNITIVE THEORY OF SELF-REGULATED LEARNING

Human Agency

Agency theories explain how self-processes influence one's functioning. These theories are distinguished by their focus on individuals having the means or power to act.

For example, expectancy-value theory postulates that human actions are a function of one's expectancy for performing successfully and the value or importance that one places on the desired outcome (Wigfield & Eccles, 2002). Expectancies and values can affect one's choices of activities, motivation (e.g., effort, persistence), and achievement. Attribution theory contends that the attributions (perceived causes) that one makes for the outcomes of actions affect future motivation and behavior (Graham &

Williams, 2009). People who attribute their task successes to personal qualities such as ability and effort are apt to experience higher motivation and task engagement than individuals who view external causes (e.g., luck, help from others) as responsible for outcomes. Self-determination theory predicts that human action is a function of three primary needs: competence (need for mastery), autonomy (need for control and agency), and relatedness (need for others and belonging to a group). Collectively, these needs help one feel self-determined and intrinsically motivated to engage in activities (Ryan & Deci, 2009).

Social cognitive theory defines agency as the belief that one can exert a large measure of control over the important events in one's life. This theory postulates that agency has four core properties (Bandura, 2008). *Intentionality* empowers agents to form action plans and select strategies for attaining those plans, such as creating an outline for writing an essay. *Forethought* involves setting goals and anticipating potential outcomes of various actions to guide or motivate oneself, such as setting time periods to write an essay and a completion date. *Self-reactiveness* refers to an individual's adopting personal standards, constructing appropriate courses of action, monitoring activities, and regulating those activities through evaluative self-reactions. For example, progress in writing an essay can be compared with the outline. These self-reactive processes enable a person to shift from forethought to self-regulation. *Self-reflectiveness* concerns examining the results of one's thoughts and actions, such as proofreading an essay for its fidelity to the outline and cohesiveness. People can reflect on the meaning of their pursuits, their personal efficacy, and the soundness of their thoughts and actions. Bandura (2008) deemed the ability to reflect upon one's functioning to be the most distinctly human agentic core property.

Bandura posited that self-efficacy beliefs play a key role in agentic functioning because of their impact on cognitive, affective, motivational, and decisional processes. *Self-efficacy* refers to one's perceived capabilities to learn or perform actions at designated levels of proficiency (Bandura, 1997). To form self-efficacy judgments, individuals must assess not only their knowledge of a particular task but also their capability to perform the task at a particular level of skill. Although self-efficacy beliefs are hypothesized to play an key role in change, Bandura (1986) cautioned that self-directed change requires more than strong motivational beliefs: "Neither intention nor desire to change alone has much effect if people lack the means for exercising influence over their own behavior" (p. 336), but how do they become more self-regulated?

Bandura (1986) contended that human functioning involves a dynamic interplay among personal, behavioral, and environmental influences. In this conception of *triadic reciprocality*, personal variables (e.g., cognitions, affects), behaviors, and environmental variables interact and influence one another. These interactions can be exemplified using self-efficacy, a personal variable. Researchers have shown that self-efficacy influences such behaviors as choice of tasks, persistence, effort, and achievement (Schunk & Pajares, 2004). But behaviors also can affect self-efficacy. As students work on tasks, they observe their progress in learning. Progress indicators such as how much of a task they have completed convey to students that they are capable, which enhances self-efficacy.

The interaction between self-efficacy and environmental variables has been highlighted in research on students with learning disabilities, many of whom hold low self-efficacy for performing well (Licht & Kistner, 1986). Persons in students' environments may react to them based on typical attributes rather than their actual behaviors. Thus, teachers may believe that such students are less capable than average learners and hold correspondingly lower expectations. Teachers' feedback can affect self-efficacy. A teacher who says, "This problem is probably too hard for you" may lower the students' self-efficacy.

The link between behaviors and environments is seen in many instructional sequences where teachers present information and ask students to attend to a slide. Environmental influence on behavior occurs when students attend to the slide without much conscious deliberation. The influence of behaviors on environmental variables can be seen when teachers ask questions in class and students reply incorrectly. The teachers are apt to reteach the troublesome points rather than continue the lesson.

People develop a sense of agency by using vicarious (e.g., modeling), symbolic (e.g., language), and self-regulatory processes (discussed later) to alter their thinking and behaviors and remain motivated to learn (Schunk, 2012). Much human learning occurs vicariously in the absence of performance by learners at the time of learning. This capability allows people to save time compared with performing every behavior to be learned and to shape their lives because they select environmental features to which they want to attend. For example, preservice teachers who engage in internships and student teaching attend closely to the actions and guidance of their mentor teachers, believing that the mentors are excellent models of teaching practice.

Models serve to inform and motivate. By observing models, observers learn new skills, strategies, and behaviors that help them succeed. Models also can motivate observers to learn, especially when observers perceive themselves as similar to models in important ways. Perceived similarity can convey behavioral appropriateness and raise observers' self-efficacy, as they may believe that if the models can learn, they can too.

Individuals possess the capability for symbolic representations using language, mathematical and scientific notation, iconography, and cognition. People use symbolic processes to interpret outcomes of their actions and guide future actions (Bandura, 1986). Symbolic processes also foster communications with others, which can result in further learning. Individuals do not merely react to events in their lives but rather display a sense of agency by generating actions to solve problems. The possibilities for learning are seen in educational activities such as collaborative learning and group discussions, where students employ their symbolic capabilities (e.g., language) to collectively produce outcomes.

Along with a sense of self-efficacy, social cognitive theory emphasizes goal setting as a key motivational process (Bandura, 1997; Locke & Latham, 1990, 2002; Zimmerman, 2008a), Learners who set a goal and feel efficacious for attaining it engage in activities that they believe will lead to goal attainment. As they work on the task and observe their goal progress their sense of self-efficacy is substantiated, which strengthens their motivation and leads to goal attainment. Once learners attain their goals they are motivated to set new goals.

Goals figure prominently in theoretical conceptions of self-regulated learning. Before engaging in a task, learners set goals and decide on strategies to use. They also hold an initial sense of self-efficacy for learning. During task engagement they regulate their cognitions, behaviors, and affects, and metacognitively monitor their goal progress. During breaks and when tasks are completed, they reflect on their experiences and progress to decide on their next steps. The perception of goal progress strengthens self-efficacy and motivates them to continue to learn.

The importance of goals in self-regulated learning is underscored by the results of a meta-analysis by Sitzmann and Ely (2011). Based on theories and research, these authors formulated a heuristic model comprising three types of constructs that constitute self-regulated learning: regulatory agents, regulatory mechanisms, and regulatory appraisals. Regulatory agents initiate self-regulated learning toward its goal, regulatory mechanisms help promote goal progress in an effective manner, and regulatory appraisals provide evaluative information on progress and influence continued goal striving. Sitzmann and Ely identified as being of primary importance one regulatory agent (goal level), six regulatory mechanisms (attention, metacognitive strategies, time management, environmental structuring, motivation, and effort), and two regulatory appraisals (attributions and self-efficacy). In this conceptualization, goal level denotes the standard that one is attempting to attain. Collectively these nine constructs define the process of self-regulated learning and highlight how self-regulated learners help control their learning.

Bandura (1986) identified three sequential subfunctions in developing one's self-regulation. *Self-observation* refers to efforts to monitor selectively certain aspects of one's behavior and ignore other aspects, such as a writer's focus on grammatical errors rather than on the quantity of text that is created. Bandura has warned that self-observation is not merely a mechanical audit of one's performance; rather, it is influenced by a number of factors, such as preexisting self-conceptions, valuing of outcomes, fatigue, and mood. For example, students in a despondent mood are more likely to focus on academic failures than on successes (Kuiper, MacDonald, & Derry, 1984). Self-observation is often difficult to separate from other self-regulatory processes, such as through self-evaluative judgments, which brings us to a second subfunction.

The second subfunction of *self-judgment* refers to one's application of personal standards to evaluate self-observations of performance, such as when a student sets a standard that a grade of B or lower on a class assignment is unsatisfactory. The formation of a standard for self-appraisal involves integrating information from three sources: one's own performance level, one's internal standards, and others' performances (Bandura, 1986). Self-evaluative judgments are affected by social and self-comparisons. Social comparisons refer to judgments of one's competence relative to others, and individuals who are regarded as similar or slightly higher in ability are preferred. Self-comparisons refer to judgments based on one's current behavior and one's prior performance.

The third subfunction, *self-reactions,* refers to feelings of satisfaction or dissatisfaction stemming from evaluative judgments of one's performances, such as being disappointed with a 75% on a spelling test. Bandura (1986) stressed that when students make their self-satisfaction or self-rewards contingent on certain accomplishments, they can motivate themselves to expend greater effort to improve their performances during subsequent attempts to learn. In this way, people can promote their skills and avoid problematic outcomes, such as failing grades in school or procrastination about studying.

Self-evaluative standards do more than sustain behavior, they also represent aspirations that can affect self-motivation and learning when they are cast in the form of goals (Bandura, 1986). Subsequently, we analyze the properties of goals that can activate the self-evaluative process governing self-motivation. But first we describe a cyclical phase model of self-regulation based on Bandura's social cognitive theory of human agency.

Cyclical Nature of Self-Regulated Learning

Most theories of self-regulated learning are distinguished by the presence of cyclical feedback loops, which describe how input regarding one's performance or outcomes is used to make subsequent changes (Hattie & Timperly, 2007). One's sources of cyclical feedback can be diverse. A first form is social feedback involving praise or guidance from teachers, coaches, parents, or peers. A second type is physical environment forms of feedback that emerge from task or contextual outcomes. A third form of feedback stems from personal sources, such as covert, physiological, or behavioral outcomes.

As a result of continuing research on the cyclical nature of feedback loops, a social cognitive cyclical model has become more detailed and complete (Schunk, 2012; Zimmerman, 2000, 2008b). Feedback loops involve a cycle of three sequential phases as shown in Figure 4.1. The first phase, *forethought*, precedes efforts to learn and is composed of learning processes and motivational beliefs that influence one's willingness and preparation to learn or perform. The second phase, *performance*, occurs during efforts to learn, and it involves learning and motivational processes that influence one's concentration and action. The third phase, *self-reflection*, occurs after efforts to perform, and it involves reactions to performance-phase outcomes. These self-reflections, in turn, influence forethought processes and beliefs regarding subsequent efforts to learn, thus completing the self-regulatory cycle.[1]

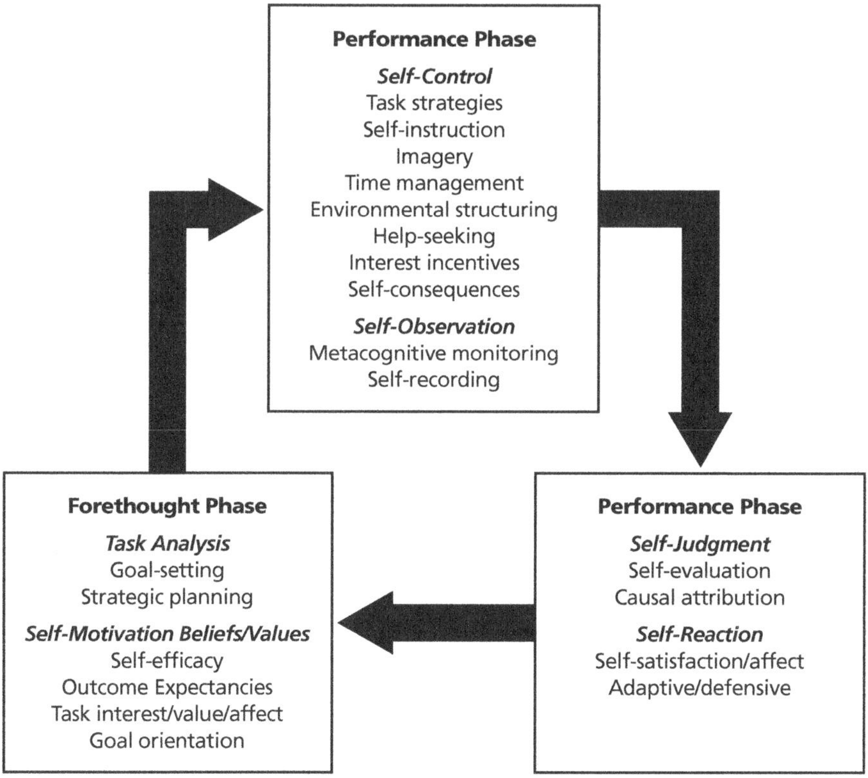

Figure 4.1 A cyclical phase model of self-regulation that integrates metacognitive processes and key measures of motivation.

Although all learners attempt to self-regulate in some fashion (Winne, 1997), this cyclical model distinguishes between proactive and reactive learners. *Proactive learners* self-regulate more effectively because they engage in high-quality forethought processes, whereas *reactive learners* regulate less effectively because they rely mainly on feedback from others to interpret their performance outcomes. Without forethought structuring, the value of performance-phase feedback is limited, and the possibility of unfortunate self-reflective-phase inferences is greatly increased, such as attributing errors to a low ability.

The forethought phase involves two major categories. *Task analysis* refers to breaking a task and its context into its components of goal setting and strategic planning (Winne & Hadwin, 1998). *Goal setting*—the focus of this chapter—involves specifying outcomes that one intends to attain, such as completing an English essay during a 2-hour writing period. Because of their superior task-analytic skills developed from education and experience, proactive learners can set clear goals for themselves. In contrast, due to their superficial task analyses, reactive students set vague (if any) goals for themselves. Various types of goals have been studied (discussed later in this chapter). Effective task analyses also enable proactive students to plan effective strategies to aid cognition, control affect, and direct motoric execution. By contrast, the superficial task analyses of reactive learners preclude them from planning a detailed strategy and compel them to rely on vague methods of learning, such as trying harder or concentrating more. *Strategic planning* refers to choosing or constructing advantageous learning methods that are appropriate for task and environmental setting. When students link their strategic plans to clear goals, they study or practice better.

Because task analysis, goal setting, and strategic planning require personal initiative and persistence, they require high levels of *self-motivation*. Proactive learners are motivated by a variety of sources, whereas reactive learners display inferior forms of motivation and as a result are less self-motivated to analyze tasks, select goals, or plan strategically than proactive learners. One key source of self-motivation is *self-efficacy*, which is related to performance-phase processes, such as choice of activities, effort, and persistence (Schunk, 2012; Zimmerman & Kitsantas, 1996). A student's self-efficacy perceptions can affect his or her use of learning strategies in diverse areas, such as writing (Schunk & Swartz, 1993a, 1993b) and time-management (Britton & Tessor, 1991).

Outcome expectancies, which constitute a second important source of self-motivation, refer to beliefs about the expected consequences of one's actions (e.g., receiving social recognition, obtaining a desirable job). Students' outcome expectations depend on their knowledge or awareness of potential outcomes, such as salaries, quality of life, and health and retirement benefits. The motivational effect of attractive outcomes has been widely demonstrated, but these expectations also depend on one's self-efficacy (Schunk & Zimmerman, 2008). For example, a student may believe that becoming a medical doctor is attractive. However, if students lack a sense of self-efficacy for learning chemistry, they are unlikely to be motivated to enroll in these collegiate courses.

A key point is that students' motivation to self-regulate their learning based on outcomes may be influenced by more than one motive. Expectancy-value research shows that although expectancies for success bear a strong positive relation to achievement, the value component influences students' choices (Wigfield & Eccles, 2002). Thus, even when outcome expectations are positive (i.e., students expect favorable outcomes from actions), learners are not apt to choose to engage in activities unless they value the expected outcomes.

Task interest, valuing, and *affect* compose a third source of students' forethought-phase motivation. These three closely associated motives refer to one's liking or disliking a task and its context because of their inherent properties rather than for their instrumental qualities in gaining other outcomes. This class of motives would include measures of intrinsic motivation (Deci & Ryan, 1985), interest value (Wigfield & Eccles, 2002), and interest (Hidi & Renninger, 2006). Research by Ainley, Corrigan, and Richardson (2005) revealed that task interest can influence students' choice of learning strategies and their achievement goals.

Students' *goal orientation* is a fourth source of motivation to self-regulate. This term refers to their reasons for learning or beliefs about the purpose of learning. Theoretical differences among goal-orientation researchers have led to variations in the names and number of goal orientations, but there is consensus regarding a learning (mastery) goal orientation and a performance goal orientation. Students who adopt a learning-goal orientation seek to improve their competence via learning, whereas students who adopt a performance-goal orientation seek to protect their competence perceptions via favorable comparisons with the performances of others (Dweck, 2006; Dweck & Leggett, 1988). Students' learning-goal orientation stems from their belief that their mental ability can be modified incrementally, whereas a performance-goal orientation stems from a belief that their mental ability is a fixed entity.[2]

Goal orientation can be differentiated from goal setting in several ways. First, goal orientation is a motivational construct, whereas goal setting is a metacognitive-process construct. Second, during goal setting, students pursue specific academic outcomes at a particular point in time (e.g., completing a book report in two days), whereas goal orientation does not target an outcome in a time period. Third, in terms of its role in self-regulation, goal setting produces an explicit feedback loop that requires self-evaluation at a specific time, whereas a goal orientation is an open-ended commitment to engage in learning or performance activities.

The second phase of self-regulation, *performance*, involves two major categories: self-control and self-observation methods. Self-control methods include a wide variety of strategies (i.e., repeatable cognitive operations to attain a goal). During this phase, proactive learners perform self-control processes that were planned during the forethought phase, such as using an outline to prepare for a history test. By contrast, reactive learners immerse themselves in a learning task without an explicit strategy to guide them.

Important self-control strategies are task strategies, self-instruction, imagery, time management, environmental structuring, help-seeking methods, interest enhancements, and setting self-consequences. *Task strategies* refer to systematic processes for addressing specific components of a task, such as creating steps for subtracting fractions in mathematics or for serving in tennis. *Self-instruction* refers to overt or covert self-descriptions of how to carry out a task, such as reminding oneself to check the spellings while writing a book report. Although the effectiveness of one's verbalizations depends on their quality and execution, research has shown that verbalizations can improve students' learning (Schunk, 1982). As a self-control strategy, *imagery* involves forming mental pictures to assist learning and retention, such as transforming textual material into diagrams, flow charts, and concept webs. These visual representations enable students to retrieve stored information in nonverbal images (Pressley, 1976). *Time management* strategies are used to accomplish tasks on schedule by setting specific task goals, estimating time requirements for tasks, and monitoring progress in attaining those goals. Students as young as elementary school age (Stoeger & Ziegler, 2011) and as mature as college age (Schmitz & Wiese, 2006) have been found to profit from time management training.

The self-control strategy of *environmental structuring* is designed to increase the effectiveness of one's immediate environments. For example, learners often use computers to write because the word processing program provides feedback regarding spelling and grammar. As a self-control strategy, *help seeking* involves soliciting assistance when learning or performing, such as seeking out a baseball coach to teach a pitcher to throw a curveball. If a student's goal is to learn a skill, then help seeking can be viewed as a social form of information seeking.

Self-control strategies are designed to improve performance-phase motivation directly (e.g., increase effort). *Interest enhancement* refers to increasing the attractiveness of a task strategically; for example, by introducing the element of competition into a boring assigned reading (Wolters, 2003). Setting *self-consequences* is another motivational strategy to increase self-control. It involves setting rewarding or punishing contingencies for oneself (e.g., delaying listening to one's favorite music until assigned homework is completed). Students who set consequences for themselves achieve better in school (Zimmerman & Martinez-Pons, 1986).

To be effective, these self-control strategies need to be adapted to learners' task outcomes. Because of the importance of this strategic feedback, the accuracy of one's self-observation is related to students' efforts to control their performances (Bandura 1986). Proactive learners rely on systematic forms of self-observation to guide their efforts to exert control, whereas reactive learners have trouble observing a particular process (e.g., discerning a grammatical error when writing) because they lack specific forethought-phase goals or plans to focus their attention.

Two key forms of self-observation have been studied: metacognitive monitoring and self-recording. *Metacognitive monitoring* or *self-monitoring* involves informal mental tracking of one's performance processes and outcomes; *self-recording* involves creating formal records of learning processes or outcomes, such as a graph of a student's mathematical division errors in his or her assignments. Having a record of one's efforts to learn is advantageous because it increases the reliability, specificity, and time span of self-observations. Self-recording can also provide information about the context of a personal event (e.g., records of where and with whom one is studying). Proactive learners use systematic forms of self-observation to guide their efforts to maintain control. They may make a list of tasks they need to accomplish before beginning their study or homework and then check off each task as they complete it. Reactive learners seldom engage in systematic forms spontaneously.

Self-observation of one's performance can be challenging even for proactive self-regulators, especially when the amount of information exceeds their capability to process it. This limitation can lead to poorly organized or superficial tracking, but these shortcomings can be avoided if students learn to track key processes. For example, they might focus on their wrist positions when shooting basketball free throws.

The third phase of self-regulation is *self-reflection*, which is composed of two self-regulatory subfunctions: *self-judgment* and *self-reaction*. *Self-evaluation* judgments involve comparisons of one's performance with a standard. Although a number of evaluative standards have been identified, three have been widely discussed: self-comparisons with prior levels of performance, comparisons of the degree to which a student masters each component of a skill (0% to 100%), and social comparisons with the performances of siblings, peers, and others. Proactive learners are guided by specific forethought-phase goals and tend to evaluate based on attainment of those goals. Because reactive students lack specific forethought-phase goals, they often fail to evaluate, or if they do, they may resort to social comparisons with classmates to judge their personal effectiveness. Contextual factors often dictate which type of standard is operative, such as when teachers use mastery standards or social standards to grade students' performance. However, teachers or coaches giving individualized instruction often rely on self-standards to judge students' progress between lessons. A self-standard of comparison has an important advantage: It emphasizes self-improvement rather than surpassing the performance of other students who may have started with an advantageous skill level. Students' goal setting during the forethought phase will influence the standard they use to evaluate during the self-reflection phase.

Causal attribution is a second type of self-judgment. Attributions are perceived causes of outcomes, such as one's ability, effort, and use of strategies. There is concern (Schunk, 2008; Weiner, 1992) that certain types of attributions for performance outcomes can undermine self-motivation, such as attributing errors to uncontrollable factors like insufficient talent or ability—an outcome experienced often by reactive students. By contrast, proactive students who attribute errors to controllable factors, such as use of a particular strategy, can sustain motivation during periods of poor performance (e.g., Zimmerman & Kitsantas, 1997, 1999). The relation between causal attributions and self-evaluations can be interactive. For example, when students judge their academic performance as successful, causal attributions to internal factors such as ability or effort should motivate subsequent efforts to learn. However, when reactive students evaluate their performance as unsuccessful, they may attribute performance outcomes to fixed ability—an uncontrollable cause that will undermine their motivation. Because proactive students evaluate based on self-chosen goals, they typically attribute errors to ineffective strategies, which are classified as controllable causes. Attribution of one's results to controllable causes leads to greater satisfaction than attributions to uncontrollable causes.

A second key category of the self-reflection phase is composed of two forms of *self-reaction*: self-satisfaction and adaptive/defensive decisions. *Self-satisfaction* is defined as cognitive and affective reactions to one's self-judgments. Self-satisfaction has been studied because students prefer learning activities that previously led to satisfaction and positive affect, and they tend to avoid those that produce dissatisfaction and negative affect (e.g., anxiety; Bandura, 1991). Reactive learners' attribution of errors to uncontrollable causes leads them to feel dissatisfied, which in turn discourages further efforts to learn. By contrast, proactive learners' attribution of errors to controllable causes leads them to feel satisfied, which sustains their learning (Cleary & Zimmerman, 2001).

Adaptive decisions refer to students' willingness to engage in further cycles of learning by continuing their use of a strategy or by modifying it, whereas *defensive* decisions avoid further efforts to learn in order to shield a student from future dissatisfaction and aversive affect. Helplessness, procrastination, task avoidance, cognitive disengagement, and apathy are all forms of defensiveness. It is important to note that both forms of students' self-reactions are related to self-judgments during the self-reflection phase. For example, favorable self-evaluations of one's performance and attributions to controllable causes can lead to increased self-satisfaction and continued efforts to learn adaptively. Proactive learners' high level of satisfaction can sustain their strategy adjustments until they develop an effective approach (Cleary & Zimmerman, 2001). Conversely, reactive learners' preoccupation with outcomes leads them to avoid future learning opportunities or defensively disclaim personal responsibility for adverse outcomes. Thus, the strategic-process goals set by proactive self-regulators during forethought lead to greater satisfaction and more effective forms of adaptation.

In a cyclical model of self-regulation, the effects of forethought-phase processes can extend well beyond this phase. For example, learners' goals also can affect their self-observations during the performance phase and self-evaluation judgments and adaptation self-reactions during the self-reflection phase. We turn next to the role of goal setting in cyclical self-regulation.

GOAL SETTING

Conceptual Basis

Cognitive perspectives postulate that individuals base their goal-setting decisions on such cognitive factors as their beliefs about their capabilities (self-efficacy), memories of past performances, beliefs about anticipated outcomes of actions (outcome expectations), and judgments of what goals are appropriate in the situation (Locke & Latham, 1990). But goal setting is not entirely a cognitive process because motivational factors also are important. Although cognition and motivation cannot fully be disentangled since they intertwine, motivational variables with cognitive representations such as self-efficacy, values, interests, and outcome expectations influence goal setting.

It is useful to think of goals as having two central attributes: content and intensity (Locke & Latham, 1990). *Goal content* refers to the object or result that one wishes to attain, such as scoring at least 90 on an exam or successfully completing a group project. Goal content can vary qualitatively; for example, students may set academic, social, and athletic goals. It also can vary quantitatively; students may set many or few goals, short- and long-term goals, and goals that vary in difficulty and specificity.

Goal intensity refers to such variables as the scope of the goal-setting process, the effort involved in setting goals, the importance of goals in a goal hierarchy (assuming multiple goals), the importance of the goal, and the individual's commitment to attaining the goal (Locke & Latham, 1990).

Although these two dimensions can be experimentally distinguished, they are not always so clear-cut in practice. For example, it often requires greater intensity (effort) to set clear, specific, short-term goals (e.g., study the first 10 pages of Chapter 3 tonight) than more-general long-term goals (e.g., do some studying this week).

The core principle of theories emphasizing goal setting is that goals are immediate regulators of human actions, although they are not the only ones (Locke & Latham, 1990). Goal theories also highlight the importance of *goal commitment,* which refers to how dedicated an individual is to attaining the goal. Where commitment to a goal is low or lacking, then for practical purposes the individual does not have a goal.

Types of Goals

Goals guide and motivate learning and performance, but not all are equally effective. Six properties of goals can make a difference (see Table 4.1). The *specificity* of a goal is an important property (Locke & Lathan, 1990). Goals that focus on specific aspects of performance, such as "Learn the words on this spelling list," can enhance learning and activate self-standards more effectively than general goals, such as "Do your best." Specific goals, which make self-evaluation more accurate and more revealing of progress as it occurs, can boost self-efficacy (Bandura & Schunk, 1981). There is extensive research indicating the effectiveness of specific goals. For example, Schunk (1983a) taught elementary school students to solve long-division problems using instruction and practice. Some students were given a specific number of problems to solve, whereas other students were

TABLE 4.1 Properties and Effects of Goals

Property of Goals	Effects of Goals
Specificity	Goals with specific standards of performance increase acquisition and motivation more than general goals.
Proximity	Short-term goals increase acquisition and motivation more than long-term goals.
Difficulty	Challenging but attainable goals increase acquisition and motivation more than easy or hard goals.
Origin	Self-set goals increase acquisition and motivation more than assigned goals.
Congruence	Goals that are mentally or socially compatible increase learning and motivation more than conflicting goals.
Focus	Learning-process goals increase acquisition and motivation more than performance outcomes until the point of automaticity.

given a general goal to work productively. Half of the students in each group received comparative-attainment information on the number of problems that their peers completed. To each child, the teacher said that he or she had worked with many children and that half of them finished the number of problems given as the goal. The results showed that setting specific goals enhanced self-efficacy beliefs, but setting specific goals and providing comparative information produced the highest self-efficacy and achievement.

Goals can be distinguished also by their *proximity* in time. An example of a short-term proximal goal is to memorize a list of Spanish vocabulary words during the next 30 minutes. In contrast, an example of a long-term distal goal is to learn the Spanish word list in the next 3 days. Because short-term goals are achieved or failed more quickly, the timely feedback they produce can be more helpful for motivation and learning.

The effectiveness of short-term goals was demonstrated in a study by Bandura and Schunk (1981). Elementary students were given subtraction instruction and practice involving seven curricular packets that were intended to be studied in seven sessions. One third of the students were given the goal of completing one packet by the end of each session; another third were given the distal goal of completing all the packets by the end of the seven sessions; and the final third of the students were given a general goal of working productively. Students given proximal goals displayed the highest subtraction self-efficacy, achievement, and interest. Students given the distal goal did no better than the general goal group on any of the dependent measures.

However, distal goals can be advantageous when they are organized in a *hierarchy* with short-term goals (Carver & Scheier, 2000). For example, a student might link the attainment of the proximal goal of daily studying to the intermediate goal of passing a course in anatomy, to the long-term goal of becoming a physical therapist. When integrated hierarchically, short-term goals give proximal feedback about learning progress, whereas long-term or distal goals project a person's self-regulatory perspective farther into the future. Setting hierarchical goals enables learners to work productively over long periods of time without needing additional sources of motivation or direction (Locke & Latham, 1990). Short-term goals provide a start on the path of learning, whereas long-term goals provide a destination.

A third important property of goals is their *difficulty*, which refers to the level of task proficiency required to succeed (Locke & Latham, 1990). Difficult goals require greater effort, but they also convey higher self-efficacy when individuals attain them. However, setting difficult goals has drawbacks if students fail to attain those goals, such as undermining their effort and diminishing their self-efficacy. One solution to this problem is to set *challenging* goals or those that are attainable but do not greatly exceed a student's level of proficiency. Challenging goals can be adjusted based on a student's prior goal attainment.

The effectiveness of setting challenging goals was investigated in a study of mathematical long-division learning (Schunk, 1983b). The teacher gave half of the students a difficult but attainable goal of completing a certain number of problems, and the other half of the students were given an easier goal of completing fewer problems. To encourage the students to believe that the goals were not too difficult, half of the students in the two goal-difficulty conditions were informed directly by the teacher that they could attain the goal (i.e., "You can work ________ problems."). The other half of the students were informed that students who were similar to them had been able to work the designated number of problems. The results showed that direct feedback led to higher perceptions of self-efficacy than did social-comparative information. Students who set difficult goals showed higher levels of motivation. Students who set difficult goals and received direct attainment feedback displayed the highest self-efficacy and achievement.

A fourth property of goals is their *origin*: There is evidence that self-set goals are more effective than goals set by others, such as teachers or parents. Schunk (1985) gave 6th-grade students with learning disabilities subtraction instruction and practice. One third of the students set daily goals for themselves, another third of the students were assigned comparable goals, and a third of the students studied without goals. Students who set their own goals displayed the highest self-efficacy and subtraction achievement.

A fifth property of goals is their degree of *congruence* with one another (Locke, Smith, Erez, Chah, & Schaffer, 1994). Whereas incongruent goals can diminish their effectiveness, congruent goals can increase it. Often, students must deal with competing goals (e.g., academic and social). Students may be pressured to set low-achievement goals to avoid being thought of as nerdy. Steinberg, Brown, and Dornbusch (1996) reported that fewer than 32% of high school students think that it is important to get good grades in school. One student in six hid their interest in succeeding in class because of concerns about reactions from friends. More than 50% of the students never discussed their schoolwork with friends. When students reach high school, they may be influenced more by their friends than their parents. Clearly, students have to contend with academic conditions that can lead to high levels of conflict in their goal setting. The consequences of setting incongruous goals on performance can be significant (Locke et al., 1994). Teachers and parents can teach students how to set challenging but realistic goals. For example, students can set a goal and monitor their progress. Teachers and parents can provide feedback to students that they are on track to attain their goal or about how to modify their goal to make it more realistic.

A sixth property of goals is their *focus*. Social cognitive theory distinguishes between two distinct but related purposes: to increase learning or to enhance performance of previously learned behaviors. A learning goal focuses one's attention on processes (or the means) to improve acquisition, such as strategies or subskills for solving mathematical word problems. A performance goal focuses on producing task outcomes (or the ends) of learning, such as percentages of problems that were correctly solved. Similar distinctions have been named "performance versus outcomes" in athletics (Burton, 1979), "learning versus performance" in work settings (Locke & Latham, 2002), and "learning process versus product" in academics (Schunk & Swartz, 1993a, 1993b).

The importance of these goals for achievement stems from the differential effects they have on learners' cognitive processes and motivational beliefs. Cognitively, learning goals emphasize the benefits of task strategies, such as improved retention and transfer (Pressley & McCormick, 1995). Motivationally, learning goals convey the message that success is attainable when one masters the right strategy or component skill. This mastery experience strengthens perceptions of self-efficacy and motivates learners to exert greater effort, persistence, and adherence to the strategy (Bandura, 1986; Schunk, 1989). In contrast, students' focus on performance outcomes (whether positive or negative) can reduce their awareness of shortcomings in their strategies or subskills, which can limit their performance outcomes and lead to unfortunate social comparisons based on outcomes (Schunk 1996). Locke and Latham (2002) contend that learning tasks are more complex than performance tasks because the former involve the discovery of strategies whereas the latter have been automatized. Automaticity occurs when an act can be performed without reflection or intent (English & English, 1958), which can result from overlearning.

There has been extensive research showing that process goals lead to not only better acquisition but also stronger self-efficacy. For example, Schunk and Swartz (1993a, 1993b) gave students in regular and gifted classes a process goal of using a strategy for writing paragraphs or a product goal (i.e., performance outcomes) of writing paragraphs. Half of the students who set a process goal received feedback periodically on their progress in learning the strategy. The remaining half did not receive progress feedback. These researchers discovered that the process goal with feedback proved to be the most effective and that the process goal without feedback led to higher writing achievement outcomes than did the product goal.

In a study of goal setting and self-monitoring while acquiring an athletic skill, Zimmerman and Kitsantas (1996) compared a learning-process goal with a performance outcome (i.e., product) goal. All students were novices to dart throwing, and all were provided with identical background knowledge of the task: They were shown a strategy for sighting, throwing, and following through. The experiment involved a 12-minute practice session, and students in the learning-process group were told that to do well in dart throwing they should concentrate on properly executing the strategy. Students in the performance-outcome condition were told to earn the highest numeric score on a concentric circle target. Half of the students in the learning-process-goal group recorded their deficient strategy steps, and half of the performance outcome group recorded their target scores during practice. After practice, the students were tested on dart-throwing proficiency, self-efficacy, intrinsic interest, and self-reactions. A no-goal control group was given the same background knowledge of dart throwing but was not allowed to practice. The results revealed that students who set learning-process goals displayed significantly greater dart-throwing skill, self-efficacy, intrinsic interest, and self-reactions than students who set performance outcome goals. Students who self-recorded showed significantly higher dart-throwing skill, self-efficacy and self-reactions than did students who did not self-record. The performance goal subgroup that did not self-record failed to surpass the control group on any dependent measure. Correlational analyses revealed that goal setting was more strongly related to dart-throwing skill (.79) than was self-recording (.27), but together, goal setting and self-recording accounted for 71% of the variance in dart skill.

However, the greater effectiveness of learning goals is not absolute but rather can depend on one's attainment of automaticity when students' goals can be shifted toward optimizing performance outcomes. The advantages of automaticity or implicit mental functioning have been widely reported by athletic coaches. For example, the British table tennis champion Syed (2010) described the advantage of implicit processing as "it frees up attention to focus on higher aspects of a skill" (p. 191).

This shifting-goal hypothesis was tested in two studies. Zimmerman and Kitsantas (1997) hypothesized that students who shifted from learning-process goals to performance-outcome goals after attaining automaticity would surpass a fixed goal-learning-process group, which in turn would surpass a fixed goal-performance-outcome group. The Zimmerman and Kitsantas (1996) dart-throwing task was used, as was self-recording. Students in the shifting group changed goals after 12 minutes of a 20-minute practice session. The results revealed support for the hypotheses: The shifting-goal group surpassed the learning-process-goal group, which in turn surpassed the performance-outcomes-goal group in posttest dart-throwing skill, self-reactions, intrinsic interest, and self-efficacy. Students who self-recorded their results displayed significantly greater dart-throwing skill, self-efficacy, and self-reactions than did students who did not self-record.

These shifting-goal results lead to the question of whether they generalize to acquisition of academic skills. To address this issue, a study of writing revision was conducted with high school girls (Zimmerman & Kitsantas, 1999). The task required participants to revise highly redundant passages. The revisions could be objectively scored in terms of missing information and for redundancies. All participants were initially taught a three-step revision strategy. Following training, a practice session was conducted. Girls in the learning-process-goal group focused on strategic steps for revising each writing task, those in the performance outcome group focused on decreasing the number of words in their revised passages, and girls in a shifting-goal group started with learning-process goals and changed to performance-outcome goals after automaticity occurred. Half of the participants in each goal group were asked to self-record their learning processes or performance outcomes.

Girls who shifted goals from learning processes to performance outcomes after having achieved automaticity surpassed the writing-revision skill of girls who adhered to learning-process goals. Girls who focused on outcomes displayed less writing-revision skill than the shifting- or process-goal groups, and self-recording enhanced writing acquisition for all goal groups. In addition to their acquisition of superior writing-revision skill, students who shifted goals displayed advantageous forms of self-motivation, such as greater attributions to controllable causes (i.e., strategy use), enhanced self-satisfaction, more optimistic self-efficacy beliefs, and greater task interest. These results support the point that goal setting can have widespread effects on diverse tasks.

Adjunctive Self-Regulatory Processes

We now turn to the combined effects of goal setting with other self-regulatory processes and sources of motivation on learning and performance. One self-regulative process that has been studied in combination with goal setting is *self-recording*. Recall that when setting both learning-process goals and performance-outcomes goals, students who kept a record of their practice outcomes acquired a significantly higher level of skill on an academic writing task (Zimmerman & Kitsantas, 1999) and an athletic dart-throwing task (Zimmerman & Kitsantas, 1997). Students who self-recorded also produced significantly greater self-satisfaction reactions, intrinsic interest in the task, and self-efficacy beliefs than did students who did not self-record.

Goal setting also influenced the students' attributions for their errors. The learning-process-goal group attributed their errors to strategy deficiencies, whereas the performance-outcome group attributed their mistakes to insufficient effort, a lack of ability, or task difficulty. Interestingly, strategy attributions positively related to athletic or academic skill, self-satisfaction reactions, self-efficacy beliefs, and intrinsic interest, whereas attributions to effort and ability negatively related to these outcomes. Having a tangible record of one's goal-setting outcomes enhances not only acquisition of two different skills but also self-reflection-phase causal attributions to strategy use and self-satisfaction reactions and forethought-phase self-efficacy and intrinsic interest.

A second self-regulatory process that has been studied in conjunction with goal setting is *self-evaluation.* Often students do not self-evaluate their competencies spontaneously, but they can be persuaded to periodically assess their progress when acquiring a valued skill. In two studies, Schunk (1996) gave fourth graders instruction and practice on fractions, along with either a learning goal (e.g., learn a strategy for solving problems) or a performance goal (e.g., solving problems). In an initial study, half of the students in each goal condition evaluated their problem-solving capabilities at the end of each of six daily sessions. Whether the students were given a learning goal with or without self-evaluation or a performance goal with self-evaluation, they surpassed students given a performance goal without self-evaluation in fractions skill, self-efficacy, and motivation. In the second study, students in each goal condition evaluated their progress in skill acquisition. Students in the learning-goal and self-evaluation group displayed higher motivation and achievement than did students in the performance-goal and self-evaluation group. These two studies showed that systematic efforts to self-evaluate can enhance the effectiveness of both learning and performance goals.

Similarly, Schunk and Ertmer (1999) investigated goal setting and self-evaluation with college students in learning computer skills in three study sessions. In the first of two studies, students who set a learning-process goal and self-evaluated their learning progress after the second session reported higher self-efficacy, self-judged learning progress, self-regulatory competence, and strategy use. Students' opportunity to self-evaluate enhanced their self-efficacy beliefs. In the second study, self-evaluation was extended to all three sessions. Frequent self-evaluations produced comparable results for both learning and process goals. The results suggest that infrequent self-evaluation complements process goals, but frequent self-evaluation outweighs the benefits of process-goal setting.

A third self-regulatory process that has been studied in conjunction with goal setting is *goal-progress feedback.* Often students fail to monitor their goal progress spontaneously, but they can be prompted to do so by providing them with periodic feedback regarding their goal progress while acquiring a skill.

There is evidence of the combined effectiveness of goal setting and goal-progress feedback. In a study by Schunk and Rice (1991), students with reading problems were taught a strategy to answer comprehension questions. Students were given a product (performance) goal of answering the questions, a process goal of learning to use the strategy, or a process goal plus progress feedback (combined). The feedback linked performance with strategy use and conveyed that they were making progress toward their goal. On the posttest, the combined group surpassed the process-goal and the product-goal groups in self-efficacy and achievement. The studies summarized earlier by Schunk and Swartz (1993a, 1993b) also showed that combining process goals with feedback promoted self-efficacy and achievement.

The studies in this section demonstrate the effectiveness of three adjunctive processes: self-recording, self-evaluation, and goal-progress feedback. Setting goals does not ensure their usefulness in judging the meaning of personal feedback. This research showed how these performance-phase processes can not only augment the impact of forethought-phase goals on acquisition of a skill but also induce an array of supportive self-reflection-phase reactions.

CALIBRATION

According to a cyclical view of self-regulation, students who engage in high-quality task analysis, choose an effective strategy, and implement it as a process goal are more likely to monitor their acquisition of skill accurately than reactive learners (Stone, 2000; Zimmerman, 1990). It has been hypothesized that these self-regulated learners are well calibrated (Zimmerman, Moylan, Hudesman, White, & Flugman, 2011). *Calibration* is a measure of metacognitive monitoring that assesses the gap between one's perceptions of competence about performing a particular task and one's actual performance.

Social cognitive researchers have investigated students' calibration based on measures of self-efficacy. In prior research, they have widely reported positive correlations between the *strength* of students' self-efficacy beliefs and their academic motivation and achievement (e.g., Schunk & Pajares, 2004). Research has uncovered another dimension of self-efficacy measures: their accuracy or calibration (e.g., Chen & Zimmerman, 2007). The calibration of self-efficacy can be measured when task-specific measures of self-efficacy are employed, such as a student's confidence about an answer to an ecological science problem. Researchers (Klassen, 2002; Pajares & Miller, 1994) have found that students often overestimate their efficacy judgments; underestimates of self-efficacy occur less frequently. As is the case when setting challenging goals, students' self-efficacy judgments should not greatly exceed their actual capabilities because overoptimism can lead to insufficient efforts to learn (Ghatala, Levin, & Pressley, 1989). Well-calibrated people monitor more accurately, and this high-quality feedback enables them to learn and perform a task more effectively (Schunk & Pajares, 2004).

In contrast to the literature on self-efficacy calibration, the literature on self-evaluation judgments of competence after performing a particular task is more extensive. Although there is evidence that students' self-evaluations of the correctness of their answers are only slightly above chance, students who engage in frequent self-evaluation tend to attain higher academic outcomes than those who do not self-evaluate their performance (Chen, 2003;

Kitsantas, Reiser, & Doster, 2004; Schunk, 1996). Of particular concern is the finding that low-achieving students are less accurate and more overconfident than high-achieving students, who tend to be slightly underconfident (Bol & Hacker, 2001). Efforts to improve students' self-evaluative accuracy have been largely unsuccessful (Bol & Hacker, 2001; Hacker & Bol, 2004).

The resistance of overconfident students to improving their self-evaluation accuracy may be due to adverse sources of motivation. For example, negative outcomes can result from inaccurate perceptions of one's capability. Students who overestimate their competence substantially are more likely to select difficult problems to solve and therefore fail, which can undermine their motivation to continue learning (Bandura, 1986; Schunk & Pajares, 2004). The question thus arises of how one breaks this cycle. Can calibration be taught to at-risk students in a real-world setting, and does it enable them to self-regulate their learning processes better and attain greater academic skill? We address this issue next.

GOAL SETTING APPLICATIONS

In this section, we describe two applications designed to improve students' self-regulated learning skills. Each of these applications highlights the key influence of goal setting.

An Intervention to Improve Calibration and Self-Reflection

Zimmerman et al. (2011) conducted an intervention study with at-risk technical-college students who were studying mathematics. The project investigated the effects of self-reflection training on students' metacognitive calibration judgments and motivational beliefs. These learners were helped to interpret their academic grades as sources of self-reflective feedback rather than personal limitation. The students were enrolled in developmental (remedial) mathematics or introductory college-level mathematics courses. They were randomly assigned to either an intervention or a control classroom of their respective courses. Teachers in intervention classrooms used modeling techniques and assessment practices designed to enhance self-reflection processes. Students in intervention classrooms were given frequent opportunities to improve their achievement using a self-reflective-feedback form to self-regulate their learning and problem solving.

Self-reflective feedback was provided during every second or third class session. Students in the intervention classrooms were administered a quiz composed of four or five problems as a vehicle for frequent feedback to students and teachers. The quiz forms asked students to render task-specific self-efficacy judgments before solving individual problems and self-evaluative judgments after attempting to solve each problem. After the instructor graded the quizzes, students in the intervention group could correct their quiz errors by completing the self-reflection forms and by receiving quiz-grade incentives.

The students' self-reflection form guided their self-regulatory processes concerning erroneous answers on a quiz and self-regulatory efforts to solve transfer problems (see Figure 4.2). Goal setting was implicit in the structure

SRL Math Revision Sheet, Quiz #____ Item #____
Student: ____________________ **Date:** ________
Instructor: ____________________

Now that you have received your corrected quiz, you have the opportunity to improve your score. Complete all sections thoroughly and thoughtfully. Use a separate revision sheet for each new problem.

PLAN IT 8pts

1. a. How much time did you spend studying for this topic area? _______

 b. How many practice problems did you do in this topic area ____________________ in preparation for this quiz?

 (circle one) 0 – 5 / 5 – 10 / 10+

 c. What did you do to prepare for this quiz? (use study strategy list to answer this question)

2. After you solved this problem, was your confidence rating too high (i.e. 4 or 5)? yes no

3. Explain what strategies or processes went wrong on the quiz problem.

PRACTICE IT 8pts

4. Now re-do the original quiz problem and write the strategy you are using on the right.

Definitely not confident   Not confident   Undecided   Confident   Very confident

5. How confident are you now that you can correctly solve this similar item?

1 2 3 4 5

6. Now use the strategy to solve the alternative problem. 4pts

7. How confident are you now that you can correctly solve a similar problem on a quiz or test in the future? 4pts

1 2 3 4 5

Figure 4.2 Math revision self-reflection form. Reprinted with permission from Zimmerman et al. (2011).

of the form because it focused the students on attaining learning-process goals (e.g., discovering strategies), as well as on performance-outcome goals (e.g., earning grade incentives). The form required students to compare their self-efficacy and self-evaluative judgments with their answer to the quiz item, explain their ineffectual strategies, develop a new more effective strategy, and indicate their confidence for solving a new problem. If the answer to the problem was incorrect and the students unaware why it was wrong, they were encouraged to seek help from an instructor, tutor, or peer. Initially, instructors modeled the completion of the self-reflection forms, and then they supported their students with in-class practice. Students were given the formula for scoring the calibration of their answers on the self-reflection forms.

The results revealed that students in self-regulation classes outperformed those in control classes on three periodic instructor-developed mathematics tests, as well as on the course final examination. Although there was substantial evidence of overconfidence by these at-risk technical-college students, students in self-regulation classes were better calibrated in their task-specific self-efficacy beliefs and in their self-evaluative judgments than students in control classes. Significant relations among self-regulated learning processes were found: Students' self-efficacy and self-evaluation judgments regarding their performance on periodic tests were positively correlated with their achievement on the periodic tests. Self-efficacy for the third and final exam, standards for self-satisfaction, and self-reported learning-strategy use were positively correlated with final-exam achievement.

Self-regulation-class instructors observed that students varied considerably in their use of the self-reflection form. For students in the developmental (remedial) course, high self-reflectors displayed significantly greater achievement on the second and third periodic tests and on the final exam. High self-reflectors did not surpass low self-reflectors significantly on the first periodic test. For students in the introductory course, high self-reflectors significantly outperformed low self-reflectors on the three periodic tests and the final exam. It appears that students with greater mathematics background were better able to profit from self-regulatory training on the first periodic exam.

These students can be described as at-risk because they were not yet admitted to this technical college as regular students. To enroll in credit-bearing courses and make progress toward obtaining a degree, students were required to pass a college-wide entrance test. A significantly greater percentage of students from the self-regulation classes passed the entrance test than students in control classes.

These results show that a self-regulated-learning intervention designed to improve students' self-reflection improved the accuracy or calibration of their self-monitoring of their problem-solving performance. This intervention also increased the students' achievement in entry-level courses in college mathematics. Awarding an academic grade is a key social interaction between a teacher and a student. In traditional forms of mathematics assessment, feedback regarding errors is often presented adversely as signs of imperfection. By contrast, during self-regulative assessment, feedback regarding errors is presented as additional opportunities for learning. The self-reflection form was designed as a way to empower at-risk students to change their perspective on acquiring skills. The results of the college entrance tests revealed that the career paths of these students had improved significantly.

An Intervention Involving Goal Setting and Writing

Many studies have been conducted examining self-regulated learning and effective writing performance based on the Self-Regulated Strategy Development (SRSD) model (Harris & Graham, 1992, 1996). This model involves six stages of instruction: (a) Develop and activate knowledge needed for writing and self-regulation; (b) Discuss It; (c) Model It; (d) Memorize It; (e) Support It; and (f) Independent Performance (Harris, Graham, Friedlander, & Laud, 2013).

Developing and activating knowledge for writing and self-regulation involves teachers helping students obtain the background knowledge about the genre being addressed and developing declarative, procedural, and conditional knowledge (Harris et al., 2013), as well as learning about self-regulation and what it entails (e.g., goal setting, modeling, strategic planning). In the second stage, *Discuss It*, goal setting is emphasized as students define the objective of the writing activity and break this objective into small attainable goals. One strategy used to assist with goal setting is to draw a graph of story elements when writing a short story. These first two stages are similar to the forethought phase of self-regulated learning. They involve preparing to engage in the learning task of writing and understanding what skills the task involves to set plans in place.

In the third stage, *Model It*, the teacher models how to write a composition. The teacher at times is a coping model—one who makes mistakes and then corrects the errors. Throughout this stage, the teacher and students monitor their progress toward goal attainment and evaluate performance (Graham, Harris, & Troia, 1998). During this stage, the teacher models self-statements to promote positive self-efficacy to complete the task. Students are asked to record their own self-statements while writing, which helps students self-monitor their progress and provides the teacher and students with information about feelings of self-efficacy during the writing task. The teacher also models self-reinforcement to show students how to praise and acknowledge themselves for good work. During the fourth stage, *Memorize It*, students use a mnemonic, phrase, or other memorization strategy to help them remember the steps of the writing strategy. This stage helps students use the strategy on their own, maintain the skills, and transfer it to different contexts in a self-regulatory way in the absence of the teacher. Both of these stages roughly map against the performance phase of self-regulated learning.

During the fifth stage, *Support It*, the teacher and students compare and evaluate their writing before and after the SRSD instruction. Students are encouraged to work collaboratively with their peers as the teacher's role diminishes to scaffolding and encouraging students to work independently. The teacher remains available for support as needed and works with students to help them maintain the SRSD approach and transfer it to other writing activities (Harris et al., 2013). This stage also is marked by an increased use of self-regulation strategies, such as working on the goals previously set, setting new ones, self-monitoring, self-reinforcement, and using performance strategies such as imagery and managing one's environment (Harris et al., 2013). In the sixth stage, *Independent Performance*, students use the writing strategies independently. They have reached independence when they are able to write an essay using all of the story elements and meet their goals without the teacher's assistance. These two stages are closely aligned with the self-reflection phase where students are reflecting and evaluating their performance and working independently of the teacher in contexts outside of the classroom.

Lienemann, Graham, Leader-Janssen, and Reid (2006) applied the SRSD model with 2nd-grade students diagnosed as at risk for failure. Prior to the intervention, 2nd-grade writing instruction consisted of teaching basic skills such as handwriting and spelling. Some 10 students were identified who completed a writing-skill assessment (write a complete and interesting story). Of these students, six scored below the 25th percentile. These students were also given a reading assessment and all but one scored below reading grade level.

Each student was assigned to one of two instructors trained in SRSD, and students were asked to write three stories prior to the intervention to establish baselines. SRSD was used to individually teach students how to plan and write stories for sessions lasting 30–45 minutes until mastery was achieved (ranging from 6 to 8 sessions). Self-regulated learning strategies such as goal setting, self-monitoring, self-instruction, and self-reinforcement were explicitly taught. The beginning stages of training focused on teaching students how to plan and use strategies, as well as what the seven elements of a good story are: WHO the main character is, WHERE the story takes place, WHEN the story occurs, WHAT the main character(s) do or plan to do, WHAT happens next, HOW the story concludes, and HOW the character(s) feel about their experiences (Reid & Lienemann, 2006).

Throughout the sessions, the instructors discussed and identified instances of transfer and goal setting, and they modeled how to plan and write a story, keeping the goal in mind of including all of the seven elements in the story while making the story fun to write. The students observed the instructors use self-instructions, self-monitoring, and self-reinforcement as they worked on their goals. The learners helped the instructors by identifying the story elements and recording their notes on the graphic organizers until they were engaged in the writing themselves. Once students were engaged in writing, the instructors used scaffolding until the students were writing and checking their writing goals independently. Students were considered to have mastered the training once they were able to write their own stories using all of the seven story elements without the instructor's help.

The results showed that teaching young struggling writers self-regulated learning strategies for writing was effective in improving the quality and length of writing. Five of the six students showed an increase in story quality up to 277%; the sixth learner increased by 113% because his stories did not increase in length after instruction. The reading level for four of the six students increased as well. This study demonstrates the benefits of teaching goal setting within the framework of self-regulated learning among young school children who previously had struggled to write.

CONCLUSION

Considerable progress has been made in recent years in identifying key self-regulatory processes and sources of motivation that underlie a learner's sense of agency. Becoming a self-directed agent involves not only self-efficacy but also using self-regulatory processes during the forethought, performance, and self-reflection phases. Goal setting is a key self-regulatory process that can help learners develop a sense of agency. For example, monitoring one's performance accurately requires setting effective goals during forethought and accurate self-evaluation during self-reflection. In the absence of effective goal setting, learners are at a disadvantage when adapting their performance. Fortunately, researchers have investigated how to set effective goals and evaluate one's goal progress. But it can be asked whether this self-regulation research makes a difference in dealing with entrenched learning problems in real-world settings.

To answer this question, we describe two intervention studies designed to enhance students' self-regulated learning using goal setting. The first application shows how self-regulatory support can be provided for at-risk students enrolled in introductory mathematics classes at a community college. The second application demonstrates the effectiveness of the SRSD program in improving struggling writers' skills. Collectively, these applications show how students who receive self-regulated learning instruction can become agents of their own academic destinies. In addition to the development of competencies, this seems like a laudable educational goal that will help create better citizens.

NOTES

1. Figure 4.1 is designed to explain self-regulation in terms of real-time functioning, and phases are defined as events that occur before, during, and after performance. Within the forethought phase, correlations between task analysis and self-motivation processes are possible theoretically, but causality cannot be inferred because both sets of processes occur at the same point in time. Causes must precede effects in time. However, causality can be inferred among between-phase processes, such as forethought-phase goal setting and performance-phase self-recording, because these phases are related sequentially. The possibility of causal relations of self-regulatory processes across the three phases is the reason that the phases are connected by arrows.
2. Researchers have proposed a second dimension of approach-avoidance that when crossed with type of orientation yields a 2 × 2 classification: mastery-approach, mastery-avoidance, performance-approach, performance-avoidance (Elliot, 1999; Pintrich, 2000). A mastery-approach orientation is positively linked with use of self-regulatory processes (Kaplan, Lichtinger, & Gorodetsky, 2009), whereas the relations between other goal orientations and self-regulation are more variable.

REFERENCES

Ainley, M., Corrigan, M., & Richardson, N. (2005). Students, tasks and emotions: Identifying the contribution of emotions to students reading of popular culture and popular science texts. *Learning and Instruction, 15*, 433–447.

Bandura, A. (1986). *Social foundations of thought and action: A social cognitive theory.* Englewood Cliffs, NJ: Prentice-Hall.

Bandura, A. (1991). Self-regulation of motivation through anticipatory and self-reactive mechanisms. In R. A. Dienstbier (Ed.), *Perspectives on motivation: Nebraska symposium on motivation* (Vol. 38, pp. 69–164). Lincoln: University of Nebraska Press.

Bandura, A. (1997). *Self-efficacy: The exercise of control.* New York, NY: Freeman

Bandura, A. (2008). Toward an agentic theory of the self. In H. W. Marsh, R. G. Craven, & D. McInerney (Eds.), In *Self-processes, leaning, and enabling human potential: Dynamic new processes* (pp. 15–49). Charlotte, NC: Information Age.

Bandura, A., & Schunk, D. H. (1981). Cultivating competence, self-efficacy, and intrinsic interest through proximal self-motivation. *Journal of Personality and Social Psychology, 41*, 586–598.

Bol, L., & Hacker, D. (2001). The effect of practice tests on students' calibration and performance. *Journal of Experimental Education, 69*, 133–151.

Britton, B. K., & Tessor, A. (1991). Effects of time management practices on college grades. *Journal of Educational Psychology, 83*, 405–410.

Burton, D. (1979). The impact of goal specificity and task complexity on basketball skill development. *The Sport Psychologist 3*, 3–47.

Carver, C., & Scheier, M. F. (2000). On the structure of behavioral self-regulation. In M. Boekaerts, P. R. Pintrich, & M. Zeidner (Eds.), *Handbook of self-regulation* (pp. 41–84). San Diego, CA: Academic.

Chen, P. P. (2003). Exploring the accuracy and predictability of the self-efficacy beliefs of seventh-grade mathematics students. *Learning and Individual Differences, 14,* 79–92.

Chen, P., & Zimmerman, B. (2007). A cross-national comparison study on the accuracy of self-efficacy beliefs of middle-school mathematics students. *Journal of Experimental Education, 75,* 221–244.

Cleary, T., & Zimmerman, B. J. (2001). Self- practice by experts, non-experts, and novices. *Journal of Applied Sport Psychology, 13,* 61–82.

Deci, E., & Ryan, R. M. (1985). *Intrinsic motivation and self-determination in human behavior.* New York, NY: Plenum.

Dweck, C. S. (2006). *Mindset: The new psychology of success.* New York, NY: Random House.

Dweck, C. S., & Leggett, E. L. (1988), A social-cognitive approach to motivation and personality. *Psychological Review, 95,* 256–273.

Elliot, A. J. (1999). Approach and avoidance motivation and achievement goals. *Educational Psychologist, 34,* 169–189.

English, H. B., & English, A. C. (1958). *A comprehensive dictionary of psychological and psychoanalytical terms.* New York, NY: McKay.

Ghatala, E. S., Levin, J. R., & Pressley, M. (1989). Improving childrens' regulation of their reading PREP time. *Contemporary Educational Psychology, 14,* 49–66.

Graham, S., Harris, K. R., & Troia, G. A. (1998). Writing and self-regulation: Cases from the self-regulated strategy development model. In D. H. Schunk & B. J. Zimmerman (Eds.), *Self-regulated learning: From teaching to self-reflective practice* (pp. 20–41). New York, NY: Guilford.

Graham, S., & Williams, C. (2009). An attributional approach to motivation in school. In K. R. Wentzel & A. Wigfield (Eds.), *Handbook of motivation at school* (pp. 11–33). New York, NY: Routledge.

Hacker, D., & Bol, L. (2004). Metacognitive theory: Considering the social-cognitive influences. In D. M. McInerney & S. Van Etten (Eds.), *Research on sociocultural influences on motivation and learning: Big theories revisited* (Vol. 4, pp. 275–297). Greenwich, CT: Information Age.

Harris, K. R., & Graham, S. (1992). Self-regulated strategy development: A part of the writing process. In M. Pressley, K. R. Harris, & J. Guthrie (Eds.), *Promoting academic competence and literacy in school* (pp. 277–309). San Diego, CA: Academic.

Harris, K. R., & Graham, S. (1996). *Making the writing process work: Strategies for composition and self-regulation.* Cambridge, MA: Brookline.

Harris, K. R., Graham, S., Friedlander, B., & Laud, L. (2013). Bring powerful writing strategies into your classroom! Why and how. *Reading Teacher, 66,* 538–542.

Hattie, J., & Timperley, H. (2007). The power of feedback. *Review of Educational Research, 77,* 81–112.

Hidi, S., & Renninger, K. A. (2006). The four-phase model of interest development. *Educational Psychologist, 41,* 111–127.

Kaplan, A., Lichtinger, E., & Gorodetsky, M. (2009). Achievement goal orientations and self-regulation in writing: An integrative perspective. *Journal of Educational Psychology, 101,* 51–69.
Kitsantas, A., Reiser, B., & Doster, J. (2004). Goal setting, cues, and evaluation during acquisition of procedural skills: Empowering students' learning during independent practice. *Journal of Experimental Education, 72,* 269–287.
Klassen, R. (2002). A question of calibration: A review of the self-efficacy beliefs of students with learning disabilities. *Learning Disability Quarterly, 25,* 88–103.
Kuiper, N. A., MacDonald, M. R., & Derry, P. A. (1984). Parameters of a depressive self-schema. In J. Suls & A. Greenwald (Eds.), *Psychological perspectives on the self* (Vol. 2, pp. 191–217). Hillsdale, NJ: Erlbaum.
Licht, B. G., & Kistner, J. A. (1986). Motivational problems of learning-disabled children: Individual differences and their implications for treatment. In J. K. Torgesen & B. W. L. Wong (Eds.), *Psychological and educational perspectives on learning disabilities* (pp. 225–255). Orlando, FL: Academic.
Lienemann, T. O., Graham, S., Leader-Janssen, B., & Reid, R. (2006). Improving the writing performance of struggling writers in second grade. *Journal of Special Education, 40,* 66–78.
Locke, E. A., & Latham, G. P. (1990). *A theory of goal setting and task performance.* Upper Saddle River, NJ: Prentice Hall.
Locke, E. A., & Latham, G. P. (2002). Building a practically useful theory of goal setting and task motivation: A 35-year odyssey. *American Psychologist, 57,* 705–717.
Locke, E. A., Smith K., Erez, M., Chah, D., & Schaffer, A. (1994). The effects of intra-individual goal conflict on persistence. *Journal of Management, 20,* 67–91.
Pajares, F., & Miller, M. D. (1994). Role of self-efficacy and self-concept beliefs in mathematical problem solving: A path analysis. *Journal of Educational Psychology, 86,* 193–203.
Pintrich, P. R. (2000). The role of goal orientation in self-regulated learning. In M. Boekaerts, P. R. Pintrich, & M. Zeidner (Eds.), *Handbook of self-regulation* (pp. 451–502). San Diego, CA: Academic.
Pressley, G. M. (1976). Mental imagery helps eight-year-olds remember what they read. *Journal of Educational Psychology, 68,* 355–359.
Pressley, M., & McCormick, C. B. (1995). *Advanced educational psychology: For educators, researchers, and policymakers.* New York, NY: Harper/Collins.
Reid, R., & Lienemann, T. O. (2006). Self-regulated strategy development for written expression with students with attention deficit/hyperactivity disorder. *Exceptional Children, 73,* 53–68.
Ryan, R. M. (Ed.) (2012). *The Oxford handbook of human motivation.* Oxford, England: Oxford University Press.
Ryan, R. M., & Deci, E. L. (2009). Promoting self-determined school engagement: Motivation, learning, and well-being. In K. R. Wentzel & A. Wigfield (Eds.), *Handbook of motivation at school* (pp. 171–195). New York, NY: Routledge.
Schmitz, B., & Wiese, B. S. (2006). New perspectives for the evaluation of training sessions in self-regulated learning: Time-series analyses of diary data. *Contemporary Educational Psychology 31,* 64–96.
Schunk, D. H. (1982). Verbal self-regulation as a facilitator of children's achievement and self-efficacy. *Human Learning, 1,* 265–277.

Schunk, D. H. (1983a). Developing children's self-efficacy and skills: The role of social comparison information and goal setting. *Contemporary Educational Psychology, 8,* 76–86.

Schunk, D. H. (1983b). Goal difficulty and attainment information: Effects on children's achievement behaviors. *Human Learning, 2,* 107–117.

Schunk, D. H. (1985). Participation in goal setting: Effects on self-efficacy and skills of learning disabled children. *Journal of Special Education, 19,* 307–317.

Schunk, D. H. (1989). Social cognitive theory and self-regulated learning. In B. J. Zimmerman & D. H. Schunk (Eds.), *Self-regulated learning and academic achievement: Theory, research, and practice* (pp. 83–110). New York, NY: Springer-Verlag.

Schunk, D. H. (1996). Goal and self-evaluative influences during children's cognitive skill learning. *American Educational Research Journal, 33,* 359–382.

Schunk, D. H. (2008). Attributions as motivators of self-regulated learning. In D. H. Schunk & B. J. Zimmerman (Eds.), *Motivation and self-regulated learning: Theory, research and applications* (pp. 245–266). New York, NY: Taylor & Francis.

Schunk, D. H. (2012). Social cognitive theory. In K. R. Harris, S. Graham, & T. Urdan (Eds.), *APA educational psychology handbook. Vol. 1: Theories, constructs, and critical Issues* (pp. 101–123). Washington, DC: American Psychological Association.

Schunk, D. H., & Ertmer, P. A. (1999). Self-regulatory processes during computer skill acquisition: Goal and self-evaluative influences. *Journal of Educational Psychology, 91,* 251–260.

Schunk, D. H., & Pajares, F. (2004). Self-efficacy in education revisited: Empirical and applied evidence. In D. M. McInerney & S. Van Etten (Eds.), *Research on sociocultural influences on motivation and learning: Big theories revisited* (Vol. 4, pp. 115–138). Greenwich, CT: Information Age.

Schunk, D. H., & Rice, J. M. (1991). Learning goals and progress feedback during reading comprehension instruction. *Journal of Reading Behavior, 23,* 351–364.

Schunk, D. H., & Swartz, C. W. (1993a). Goals and progress feedback: Effects on self-efficacy and writing achievement. *Contemporary Educational Psychology, 18*(3), 337–354.

Schunk, D. H., & Swartz, C. W. (1993b).Writing strategy instruction with gifted students: Effects of goals and feedback on self-efficacy and skills. *Roeper Review, 15,* 225–230.

Schunk, D. H., & Zimmerman, B. J. (Eds.). (2008). *Motivation and self-regulated learning: Theory, research, and applications.* Mahwah, NJ: Erlbaum.

Sitzmann, T., & Ely, K. (2011). A meta-analysis of self-regulated learning in work-related training and educational attainment: What we know and where we need to go. *Psychological Bulletin, 137,* 421–442.

Steinberg, L., Brown, B. B., & Dornbusch, S. M. (1996). *Beyond the classroom: Why school reform has failed and what parents need to do.* New York, NY: Simon & Schuster.

Stoeger, H., & Ziegler, A. (2011). Self-regulatory training through elementary-school students' homework completion. In B. J. Zimmerman & D. H. Schunk (Eds.), *Handbook of self-regulation of learning and performance* (pp. 87–101). New York, NY: Routledge.

Stone, N. J. (2000). Exploring the relationship between calibration and self-regulated learning. *Educational Psychology Review, 12,* 437–475.

Syed, M. (2010). *Bounce.* New York, NY: HarperCollins.

Weiner, B. (1992). *Human motivation: Metaphors, theories, and research.* Newbury Park, CA: Sage.

Wigfield, A., & Eccles, J. S. (2002). The development of competence beliefs and values from childhood through adolescence. In A. Wigfield & J. S. Eccles (Eds.), *Development of achievement motivation* (pp. 92–120). San Diego, CA: Academic.

Winne, P. H. (1997). Experimenting to bootstrap self-regulated learning. *Journal of Educational Psychology, 89,* 397–410.

Winne, P. H., & Hadwin, A. F. (1998). Studying as self-regulated learning. In D. J. Hacker, J. Dunlosky, & A. C. Graesser (Eds.), *Metacognition in educational theory and practice* (pp. 277–304). Hillsdale, NJ: Erlbaum.

Wolters, C. A. (2003). Regulation of motivation: Evaluating an underemphasized aspect of self-regulated learning. *Educational Psychologist, 38,* 189–205.

Zimmerman, B. J. (1990). Self-regulating academic learning and achievement: The emergence of a social cognitive perspective. *Educational Psychology Review, 82,* 297–306.

Zimmerman, B. J. (2000). Attaining self-regulation: A social cognitive perspective. In M. Boekaerts, P. R. Pintrich, & M. Zeidner (Eds.), *Handbook of self-regulation* (pp. 13–39). San Diego, CA: Academic.

Zimmerman, B. J. (2008a). Goal setting: A key proactive source of academic self-regulation. In D. H. Schunk & B. J. Zimmerman (Eds.), *Motivation and self-regulated learning: Theory, research, and applications* (pp. 267–295). New York, NY: Taylor & Francis.

Zimmerman, B. J. (2008b). In search of self-regulated learning: A personal quest. In H. W. Marsh, R. G. Craven, & D. McInerney (Eds.), In *Self-processes, leaning, and enabling human potential: Dynamic new processes* (pp. 171–191). Charlotte NC: Information Age.

Zimmerman, B. J., & Kitsantas, A. (1996). Self-regulated learning of a motoric skill: The role of goal setting and self-monitoring. *Journal of Applied Sport Psychology, 8,* 69–84.

Zimmerman, B. J., & Kitsantas, A. (1997). Developmental phases in self-regulation: Shifting from process to outcome goals. *Journal of Educational Psychology, 89,* 29–36.

Zimmerman, B. J., & Kitsantas, A. (1999). Acquiring writing revision skill: Shifting from process to outcome self-regulatory goals. *Journal of Educational Psychology, 91,* 1–10.

Zimmerman, B. J., & Martinez-Pons, M. (1986). Development of a structured interview for assessing students' use of self-regulated learning strategies. *American Educational Research Journal, 23,* 614–628.

Zimmerman, B. J., Moylan, A., Hudesman, J., White, N., & Flugman, B. (2011). Enhancing self-reflection and mathematics achievement of at-risk urban technical college students. *Psychological Test and Assessment Modeling, 53,* 108–127.

Zimmerman, B. J., & Schunk, D. H. (Eds.) (2011). *Handbook of self-regulation of learning and performance.* New York, NY: Routledge.

CHAPTER 5

DIMENSIONAL COMPARISON THEORY

An Extension of the Internal/External Frame of Reference Model

Herbert W. Marsh
Australian Catholic University
King Saud University (Saudi Arabia)
University of Oxford (UK)

Philip D. Parker
Australian Catholic University

Rhonda G. Craven
Australian Catholic University

INTRODUCTION

Self-concept is an important outcome variable that also facilitates the attainment of other desirable outcomes. Its formation is shaped in part by the frames of reference and/or standards of comparison used to evaluate

Self-Concept, Motivation, and Identity, pages 115–150

one's accomplishments. The internal/external frame of reference (I/E) model posits paradoxical relations between achievement and self-concept in mathematical and verbal domains: achievement in each domain has a positive effect on self-concept in the matching domain (e.g., mathematics achievement on mathematics self-concept) but a negative (contrast) effect on self-concept in the nonmatching domain (e.g., mathematics achievement on verbal self-concept). Extending the I/E model, Dimensional Comparison Theory (DCT) posits that self-evaluations are based on dimensional comparisons (e.g., how my accomplishments in one domain compare with my accomplishments in another domain) as well as the more traditional social and temporal comparisons. Extending the traditional tests of the I/E model, DCT predicts strong contrast effects only for contrasting domains that are at the opposite ends of the theoretical continuum of academic self-concept (far comparisons; e.g., the negative effect of math achievement on verbal self-concept), but much weaker negative contrast or even positive assimilation effects for complementary domains that are close to each other (near domains; e.g., positive effects of math achievement on physics self-concept; positive effects of native language on foreign language self-concept). Here we illustrate new predictions, theoretical insights, and methodology associated with the I/E model and its extension into DCT in multiple academic domains (e.g., native language, foreign language, history, biology, physics, and math), showing significant contrast effects for far comparisons and significantly smaller contrast or assimilation effects for near domains.

Overview of Self-Concept

Self-concept is fundamental to psychological well-being and an important psychological construct that facilitates the attainment of personal goals such as educational attainment. It has been established as one of the most important constructs in the social sciences, is one of the oldest constructs in psychology, and is also a major focus across many social science disciplines. The self-concept construct is central to the positive psychology revolution, which focuses on how healthy, normal, and exceptional individuals can get the most from life (e.g., Diener, 2000; Marsh & Craven, 2006; Seligman & Csikszentmihalyi, 2000). Following from Shavelson, Hubner, and Stanton (1976) self-concept refers to an individual's relatively stable and organized perception and evaluation of themselves within socially important domains that are formed through experience with and interpretations of one's environment. Self-concepts are influenced especially by evaluations by significant others, reinforcements, and attributions for one's own behavior. Self-concept is not an entity within the person but a hypothetical construct that is potentially useful in explaining and predicting how a person acts.

Particularly in education settings, a positive academic self-concept (ASC) is both a highly desirable goal and a means of facilitating subsequent academic accomplishments, academic achievement, subject choice and coursework selection, academic persistence, and long-term educational attainment (e.g., Chen, Yeh, Hwang, & Lin, 2013; Guay, Larose, & Boivin, 2004; Marsh, 1991, 2007; Marsh & Craven, 2006; Pinxten, De Fraine, Van Damme, & D'Haenens, 2010). For example, Marsh and Yeung (1997; see also Parker et al., 2012) found that ASCs predicted future coursework selection better than academic achievement. Moreover, Marsh and O'Mara (2008, 2010) found that ASCs predicted long-term educational attainment 5 years after high school graduation better than school grades, IQ, standardized tests, or socioeconomic status.

Self-concept research since the 1980s has seen a renaissance, characterized by growth in the quality and sophistication of theoretical models, quantitative methodology, measurement instruments, and research design. Particularly in educational psychology, much of this progress was due to a stimulating interplay between theory, research, measurement and practice. The impetus for this resurgence came from the classic review article by Shavelson et al. (1976), who posited self-concept as a multidimensional (i.e., people do not just maintain a global self-esteem but feel differently about themselves in different domains) and hierarchical (i.e., global self-esteem represents some global composite of domain-specific self-concepts) construct in which different facets of academic self-concept are substantially correlated and form a single higher-order academic self-concept factor. This multidimensional, hierarchical perspective is consistent with similar theoretical models of achievement (e.g., Vernon, 1950) and with the positive relations routinely observed between achievements in different school subjects (Marsh, 2007). However, subsequent research revealed that mathematics self-concept (MSC) and verbal self-concept (VSC) in particular, were nearly uncorrelated. This led Marsh and Shavelson (1985) to propose the Marsh/Shavelson revision of the original model, in which they posited two higher-order academic self-concept factors (mathematics/academic and verbal/academic), a continuum of core academic self-concept factors ranging from MSC at one end to VSC at the other end, and an ordering of academic self-concepts in other domains along this continuum (see Figure 5.1). Thus, the original Shavelson et al. (1976) model has been heuristic, but further research within this paradigm has led to its revision. Indeed, this is how the interplay between theory and research is supposed to work. However, subsequent research largely focused on individual components of self-concept, and there has been surprisingly little research on the underlying continuum posited by Marsh and Shavelson (1985). In this chapter, we review some research that explicitly addresses this continuum in relation to frame of reference effects based on internal, dimensional comparisons

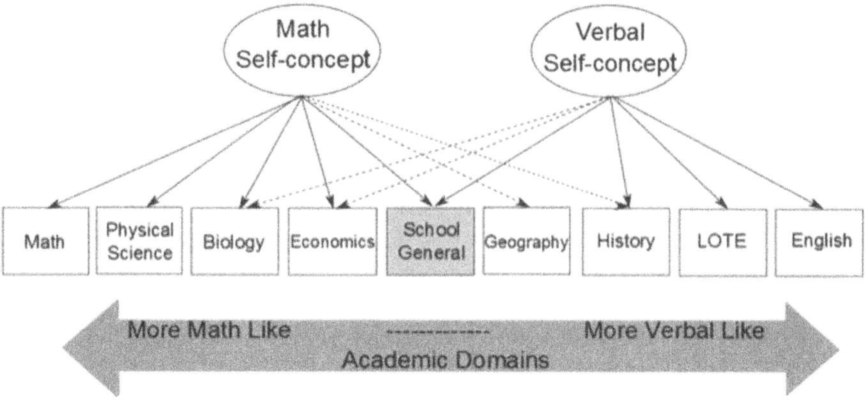

Figure 5.1 The Marsh/Shavelson revised academic self-concept model, including a wider variety of specific academic facets. Adapted with permission from Marsh (2007). LOTE = language other than English.

in which individuals compare their accomplishments in one domain with those in other domains.

Self-Concept and Frames of Reference

Since the idea was proposed as long ago as the 19th century by William James (1890/1963), psychologists have long understood that self-concepts are based in part on one's own perception of their objective achievements in relation to frames of reference. Indeed, self-concept theory emphasizes that perceptions of the self cannot be adequately understood if the role of frames of reference is ignored (Marsh, 2007). The same objective characteristics and accomplishments can lead to disparate self-concepts, depending on the frames of reference or standards of comparison that individuals use to evaluate themselves, and these self-beliefs have important implications for future academic choices, academic performance, and other academic behaviors. The two most frequently posited frames of reference are based on temporal and social comparisons (Albert, 1977; Festinger, 1954; Möller, 2005; Möller, Pohlmann, Köller, & Marsh, 2009; Möller, Retelsdorf, Köller & Marsh, 2011); self-perceptions are based in part on how current accomplishments compare with our past performances (temporal comparisons) and in part on how our accomplishments compare with those of others within our current context (social comparisons; e.g., classmates in our school or class). However, particularly in educational settings, a growing body of research based on the I/E model (Marsh, 1986) demonstrates that self-perceptions may also be the result of internal or dimensional comparisons in which accomplishments in one school subject can serve as a frame of reference for another school subject (e.g., Möller & Köller, 2001a; Möller & Marsh, 2013; Möller et al., 2009).

THE INTERNAL/EXTERNAL (I/E) FRAME OF REFERENCE MODEL

Dimensional comparison research has largely evolved from the I/E model, which initially was developed to explain why math and verbal self-concepts are almost uncorrelated, even though corresponding areas of academic achievement are substantially correlated (typically .5 to .8, depending on how achievement is measured; for further discussion on this point, see Marsh, 2007). People think of themselves as mostly math or mostly verbal persons, even though individuals who are good at one also tend to be good at the other (see Marsh, 1986). Why is there this stark contrast between academic self-perceptions and corresponding objective accomplishments?

Marsh (1986, 1990b; Marsh, Byrne, & Shavelson, 1988) developed the I/E model to explain the specificity of math and verbal self-concept. According to the I/E model, academic self-concept in a particular school subject is formed in relation to an external (social comparison) reference, in which students compare their self-perceived performances in a particular school subject with the perceived performances of other students in the same school subject. However, the model also posits an internal (ipsative-like) reference in which students compare their self-perceived performances in one particular school subject with self-perceived performances in other school subjects. Hence, students may have a favorable math self-concept if math is their best subject, even if they are not particularly good at math relative to other students. The external comparison process leads to a positive math-verbal correlation (because math and verbal achievements are substantially correlated; the internal comparison process leads to a negative math-verbal correlation (because of the ipsative comparison process, in which being particularly good in one subject is taken to imply that one is relatively less good at other subjects—a zero-sum process). The combination of the two counterbalancing processes results in a near-zero correlation, depending on the relative importance of each comparison process.

Stronger tests of the I/E model are possible when math and verbal achievements are regressed on MSC and VSC (see Figure 5.2). The external comparison process predicts, not surprisingly, that good math skills lead to higher MSCs and that good verbal skills lead to higher VSCs. More surprising is the internal comparison process, which predicts that good math skills should lead to *lower* VSCs (once the positive effects of good verbal skills are controlled): The better I am at mathematics, the poorer I perceive myself to

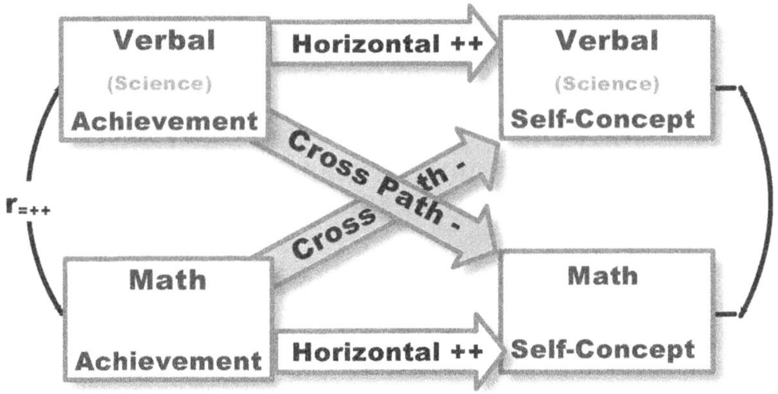

Figure 5.2 The "classic" internal/external frame of reference (I/E) model relating verbal and math achievement to verbal and math self-concept. According to predictions from the I/E model, the horizontal paths from achievement to self-concept in the matching domains (content area) are predicted to be substantial and positive (++), whereas the cross-paths from achievement in one domain area to self-concept in a nonmatching domain (shaded in grey above) are predicted to be negative (–). In the present investigation, we evaluate the generalizability of these predictions to the science domain, relating science and math achievement to science and math self-concepts. Adapted with permission from Marsh (2007).

be in verbal subjects (relative to my good math skills). Similarly, better verbal skills should lead to *lower* MSCs (once the positive effects of good math skills are controlled). In models used to test this prediction (Figure 5.3), the horizontal paths leading from math achievement to MSC and from verbal achievement to VSC (the grey horizontal lines in Figure 5.2) are predicted to be substantially positive (indicated by "++" in Figure 5.2). However, the cross-paths leading from math achievement to VSC and from verbal achievement to MSC (the dark lines in Figure 5.2) are predicted to be negative.

Generalizability of Empirical Support for the I/E Model

Marsh (1986), summarizing the results of 13 studies of the relations between math and verbal achievements and self-concepts in the corresponding domains, proposed the I/E model. In these studies, although there were consistently high correlations between math and verbal achievements (.42 to .94), there were weak or even negative correlations between MSCs and VSCs (–.10 to .19). In the I/E path diagram (Figure 5.2), the (horizontal) paths from math achievement to MSC and from verbal achievement to VSC are substantial and positive. However, the (cross) paths from math achievement to VSC and from verbal achievement to MSC are significant and negative.

Generalizability to Different Groups

Subsequent research (see reviews by Marsh, 2007; Möller et al., 2009) provides strong support for the generalizability of these findings. This pattern of results was subsequently replicated for responses to each of three different self-concept instruments (Marsh et al., 1988), for the nationally representative samples of U.S. high school students in the High School and Beyond Study and in the National Longitudinal Study, and for different indicators of achievement (e.g., test scores, school grades), as well as over time (e.g., Marsh, Kong, & Hau, 2001). In a large cross-cultural study, Marsh and Hau (2004; also see Marsh, Hau, Artelt, Baumert, & Peschar, 2006) demonstrated that support for the I/E model generalized over large, nationally representative samples of 15-year-olds from each of 26 countries. In a meta-analysis of 69 datasets Möller et al. (2009) reported that math and verbal achievements were highly correlated (.67), while self-concepts were nearly uncorrelated (.10). The horizontal paths from achievement to ASC in the matching domains were positive (.61 for math, .49 for verbal), but cross-paths were negative from math achievement to VSC (–.21) and verbal achievement to MSC (–.27). The strong support for the generalizability of the I/E predictions led these authors to conclude, "The results of our meta-analyses indicate that the relations described in the classical I/E model are not restricted to a particular achievement or self-concept measure or to specific age groups, gender groups, or countries" (p. 1157).

Generalizability to Different Research Designs

Although support for the I/E model is largely based on cross-sectional or longitudinal and quasi-experimental studies, Möller and colleagues have tested the I/E in three laboratory studies with random assignment to treatment and groups. Möller and Köller (2001a, 2001b) independently manipulated the external comparison process (based on performance feedback relative to other students) and the internal comparison process (based on feedback relative to performances by the same student on achievement in two subject-specific tasks). In each study, dimensional comparison information had the expected effects (e.g., positive math feedback enhanced MSC and weakened VSC). This pattern of results was replicated in their third study and in subsequent research (Pohlmann & Möller, 2009) that evaluated the dimensional comparison process in combination with social comparison feedback. These true experimental studies provide strong support for both the internal and external comparison processes posited in the I/E model and for causal interpretation of the two processes.

Generalizability to Everyday Life

Möller and Husemann (2006) evaluated processes underlying dimensional comparisons in everyday life. They adapted and extended an introspective methodology based on social psychology research to study everyday social comparisons. In two studies using a diary instrument, university (Study 1) and high school (Study 2) students recorded their spontaneous comparisons over a 2-week period. Comparison dimensions used by each participant were classified into 14 categories by the participant him or herself. Although "academic matters" was the most frequent category in both studies, the combined number of comparisons in the four social categories (friends, partner, family, acquaintances) was substantial, as was the physical appearance category, and each of the 14 categories was employed in at least 1% of the comparisons. In traditional I/E studies, the number of upward and downward paths (i.e., comparison between a stronger domain and a weaker domain, or between a weaker and a stronger domain) is necessarily equal. However, this need not be the case for spontaneous internal comparisons, a finding that is a major contribution of their research. Möller and Husemann found that a majority of the internal comparisons were upward comparisons (i.e., participants rated themselves worse in the main domain than the comparison domain), although downward comparisons were common as well. The results also make it clear that dimensional comparisons are made spontaneously in everyday life and that even within a student population where academic concerns are likely to be important, spontaneous dimensional comparisons are common in the social, physical, and emotional domains.

Generalizability to Long-Term Academic Outcomes

Importantly, the I/E framework has recently been extended to predict long-term educational choices. For example, Nagy et al. (2008) and Nagy, Trautwein, Baumert, Köller, and Garrett (2006) have shown that math achievement, task value, and self-concept have a positive effect on choosing math-related advanced courses but a negative effect on choosing verbal-related advanced courses. Parker et al. (2012; Parker, Marsh, Ciarrochi, Marshall, & Abduljabbar, 2014; also see Parker, Nagy, Trautwein, & Lüdtke, 2014) have shown that math and verbal achievement and self-concept positively predicted final school year matriculation examination results, university entry, and subsequent choice of university major. In particular, math achievement and self-concept positively predicted entry into university majors in math and the physical sciences, but negatively predicted entry into the humanities. Such research suggests that dimensional comparison processes associated with the I/E model mean that young people use a profile of their perceived strengths and weaknesses in order to make educational decisions.

Generalizability to Different Constructs

The I/E model was originally developed to explain relations between achievement and ASC in the math and verbal domains. Xu et al. (2013)

evaluated the extent to which negative cross-paths in particular, from achievement in one domain, negatively predict outcomes in a variety of Student Approaches to Learning (SAL) constructs. Across 13 different SAL constructs, both math and verbal cross-paths were significantly negative for four SAL factors, namely, self-concept, interest, performance approach, and competitive learning preferences. There was partial support (one of two cross-paths—typically math achievement, which was significantly negative, while the other cross-path was nonsignificant) for task-value importance, task-value usefulness, mastery goals, approach-avoidance goals, co-operative-learning preferences, memorization, learning-control strategies, and effort/persistence learning strategies. Only for elaboration learning strategies were the effects of both cross-paths nonsignificant. However, there were no instances in which achievement in one domain had a favorable effect on any of the SAL constructs in a different domain. These results thus indicate that dimensional comparisons are present across constructs other than self-concept. Further, there is little evidence for the presence of assimilation effects for any SAL areas.

Generalizability to Perceptions by Significant Others

There is extensive theoretical and empirical self-concept research linking individual self-concept responses to those of significant others (e.g., family members, teachers, friends); this stems in part from a symbolic interactionist perspective, which views self-perceptions as the product of interactions with others (Shrauger & Schoeneman, 1979; also see Marsh, Barnes, & Hocevar, 1985). Furthermore, longitudinal self-concept studies suggest that parents' perceptions are influential. For example, longitudinal research has demonstrated that parents' perceptions have a stronger effect on their children's self-perceptions than their child's actual academic grades (e.g., Eccles, Adler, & Kaczala, 1982; Schoon & Parsons, 2002). Hence, it is useful to evaluate support for I/E predictions based on responses by significant others.

Although this is not specifically focused on in the I/E model, Marsh and Byrne (1993) noted that responses for math and verbal self-concept scales were negatively correlated for responses both by students (–.26 and –.11, respectively) and by significant others (–.06 and –.04, respectively), thereby providing tentative support for an I/E model in the responses of significant others. In contrast, for young children in primary school, Marsh and Craven (1997) suggest that math and verbal self-concepts inferred by teachers and parents are not nearly as differentiated as self-concept responses by children themselves. However, because neither of these studies included achievement scores, it was not possible to test the I/E model.

Dai (2002) found support for I/E predictions based on self-concept responses by Chinese adolescents, but reported that parents apparently did not use the internal comparison process when assessing the academic abilities of their children. However, whereas the adolescents themselves rated their academic self-concepts, parents were asked to rate the academic abilities of their children, not their academic self-concepts. In this respect, the results do not really address the issue of whether the internal-comparison process would have been evident if parents had rated the academic self-concepts of their children rather than their academic abilities.

In order to address limitations in the I/E research literature, Van Zanden, Seaton et al., (2015; also see Van Zanden, Marsh, et al., 2015), evaluated ASC responses by 486 Australian high school students and inferred self-concept ratings by their parents. Van Zanden, Seaton et al. began by demonstrating support for the measurement invariance of the self-concept responses across the student and parent samples, and support for the convergent and discriminant validity of the math and verbal self-concept scales. SEMs provided support for I/E predictions based both on student and parent responses. Horizontal paths were significantly positive for responses for both students and parents, whereas cross-paths were significantly negative for both students and parents. In summary, the Van Zanden, Seaton et al. study is apparently the only one to have provided appropriate tests of the I/E model based on the responses of students and significant others, and the first to demonstrate support for I/E predictions based on responses by parents, as well as to underline the important role that parents play in the academic development of their children. Nevertheless, the results from these different studies indicate the need for further research that juxtaposes I/E predictions for responses by students with those based on responses by parents, teachers, and significant others more generally.

Extensions of I/E Studies: Integration With Other Academic Self-Concept Models

In addition to the I/E model, other theoretical models of relations between ASC and achievement have dominated recent ASC research: the reciprocal effects model (REM) and the Big-Fish-Little-Pond Effect (BFLPE), described below. Although both these models have much theoretical and empirical support, they are traditionally based on responses to a single domain of academic self-concept. However, in both cases, some work has been done toward integrating them with the I/E model.

Reciprocal Effects Model (REM)

Although the research reviewed here demonstrates that ASC and academic achievement are substantially correlated, a critical question is the causal ordering of these two constructs. Traditional approaches to this question (Calsyn & Kenny, 1977; also see Marsh, 1990a) took an "either/or" approach—either achievement causes ASC (a skill-development model) or ASC causes achievement (a self-enhancement model). However, Marsh (1990a) argued on a theoretical and statistical basis for a dynamic REM integrating the skill-development and self-enhancement models, in which both ASC and achievement are causes and effects of each other. In the prototypical REM (see Figure 5.3), both achievement and ASC are represented with multiple indicators, each measured on three or more occasions. Although the REM predicts that both sets of paths are statistically significant, the linkages from prior self-concept to subsequent achievement are particularly

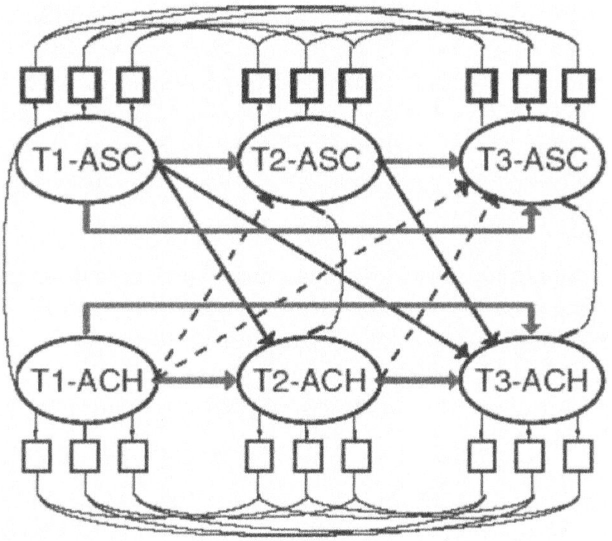

Figure 5.3 Prototype causal-ordering model for testing self-enhancement, skill-development, and reciprocal-effects models. In this full-forward, multiwave, multivariable model, multiple indicators of academic self-concept (ASC) and achievement (ACH) are collected in three successive waves (T1, T2, and T3). Each latent construct (represented by an oval shape) has paths leading to all latent constructs in subsequent waves. Within each wave, academic self-concept and achievement are assumed to be correlated; in the first wave, this correlation is a covariance between two latent constructs, and in subsequent waves, it is a covariance between residual factors. Curved lines at the top and bottom of the figure reflect correlated uniquenesses between responses to the same measured variable (represented by boxes) collected on different occasions. Paths connecting the same variable on multiple occasions reflect stability (the solid gray paths), but these coefficients typically differ from the corresponding test-retest correlations (which do not include the effects of other variables). Dashed lines reflect effects of prior achievement on subsequent self-concept, whereas solid black lines reflect the effects of prior self-concept on subsequent achievement. Adapted with permission from Marsh (2007).

important in relation to self-concept theory and practice. Following from the classic demonstration of the REM (Marsh, 1990a), there is substantial support for the generalizability of the findings over age, nationality, different self-concept instruments, and different ways of measuring achievement (Marsh & Craven, 2006; also see meta-analysis by Valentine & DuBois, 2005; Valentine, DuBois, & Cooper, 2004).

Of central importance to this chapter, REM analyses typically are based on multiple waves of (longitudinal) data for a single domain of ASC (e.g., MSC, VSC, or global ASC), whilst I/E analyses typically are based on multiple domains (e.g., MSC and VSC) collected on a single occasion. However, longitudinal extensions to the I/E model have supported the domain specificity, that is, the underlying basis of the I/E model (e.g., Marsh, et al., 2001; Möller et al., 2011; Parker, Marsh, Seaton, & Van Zanden, 2014). Extending the Marsh et al. (2011) study, Möller et al. (2011) proposed and found support for the Reciprocal Internal/External frame of reference model (RI/EM), an integration of the REM and I/E models, based on three waves of data for students in grades 5–8. Consistent with *a priori* predictions based on the

- I/E model, math and verbal achievement had positive effects on matching areas of ASC (horizontal paths) and negative effects on nonmatching areas of self-concept (cross-paths).
- REM, prior ASCs and achievement (school marks) each had positive effects on subsequent measures of ASC and achievement in matching domains.

The unique, new feature of this integrated RI/EM was the negative effect of prior ASC in matching domains on subsequent achievement in the nonmatching domain (i.e., prior math self-concept on subsequent verbal achievement and prior verbal self-concept on subsequent math self-concept). Consistent with the logic of the RI/EM, these cross-paths from prior ASC in one domain to achievement in a different domain were negative, but the effects were small and not always statistically significant in the Möller et al. (2011) study. However, this pattern in support of the RI/EM was again found in the Van Zanden et al., (2015; also see Van Zanden, Marsh, et al., 2015) study based on achievement test scores for high school students. In particular, even after controlling for prior math and verbal achievement, prior MSC had positive effects on subsequent math achievement but negative effects on subsequent verbal achievement, whereas prior VSC had positive effects on subsequent verbal achievement but negative effects on subsequent math achievement.

More recently, Parker, Marsh, Morin, Seaton, and Van Zanden (2015) expanded this integration of the I/E and REM models to test the implicit assumption of the I/E model that as self-concept in one domain goes up, self-concept in contrasting domains goes down. Capitalizing on recent research suggesting that self-concept composes both trait and state residual (fluctuations from trait) components (e.g., Morin, Maïano, Marsh, Janosz, & Nagengast, 2011), they applied new and evolving statistical models of latent growth to test this assumption, based on six waves of self-concept data for each of four different adolescent age cohorts. There was clear support for traditional I/E predictions based on cross-lagged models, relating math and verbal achievement to math and verbal self-concepts. Nevertheless, the traditional cross-lagged and traditional growth models provided little evidence that trajectories of math and verbal self-concepts are negatively related. However, Parker et al. (2014) then tested autoregressive cross-lagged models, which enabled them to separate the state and trait components of math and verbal self-concept trajectories. The results based on this more sophisticated statistical model suggested that a short-term (state residual component) increase above the overall (trait-component) trajectory in one self-concept domain resulted in a short-term (state residual) decline from trend in self-concept in another domain. Likewise, the relationships between state achievement and state residual self-concept were consistent with the IE model. These results may suggest that dimensional comparisons in response to state-like events (e.g., doing much better or worse than expected on a math test) acts as a mechanism to maintain stable academic self-concept. Thus, for example, an event that leads to a student doubting their ability in math may result in a rise in their English self-concept, thus helping to promote a stable growth trajectory in overall academic self-concept. In this way, the multidimensionality of academic self-concept and dimensional comparisons could help to sustain resilience mechanisms that lead to maintaining a stable academic self-perception overall. This stable academic self-perception overall may in turn produce positive outcomes such as long-term educational attainment (Guay et al., 2004).

The Big-Fish-Little-Pond Effect (BFLPE)

Marsh (1984; see also Marsh & Parker, 1984; Marsh et al., 2008) proposed the Big-Fish-Little-Pond Effect (BFLPE) to encapsulate frame of reference effects through integrating theoretical models and empirical research from diverse disciplines (e.g., relative deprivation theory, social comparison theory, psychophysical judgment, social judgment). In the BFLPE model, students are hypothesized to compare their abilities with the abilities of their classmates and to use this social comparison impression as one basis for forming their own self-concept (Figure 5.4); individual ability is positively related to academic self-concept (the brighter I am the higher my ASC) but school-average ability has a negative effect on ASC (the brighter my classmates, the lower my ASC). Hence, ASC depends not

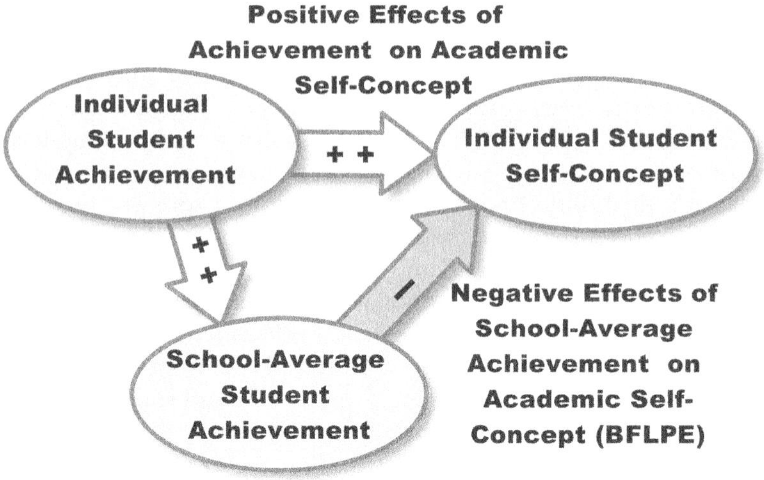

Figure 5.4 Path model predictions based on the Big-Fish-Little-Pond Effect. Adapted with permission from Marsh (2007).

only on a student's academic accomplishments but also on those of his/her classmates. Support for the BFLPE generalizes across student groups, subject domains, ASC instruments and cultures (see review by Marsh, 2007; also see Marsh et al., 2008). However, of critical importance, similarly to the REM, nearly all of this research is based on a single domain of ASC: typically MSC, VSC, or global ASC.

Indeed, integration of these two theoretical models suggests that the negative BFLPE could be accompanied by a compensatory positive effect (the BFLP-CE) when both math and verbal domains are considered simultaneously. The I/E model suggests that processes that change self-concept in one domain have a compensatory effect on self-concept in another domain, leading to the predictions that (a) school-average ability in math has a negative effect on MSC (the BFLPE) but a positive effect on VSC (the BFLP-CE); (b) school-average verbal ability in the verbal domain has a negative effect on VSC (BFLPE) but a positive effect on MSC. For example, if a student surrounds him/herself with math geniuses, their math self-concept will decline (BFLPE). Provided the student's math genius peers are not also wordsmiths, the decline in math self-concept may be associated with a compensatory increase in verbal self-concept (BFLP-CE). Marsh (1990b) provided initial support for this integration of the I/E and BFLPE models, showing that school-average math ability negatively predicted MSC but positively predicted VSC, and vice versa for English achievement. However, compensatory effects found by Marsh were small, and finding appropriate tests of the integrated BFLP-CE model has proved difficult, because school-average math and verbal achievements typically are so highly correlated (*rs* > .95) that school contexts in the two domains cannot be easily differentiated. However, he suggested that the school-average contextual effects might be better differentiated in themed or "magnet" schools, in which students are chosen primarily on the basis of accomplishments in one particular academic domain rather than on academic accomplishments more generally.

Integrating recent advances in latent variable and multilevel models, Parker, Marsh, Lüdtke, and Trautwein (2013) extended the Marsh (1990b) suggestions, capitalizing on an important feature of the German educational system; some academically selective schools select students on the basis of overall achievement, but others have a subject-specific theme and select students who excel in a particular area rather than overall. There were BFLPEs for both types of selective school, but the BFLP-CE, based on the I/E model, was only evident for the themed (magnet) schools; this is consistent with theoretical predictions.

Theoretical Extensions of the Internal/External Frame of Reference Model

Denissen, Zarrett, and Eccles (2007; Eccles, 2009; Guo, Marsh, Parker, Morin & Kaur, 2015; Parker et al., 2012) subsequently integrated the I/E model into traditional expectancy-value theory (EVT). EVT (Eccles et al., 1983; Eccles & Wigfield, 1995; Wigfield, 1994; Wigfield & Eccles, 2002; Wigfield, et al., 1997) posits that expectancy (often operationalized as self-concept) and components of value (e.g., intrinsic, extrinsic, cost) predict a wide range of future outcomes. Although self-perceived competence is related to several different value constructs in the EVT model, the relations with intrinsic value and interest were consistently the strongest (Wigfield & Eccles, 2002). Whereas, in both cross-sectional and longitudinal studies, expectancy beliefs are closely associated with performance, interest and other value beliefs tend to be better predictors of choice, effort, and persistence at achievement-related activities (e.g., Bøe, Henriksen, Lyons, & Schreiner, 2011; Eccles et al., 1983; Eccles, Adler & Meece, 1984; Guo et al., 2015; Marsh, Trautwein, Lüdtke, Köller, & Baumert, 2005; Meece, Wigfield & Eccles, 1990; Nagengast et al., 2011; Wigfield et al., 1997).

Value, and particularly expectancy, constructs are highly domain specific, as emphasized in I/E studies (e.g., Denissen et al., 2007). Consistent with this evidence, EVT studies are often based on constructs representing a specific single domain (e.g., mathematics). Further reinforcing the link between EVT and the I/E model, Eccles (2009) emphasized "that both external and internal comparison processes are key—people assess their own skills by comparing their performances with those of other people and with their own performances across domains" (p. 82) and demonstrated how this internal dimensional comparison process has a critical influence on academic choice behavior (e.g., choice of university major; see Parker et al., 2012; Parker, Marsh, Ciarrochi, et al., 2014).

Pekrun and colleagues (Goetz, Frenzel, Pekrun & Hall, 2006; Pekrun, 2006) extended their control-value theory of achievement emotions to incorporate the I/E model. This was done to explain the domain specificity of students' achievement emotions based on their hypothesis that "the mechanisms addressed by Marsh's (1986) I/E model could operate for students' emotions as well" (Goetz et al., 2006, p. 7). They found that emotions were substantially more domain specific than achievement in different math and verbal subjects, and that enjoyment was the most domain specific emotion. Goetz, Frenzel, Hall, and Pekrun (2008) subsequently found support for the I/E model in relation both to self-concept and to enjoyment but showed that achievement/enjoyment relations were mediated by self-concept. Goetz, Cronjaeger, Frenzel, Lüdtke, and Hall (2010) subsequently found that self-concept and emotional associations were stronger within quantitative domains (math and physics) and within verbal domains (English and German) than between quantitative and verbal domains, and that the relations grew stronger with age. Because enjoyment is a key component of intrinsic motivation, their research complements EVT studies showing the domain specificity of intrinsic motivation (see also Guay et al., 2010).

Developmental and Cross-Cultural Support for the I/E Model Based on TIMSS Data

Marsh, Abduljabbar et al. (2014) evaluated support for the generalizability of I/E predictions in relation to math and science domains based on nationally representative matched samples of 4th- and 8th-grade students from 13 diverse countries (117,321 students from 6,499 classes). The study has important developmental and cross-cultural implications, as it was the first to test the I/E model with the Year-4 sample from TIMSS and the first to compare results from nationally representative samples of Year-4 and Year-8 students from each of 13 diverse Asian, Western, and Middle-Eastern Islamic countries.

Developmentally, previous research provides clear evidence that young children's ASCs become more differentiated with age and that relations between self-concept and achievement—the horizontal paths in the I/E model (see Figure 5.1) grow stronger over the preadolescent to early-adolescent developmental stages (e.g., Marsh, 1989, 1990a, 1990b). There is, however, relatively little developmental work on how the strength of the internal or dimensional comparison process—the cross-paths in the I/E model (see

Figure 5.1)—varies with age. Whilst a few studies of primary school-aged students were included in Möller et al.'s (2009) meta-analysis, this developmental aspect of their study was not systematically evaluated, due in part to the paucity of available data from young children. Employing new statistical models, Marsh, Abduljabbar et al. (2014) have shown support for *a priori* developmental hypotheses that the I/E predictions generalize over age cohorts. However, the paths were stronger—more positive horizontal paths and more negative cross-paths—for the older age cohort.

Cross-culturally, there is good support for the generalizability of I/E predictions for older students—nationally representative samples of 15-year-olds from 26 countries—based on PISA (Marsh & Hau, 2004). Indeed, remarkably, there were no significant differences in support for the I/E predictions, according to country of residence, in the Möller et al. (2009) meta-analysis, which included results from the Marsh and Hau (2004) PISA study. However, most of the studies in the Möller et al. (2009) meta-analysis, aside from a few conducted in Asian countries, were conducted in Western countries (7 Asian, 12 Australian, 7 U.S., and 39 European samples were included in the analysis of country as a moderator). Although the meta-analysis included responses by students from "other nationalities," Möller et al. argued that the number of studies doing so, including two studies based on Middle Eastern Islamic samples (Abu-Hilal, 2002; Abu-Hilal & Bahri, 2000), was too small to warrant inclusion in analyses of country as a moderator. However, Abu-Hilal and Bahri (2000) suggest that schools in Middle Eastern Islamic countries place less emphasis on evaluative and diagnostic feedback such that ASCs are less differentiated and less correlated with achievement—more like the results found with younger students in Western research. Consistent with *a priori* predictions based on research by Abu-Hilal and colleagues, Marsh, Abduljabbar et al. (2014) have shown support for the I/E model was systematically weaker in the Middle Eastern Islamic countries, particularly for the younger-age cohort. Indeed, consistent with speculations by Abu-Hilal and Bahri (2000), support for the I/E model for 8th-grade Middle Eastern Islamic students was similar to that found for the 4th-grade cohort in the Western countries.

In some ways, the extremely good support for the I/E model, based on TIMSS measures of math and science, is surprising. Most support for the I/E model is based on math and verbal self-concepts, which represent the endpoints of the continuum of academic self-concepts posited in the Marsh/Shavelson model. However, for two domains that are closer together along this continuum—such as the math and science domains in the TIMSS study—stronger skills in one domain need not be expected to have this negative effect on self-concept. Although Marsh, Abduljabbar et al. (2014) did not find support for this suggestion in their study, we note that their focus was on a generic science scale that may obscure potentially distinct subdomains of science self-concept. Thus, for example, in their German sample, where physics is taught as a separate subject, Möller, Streblow, Pohlmann, and Köller (2006) found small positive effects of math achievement on physics self-concept and of physics achievement on math self-concept. We also note that contrasting contextual effects could be reinforced by the simultaneous presentation of items from only two subject domains, leading students to contrast themselves in relation to the two subjects. An interesting direction for further research is to explore individual student differences and the domains or conditions in which cross-paths are positive rather than negative (i.e., where there is assimilation rather than contrast). In particular, it is important to expand this research to include a greater diversity of school subjects, to provide stronger tests of the new theoretical predictions based on Dimensional Comparison Theory.

DIMENSIONAL COMPARISON THEORY: EXTENDING THE I/E MODEL TO INCORPORATE ASSIMILATION AND CONTRAST BASED ON NEAR AND FAR COMPARISONS

Although I/E predictions have mostly been tested in relation to the math and verbal domains, the theoretical underpinning of the I/E model and its extension into DCT is based on a continuum of academic domains that vary between the mathematical and verbal end points (Figure 5.1). This hypothesized continuum is based on a higher-order factor analysis (Marsh et al., 1988) in which the similarity between different academic domains is operationalized as correlations among the different domains. In I/E studies, there is consistent support for negative cross-paths (Figure 5.1 and Figure 5.5A) based on comparisons of maximally dissimilar dimensions at these end points. In the broader social comparison literature, these negative effects are referred to as contrast effects (see Marsh, Möller et al., 2015; Möller, Helm, Müller-Kalthoff, Nagy, & Marsh, 2015; Möller & Marsh, 2013). DCT posits that the negative (contrast) effects will diminish and may even become positive (assimilation) effects when dimensional comparisons are based on domains that are close together on the academic continuum. Thus, for example, Möller et al. (2006) found that math achievement had a positive (assimilation) effect on physics self-concept. Similarly, recent research (Parker et al., 2013) based on PISA data indicates that paths leading to MSC (the only self-concept domain assessed) were positive for math achievement and negative for verbal achievement, but that the path from science achievement (a domain close to math on the underlying academic continuum) to MSC was also positive—an assimilation effect. Other researchers have focused on dimensional comparison effects for multiple verbal domains (e.g., native language and nonnative language), typically

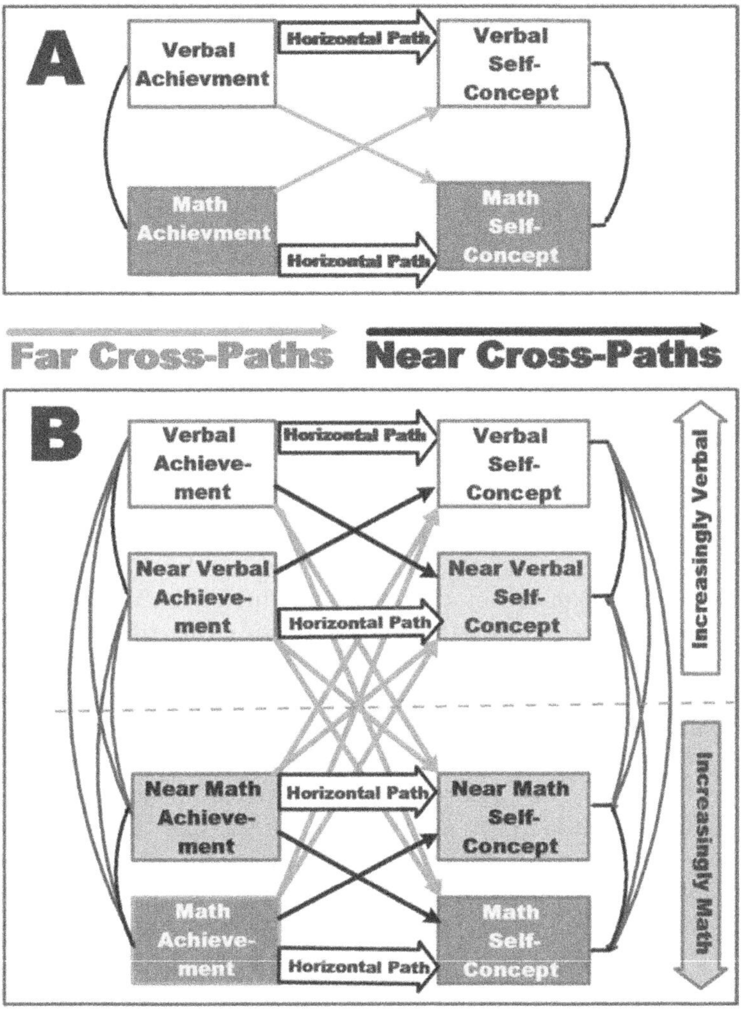

Figure 5.5 (A) The "classic" internal/external frame of reference (I/E) model relating verbal and math achievement to verbal and math self-concept. According to predictions from the I/E model, the horizontal paths from achievement to self-concept in the matching domains (content area) are predicted to be substantial and positive, whereas the cross-paths from achievement in one domain area to self-concept in a nonmatching domain are predicted to be negative (contrast). (B) Extending the I/E model to include the verbal domain, one or more verbally related domains, the math domain, and one or more math-related domains. Far cross-paths (any of the math domains to any of the verbal domains) are again predicted to be negative. However, the near cross-paths (relating the different verbal domain to each other, or the different math domains to each other) are predicted to be significantly less negative, nonsignificant, or even positive (assimilation).

in combination with the math domain. Although these studies (e.g., Xu et al., 2013) typically have found contrast effects (negative cross-paths) from both verbal domains to MSC, the results relating the two verbal domains have not been entirely consistent (Marsh et al., 2001; Marsh & Yeung, 2001; Nagy et al., 2006; Yeung & Lau, 1998), suggesting that neither assimilation nor contrast effects were particularly strong.

Near Versus Far Comparisons

The classic I/E model (Figure 5.5A) is based only on the math and verbal domains, so that there are only "horizontal" paths between matching domains and "cross" paths between nonmatching domains. Although several I/E studies have considered additional domains (e.g., Bong, 1998; Marsh et al., 2013; Marsh & Yeung, 2001; Möller et al., 2006), none of these was based on the new theoretical DCT framework, which incorporates a range of domains other than the math and verbal domains emphasized in the classic I/E model (Figure 5.5B). This ordering of school subjects along an *a priori* verbal-to-math continuum is based on the theoretical and empirical research that led to the Marsh/Shavelson revision (Marsh, 1990b; Marsh et al., 1988; Marsh & Shavelson, 1985) of the original Shavelson et al. (1976) multidimensional, hierarchical model of self-concept (see Marsh, 2007), thereby integrating DCT with established self-concept theory and empirical results. Hence, a critically important contribution of DCT is the expansion of the scope of the theoretical perspective to include a wider variety of domains, so that the cross-paths involve "near" and "far" comparisons, based on how similar or dissimilar different school subjects are to each other. However, several recent studies provide a much stronger test of the appropriateness of this continuum to DCT: stronger in terms of the DCT theoretical basis, the range of different school subjects considered, and the statistical methods used.

Assimilation Versus Contrast Effects

Social comparison studies in the ASC literature (see review by Marsh, 2007) typically report negative (contrast) contextual effects; the negative effects of school- or class-average ability on ASC. In the broader social psychology literature, which covers a diversity of domains (mostly not academic in nature) there is also a predominance of contrast effects (e.g., Diener & Fujita, 1997). Even though some theoretical models in the social psychology literature suggest assimilation effects (e.g., Brickman & Bulman, 1977; Collins, 1996; Tesser, 1988; sometimes referred to as positive contextual effects, reflected glory effects, or contagion effects), replicable support for assimilation effects in contextual studies continues to be elusive (Diener & Fujita, 1997; Marsh et al. 2008, 2010).

A critical feature of the expansion of the I/E model into DCT is that it highlights this distinction between near and far comparisons, to test the *a priori* prediction that contrast effects based on "near" comparisons will be substantially less negative and may even be positive rather than negative (i.e., assimilation effects). Hence, similar subjects (e.g., native and foreign languages, or math and physics) may be seen as complementary rather than contrasting such that achievement in one domain contributes positively to self-concept in a complementary, near domain. This is also important in building bridges between research based on the classic I/E model, studied primarily in educational settings and the more diverse social comparison literature.

Studies based on a wide variety of school subjects are needed to provide strong tests of the newly formulated DCT and its extension of the classic I/E model. More specifically, they expand on previous research to test more explicitly the theoretical prediction that contrast effects (the negative cross-paths in Figure 5.5B) are maximized for "far" domains: those that are distant from each other on the academic continuum (Figure 5.1). However, for "near" comparisons, based on academic domains that are close to each other on the academic self-concept continuuum (e.g., native language and foreign language; see Figure 5.1), the cross-paths will be substantially less negative (weaker contrast) or even positive (assimilation). Based on this theoretical extension of the traditional I/E model, it is hypothesized that

- Matching paths from achievement to self-concept in the same domain (e.g., math achievement to math self-concept) will be substantial and positive;
- For models with only math and verbal self-concepts, the I/E predictions will be replicated—substantially positive paths for matching domains, negative (contrast) cross-paths for nonmatching domains (i.e., math achievement ⇒ verbal self-concept, verbal achievement ⇒ math self-concept);
- In the extended DCT model, which includes multiple school subjects, cross-paths relating "far" domains (e.g., math with native and nonnative languages; language with math and physics) will be significantly negative (contrast effect);
- In the extended DCT model, cross-paths relating "near" domains (e.g., native and nonnative languages; math and physics) will be significantly less negative than paths based on far comparisons.

It was left as a research question whether near paths would remain significantly negative (contrast, but less so than for far paths), nonsignificant, or even positive (assimilation effects).

STUDIES OF THE EXPANDED SET OF HYPOTHESES: EXTENSION OF THE I/E MODEL INTO DCT

A number of studies have been undertaken that were designed specifically to test this expanded set of hypotheses, based on the extension of the I/E model into DCT.

Study 1: Contrasting Near and Far Comparisons in Relation to Class Marks and Standardized Test Scores

Central to DCT is the expansion of the classic I/E model (Figure 5.5A) to include more than just math and science (Figure 5.5B) and to test key the DCT predictions that negative cross-paths (contrast) associated with maximally dissimilar (far) domains will diminish and may even become positive (assimilation) for maximally similar (near) domains. In a large, comprehensive study (15,356 Dutch 9th-grade students from 651 classes in 95 schools) Marsh, Kuyper et al. (2014) empirically tested DCT propositions formulated by Möller and Marsh (2013) as an extension of I/E theory, exploring methodological, theoretical, and substantive insights. In a series of increasingly complex SEMs, three latent academic self-concepts (Dutch, English, and math self-concept) were regressed on a set of three test scores, a set of three class marks, and the combined set of test scores and class marks in these domains. Although this was not specifically evaluated in the Möller et al. (2009) meta-analysis, their results apparently do not support our prediction that support for DCT predictions should be stronger for class marks (school grades from the last report card) than for standardized test scores. However, their meta-analysis was based largely on studies either of test scores or of class marks, which are not particularly strong in terms of evaluating differences between test scores and class marks.

In the traditional I/E model, the focus is on verbal (native language) and math constructs. In each of the models tested by Marsh, Kuyper et al. (2014), there was good support for predictions from the traditional I/E (positive horizontal paths, negative cross-paths). However, in support of predictions regarding test scores and class marks, the horizontal paths were substantially stronger for class marks (Mn = .759, SE = .008) than for test scores (Mn = .408, SE = .011). When both class marks and test scores were included in the same model, the horizontal paths based on class marks were nearly as strong (Mns = .715 vs. .759), whilst those based on test scores were substantially weaker (Mns = .177 vs. .408). Testing the extended DCT, Marsh, Kuyper et al. showed that the more dissimilar the academic domains, the more negative the cross-paths (far comparisons), whereas cross-paths relating more similar subjects (near comparisons) were much less negative and sometimes positive. In supplemental models they controlled additional background/demographic variables (academic track, gender, age, SES, and ethnicity), but the results were largely unchanged, and support for DCT predictions was marginally stronger. This study set the stage for further tests of DCT, introducing new statistical models to make comparisons of matching, near, and far paths, that will be the basis of subsequent research.

Study 2: DCT Extension to Include Five Domains

The Marsh, Kuyper et al. (2014, in review) research was important, but potentially limited in that it was based only on three domains. Marsh, Lüdtke et al. (2015) addressed this issue in a large study (1,140 German 7th- and 10th-grade students from 51 classes in six high schools) based on parallel data in five academic domains: German (native language), English (first foreign language), second foreign language, biology, and math. Achievement was based on students' most recent report card in each of the five school subjects. In the extended DCT model, they included 25 (5 × 5) paths leading from each of the five ACH domains to each of the five latent ASC factors. Each of these 25 path coefficients was classified *a priori* as representing a matching, near or far comparison, based on the theoretical ordering of ASC factors (Figure 5.1). Path coefficients involving any pair of verbally based constructs (German, English, second foreign language) or between the two math/science-like (biology and math) constructs were considered to be "near" comparisons, whilst comparisons between achievement from one group to self-concept in the other group were considered as "far" comparisons (see Figure 5.5B). In extending the classic I/E model, the critical new feature is the juxtaposition between near and far comparisons.

Marsh, Lüdtke et al. (2015) began by testing the classic I/E model based only on paths for the verbal (German: the native language for these students) and math domains. There was strong support for the replicability of the I/E model in that matching coefficients were consistently substantial and positive (Mean of coefficients = .656) and coefficients representing the far comparisons were consistently negative (Mean of coefficients = –.162). Extending this model, they asked if the size, or direction, of these contrast effects was consistent for "near" comparisons between more closely related domains that could be seen as complementary. The mean of the 8 near coefficients was not significantly different from zero (Mn = –.014, SE = .017), whilst the mean of the 12 "far" coefficients was significantly negative (Mn = –.080, SE = .010); the difference between the two groups of coefficients (near vs. far) was statistically significant (Mn = .066, SE = .017). In summary, consistent with *a priori* predictions for the extended DCT model, the contrast effects that are such a salient feature of the classic I/E model are largely limited to far comparisons in the extended DCT model. We note, however, that there were no instances of statistically significant assimilation effects (i.e., positive effects in near comparisons; the effect of achievement on a complementary self-concept domain).

Study 3: DCT Extension to Include Six Domains

In the second study (511 German 8th- and 9th-grade students from 51 classes), presented by Marsh, Lüdtke et al. (2015), the range of academic domains was extended to include six school subjects that better represented the theoretical continuum underpinning DCT (Figure 5.1). Test materials consisted of a standardized test of basic cognitive abilities (administered at the beginning of the session) and a questionnaire adapted from previous research. Strictly parallel wording was used for all domain-specific items. A total of six self-report items were used to assess self-concept and homework self-efficacy in each of the six domains (native language, foreign language, history, biology, physics, and math). Based on the *a priori* design and preliminary analyses, two of the items measured self-concept in each domain: three items measured homework self-efficacy, and one additional item cross-loaded on both self-concept and homework self-efficacy scales for each of the six domains. Again Marsh, Lüdtke et al. (2015) tested a series of CFA models, including method factors, to account for the parallel wording on items and showed the factor loadings to be invariant across the six domains. Achievement measures in each of the six domains were based on grades awarded on the midterm report card. The factor structure underlying the self-concept and homework self-efficacy responses was well-defined, and was consistent with *a priori* expectations. Correlations between self-concept, self-efficacy, and achievement scores provided strong support for the convergent and discriminant validity of the responses to all three sets of constructs. However, in relation to the underlying verbal-math continuum (Figure 5.1), these correlations suggest that biology might not be more math based than it is verbal, and that history might not be more verbal than it is math based.

Again, the research began by briefly testing the replicability of the classic I/E model (Figure 5.5A), based only on the verbal (German) and math domains. For ASC responses, there was strong support for I/E predictions, in that matching coefficients were consistently substantial and positive (Mn = .614, SE = .041) but far comparisons were consistently negative (Mn = –.143, SE = .036). For homework self-efficacy responses, there was also reasonable support for I/E predictions, in that matching coefficients were consistently positive (Mn = .319, SE = .040) but far comparisons were negative (Mn = –.088, SE = .037). In summary, there is good support for the I/E predictions in relation to ASC, but support for I/E predictions in relation to homework self-efficacy is weaker. The findings for self-efficacy are consistent with *a priori* predictions that self-efficacy is less dependent on social comparison processes (see also Parker et al., 2013). Extending this model, it can then be asked whether the size and direction of these contrast effects is consistent for "near" comparisons between more closely related domains that might be seen as complementary.

In the extended SEM model 36 (6 × 6) paths were included. These led from each of the six achievement domains to each of the six latent self-concept factors; another 36 paths led from achievement domains to the six homework self-efficacy factors. For each set of 36 paths, coefficients were classified *a priori* as matching, near and far comparisons, based on the theoretical ordering of ASC factors (Figure 5.1); path coefficients involving any pair of the verbal-based constructs (German, English, history) or between any pair of math/science (biology, physics, and math) constructs, were considered to be "near" comparisons, whilst comparisons between achievement from one group to self-concept or self-efficacy in the other group were considered to be far (e.g., math achievement to German self-concept).

The critical finding is that the mean of the 12 near coefficients is significantly positive for both self-concept and self-efficacy responses (self-concept: Mn = .048, SE = .017; self-efficacy: Mn = .029, SE = .014). In contrast, the mean of the 18 "far" coefficients is significantly negative for both self-concept (Mn = –.055, SE = .010) and self-efficacy (Mn = –.035, SE = .016). For both self-concept and self-efficacy responses, the difference between the near and far coefficients was significant. Inspection of individual paths shows that statistically significant paths for nonmatching domains involve primarily the four domains that are most extreme on the underlying verbal-math continuum: the two verbal scales (German and English), math, and physics. In order to evaluate this possibility we computed summary statistics based on just these four scales. For both self-concept and homework self-efficacy responses, contrast effects based on far comparisons were more negative (–.116 vs. –.055 for self-concept; –.070 vs. –.035 for self-efficacy), whilst assimilation effects based on near comparisons were more positive (.086 vs. .048 for self-concept, .037 vs. .024 for self-efficacy).

Study 4: DCT Extension to Include Three Science Domains

Jansen, Schroeders, Lüdtke, and Marsh (2015) extended DCT research based on a large (N = 20,050) representative sample of 9th-grade German students based on ASC and achievement measures (school grades and test scores) in math, German, biology, chemistry, and physics. Jansen et al. noted that there is mixed evidence with regard to whether contrast or assimilation effects occur for near comparisons, and that there has been limited research based on the three traditional science domains (biology, chemistry, and physics). Preliminary tests of the classic I/E model provided support for I/E predictions based on both test scores and class marks, but the support was stronger for class marks. The addition of the three science subjects had little effect on the pattern of results or on the variance explained in the math and German self-concepts, but grades in German and math had substantial effects on self-concept in the science domains. German grades had significant negative (contrast) effects on all three science self-concepts, whereas math grades had small negative (contrast) effects on biology and small positive (assimilation) effects on chemistry and physics. Similar, but weaker, patterns were found with test scores. The results demonstrated that both contrast and assimilation effects can result from dimensional comparisons. This supports the DCT proposal that domain-specific self-concepts are arranged along a continuum from verbal to quantitative domains and that their perceived proximity on this continuum predicts the occurrence of assimilation or contrast effects.

CONCLUSION

Self-evaluations are formed in relation to social and temporal comparisons—the better I perform relative to others and relative to my past accomplishments, the more positive my self-evaluations. As emphasized by the I/E model and its extension into DCT, internal dimensional comparisons among different domains provide an additional basis of comparison, with important implications for theory, achievement, individual choice behavior, policy, and practice. Indeed, a critical source of self-knowledge is knowing one's relative strengths and weaknesses in different domains. This provides a basis for academic choices, accurate self-evaluation, self-improvement, self-maintenance, and self-enhancement. The classic I/E model focused primarily on how math and verbal achievements are related to MSC and VSC (Figure 5.5A). As shown by an impressive array of correlational, longitudinal, cross-cultural, experimental, and qualitative studies, better math achievement leads to lower VSCs, and better verbal achievement leads to lower MSCs—the critical albeit paradoxical prediction of the I/E model.

In this chapter, we explore new methodological, theoretical, and substantive insights from the extension of the I/E model into DCT. A central feature of DCT and its extension of the I/E model is the distinction between near and far comparisons. Here we integrate theoretical perspectives based on the Marsh/Shavelson structural model of self-concept (Figure 5.1) with new insights from DCT. The extensive research literature based on the I/E model demonstrates that better achievement in one domain has a negative effect of ASCs in a far domain. In the broader social comparison literature, these negative effects are referred to as contrast effects (see Marsh, Möller et al., 2015; Möller, Helm et al. 2015; Möller & Marsh, 2013). DCT posits that the negative (contrast) effects will diminish and may even become positive (assimilation) effects when dimensional comparisons are based on complementary domains that are close together on the academic continuum. This extension was operationalized and new statistical tests were developed to evaluate these predictions in further studies described in this chapter.

As noted earlier, intrinsic to the DCT is the theoretical continuum of academic subjects along the math-to-verbal continuum (Figure 5.1). In this respect, it integrates well-established theoretical and empirical research based on the Marsh/Shavelson multidimensional, hierarchical model of self-concept, with the social comparison research pursued in many disciplines. Nevertheless, there is need for further research as to whether pair-wise differences between the perceived complementarity/antagonism of a whole range of academic domains can be adequately represented by this continuum in relation to DCT. For example, Goetz et al., (2010) quantified differences between school subjects based on students' responses in terms of the emotions they experienced to be associated with different school subjects.

Jansen et al. (2015) found that math and verbal achievement seemed to function to anchor for dimensional comparisons, whereas achievement in the sciences had no effect on self-concepts in other subjects. On this basis, they suggested that their results provide a possible answer to the "what with" question posed by Möller and Marsh (2013): math and verbal domains provide the basis of comparison for other domains. However, better tests of this proposal would require a more diverse set of academic domains, including more domains closer to the verbal end point of the academic continuum. Thus, for example, Marsh, Lüdtke et al. (2015) found significant paths involving all four of six domains that were placed at either extreme of the continuum—the two verbal scales (native and nonnative languages); math and physics. However, somewhat inconsistently with the hypothesized ordering domains, they found that biology self-concept was more positively correlated with German, English, and history than with physics and math, whilst history self-concept was as positively correlated with physics and biology as with English or German. Furthermore, even biology achievement had some small cross-paths in their two studies (e.g., negative effects on history and nonnative language self-concepts, and positive effects on math self-concepts). There is also the possibility that the "what with" question depends on what domains are presented and on subtle clues idiosyncratic to the particular study. Thus, for example, Jansen et al. (2015) suggested that the consistent contrast effects based on the TIMSS math and science data (see earlier discussion of Marsh, Abduljabbar et al., 2014) may owe to the fact that TIMSS is based on generic science measures rather than on domain-specific measures of science. However, another possibility is that by merely presenting two different domains to students, there is an implicit demand that they contrast responses to these two domains—whatever they are—in a manner consistent with the classic I/E model (i.e., contrasting for nonmatching domains) but perhaps not as consistent with the more nuanced predictions based on DCT.

SUMMARY

In this chapter, we have provided a comprehensive overview of the development of the I/E model from the first publication (Marsh, 1986) through to the current research that is testing new theoretical predictions based on its extension into DCT. The classic I/E model posits paradoxical relations between achievement and self-concept in mathematics and verbal domains in which achievement in each domain has a positive effect on self-concept in the matching domain (i.e., horizontal paths in Figure 5.5A) but a negative (contrast) effect on self-concept in the nonmatching domain (i.e., cross paths in Figure 5.5A). In this chapter we have briefly summarized the diversity of I/E studies that have been conducted, illustrating the generalizability of the findings across different indicators of achievement, different self-concept instruments, different cultures, and different constructs. We have briefly touched on the range of research methodologies in support of I/E predictions, including cross-sectional correlational studies, longitudinal causal ordering studies, quasi-experimental and true experimental studies, cross-cultural studies, and introspective diary studies of spontaneous comparisons in everyday life. We have illustrated how extensions of the I/E model integrate it with some of the major theoretical models of academic self-concept: the Marsh/Shavelson multidimensional, hierarchical model of academic self-concept (Figure 5.1); the longitudinal reciprocal effects model (REM) of the causal ordering of relations between self-concepts and accomplishments (Figure 5.3); the Big-Fish-Little-Pond Effect (BFLPE) model of negative (contrast) social comparison effects associated with attending academically selective schools and classes (Figure 5.4). This extensive body of research demonstrates that support for the theoretical predictions based on the I/E model is found in some of the most robust findings in educational psychology and perhaps psychology more generally.

Extending the I/E model, DCT posits that self-evaluations are based on dimensional comparisons as well as the more traditionally understood social and temporal comparisons. In particular, DCT predicts that strong contrast effects occur only for far comparisons (contrasting domains that are at the opposite ends of the theoretical continuum of academic self-concept) but are much weaker negative contrast, or even positive assimilation effects, for near domains (complementary domains that are close to each other). Here we illustrate new predictions, theoretical insights, and methodology associated with the I/E model and its extension into DCT, based on multiple academic domains (e.g., native language, foreign language, history, biology, physics and math; see Figure 5.1), showing significant contrast effects for far comparisons and significantly smaller contrast or assimilation effects for near domains.

In summary, this chapter has presented the first overview of I/E research, relating it to four "new wave" studies explicitly designed to test DCT theoretical predictions based on a comprehensive range of academic domains. All four studies provide clear support for the critical prediction that paths for achievement to ASC based on near comparisons will be less negative than those based on far comparisons. These results have important implications for theory, research, and practice. The results extend self-concept theory in new and nuanced ways and provide a fertile foundation for further research. The results imply that educators, parents, and significant others need to be aware of these effects when attempting to shore up students' academic self-concepts, and need to discourage comparisons in which good achievement in one results in poorer self-concept in contrasting domains.

ACKNOWLEDGMENTS

This chapter was supported in part by a grant from the Australian Research Council (DP130102713) awarded to the first two authors authors and (DE140100080) awarded to the third author. The authors would like to thank Marjoie Seaton, Jens Möller, Reinhard Pekrun, Malte Jansen, Oliver Lüdtke, and Matte Jansen for helpful comments leading to this chapter. Requests for further information about this chapter should be sent to Professor Herbert W. Marsh, Institute for Positive Psychology and Education, Australian Catholic University; E-mail: herb.marsh@acu.edu.au.

REFERENCES

Abu-Hilal, M. M. (2002). *Frame of reference model of self-concept and locus of control: A cross gender study in the United Arab Emirates.* Paper presented at the annual meeting of the American Educational Research Association, New Orleans, LA.

Abu-Hilal, M. M., & Bahri, T. M. (2000). Self-concept: The generalizability of research on the SDQ, Marsh/Shavelson model and I/E reference model to

United Arab Emirates students. *Social Behavior and Personality, 28*, 309–322. doi:10.2224/sbp.2000.28.4.309

Albert, S. (1977). Temporal comparison theory. *Psychological Review, 84*, 485–503. doi:10.1037/0033-295X.84.6.485

Bøe, M. V., Henriksen, E. K., Lyons, T., & Schreiner, C. (2011). Participation in science and technology: Young people's achievement-related choices in late-modern societies. *Studies in Science Education, 47*, 37–72. doi:10.1080/03057267.2011.549621

Bong, M. (1998). Tests of the internal/external frames of reference model with subject-specific academic self-efficacy and frame-specific academic self-concepts. *Journal of Educational Psychology, 90*, 102–110. doi:10.1037/0022-0663.90.1.102

Brickman, P., & Bulman, R. J. (1977). Pleasure and pain in social comparison. In J. M. Suls & R. L. Miller (Eds.), *Social comparison processes: Theoretical and empirical perspectives* (pp. 149–186). Washington, DC: Hemisphere.

Calsyn, R., & Kenny, D. (1977). Self-concept of ability and perceived evaluations by others: Cause or effect of academic achievement? *Journal of Educational Psychology, 69*, 136–145.

Chen, S., Yeh. Y., Hwang, F., & Lin, S. S. J. (2013). The relationship between academic self-concept and achievement: A multicohort–multioccasion study. *Learning and Individual Differences, 23*, 172–178.

Collins, R. (1996). For better or worse: The impact of upward social comparison on self-evaluations. *Psychological Bulletin, 119*, 51–69.

Dai, D. Y. (2002). Incorporating parent perceptions: A replication and extension study of the internal-external frame of reference model of self-concept development. *Journal of Adolescent Research, 17*, 617–645.

Denissen, J. J. A., Zarrett, N. R., & Eccles, J. S. (2007). I like to do it, I'm able, and I know I am: Longitudinal couplings between domain-specific achievement, self-concept, and interest. *Child Development, 78*, 430–447. doi:10.1111/j.1467-8624.2007.01007.x

Diener, E. (2000). Subjective well-being—The science of happiness and a proposal for a national index. *American Psychologist, 55*(1), 34–43. doi:10.1037/0003-066X.55.1.34

Diener, E., & Fujita, F. (1997). Social comparison and subjective well-being. In B. P. Buunk & F. X. Gibbons (Eds.), *Health, coping, and well-being: Perspectives from social comparison theory* (pp. 329–358). Mahwah, NJ: Erlbaum.

Eccles, J. S. (2009). Who am I and what am I going to do with my life? Personal and collective identities as motivators of action. *Educational Psychologist, 44*, 78–89. doi:10.1080/00461520902832368

Eccles, J. S., Adler, T. F., Futterman, R., Goff, S. B., Kaczala, C. M., Meece, J. L., & Midgley, C. (1983). Expectations, values and academic behaviors. In J. T. Spence (Ed.), *Achievement and achievement motives* (pp. 75–145). San Francisco, CA: Freeman.

Eccles, J., S., Adler, T. F., & Kaczala, C. M. (1982). Socialization of achievement attitudes and beliefs: Parental influences. *Child Development, 53*, 310–321. doi:10.2307/1128973

Eccles, J., Adler, T., & Meece, J. L. (1984). Sex differences in achievement. A test of alternate theories. *Journal of Personality and Social Psychology, 46,* 26–43. doi:10.1037//0022-3514.46.1.26

Eccles, J. S., & Wigfield, A. (1995). In the mind of the actor: The structure of adolescents' achievement task values and expectancy-related beliefs. *Personality and Social Psychology Bulletin, 21*(3), 215–225. doi:10.1177/0146167295213003

Festinger, L. (1954). A theory of social comparison processes. *Human Relations, 7,* 117–140.

Goetz, T., Cronjaeger, H., Frenzel, A. C., Lüdtke, O., & Hall, N. C. (2010). Academic self-concept and emotion relations: Domain specificity and age effects. *Contemporary Educational Psychology, 35*(1), 44–58.

Goetz, T., Frenzel, C. A., Hall, N. C., & Pekrun, R. (2008). Antecedents of academic emotions: Testing the internal/external frame of reference model for academic enjoyment. *Contemporary Educational Psychology, 33,* 9–33. doi:10.1016/j.cedpsych.2006.12.002

Goetz, T., Frenzel, A. C., Pekrun, R., & Hall, N. C. (2006). The domain specificity of academic emotional experiences. *The Journal of Experimental Education, 75*(1), 5–29.

Guay, F., Chanal, J., Ratellem C. F., Marsh, H. W., Larose, S., & Michel Boivin, M. (2010). Intrinsic, identified, and controlled types of motivation for school subjects in young elementary school children. *British Journal of Educational Psychology, 80,* 711–735.

Guay, F., Larose, S., & Boivin, M. (2004). Academic self-concept and educational attainment level: A ten-year longitudinal study. *Self and Identity, 3,* 53–68.

Guo, J., Marsh, H. W., Parker, P. D., Morin, A. J. S., & Yeung, A. S. (2015). Expectancy-value in mathematics, gender and socioeconomic background as predictors of achievement and aspirations: A multi-cohort study. *Learning and Individual Differences, 37,* 161–168.

James, W. (1890/1963). *Principles of psychology.* Chicago, IL: Encyclopedia Britannica. doi:10.1037/11059-000

Jansen, M., Schroeders, U., Lüdtke, O., & Marsh, H. W. (2015). Contrast and assimilation effects of dimensional comparisons in five subjects: An extension of the I/E model. *Journal of Educational Psychology.* Advance online publication. http://dx.doi.org/10.1037/edu0000021

Marsh, H. W. (1984). Self-concept: The application of a frame of reference model to explain paradoxical results. *Australian Journal of Education, 28,* 165–181.

Marsh, H. W. (1986). Verbal and math self-concepts: An internal/external frame of reference model. *American Educational Research Journal, 23,* 129–149.

Marsh, H. W. (1989). Age and sex effects in multiple dimensions of self-concept: Preadolescence to early-adulthood. *Journal of Educational Psychology, 81,* 417–430. doi:10.1037/0022-0663.81.3.417

Marsh, H. W. (1990a). The causal ordering of academic self-concept and academic achievement: A multiwave, longitudinal panel analysis. *Journal of Educational Psychology, 82,* 646–656.

Marsh, H. W. (1990b). The influences of internal and external frames of reference on the formation of English and math self-concepts. *Journal of Educational Psychology, 82,* 107–116.

Marsh, H. W. (1991). Failure of high ability schools to deliver academic benefits commensurate with their students' ability levels. *American Educational Research Journal, 28*, 445–480.

Marsh, H. W. (2007). *Self-concept theory, measurement and research into practice: The role of self-concept in educational psychology.* Leicester, England: British Psychological Society.

Marsh, H. W., Abduljabbar, A. S., Abu-Hilal, M. M., Morin, A. J. S., Abdelfattah, F., Leung, K. C., & Parker, P. (2013). Factorial, convergent, and discriminant validity of TIMSS math and science motivation measures: A comparison of Arab and Anglo-Saxon countries. *Journal of Educational Psychology, 105*(1), 108–128.

Marsh, H. W., Abduljabbar, A. S., Parker, P. D., Morin, A. J., Abdelfattah, F., & Nagengast, B. (2015). The internal/external frame of reference model of self-concept and achievement relations: Age-cohort and cross-cultural differences. *American Educational Research Journal.* (on-line prepublication)

Marsh, H. W., Barnes, J., & Hocevar, D. (1985). Self-other agreement on multidimensional self-concept ratings: Factor analysis and multitrait-multimethod analysis. *Journal of Personality and Social Psychology, 49*, 1360–1377.

Marsh, H. W. & Byrne, B. M. (1993). Do we see ourselves as others infer: A comparison of self-other agreement on multiple dimensions of self-concept from two continents. *Australian Journal of Psychology, 45*, 49–58.

Marsh, H. W., Byrne, B. M., & Shavelson, R. J. (1988). A multifaceted academic self-concept: Its hierarchical structure and its relation to academic achievement. *Journal of Educational Psychology, 80*, 366–380. doi:10.1037/0022-0663.80.3.366

Marsh, H. W., & Craven, R. (1997). Academic self-concept: Beyond the dustbowl. In G. Phye (Ed.), *Handbook of classroom assessment: Learning, achievement, and adjustment* (pp. 131–198). Orlando, FL: Academic.

Marsh, H. W., & Craven, R. G. (2006). Reciprocal effects of self-concept and performance from a multidimensional perspective: Beyond seductive pleasure and unidimensional perspectives. *Perspectives on Psychological Science, 1*, 133–163. doi:10.1111/j.1745-6916.2006.00010.x.

Marsh, H. W., & Hau, K. T. (2004). Explaining paradoxical relations between academic self-concepts and achievements: Cross-cultural generalizability of the internal-external frame of reference predictions across 26 countries. *Journal of Educational Psychology, 96*, 56–67. doi:10.1037/0022-0663.96.1.56

Marsh, H. W., Hau, K.-T., Artelt, C., Baumert, J. & Peschar, J. L. (2006). OECD's brief self-report measure of educational psychology's most useful affective constructs: Cross-cultural, psychometric comparisons across 25 countries. *International Journal of Testing, 6*, 311–360. doi:10.1207/s15327574ijt0604_1

Marsh, H. W., Kong, C. K., & Hau, K. (2001). Extension of the internal/external frame of reference model of self-concept formation: Importance of native and nonnative languages for Chinese students. *Journal of Educational Psychology, 93*, 543–553. doi:10.1037/0022-0663.93.3.543

Marsh, H. W., Kuyper, H., Seaton, M., Parker, P. D., Morin, A. J. S., Möller, J., & Abduljabbar, A. S. (2014). Dimensional comparison theory: An extension of the internal/external frame of reference effect on academic self-concept formation. *Contemporary Educational Psychology, 39*, 326–341.

Marsh, H. W., Lüdtke, O., Nagengast, B., Trautwein , U., Abduljabbar, A. S. (2015). Dimensional Comparison Theory: Paradoxical relations between self-beliefs and achievements in multiple domains. *Learning and Instruction 35,* 16–32.

Marsh, H. W., Möller, J., Parker, P., Xu, M. K., Nagengast, B. & Pekrun, R. (2015). Internal/external frame of reference model. In J. D. Wright (Ed.), *The international encyclopedia of the social and behavioral sciences* (2nd ed., pp. 430–436). Oxford, England: Elsevier.

Marsh, H. W., & O'Mara, A. (2008). Reciprocal effects between academic self-concept, self-esteem, achievement, and attainment over seven adolescent years: Unidimensional and multidimensional perspectives of self-concept. *Personality and Social Psychology Bulletin, 34,* 542–552. doi:10.1177/0146167207312313

Marsh, H. W., & O'Mara, A. (2010). Long-term total negative effects of school-average ability on diverse educational outcomes: Direct and indirect effects of the Big-Fish-Little-Pond Effect. *German Journal of Educational Psychology, 24,* 51–72. doi:10.1024/1010-0652.a000004.

Marsh, H. W., & Parker, J. W. (1984). Determinants of student self-concept: Is it better to be a relatively large fish in a small pond even if you don't learn to swim as well? *Journal of Personality and Social Psychology, 47,* 213–231.

Marsh, H. W., Seaton, M., Kuyper, H., Dumas; F., Huguet, P., Regner, I., . . . Gibbons, F. X. (2010). Phantom behavioral assimilation effects: Systematic biases in social comparison choice studies. *Journal of Personality, 78,* 671–710. doi:10.1111/j.1467-6494.2010.00630.x

Marsh, H. W., Seaton, M., Trautwein, U., Lüdtke, O., Hau, K. T., O'Mara, A. J., & Craven, R. G. (2008). The Big-Fish-Little-Pond-Effect stands up to critical scrutiny: Implications for theory, methodology, and future research. *Educational Psychology Review, 20,* 319–350. doi:10.1007/s10648-008-9075-6

Marsh, H. W., & Shavelson, R. (1985) Self-concept: Its multifaceted, hierarchical structure. *Educational Psychologist, 20,* 107–125.

Marsh, H. W., Trautwein, U., Lüdtke, O., Köller, O., & Baumert, J. (2005). Academic self-concept, interest, grades and standardized test scores: Reciprocal effects models of causal ordering. *Child Development, 76,* 397–416. doi:10.1111/j.1467-8624.2005.00853.x

Marsh, H. W., & Yeung, A. S. (1997). Coursework selection: The effects of academic self-concept and achievement. *American Educational Research Journal, 34,* 691–720. doi:10.3102/00028312034004691

Marsh, H. W., & Yeung, A. S. (2001). An extension of the internal/external frame of reference model: A response to Bong (1998). *Multivariate Behavioral Research, 36,* 389–420.

Meece, J. L.,Wigfield, A., & Eccles, J. S. (1990). Predictors of math anxiety and its consequences for young adolescents' course enrollment intentions and performances in mathematics. *Journal of Educational Psychology, 82,* 60–70.

Möller, J. (2005). "Paradoxical" effects of praise and criticism: Social, dimensional, and temporal comparisons. *British Journal of Educational Psychology, 75,* 275–295. doi:10.1348/000709904X24744

Möller, J., Helm, F., Müller-Kalthoff, H., Nagy, H, Marsh, H. W. (2015). Dimensional comparisons and their consequences for self-concept, motivation, and emotion. In J. D. Wright (Ed.) *International encyclopedia of the social & behavioral sciences* (2nd ed., pp. 430–436). Oxford, England: Elsevier.

Möller, J., & Husemann, N. (2006). Internal comparisons in everyday life. *Journal of Educational Psychology, 98,* 342–353. doi:10.1037/0022-0663.98.2.342

Möller, J., & Köller, O. (2001a). Dimensional comparisons: An experimental approach to the internal/external frame of reference model. *Journal of Educational Psychology, 93,* 826–835. doi:10.1037/0022-0663.93.4.826

Möller, J., & Köller, O. (2001b). Frame of reference effects following the announcement of exam results. *Contemporary Educational Psychology, 26,* 277–287. doi:10.1006/ceps.2000.1055

Möller, J., & Marsh, H. W. (2013). Dimensional comparison theory. *Psychological Review, 120*(3), 544–560. doi:10.1037/a0032459

Möller, J., Pohlmann, B., Köller, O., & Marsh, H. W. (2009). A meta-analytic path analysis of the internal/external frame of reference model of academic achievement and academic self-concept. *Review of Educational Research, 79,* 1129–1167. doi:10.3102/0034654309337522

Möller, J., Retelsdorf, J., Köller, O., & Marsh, H. W. (2011). The Reciprocal I/E Model: An integration of models of relations between academic achievement and self-concept. *American Educational Research Journal, 48,* 1315–1346. doi:10.3102/0002831211419649

Möller, J., Streblow, L., Pohlmann, B., & Köller, O. (2006). An extension to the internal/external frame of reference model to two verbal and numerical domains. *European Journal of Psychology of Education, 21,* 467–487. doi:10.1007/BF03173515

Morin, A. J., Maïano, C., Marsh, H. W., Janosz, M., & Nagengast, B. (2011). The longitudinal interplay of adolescents' self-esteem and body image: A conditional autoregressive latent trajectory analysis. *Multivariate Behavioral Research, 46,* 157–201.

Nagengast, B., Marsh, H. W., Scalas, L. F., Xu, M. K., Hau, K.-T., & Trautwein, U. (2011). Who took the "×" out of expectancy-value theory? A psychological mystery, a substantive-methodological synergy, and a cross-national generalization. *Psychological Science, 22*(8), 1058–1066. doi:10.1177/0956797611415540

Nagy, G., Garrett, J., Trautwein, U., Cortina, K., Baumert, J., & Eccles, J. (2008). Gendered high school course selection as a precursor of gendered careers: The mediating role of self-concept and intrinsic value. In H. Watt & J. Eccles (Eds.), *Gender and occupational outcomes: Longitudinal assessments of individual, social, and cultural influences* (pp. 115–143). Washington, DC: American Psychological Association. doi:10.1037/11706-004

Nagy, G., Trautwein, U., Baumert, J., Köller, O., & Garrett, J. (2006). Gender and course selection in upper secondary education: Effects of academic self-concept and intrinsic value. *Educational Research and Evaluation, 12,* 323–345. doi:10.1080/13803610600765687

Parker, P. D., Marsh, H. W., Ciarrochi, J. Marshall, S., & Abduljabbar, A. S. (2014). Juxtaposing math self-efficacy and self-concept as predictors of long-term achievement outcomes. *Educational Psychology, 34*(1): 29–48.

Parker, P. D., Marsh, H. W., Lüdtke, O., & Trautwein, U. (2013). Differential school contextual effects for math and English: Integrating the Big-Fish-Little-Pond

Effect and the internal/external frame of reference. *Learning and Instruction, 23,* 78–89.

Parker, P. D., Marsh, H. W., Morin, A. J., Seaton, M., & Van Zanden, B. (2015). If one goes up the other must come down: Examining ipsative relationships between math and English self-concept trajectories across high school. *British Journal of Educational Psychology, 85,* 172–191.

Parker, P. D., Nagy, P. D., Trautwein, U., & Lüdtke, O. (2014). The internal/external frame of reference as predictors of career aspirations and university majors. In J. Eccles & I. Schoon (Eds.) *Gender differences in aspirations and attainment: a life course perspective* (pp. 224–246). Cambridge, England: Cambridge University Press.

Parker, P. D., Schoon, I., Tsai, Y., Nagy, G., Trautwein, U., & Eccles, J. (2012). Achievement, agency, gender, and socioeconomic background as predictors of post-school choices: A multi-context study. *Developmental Psychology, 48,* 1629–1642.

Pekrun, R. (2006). The control-value theory of achievement emotions: Assumptions, corollaries, and implications for educational research and practice. *Educational Psychology Review, 18,* 315–341.

Pinxten, M., De Fraine, B., Van Damme, J., & D'Haenens, E. (2010). Causal ordering of academic self-concept and achievement: Effects of type of achievement measure. *British Journal of Educational Psychology, 80,* 689–709.

Pohlmann, B., & Möller, J. (2009). On the benefits of dimensional comparisons. *Journal of Educational Psychology, 101,* 248–258. doi:10.1037/a0013151

Schoon, I., & Parsons, S. (2002). Teenage aspirations for future careers and occupational outcomes. *Journal of Vocational Behavior, 60*(2), 262–288.

Seligman, M. E. P., & Csikszentmihalyi, M. (2000). Positive psychology: An introduction. *American Psychologist, 55,* 5–14. doi:10.1037/0003-066X.55.1.5

Shavelson, R. J., Hubner, J. J., & Stanton, G. C. (1976). Self-concept: Validation of construct interpretations. *Review of Educational Research, 46,* 407–444.

Shrauger, J. S., & Schoeneman, T. J. (1979). Symbolic interactionist view of self-concept: Through the glass darkly. *Psychological Bulletin, 86,* 549–573.

Tesser, A. (1988). Toward a self-evaluation maintenance model of social behavior. In L. Berkowitz (Ed.), *Advances in experimental social psychology* (Vol. 21, pp. 181–227). New York, NY: Academic.

Valentine, J. C., & DuBois, D. L. (2005). Effects of self-beliefs on academic achievement and vice-versa: Separating the chicken from the egg. In H. W. Marsh, R. G. Craven, & D. M. McInerney (Eds.), *International advances in self research* (Vol. 2, pp. 53–78). Greenwich, CT: Information Age.

Valentine, J. C., DuBois, D. L., & Cooper, H. (2004). The relation between self-beliefs and academic achievement: A meta-analytic review. *Educational Psychologist, 39,* 111–133. doi:10.1207/s15326985ep3902_3

Van Zanden, B., Marsh, H. W., Seaton, M. & Parker, P. (2015). Self-concept: From unidimensional to multidimensional and beyond. In J. D. Wright (Ed.), International encyclopedia of the social and behavioral sciences (2nd ed., pp. 460–468. Oxford, England: Elsevier.

Van Zanden, B., Seaton, M., Parker, P. D., Marsh, H. W., Gou, J., & Duineveld, J. J. (2015). Extending the internal/external model to parents: A comparison of selective and comprehensive students and their parents. Sydney: Institute for Positive Psychology and Education, Australian Catholic University.

Vernon, P. E. (1950). *The structure of human abilities.* London, England: Methuen.

Wigfield, A. (1994). Expectancy-value theory of achievement motivation: A developmental perspective. *Educational Psychology Review, 6,* 49–78.

Wigfield, A., & Eccles, J. S. (2002). The development of competence beliefs and values from childhood through adolescence. In A. Wigfield & J. S. Eccles (Eds.), *Development of achievement motivation* (pp. 92–120). San Diego, CA: Academic. doi:10.1016/B978-012750053-9/50006-1

Wigfield, A., Eccles, J. S., Yoon, K. S., Harold, R. D., Arbreton, A. J. A., Freedman-Doan, C., & Blumenfeld, P. C. (1997). Change in children's competence beliefs and subjective task values across the elementary school years: A 3-year study. *Journal of Educational Psychology, 89,* 451–469. doi:10.1037//0022-0663.89.3.451

Xu, M. K., Marsh, H. W., Hau, K.-T., Ho, I. T., Morin, A. J. S., & Abduljabbar, A. S. (2013). The internal/external frame of reference of academic self-concept: Extension to a foreign language and the role of language of instruction. *Journal of Educational Psychology, 105*(2), 489–503. doi:10.1037/a0031333

Yeung, A. S., & Lau, I. C. (1998). *The internal/external frame of reference in the self-concept development of higher education students.* Paper presented at the Conference of the Higher Education Research and Development Society of Australasia, Auckland, New Zealand.

CHAPTER 6

TOO MUCH TIME HAS BEEN SPENT ON THE TIME DEVOTED TO HOMEWORK

Motivation Is the Key Construct in Homework Research

Ulrich Trautwein
University of Tübingen

Oliver Lüdtke
Leibniz Institute for Science and Mathematics Education /Centre for International Student Assessment

Benjamin Nagengast
University of Tübingen

Barbara Flunger
University of Tübingen

Michael is a 9th-grade student with an average achievement record who sits forever over his homework, although he may not be fully concentrated the whole time. In fact, over time, he has become a master of daydreaming. But

Self-Concept, Motivation, and Identity, pages 151–171

because his parents check on whether he is completing his assignments, he typically manages to come up with some more or less convincing results after a couple of hours.

Michael's classmate Jennifer is a very talented and fairly ambitious student who never spends more than half an hour a day on her homework. She explained to her parents that homework was "my work, not yours" and argues that finishing homework is not necessary for her given that it is typically repeated and discussed at school.

Michael and Jennifer's friend Ellen attends a different school in the same town. Ellen's teachers are well-known for assigning large amounts of homework and for strict monitoring of homework completion. As Ellen knows that her teachers attach great importance to thoroughly completed homework and she wants to succeed in school, she became a hard-working student who invests a lot of time and energy in her homework. Although students at her school differ in how much time it takes them to complete their homework, the average time spent on homework is higher than in most other schools, and so is the average achievement.

These are only three of the many different patterns of the association between homework time and school achievement. They give a quick impression of why there may not be a straightforward correlation between homework time and achievement, although this association is at the core of the "battle over homework" and despite the fact that a huge number of studies over the last 100 years have been searching for such a clear, linear association (see Cooper, 2001). In the first part of this chapter, we describe and critically discuss the limitations of this approach and highlight some general issues in study design and analyses.

However, the three examples described above do not only highlight the limitations of a traditional approach, they also point to possibilities. Why does it take Michael so long before he stops daydreaming and starts finishing his homework? Is Jennifer's reasoning adaptive? What does it mean for a class to have a teacher who exercises a strict monitoring of homework completion? Using motivational constructs to answer such questions will not only yield a better understanding of the homework process but, more generally, a better understanding of the development and impact of student motivation. Accordingly, in the second part of the chapter, we describe how motivational constructs enrich the understanding of the homework process and how this research in turn adds to the study of motivation more generally. In the third part of the chapter, we describe some potentially productive avenues for future research.

Time on Homework: Wrong Questions, Unsatisfactory Answers

A considerable part of students' studying for school takes place in the form of assigned homework, notably in mathematics, reading, writing, and foreign languages. According to Cooper, Robinson, and Patall (2006, p. 1; also see Cooper, 1989), "Homework can be defined as any task assigned by schoolteachers intended for students to carry out during nonschool hours." The most important reason for assigning homework is to increase students' achievement, but additional goals that have been linked to homework assignments include a positive impact on student motivation, an improvement of self-regulation skills, and the possibility to interact with parents to let them participate in students' academic path (Cooper, 1989; Paschal, Weinstein, & Walberg, 1984; Trautwein, Schnyder, Niggli, Neumann, & Lüdtke, 2009).

Homework has met considerable attention from researchers. This is specifically true with regard to the association between time spent on homework and achievement (see Cooper, 1989). In these studies, students are typically asked to report the time they spent on average on homework (in specific subjects or in general) on a typical day or a regular school week, and this measure is related to some sort of achievement indicator. It is interesting to note that this question of "How much time did you spend on your homework?" is also posed quite often in typical classroom situations and at families' dinner tables; in the form of "too much homework," it even made it onto the cover page of *Time* magazine on January 25, 1999. There have been hundreds of published (and perhaps even more unpublished) studies that examined this association. Furthermore, there are by now a number of meta-analyses on the homework-achievement association (Cooper, 2001; Cooper et al., 2006; Hattie, 2009; Hendriks, Luyten, Scheerens, & Sleegers, 2014).

The perhaps most influential article is the award-winning meta-analysis that was published by Cooper et al. (2006). In this technically highly sophisticated meta-analysis, homework studies reported between 1987 and 2003 were included. Three study types were delineated. First, six studies had an experimental design and reported positive effects of homework, but unfortunately none of them were published in peer-reviewed journals. Second, 30 studies used data from naturalistic, cross-sectional or longitudinal studies such as the National Education Longitudinal Study or the High School and Beyond database to relate homework time to achievement, statistically controlling for confounding variables. In the large majority of these studies, homework time was the only homework indicator employed and was positively associated with achievement. Third, 32 studies reported bivariate correlations between homework time and achievement; a weighted mean correlation of $r = .24$ was calculated for these studies. In sum, according to the authors, the studies reviewed support the idea of a positive homework-achievement association. In a recent review that was also largely devoted to the association between time spent on homework and achievement, Cooper, Steenbergen-Hu, and Dent (2012) came to a similar conclusion.

Unfortunately, the Cooper et al. (2006) meta-analysis has one little, but not irrelevant, limitation: Especially in the case of the nonexperimental studies, it is largely unclear what the findings of a positive association between time spent on homework and achievement really mean because the primary studies included in the review are characterized by methodological limitations concerning the central variable, "time spent on homework." Did students report "much time on homework" because, like Michael, it took them forever to complete their assignments because of daydreaming? Do we expect low achievement when talented students save time by not completing all their homework as in the case of Jennifer? And don't we need to better differentiate why a student took/invested lots of time spent on homework? Was it because of her/his working style (like Michael) or because the teacher (as in Ellen's case) assigned lots of homework? In fact, most of the primary studies reviewed by Cooper et al. did not provide enough information on why and how time was spent on homework, and because it is unclear what was measured with "time spent on homework" in the original studies, the aggregation of various studies might be of limited informative value.

Stated more systematically, there are a number of problems (see Trautwein & Köller, 2003) with time spent on homework items such as "How much time do you typically spend on math homework each week?" that were used in most of the studies reviewed by Cooper et al. (2006). First, homework can be related to achievement at two levels (see Trautwein & Köller, 2003): (a) A homework effect at the class level (i.e., homework *assignment* effect) is found when students in classes with a higher quantity (or quality of homework; see below) have more pronounced achievement gains than do students in other classes, as is the case in Ellen's class; (b) a homework effect at the student level (i.e., a homework *completion* effect) is found when students in the same class who differ in their homework behavior (e.g., time spent on homework) show differential outcomes. It is of paramount importance to differentiate between class- and student-level effects in all studies that relate homework to achievement, but this was not consistently done in the studies reviewed by Cooper et al. (2006).

Second, the measure of time spent on homework might also capture off-task behaviors (e.g., Karweit & Slavin, 1981) or nonpersistent behaviors (see Carroll, 1963). In this sense, Trautwein and Köller (2003) argued that time spent on homework can mean quite different things. On the one hand, homework time may reflect high homework compliance and a conscientious working style. On the other hand, some students might report a high amount of time spent on homework because they are not concentrated when working on homework problems, such as Michael. Unless studies exploring the association between time spent on homework and achievement differentiate between the different types of high amounts of homework time, they may not paint a very conclusive picture of homework effects.

Third, the extent to which students are able to reliably report the time they spend on homework is unclear. How many hours of homework time will Michael, Jennifer, and Ellen report on a questionnaire? In fact, in Michael's case, what would be the correct figure? The total time he sits on his homework or only the time when he "really" works on it? And even if students are able to determine the "real" amount of time it took them, will they be willing to report an unbiased estimation since spending a lot of time on homework is typically not considered to be "cool?" Not surprisingly, there are some indications of restricted reliability of the "time spent on homework" measure (see Trautwein & Köller, 2003). For instance, Cooper, Lindsay, Nye, and Greathouse (1998) found a rather weak, albeit significant, correlation of 0.16 between student and parent reports of the amount of homework assigned. Similarly, in a study with 37 students, De Jong, Westerhof and Creemers (2000) found a correlation of $r = .32$ between a report of the average time spent on homework and a logbook recording the time spent on homework every day for a month.

Fourth, there is an often-emphasized need for attending to quality issues of the primary studies in terms of study design. For instance, measures of students' prior achievement are needed when gauging the effects of homework assignments or homework completion on change in achievement. Of course, a talented student such as Jennifer is likely to always be a successful student. But would she be even more successful if her homework compliance would be higher? Unfortunately, measures of prior achievement are missing in the majority of the published homework studies. In fact, the shortcomings of several of the studies that were included in the Cooper et al. (2006) review are quite obvious, as Cooper et al. readily acknowledged ("The authors found that all studies, regardless of type, had design flaws"; p. 1). It is safe to say that with respect to their quality, a large majority of the studies would not have made it into a research synthesis of the U.S. Institute of Education Sciences' What Works Clearinghouse (see What Works Clearinghouse, 2014; Valentine & Cooper, 2003), which only includes studies of high quality.

Fifth, the Cooper et al. (2006) review has had impact on several educational authorities around the world, but it is based on studies conducted in the United States only. It is interesting to see that a recent meta-analysis (Hendriks et al., 2014) with broader inclusion criteria in terms of geographical origin established less impressive support for homework time. Hendriks et al. (2014, p. 70) used the so-called vote-counting strategy (i.e., they counted studies with positive, neutral, and negative effects) and referred to effects identified in 68 samples of 26 studies. In total, 42 negative effects, 43 non-significant effects, and 45 positive effects were found for the association of homework time and individual students' achievement. Similarly, in a study in which multilevel analysis was applied to school-achievement study data in a multicountry study, Dettmers, Trautwein and Lüdtke (2009) found the association between homework time and achievement to vary considerably across countries. More specifically, this cross-cultural study analyzed the relationship between homework time and mathematics achievement drawing on data from 231,759 students in 9,791 schools and 40 countries who participated in the Programme for International Student Assessment (PISA) 2003. Multilevel analyses found a positive association between school-average homework time and mathematics achievement in almost all countries, but the size of the association decreased considerably once socioeconomic background and school track were controlled. At the student level, the authors found 11 statistically significant positive associations between homework time and achievement, but also 12 statistically significant negative associations across the 40 countries after controlling for socioeconomic background and school track. From a theoretical point of view, it would be highly interesting to study if characteristics of learning environments moderate the impact of homework assignments/homework completion on achievement.

Some of the limitations outlined above can be overcome (and have been overcome) by conducting or using data from studies with adequate designs. For instance, the multilevel structure of homework data has been taken into account in the Hendricks et al. (2014) meta-analysis. Furthermore, measures of prior achievement and a statistical approach that controls for important covariates have been implemented in a number of studies, primarily in non-U.S. contexts. However, even with improved studies, the results of the "time spent on homework" research agenda may be less productive than what can be hoped for because it has not addressed what's at the heart of the homework process: the issue of student motivation.

STUDENT MOTIVATION: DRIVING HOMEWORK PROBLEMS, DRIVING HOMEWORK COMPLETION

A Multilevel, Domain-Specific Homework Model

Research on the association between "time spent on homework" (or, more general, "homework") and achievement has largely been a topic in the fields of educational research and research on educational effectiveness, and this research has always met specific attention in the public when the pros and cons of homework are discussed (e.g., Cooper, 2001). Somewhat less prominent, homework has also featured as a recurrent element in psychological research. However, homework was typically not the main issue in this research but rather a situation/stimulus that was used to test the power/applicability of a theory.

Importantly, in research on self-determination theory (Deci & Ryan, 2002), the homework situation has repeatedly served to study the effects of controlled vs. autonomous motivation (for a recent example, see Katz, Eilot, & Nevo, 2014). A very productive stream of research that uses self-determination theory focuses on the role of parents for student motivation in the context of homework, as exemplified, for instance, by the research programs of Grolnick (e.g., Grolnick, 2003; Grolnick & Slowiaczek, 1994) and Pomerantz (e.g., Pomerantz & Eaton, 2001; Pomerantz, Wang & Ng, 2005). This work highlights the importance of taking into account students' need for autonomy when the process of homework completion is analyzed.

A second stream of research in which homework serves prominently is research on self-regulation (e.g., Oettingen, Hönig, & Gollwitzer, 2000; Schmitz & Skinner, 1993; also see Boekaerts, 1999; Zimmerman, Bonner, & Kovach, 1996). In this research, homework is used as a prototypical situation in which self-regulation skills are necessary and highly effective; furthermore, homework situations are used in intervention studies as a means to practice self-regulation skills such as defining goals, modulating affect, and regulating cognition and behavior in a way that helps the learners to attain personal goals.

The sound theoretical underpinning that characterized the psychological homework studies allowed them to make a strong contribution to the understanding of the homework process. However, there are also some limitations of these studies. Importantly, unlike in educational research on homework, the question of the "effects" of homework does not play a pivotal role; in a related vein, standardized achievement measures only play a comparatively minor role. In other words, these studies do not directly contribute to our understanding of the homework-achievement association. Moreover, because the samples are typically rather small and their representativeness is unknown, the generalizability of the results to real educational contexts is unclear.

In our own research, we have attempted to bring together the strength of both the educational and the psychological approaches to homework. More specifically, following the conceptualization of use-inspired basic research (Stokes, 1997), the starting point of our research program has been a "real-world question": (How) do homework assignments and homework completion contribute to students' educational progress? However, this real-world question has had to be rephrased using theoretical language and translated into a research model. In our research, motivation has been used

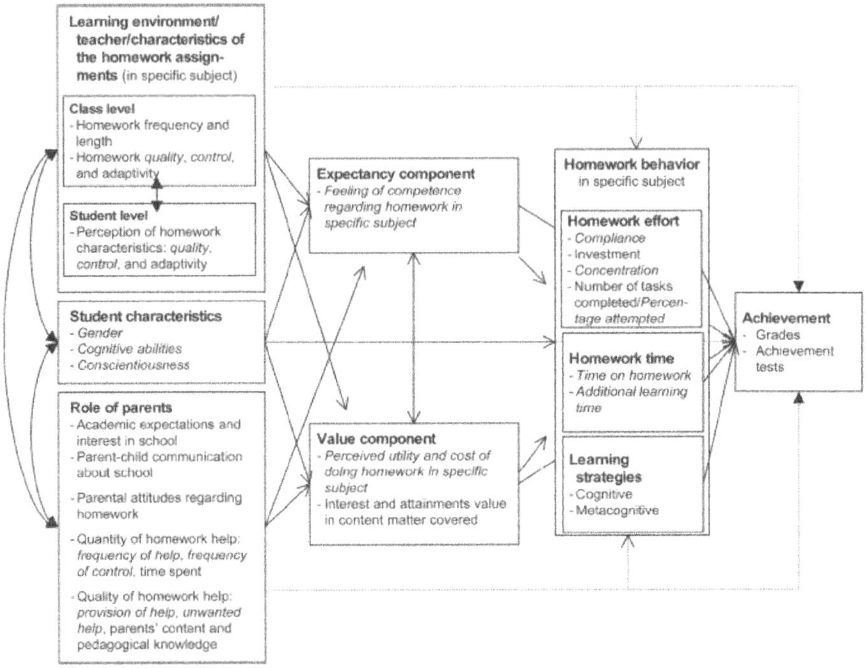

Figure 6.1 A multilevel, domain-specific homework model (adapted from Trautwein, Lüdtke, Schnyder et al., 2006)

as a key to understanding the homework process (see Figure 6.1). In the next step, data sets have been identified or created that provide a sound basis for testing the predictions with adequate statistical tools. Ideally, the product of a use-inspired basic research program is both of theoretical and practical interest.

Our conceptual model (for a detailed description, see Trautwein, Lüdtke, Kastens, & Köller, 2006; Trautwein, Lüdtke, Schnyder, & Niggli, 2006) combines elements of educational effectiveness research with, among other approaches, expectancy-value theory (Eccles, 1983; Eccles & Wigfield, 2002), self-determination theory (Deci & Ryan, 2002; Grolnick & Slowiaczek, 1994), and research on learning and instruction (e.g., Weinert & Helmke, 1995). A graphical depiction of the multilevel, multidimensional homework model is shown in Figure 6.1. It takes into account the three protagonists in the homework process (students, teachers, and parents) and covers six major groups of variables (achievement, homework behavior, homework motivation, student characteristics, parental behavior, and the learning environment).

The model predicts that homework behavior is related to achievement outcomes. Within homework behavior, there is a differentiation between homework effort, homework time, and learning strategies. No predictions are made with regard to homework time when assessed by means of the traditional "time on homework" self-report measure; because of the inherent problems with this variable described above, the direction of the effect of homework time is not easily predictable (but see below for a combined use of time on homework and homework effort). Conversely, it is assumed that the effort students spend on their homework assignments (i.e., doing their best to solve the tasks assigned) is positively related to their achievement. Homework effort is defined as the degree to which students seriously work on their homework tasks and the degree to which they comply with their assignments (e.g., Trautwein & Köller, 2003). In other words, homework effort refers to the amount of homework worked on thoroughly even if students are not able to solve all tasks correctly. Students with high homework effort do their best to complete their homework and do not copy it from classmates. In line with the prediction of the model, several studies have found a positive association between homework effort and achievement (e.g., Natriello & McDill, 1986; Schmitz & Skinner, 1993; Trautwein, 2007; Trautwein et al., 2006; Trautwein, Niggli, Schnyder, & Lüdtke, 2009). Similar predictions were made with regard to learning strategies, although these variables have not appeared prominently in our subsequent research.

In line with expectancy-value theory (see Eccles & Wigfield, 2002), homework effort is conceptualized as strongly influenced by expectancy and value beliefs (see Trautwein et al., 2006, for more details on an operationalization of these constructs). The expectancy component reflects a student's belief in being able to complete a given homework assignment successfully (e.g., "If I make an effort, I can do all my [subject] homework" and "I often feel completely lost in my [subject] homework" [reverse scored]). The value component describes students' reasons for doing a task (Eccles & Wigfield, 2002) in terms of the importance of succeeding in a specific domain, the enjoyment of engaging in the activity, the utility of the activity, and the associated costs of the activity. Items that we have used in our own research (e.g., "There is no point in my doing [subject] homework" [reverse scored] and "[Subject] homework helps me understand the material covered in the lesson better.") have had some emphasis on utility and cost. More research which distinguishes between domains and facets of value beliefs (see Gaspard et al., in press) might be very fruitful.

Subsequent research has indeed shown that expectancy and value beliefs are potent predictors of homework effort (e.g., Trautwein et al., 2006). In fact, this relation holds in both between-person and within-person analyses. In other words, in between-person analyses, students with higher expectancy and value beliefs in a specific subject are more likely to spend some effort on their homework in that subject than students with lower expectancy and value beliefs (Trautwein & Lüdtke, 2009; Trautwein, Lüdtke, Kastens et al.,

2006). Furthermore, using within-person analyses, it was shown that students typically spent more effort on homework in those subjects in which they have higher expectancy and value beliefs compared to their other subjects (Trautwein & Lüdtke, 2007; see also Nagengast, Trautwein, Kelava, & Lüdtke, 2013). It was additionally shown that there was a low association (low and mostly nonsignificant regression coefficients) among expectancy and value beliefs on the one hand and time on homework on the other, although there was a tendency for students with lower expectancy beliefs to report spending more time on homework. This would mean that students with a problematic motivational profile—Michael from the opening paragraph is a good example—may spend quite a lot of time on something that they do not enjoy, and this investment does not seem to be particularly effective.

In line with self-determination theory (see Deci & Ryan, 2002), the homework model further predicts that the quality of parental homework assistance is associated with homework expectancy and value beliefs and with homework effort. This hypothesis is largely in line with the theoretical and empirical accounts by the research groups lead by Grolnick and Pomerantz (Pomerantz & Eaton, 2001; Pomerantz, Grolnick, & Price, 2005). Furthermore, support for such a pattern of relationships was also found in our own studies (see Dumont et al. 2012; Dumont, Trautwein, Nagy, & Nagengast, 2014).

Moreover, student characteristics such as students' academic achievement, cognitive abilities, and conscientiousness are predicted to affect homework effort, partly mediated by student motivation (expectancy and value beliefs). Although we found partial support for this hypothesis (e.g., Trautwein, Lüdtke, Schnyder et al., 2006), it was also shown that conscientiousness and motivation (especially competence beliefs) seem to constitute rather independent predictors of homework effort.

Finally, the model comprises core characteristics of homework assignments, including homework frequency, homework length, homework control exerted by teachers, and the quality of the homework assignments. Again, it is postulated that homework motivation (expectancy and values) serves as a mediator between these characteristics and homework effort. Studies by Trautwein, Niggli, et al. (2009) as well as Dettmers, Trautwein, Lüdtke, Kunter, and Baumert (2010) confirmed this prediction. It is important to note that most constructs included in the model have to be assessed and modeled in a domain-specific way (e.g., math/English/science task value and competence beliefs).

Driving the Understanding of Student Motivation

In our view, the studies which used the multilevel, domain-specific homework model as a conceptual basis helped to get a somewhat more complete picture of when homework assignments and homework completion is successful. For instance, it can be used to get an idea of why Michael's "time investment" is not associated with great success (he is wasting time and does not really work hard on the assignments) and why this is the case (he may have rather low expectancy and value beliefs for at least some of his school subjects). Similarly, it helps to understand why the nature of Ellen's time investment is quite different from Michael's time investment (her teachers place great importance on ambitious academic goals and assign a high homework load.)

At the same time, homework provides a good opportunity to understand motivational issues more generally, as the two following examples demonstrate. The first example comes from a study in which we studied differences between classwork and homework effort (see Trautwein, Lüdtke, Kastens et al., 2006, Study 2). In this study, we were interested in the relation of classwork effort and homework effort to a number of predictors, including expectancy and value beliefs as well conscientiousness. One of the main findings of this study was that the difference between effort on homework and effort on classwork was higher among students low on conscientiousness. Students low on conscientiousness reported putting less effort into their homework than their classwork, but no such effect was found for students high on conscientiousness. This finding highlights the need to simultaneously attend to personality dimensions and the differential affordances and constraints of different learning settings in motivational research. The differences between classwork and seatwork provide a perfect opportunity to study such differences.

A second example concerns aspects of teaching quality and their effects on students' motivation, homework behavior, and achievement. As described in the opening part of this chapter, Ellen's teachers enforce homework completion using rather strict policies. But do all the students in the class experience the assignments in a similar way? And what to do if students describe their homework in different ways? As already described above, homework time is a perfect example of a variable that contains both "class level effects" (i.e., the "amount" the teacher assigns) and "student-level effects" (i.e., the differing characteristics of students such as prior knowledge and motivation that impact the time spent on homework). In fact, studies by Trautwein, Schnyder, et al. (2009) and Dettmers et al. (2010) highlight the need to take both sources of variance into account. But homework time is not the only example for the importance of class-level and student-level effects. For instance, Dettmers et al. scrutinized the role of two indicators of homework quality which they called selection (appropriate, high-quality tasks, an example item being "our math teacher almost always chooses homework assignments really well") and challenge (i.e., the level of difficulty; item example: "Our math homework assignments are often too easy" [reverse scored]). Results showed that the intraclass correlation (ICC), an indicator for the reliability of aggregated individual student judgments, was .18 for homework selection and .11 for homework challenge. Thus, 18% of the variance in homework selection and 11% of the variance in homework challenge was located between classes. The somewhat lower ICC for homework challenge may signal larger differences in individual perceptions of this variable than that of homework selection (see Lüdtke, Robitzsch, Trautwein, & Kunter, 2009). Perceptions of homework challenge may be more dependent on interindividual differences in, for instance, cognitive abilities or prior knowledge, than perceptions of homework selection. As homework provides (at least according to theoretical accounts) good opportunities for bringing in individualized elements into instruction, the Dettmers et al. (2010) article may be used as a blueprint for how to differentiate between class-level and student-level effects.

Future Directions

When the issue of homework is understood as an opportunity for use-inspired basic research, it is easy to discover a huge number of important open questions that await an answer. In the following, we would like to point the readers' attention to just three of these issues.

Time and Effort

Throughout this chapter, we have argued that the use of the "time spent on homework" measure is questionable. Despite these apparent weaknesses in terms of reliability and validity and the inconsistent pattern of results with regard to achievement outcomes, there might still be a role for homework time as a useful variable in homework research. This is the case when it is not used as a stand-alone indicator (and misunderstood as indicating "effort") but rather combined with other measures of homework effort. More specifically, we will argue that a high amount of time spent on homework can either reflect a conscientious working style (which is also associated with favorable achievement outcomes) or an inefficient, time-wasting working style (which is associated with less favorable achievement outcomes), and this in turn can be used as a predictor or criterion variable in motivational research.

As the dissimilar patterns in the homework behavior of Michael, Jennifer, and Ellen suggest, students' differences in homework behavior might be characterized by a specific interplay of "high" and/or "low" levels of homework effort and time spent on homework, which could be discerned as learning profiles. In Figure 6.2, a graphical, simplified depiction of possible combinations of homework time and homework effort in the form of "learning types" is provided. (1) Students who put a lot of time and energy in their homework show high levels in homework time and homework effort. These students can be labeled as "high-effort learners." Ellen

		Homework Effort	
		high	*low*
Homework Time	*high*	the high-effort learner	the struggling learner
	low	the fast learner	the minimalist

Figure 6.2 Possible homework learning types.

represents a "high-effort learner," as she spends a lot of time on her homework while working on it very carefully. (2) By comparison, Michael would report a high amount of time spent on homework, but concurrently give an account of low homework effort. That is, when doing homework, he has difficulties in not starting to day-dream and getting distracted. Therefore, he can be characterized as a "struggling learner" because he has troubles meeting the demands of the homework tasks. "Struggling learners" might also be students who spend a great amount of time on homework but due to lack of care and attention cannot turn their investment into a favorable learning style. (3) Jennifer puts neither a lot of time nor great effort into homework. Taking into account the little time she schedules for her daily homework in a regular week, she and other students with these homework habits might be called "minimalists." (4) A further subgroup of students might emerge that could be characterized by the co-occurrence of a low amount of homework time and high amount of effort. According to the quantity of homework that these students manage to complete accurately within a short time, these students can be labeled as "fast learners."

High levels in homework time may not automatically translate into high achievement outcomes in all learning types. Rather, the different ways that homework effort co-occurs in these learning types might be the crucial factor in determining successful learning behavior. That is, students who invest a great amount of time and effort in their homework (i.e., the "high-effort learners") might show more favorable achievement outcomes than students who work for a long time period with low effort (i.e., the "struggling learners"). Moreover, low levels in homework time may not automatically be associated with low achievement outcomes, although the "minimalists" seem to be at greater risk for school failure compared to the other learning types given the little time they invest in homework.

So far, interindividual differences in students and the possibility to identify distinct learning types in these differences have been to some degree overlooked in educational research when studying the effects of time. That is, it can be summarized that "different effects for different kinds of students are usually not included.... There is also strong suggestion in the literature that sufficient time is especially important for the weaker students" (Scheerens & Hendriks, 2014, p. 12). This limitation applies for research on homework time as well. Therefore, further studies are needed to test these predictions. These studies will have practical implications because they will deal with an important real-world problem: the unnecessary waste of time by many students when doing homework. However, they will also have the potential to contribute to psychological and educational theory in describing motivational profiles and the predictors and consequences of specific profiles.

The person-centered approach is the technique best suited for the objective to identify and yield a better understanding of qualitatively different homework learning types in students, by examining homework effort and homework time in conjunction. The basic principle of the person-oriented approach is to group students with a similar profile of indicator variables (e.g., Bergman, Magnusson, & El-Khouri, 2002). Therefore, distinct types can be identified and their prevalence can be evaluated (e.g., Vermunt & Magidson, 2002). Thus, in search of homework learning profiles and their differences in academic achievement, Flunger et al. (in press) reanalyzed a 2-wave study on the French homework of 1,915 Swiss 8th-grade students with a person-centered approach, exploring the interplay of homework effort and homework time. And indeed, four learning types were yielded that could be identified according to their mean profiles in homework time and homework effort as "fast learners," "high-effort learners," "struggling learners," and "minimalists." Moreover, next to the hypothesized groups, one learning type was found that seemed to hold a median level of homework effort and spend little time on homework. This group was labeled as "average students."

In order to investigate the achievement gains of students classified as distinct learning types over time, the learning types were compared with regard to both a French-achievement test and French grades in longitudinal analyses. Therefore, the differences of the learning types in the Time 2 academic achievement were investigated in separate analyses for each outcome, while controlling for the effect of previous achievement at Time 1, respectively. In these analyses, "fast learners" were shown to have the highest achievement test scores and grades, "struggling learners" to have the lowest achievement test scores and lowest grades. Moreover, the "high-effort learners" were shown to have favorable achievement outcomes in terms of school grades. The "minimalists" constitute an interesting subgroup because they showed a more positive development than the "struggling learners," despite similarly low scores on homework effort.

These findings indicate that the simultaneous considerations of homework time and effort might enable researchers to kill two birds with one stone: the oversimplification in the conceptualization of homework time, and the missing investigation of differential associations for distinct students. In sum, a better understanding of the meaning of time individual students spend on homework can be yielded when students' homework effort is considered in conjunction with homework time.

Using New Technologies to Assess Learning Behavior

Another approach that also overcomes the uncritical usage of a "time on homework" measure is the turn to new assessment technologies to assess learning behavior. A number of researchers have highlighted the role of technological progress (e.g., Mehl & Conner, 2011) that could also transform educational assessments. For instance, experience sampling methods using "beepers" have been used to focus students' emotions during homework (Goetz et al., 2012). In this study, students were repeatedly asked to report on their emotions during homework completion. More recent advancements can be used to assess additional parameters, such as physiological measures. In this vein, researchers have argued that the next generations of smartphones have the potential to instigate the next revolution in data collection in psychological and educational research (see Miller, 2012, "Smartphone Psychology Manifesto") and implicate unprecedented opportunities for assessing psychological processes in real-life situations.

Similarly, the shift to using electronic learning resources at school and for homework may open up a window of opportunity to assess students' learning and homework behavior in a more detailed way. For instance, if students work with an electronic textbook on a tablet computer, it is possible to record the traces of all learning activities. In a next step, these traces can be used to yield indicators/categories of learning behavior, either by using predefined algorithms or by ways of data-mining procedures.

Projected even further into the future, there is the potential for brain-computer interaction technology to assess mental states (such as being bored or overtaxed by homework tasks) during learning and homework completion (see Gerjets, Walter, Rosenstiel, Bogdan, & Zander, in press). This in turn might one day in the (far) future be used for adaptively and automatically tailoring instruction (including homework assignments) to students' competence and needs.

Do Homework Assignment and Completion Make Students "Grittier"?

From an educational point of view, a main question for future research is clearly how to increase academic effort in students like Michael with low levels of motivation. In the long run, increased academic effort is likely to lead to improved academic achievement. There seem to be three major targets for interventions: student motivation, conscientiousness, and self-regulation skills.

Motivational Interventions

Conceptually, task-value beliefs and expectancy beliefs seem to be logical targets for educational interventions. Evidence from educational psychology suggests that both expectancy beliefs and value beliefs can be systematically increased in favorable learning environments (Guthrie, Wigfield, & Perencevich, 2004; Pintrich, 2003). For instance, effective teachers use a variety of means to make their lessons and homework assignments interesting, such as working with new or personally relevant materials, providing autonomy support, and offering appropriate scaffolding for difficult tasks (e.g., Hidi & Renninger, 2006). Increasing the situational interestingness of the learning environment is believed to positively affect the learning of all students, irrespective of their prior levels of individual interest.

At the same time, designing highly interesting lessons is difficult, time-consuming, and probably not a viable solution for all motivational difficulties. Even highly committed and effective teachers will not be able to make all their lessons and homework assignments so interesting that they immediately engage all unmotivated students. Researchers have therefore identified a need for strategies to transform situational interest into more stable individual interest. Two important factors here would seem to be personal relevance and the repeated experience of positive affect when dealing with a subject (Pintrich, 2003).

However, increasing individual interest in a subject also has potential drawbacks. Academic interest is domain specific. Interests become differentiated in adolescence, resulting in pronounced interest profiles (e.g., Denissen, Zarrett, & Eccles, 2007) and associated profiles of academic engagement. This differentiation process is an important aspect of identity development and facilitates adaptive academic and vocational choices. From this perspective, interest profiles, including some low-interest subjects, may in fact be a desirable outcome of schooling. In a related vein, as a result of intraindividual comparison processes, increased individual interest in one subject area is likely to be associated with increased effort in that area, but with decreased effort in others (see Trautwein & Lüdtke, 2007). Somewhat paradoxically then, effective teachers who increase students' interest in the subject they teach might make life harder for their colleagues.

Conscientiousness

At first glance, attempts to foster conscientiousness may seem less promising. To date, there is no evidence that certain learning environments are conducive to the development of high conscientiousness. Moreover, rank-order correlations for conscientiousness are high across the life span

(Roberts & DelVecchio, 2000), indicating that interindividual differences in conscientiousness are quite stable. However, it might be somewhat rash to strike conscientiousness from the list of targets for intervention for several reasons. First, conscientiousness is related to academic effort across a broad spectrum of academic domains, making it a potentially powerful lever for improving academic effort and achievement. Second, several authors have recently reported replicable associations between life experiences and changes in personality traits, indicating that conscientiousness may be more strongly associated with environmental characteristics than previously thought (Bleidorn, 2012; Lüdtke, Roberts, Trautwein, & Nagy, 2011). For instance, features of the work environment seem to be associated with changes in conscientiousness (Roberts, Caspi, & Moffitt, 2003), environmental characteristics at college (e.g., quality of interactions with the university, affective response to grades) correlate with change in conscientiousness (Robins, Noftle, Trzesniewski, & Roberts, 2005), and social investment is associated with both trait levels and changes in conscientiousness (Lodi-Smith & Roberts, 2007).

Self-Regulation Interventions

Finally, self-regulation is typically depicted as a competence that can and should be taught and learned at school (Boekaerts, 1999) and expresses itself in motivational, metacognitive, and cognitive strategies that increase the effectiveness and efficiency of learning behavior. Further research is needed to study the degree to which effective homework assignments and successful completion of homework assignments positively impact self-regulation. Moreover, given the considerable conceptual overlap between the constructs of self-regulation and conscientiousness, it will be important to study whether increases in self-regulation predict increases in conscientiousness over time.

CONCLUSION

Many researchers have spent a lot of time on establishing the association between "time spent on homework" and achievement. As we hope to have shown in this chapter, this line of research may not yield the most reliable, valid, or useful results. As an alternative, we call for research programs on student motivation that take use of the full potential of the homework situation. The many Michaels, Jennifers, and Ellens around the world have already waited too long for robust findings on efficient study behavior in the homework context and for effective interventions programs.

REFERENCES

Bergman, L. R., Magnusson, D., & El-Khouri, B. M. (2002). *Studying individual development in an interindividual context: A person-oriented approach* (Vol. 4). New York, NY: Psychology.

Bleidorn, W. (2012). Hitting the road to adulthood: Short-term personality development during a major life transition. *Personality and Social Psychology Bulletin, 38,* 1594–1608.

Boekaerts, M. (1999). Self-regulated learning: Where we are today. *International Journal of Educational Research, 31,* 445–457.

Carroll, J. B. (1963). A model of school learning. *Teachers' College Record, 64,* 723–733.

Cooper, H. (1989). *Homework.* White Plains, NY: Longman.

Cooper, H. (2001). *The battle over homework* (2nd ed.). Thousand Oaks, CA: Corwin.

Cooper, H., Lindsay, J. J., Nye, B., & Greathouse, S. (1998). Relationships among attitudes about homework, amount of homework assigned and completed, and student achievement. *Journal of Educational Psychology, 90,* 70–83.

Cooper, H., Robinson, J. C., & Patall, E. A. (2006). Does homework improve academic achievement? A synthesis of research, 1987–2003. *Review of Educational Research, 76,* 1–62.

Cooper, H., Steenbergen-Hu, S., & Dent, A. L. (2012). Homework. In K. R. Harris, S. Graham, & T. Urdan (Eds.), *APA educational psychology handbook, Vol 3: Application to learning and teaching* (pp. 475–495). Washington, DC: American Psychological Association.

De Jong, R., Westerhof, K. J., & Creemers, B. P. M. (2000). Homework and student math achievement in junior high schools. *Educational Research and Evaluation, 6,* 130–157.

Deci, E. L., & Ryan, R. M. (Eds.). (2002). *Handbook of self-determination research.* New York, NY: University of Rochester Press.

Denissen, J. J., Zarrett, N. R., & Eccles, J. S. (2007). I like to do it, I'm able, and I know I am: Longitudinal couplings between domain-specific achievement, self-concept, and interest. *Child Development, 78*(2), 440–447.

Dettmers, S., Trautwein, U., & Lüdtke, O. (2009). The relationship between homework time and achievement is not universal: Evidence from multilevel analyses in 40 countries. *School Effectiveness and School Improvement, 20*(4), 375–405.

Dettmers, S., Trautwein, U., Lüdtke, O., Kunter, M., & Baumert, J. (2010). Homework works if homework quality is high: Using multilevel modeling to predict the development of achievement in mathematics. *Journal of Educational Psychology, 102,* 467–482.

Dumont, H., Trautwein, U., Lüdtke, O., Neumann, M., Niggli, A., & Schnyder, I. (2012). Does parental homework involvement mediate the relationship between family background and educational outcomes? *Contemporary Educational Psychology, 37,* 55–69.

Dumont, H., Trautwein, U., Nagy, G., & Nagengast, B. (2014). Quality of parental homework involvement: Predictors and reciprocal relations with academic functioning in the reading domain. *Journal of Educational Psychology, 106,* 144–161.

Eccles, J. S. (1983). Expectancies, values, and academic choice: Origins and changes. In J. Spence (Ed.), *Achievement and achievement motivation* (pp. 87–134). San Francisco, CA: Freeman.

Eccles, J. S., & Wigfield, A. (2002). Motivational beliefs, values, and goals. *Annual Review of Psychology, 53,* 109–132.

Flunger, B., Trautwein, U., Nagengast, B., Lüdtke, O., Niggli, A., & Schnyder, I. (in press). The janus-faced nature of time spent on homework: Using latent profile analyses to predict academic achievement over a school year. *Learning and Instruction.*

Gaspard, H., Dicke, A.-L., Flunger, B., Schreier, B., Häfner, I., Trautwein, U., & Nagengast, B. (in press). More value through greater differentiation: Gender differences in value beliefs about math. *Journal of Educational Psychology.*

Gerjets, P., Walter, C., Rosenstiel, W., Bogdan, M., & Zander, T.O. (in press). Cognitive state monitoring and the design of adaptive instruction in digital environments: Lessons learning from cognitive workload assessment using a passive brain-computer interface approach. *Frontiers in Neuroscience.*

Goetz, T., Nett, U. E., Martiny, S. E., Hall, N. C., Pekrun, R., Dettmers, S., & Trautwein, U. (2012). Students' emotions during homework: Structures, self-concept antecedents, and achievement outcomes. *Learning and Individual Differences, 22,* 225–234.

Grolnick, W. S. (2003). *The psychology of parental control: How well-meant parenting backfires.* Mahwah, NJ: Erlbaum.

Grolnick, W. S., & Slowiaczek, M. L. (1994). Parents' involvement in children's schooling: A multidimensional conceptualization and motivational model. *Child Development, 65,* 237–252.

Guthrie, J. T., Wigfield, A., & Perencevich, K. C. (Eds.). (2004). *Motivating reading comprehension: Concept-oriented reading instruction.* Mahwah, NJ: Erlbaum.

Hattie, J. (2009). *Visible learning.* London, UK: Routledge.

Hendriks, M., Luyten, H., Scheerens, J., & Sleegers, P. (2014). Meta-analyses. In J. Scheerens (Ed.), *Effectiveness of time investments in education* (pp. 55–142). Berlin, Germany: Springer.

Hidi, S., & Renninger, K. A. (2006). The four-phase model of interest development. *Educational Psychologist, 41,* 111–127.

Karweit, N., & Slavin, R. E. (1981). Measurement and modeling choices in studies of time and learning. *American Educational Research Journal, 18*(2), 157–171.

Katz, I., Eilot, K., & Nevo, N. (2014). "I'll do it later": Type of motivation, self-efficacy and homework procrastination. *Motivation and Emotion, 38,* 111–119. doi:10.1007/s11031-013-9366-1

Lodi-Smith, J. L., & Roberts, B. W. (2007). Social investment and personality: A meta-analytic analysis of the relationship of personality traits to investment in work, family, religion, and volunteerism. *Personality and Social Psychology Review, 11,* 68–86.

Lüdtke, O., Roberts, B., Trautwein, U., & Nagy, G. (2011). A random walk down university avenue: Life paths, life events, and personality trait change at the transition to university. *Journal of Personality and Social Psychology, 101,* 620–637.

Lüdtke, O., Robitzsch, A., Trautwein, U. & Kunter, M. (2009). Assessing the impact of learning environments: How to use student ratings in multilevel modelling. *Contemporary Educational Psychology, 34,* 120–131.

Mehl, M. R., & Conner, T. S. (2011). *Handbook of research methods for studying daily life.* New York, NY: Guilford.

Miller, G. F. (2012). The smartphone psychology manifesto. *Perspectives on Psychological Science, 7*(3), 221–237.

Nagengast, B., Trautwein, U., Kelava, A. & Lüdtke, O. (2013). Synergistic effects of expectancy and value on homework engagement: The case for a within-person perspective. *Multivariate Behavioral Research, 48,* 428–460.

Natriello, G., & McDill, E. L. (1986). Performance standards, student effort on homework, and academic achievement. *Sociology of Education, 59,* 18–31.

Oettingen, G., Hönig, G., & Gollwitzer, P M. (2000). Effective self-regulation of goal attainment. *International Journal of Educational Research, 33,* 705–732.

Paschal, R. A., Weinstein, T., & Walberg, H. J. (1984). The effects of homework on learning: A quantitative synthesis. *Journal of Educational Research, 78,* 97–104.

Pintrich, P. R. (2003). A motivational science perspective on the role of student motivation in learning and teaching contexts. *Journal of Educational Psychology, 95,* 667–686.

Pomerantz, E. M., & Eaton, M. M. (2001). Maternal intrusive support in the academic context: Transactional socialization process. *Developmental Psychology, 37,* 174–186.

Pomerantz, E. M., Grolnick, W. S., & Price, C. E. (2005). The role of parents in how children approach achievement. In A. J. Elliot & C. S. Dweck (Eds.), *Handbook of competence and motivation* (pp. 259–278). New York, NY: Guilford.

Pomerantz, E. M., Wang, Q., & Ng, F. F.-Y. (2005). Mothers' affect in the homework context: The importance of staying positive. *Developmental Psychology, 41,* 414–427. doi:10.1037/0012-1649.41.2.414

Roberts, B. W., & DelVecchio, W. F. (2000). The rank-order consistency of personality from childhood to old age: A quantitative review of longitudinal studies. *Psychological Bulletin, 126,* 3–25.

Roberts, B. W., Caspi, A., & Moffitt, T. (2003). Work experiences and personality development in young adulthood. *Journal of Personality and Social Psychology, 84,* 582–593.

Robins, R. W., Noftle, E. E., Trzesniewski, K. H., & Roberts, B. W. (2005). Do people know how their personality has changed? Correlates of perceived and actual personality change in young adulthood. *Journal of Personality, 73,* 489–521.

Scheerens, J., & Hendriks, M. (2014). State of the art of time effectiveness. In *Effectiveness of time investments in education* (pp. 7–29). Springer International.

Schmitz, B., & Skinner, E. (1993). Perceived control, effort, and academic performance: Interindividual, intraindividual, and multivariate time-series analyses. *Journal of Personality and Social Psychology, 64,* 1010–1028.

Stokes, D. E. (1997). *Pasteurs's quadrant: Basic science and technological innovation.* Washington, DC: Brookings Institution.

Trautwein, U. (2007). The homework-achievement relation reconsidered: Differentiating homework time, homework frequency, and homework effort. *Learning and Instruction, 17,* 372–388.

Trautwein, U., & Köller, O. (2003). The relationship between homework and achievement: Still much of a mystery. *Educational Psychology Review, 15*, 115–145.

Trautwein, U., & Lüdtke, O. (2007). Students' self-reported effort and time on homework in six school subjects: Between-student differences and within-student variation. *Journal of Educational Psychology, 99*, 432–444.

Trautwein, U., & Lüdtke, O. (2009). Predicting homework motivation and homework effort in six school subjects: The need to differentiate between the student and class levels. *Learning and Instruction, 19*, 243–258.

Trautwein, U., Lüdtke, O., Kastens, C., & Köller, O. (2006). Effort on homework in grades 5 through 9: Development, motivational antecedents, and the association with effort on classwork. *Child Development, 77*, 1094–1111.

Trautwein, U., Lüdtke, O., Schnyder, I., & Niggli, A. (2006). Predicting homework effort: Support for a domain-specific, multilevel homework model. *Journal of Educational Psychology, 98*, 438–456.

Trautwein, U., Niggli, A., Schnyder, I., & Lüdtke, O. (2009). Between-teacher differences in homework assignments and the development of students' homework effort, homework emotions, and achievement. *Journal of Educational Psychology, 101*, 176–189.

Trautwein, U., Schnyder, I., Niggli, A., Neumann, M., & Lüdtke, O. (2009). Chameleon effects in homework research: The homework-achievement association depends on the measures used and the level of analysis chosen. *Contemporary Educational Psychology, 34*, 77–88.

Valentine, J. C., & Cooper, H. M. (2003). *The Department of Education's What Works Clearinghouse Study Design and Implementation Device: Version 1.0.* Washington, DC: Department of Education, What Works Clearinghouse.

Vermunt, J. K., & Magidson, J. (2002). Latent class cluster analysis. *Applied Latent Class Analysis*, 89–106.

Weinert, F. E., & Helmke, A. (1995). Interclassroom differences in instructional quality and interindividual differences in cognitive development. *Educational Psychologist, 30*, 15–20.

What Works Clearinghouse. (2014). *Procedures and standards handbook, Version 3.0.* Washington, DC: Institute of Education Sciences, U.S. Department of Education.

Zimmerman, B. J., Bonner, S., & Kovach, R. (1996). *Developing self-regulated learners: Beyond achievement to self-efficacy.* Washington, DC: American Psychological Association.

CHAPTER 7

SOCIAL COGNITIVE CAREER THEORY

A Theory of Self (Efficacy) in Context

Steven D. Brown
Loyola University Chicago

Robert W. Lent
University of Maryland

Social Cognitive Career Theory (SCCT) was developed by Lent, Brown, and Hackett (1994) to provide a unifying framework for understanding, explaining, and predicting processes through which people (a) develop educational and vocational interests, (b) make and remake educational and occupational choices, and (c) achieve success and stability in educational and occupational pursuits. Two additional SCCT models have been more recently introduced—one focusing on educational and work satisfaction (Lent & Brown, 2006, 2008) and the other on career self-management (Lent & Brown, 2013). The satisfaction model incorporates core SCCT constructs to explain and predict students and workers' levels of school and work satisfaction. The self-management model, which also uses core SCCT

Self-Concept, Motivation, and Identity, pages 173–200

constructs, focuses on how people direct (or can be helped to direct) their own career and educational behavior in diverse contexts.

The interest, choice, performance, and satisfaction models focus on such *content* questions as predicting the types of educational and vocational activity domains toward which people will gravitate (e.g., whether to major in math or English, whether to become a physician or house painter) and how they achieve satisfaction and success in these domains. The career self-management model differs from the other four models by focusing on *process* questions related to how people achieve their own career and educational goals—how, for example, they make career and educational decisions (rather than what decisions they make), negotiate transitions from school to work, find jobs, pursue work and educational goals, maintain motivation, manage multiple roles, deal with career and educational setbacks, and transition from work to retirement.

From the outset, the goals of SCCT were both theoretical and practical. Theoretically, SCCT provides a series of testable propositions and models about both content and process aspects of career and educational development. Practically, SCCT offers templates for designing remedial and preventive career and educational interventions. For example, the choice model was designed to direct research on how educational and occupational choices are made under favorable circumstances as well when choices may be limited by poverty, economic realities, discrimination, and other unfavorable conditions. It was also designed to suggest how people can be helped to make more satisfying choices under both favorable and unfavorable conditions. Similarly, the more recent self-management model was intended to not only explain, for example, how people manage (for better or worse) retirement transitions but also how people can be helped to better manage such transitions or even prevent difficulties before they occur.

All SCCT models are based on Bandura's (1986, 1997) general social cognitive theory, a theory of motivation and self-regulation that has been applied to many areas of psychosocial functioning. Self-efficacy (Bandura, 1977), a central construct of social cognitive theory, has especially captured the interest of researchers and practitioners in diverse disciplines. Hackett and Betz (1981) and Betz and Hackett (1981) were the first to see the potential utility of self-efficacy in explaining various aspects of career behavior, especially women's underrepresentation in male-dominated majors and fields (e.g., STEM careers). Their investigations served to spark a great deal of subsequent work linking self-efficacy to the types of educational and occupational choices people make and other aspects of career development among diverse samples of students and workers (see Lent, 2013b).

We will first define self-efficacy more explicitly and differentiate it from other "self" constructs like self-concept and self-esteem. We will then briefly summarize meta-analytic research on the relationship of self-efficacy to key educational and career outcomes. However, the bulk of the chapter will be devoted to placing self-efficacy into two key contexts. First, we will place it in the context of other key person-oriented constructs in SCCT. The goal is to provide a fuller and more complete account of how interests are formed and revised, choices are made and remade, performance is attained and improved, satisfaction is achieved and promoted, and how people manage and can be helped to manage the routine and not-so-routine events that they encounter as they establish, maintain, and leave their careers. Second, the chapter will emphasize that self-efficacy and other key person variables also occur in another, larger context; namely, the environmental context in which one grows up and currently lives. A full understanding of educational and career behavior of any individual or group of individuals requires an understanding of the cultural, economic, and social conditions of their lives. SCCT offers testable propositions about how contextual influences may facilitate or limit the types of interests people develop, the choices they make, the levels of performance and satisfaction they attain at school and work, and their abilities to manage their own careers.

SELF-EFFICACY: WHAT IT IS, WHAT IT IS NOT, AND TO WHAT DOES IT RELATE

Although self-efficacy is not the only person-centered construct in social cognitive theory, it has clearly been the most widely researched in educational and vocational psychology. In this section, we define self-efficacy, distinguish it from other concepts of the self, and briefly summarize meta-analytic research testing SCCT's hypotheses concerning self-efficacy beliefs.

What Is Self-Efficacy?

Self-efficacy refers to people's beliefs about their capabilities to organize and execute behaviors necessary to reach particular goals or succeed in different domains of activity. Thus, one critical defining characteristic of self-efficacy is that it is domain or context specific. For example, an individual might feel very efficacious about his or her math abilities but less efficacious about his or her social skills. Or one child might feel very efficacious at academic tasks while another child may doubt his or her academic capabilities.

In addition to being context specific, self-efficacy functions as a prime motivator of human behavior. Specifically, Bandura (1986) hypothesized that self-efficacy beliefs help determine whether people will initiate (versus avoid) a given behavior, how much effort they will expend on it, how long they will sustain effort in the face of obstacles and other aversive experiences, and ultimately how well they will perform. Thus, a person who feels substantially more efficacious about his or her math than writing skills will be more likely to approach versus avoid math activities (e.g., elect to take math courses versus writing courses), put more effort into math than writing activities, and persist longer in math than writing pursuits when confronted with difficulties. As a result of choosing, practicing, and persevering at math tasks, the person will probably perform better in courses, leisure activities, and occupations that involve math than in those involving writing. Similarly, children with strong self-efficacy beliefs for a variety of academic learning activities will be more likely to engage in school work than children with weaker academic self-efficacy beliefs. They will also work harder, persist longer, and ultimately perform better in school than less academically efficacious students.

SCCT's interest development, choice, performance, and satisfaction models emphasize the motivating properties of self-efficacy beliefs. That is, SCCT hypothesizes that self-efficacy helps promote academic and career-related interests (e.g., math self-efficacy leads to math interests), choices (e.g., math self-efficacy and interest leads to math choices), and performance, persistence, and satisfaction (e.g., math self-efficacy promotes persistence and ultimately success and satisfaction at math-related activities, courses, majors, and occupations).

What Self-Efficacy Is Not

Self-efficacy has often been confused with other constructs. One common mistake is to consider self-efficacy a trait, like self-esteem, which is stable across different situations and life domains. To the contrary, self-efficacy beliefs are sets of contextualized self-beliefs that are particular to specific performance domains. Self-esteem, on the other hand, refers to general feelings of self-worth across multiple contexts. It is assessed by asking people questions about how much they like or approve of themselves in general (e.g., "On the whole, I am satisfied with myself."). By contrast, in assessing self-efficacy beliefs, people are asked how confident they are that they can perform tasks in particular performance domains (e.g., receive a B or higher in math classes). These two self-constructs differ in several ways, including globality (self-esteem) versus specificity (self-efficacy), trait (self-esteem) versus state (self-efficacy), and content (self-liking versus self-percepts concerning behavioral competencies). It is not hard to imagine, for example, that two people with similar feelings of self-worth may have very different self-efficacy beliefs in a given performance domain—one may have stronger social than musical self-efficacy beliefs, while the other may display an opposite pattern of efficacy beliefs. Scores on measures of domain-specific self-efficacy beliefs are often found to correlate weakly with measures of self-esteem. For example, Betz and Klein (1996) reported correlations between mathematics self-efficacy and self-esteem of .09 for women and .23 for men.

Self-efficacy is also sometimes confused with general self-confidence. In fact, some investigators (e.g., Sherer et al., 1982) have constructed scales to measure generalized self-efficacy beliefs (e.g., "I tend do most things well."). However, generalized self-efficacy seems to have more in common conceptually with such other decontextualized competence-oriented constructs as mastery (Pearlin & Schooler, 1978) or control (White, 1959) beliefs than with self-efficacy. Bandura has been very clear in his writings (e.g., 1986, 1997) that self-efficacy is context and domain specific and should be assessed at levels commensurate with a particular dependent variable (e.g., "I am confident I can do well on my next math test."). Consistent with Bandura, SCCT's main hypotheses about interest, choice, performance, satisfaction, and self-management distinguish domain-specific self-efficacy beliefs from more decontextualized constructs like general confidence, self-esteem, and other trait-like constructs.

Some writers also fail to distinguish between self-efficacy and self-concept. The two do tend to demonstrate more conceptual overlap when both are measured in context-specific terms (e.g., math self-efficacy and math self-concept; see Bong & Skaalvik, 2003; Marsh, Walker, & Debus, 1991) than when context-specific self-efficacy is compared with more global self-concept measures. Conceptually, the primary distinctions between the two constructs revolve around whether evaluative feelings are central to the construct and how each is operationalized. Self-concept is hypothesized to be inherently evaluative, while self-efficacy is not. Thus, for example, math self-concept involves how an individual feels about him or herself in relation to math and involves comparative judgments relative to the perceived mathematical performance of others (e.g., "How good am I at math compared to others?"). Self-efficacy, on the other hand, involves competency judgments against absolute (noncomparative) criteria (e.g., "How confident am I that I can get B or better in my math courses?"). Operationally, therefore, self-concept measures require people to make comparative judgments, while self-efficacy measures ask people to provide confidence ratings against a specified performance criterion. In addition, self-concept measures tend to focus on the *current* skills that people believe they possess, while self-efficacy refers to *prospective* judgments regarding what people can accomplish with their skills (i.e., it involves beliefs about how well people can organize and deploy their skills to achieve particular objectives); that is, "What skills I have" versus "What I can do with them."

Empirically, several investigators have found that self-efficacy and self-concept for various performance domains are empirically distinguishable (e.g., Pajares & Schunk, 2002), though this has not been a universal finding. Both self-efficacy and domain-specific self-concept are also hypothesized to relate to performance in commensurate performance domains. Although the evidence clearly supports these hypotheses, evidence for the comparative predictive powers of self-efficacy and self-concept is mixed (e.g., Bong, Cho, Ahn, & Kim, 2012; Pajares & Miller, 1994; Pietsch, Walker, & Chapman, 2003).

We would suggest that future research might profit by testing hypotheses and models about how these two constructs may jointly predict achievement as well as other important outcomes. Brown, Lent, and Gore (2000), for example, found that self-efficacy mediated (explained) the relationships between comparative ability judgments in RIASEC domains (Holland, 1997) and interests in corresponding domains. In other words, comparative ability judgments ("How do I compare to my peers.") informed self-efficacy beliefs, which in turn related (as hypothesized by SCCT) to domain-specific interests. It therefore may be that self-concept can function as a source of efficacy information in various performance domains, influencing interest, persistence, and performance via its effect on domain-specific competence expectations.

Such a hypothesis is also consistent with Eccles's expectancy-value theory of task-choice. For example, Eccles (2009) hypothesized that ability self-concepts represent one source of information regarding people's expectations of success in various performance domains. It is then people's expectations of success that relate to the types of tasks that they undertake and the choices they make. Parenthetically, expectations of success seem to be quite similar to self-efficacy beliefs in Eccles's model, and Eccles even uses research on self-efficacy beliefs (e.g., Betz & Hackett, 1986) to support the hypothesized links between expectations of success and choice activities (see Eccles, 2009).

Finally, some writers (e.g., Heggestad & Kanfer, 2005) have suggested that self-efficacy beliefs are simply self-reported proxies for more objectively measured skills (i.e., they are redundant constructs), while others (e.g., Gottfredson, 2005; Lubinski, 2010) think that social cognitive theory ignores abilities altogether. To the contrary, SCCT neither ignores the influence of abilities nor sees self-efficacy as a simple proxy for abilities. Rather, abilities (in the form of objectively measured competencies or past performance accomplishments) are hypothesized to have both direct and indirect effects (via self-efficacy beliefs) on domain-specific performance. The hypothesized direct effect of ability on performance (which is often overlooked by some writers) clearly acknowledges the key role of ability and implies that self-efficacy is not merely a substitute for ability. The indirect effect represents ability as an important source of self-efficacy information. Persons with higher abilities or more frequent performance accomplishments in a domain may outperform those of lower ability both because they possess requisite skills *and* because they develop stronger and more robust self-efficacy beliefs in that domain. Self-efficacy adds value by enabling people to organize and deploy their skills more effectively.

The relationship of abilities and accomplishments to self-efficacy beliefs is however not perfect because people need to attend to, interpret, encode, and recall information relevant to past accomplishments and ability indicators. Thus, two people with equal abilities in an area may not process their experiences in the same way—one may discount a success experience by attributing it to an external cause, while the other may accurately encode it as a success experience. As a result, the one person will hold weaker efficacy percepts in that performance domain than will the other. The first individual may, as a result, express less interest, set less-challenging goals, give up more easily, and report less satisfaction in a particular performance domain than the other person, despite having equal levels of measured ability in that domain.

In addition to prior performance accomplishments, self-efficacy beliefs are influenced by vicarious experiences, social persuasion, and physiological and affective states. For example, self-efficacy may be bolstered by exposing children to demographically similar models who have experienced success in a given performance domain. Social interactions with others that reinforce performance accomplishments will tend to raise self-efficacy beliefs, while belittlement will lower them. Likewise, the experience of positive (or negative) affect while engaged in a given performance task will likely strengthen (or weaken) appraisals of self-efficacy.

Research tends to support the view that self-efficacy plays a unique role relative to abilities in educational and career development. For example, self-efficacy beliefs have been shown to account for unique variance in work and school performance over and above that accounted for by objective measures of ability and past performance (Brown, Lent, Telander, & Tramayne, 2011; Brown et al., 2008). The same two investigations (Brown et al., 2011, 2008) have also shown that self-efficacy partially mediated the relation of abilities to school and work performance. Self-efficacy has also been shown to fully mediate the relationship of abilities to work and school interests (Lent et al., 1994). These findings suggest that self-efficacy may aid the translation of abilities into performance and subsume the effect of abilities on interests. For instance, an individual with objectively strong ability in a given domain may not develop interests in that domain unless he or she develops correspondingly favorable efficacy beliefs.

To What Does Self-Efficacy Relate?

Self-efficacy is one of several core constructs in all SCCT models. When measured in context-specific ways, self-efficacy is hypothesized to relate, in the interest and choice models, to the types of interests people develop in different educational and occupational domains and to the specific educational and occupational goals (e.g., choices) they set for themselves. In the performance and satisfaction models, self-efficacy is hypothesized to relate to educational and occupational performance and persistence as well as to satisfaction in different educational and occupational pursuits. The most recent career self-management model hypothesizes that the exercise of different career-self-management tasks (e.g., making a career decision) is facilitated by task-specific self-efficacy beliefs (e.g., career decision-making self-efficacy beliefs).

Several meta-analyses, primarily involving adolescents and young adults, have tested SCCT's hypotheses about the relations of self-efficacy beliefs to educational and occupational interests and choices (Lent et al., 1994; Rottinghaus, Larson, & Borgen, 2003). Bivariate effect-size estimates (correlations) between self-efficacy beliefs and interests have ranged from .52 (Lent et al., 1994) to .59 (Rottinghaus et al., 2003), while the interest-choice correlation was reported to be .60 in one meta-analysis (Lent et al., 1994). Although these relationships are substantial when considered at the bivariate-level, they become reduced when all core SCCT variables are included (e.g., Sheu et al., 2010).

Meta-analyses of the relationships between self-efficacy beliefs and performance outcomes have found that self-efficacy relates to both educational (Multon, Brown, & Lent, 1991) and occupational (Sardi & Robertson, 1993; Stajkovic & Luthans, 1998) performance and persistence indicators, both at the bivariate and multivariate levels (i.e., when additional SCCT variables are modeled meta-analytically; Brown et al., 2011, 2008). Finally, although predating the appearance of the new SCCT career management model (Lent & Brown, 2013), at least two meta-analyses have provided data relevant to it. Choi et al. (2012) reported strong (inverse) meta-analytic relations between career decision-making self-efficacy beliefs and career indecision. Kanfer, Wanberg, and Kantrowitz (2001) offered meta-analytic evidence for bivariate relationships between job-search self-efficacy beliefs and job-search outcomes (e.g., employment status, time to employment, number of job offers).

The results of these meta-analyses provide strong support for the relationships of self-efficacy beliefs to educational and vocational interests, choice, performance, and persistence. However, as noted, meta-analyses at the bivariate level provide somewhat inflated estimates of the influence self-efficacy beliefs because they do not account for the variance that self-efficacy shares with other key SCCT person and contextual variables. Research has also suggested that the more complete SCCT models provide a more nuanced and useful lens through which to view the interest development, choice making, performance, satisfaction, and career management processes. These models emphasize the interplay between self-efficacy and the other social cognitive predictors. We will turn next to the fuller models, which collectively constitute Social Cognitive Career Theory.

SOCIAL COGNITIVE CAREER THEORY

In our full SCCT models, self-efficacy is seen as operating in tandem with several other person, behavioral, and contextual variables. Among its other cognitive-person variables, SCCT highlights the roles of *outcome expectations* and *goals* in addition to self-efficacy beliefs. Outcome expectations refer to persons' beliefs about the consequences (positive, negative, or neutral) of performing a particular behavior. Outcome expectations differ from self-efficacy beliefs in that self-efficacy beliefs focus on perceived capabilities ("Can I succeed in a STEM major?"), while outcome expectations refer to perceived consequences ("What will happen if I declare a STEM major?"). For example, measures of self-efficacy in STEM fields ask about confidence in completing tasks necessary for STEM major success (e.g., earning a B or better in required science courses), while measures of outcome expectations ask about potential positive and negative outcomes of STEM major involvement (e.g., "My family will be proud of me, I will experience discrimination due to my sex."). Outcome expectations can be extrinsic (e.g., receipt of material rewards), intrinsic (e.g., experience of flow or absorption in the task itself), social (e.g., approval from others), or self-evaluative (e.g., experiencing pride). Parenthetically, Eccles's (2009) notion of "subjective task value" bears a resemblance to outcome expectations but also includes additional elements, like interests. SCCT distinguishes between outcome expectations and interests, and findings indicate that outcome expectations are very useful predictors of interests (e.g., Sheu et al., 2010).

Outcome expectations are hypothesized by Bandura (1986, 1997) to have the same sorts of motivational properties as self-efficacy beliefs. That is, positive outcome expectations will be associated with approach behavior, while negative outcome expectations will be associated with avoidance behavior. Positive outcome expectations are also associated with effort expenditure and persistence in a specific performance domain. Thus, persons with more positive outcome expectations about pursuing a STEM major will be more likely to declare majors in STEM fields, put effort into their majors, and persist in them longer than those with less positive or more negative outcome expectations.

Although the motivational properties of self-efficacy beliefs and outcome expectations are similar, the two constructs are not redundant. Rather, a consideration of the two in tandem allows for greater precision in predicting approach versus avoidance behavior, effort, persistence, and performance. Approach behavior is facilitated by strong and robust efficacy beliefs and positive outcome expectations. To use STEM majors as an example again, students will be more likely to declare majors in STEM fields if they *both* believe in their capabilities *and* envision positive extrinsic, intrinsic, social, and self-evaluative outcomes associated with majoring in STEM fields. Self-efficacy is not as likely to be associated with approach behavior (e.g., declaring a STEM major) in the presence of negative or neutral outcome expectations. Likewise, positive outcome expectations are less likely to be associated with approach behavior (declaring a STEM major) for people who do not see themselves as sufficiently capable. Finally, self-efficacy is hypothesized to relate to outcome expectations, especially in situations where outcomes are closely tied to performance (i.e., strong self-efficacy is likely to lead to positive outcome expectations in a particular performance context).

Goals refers to one's intentions to engage in a particular activity or to affect a particular outcome. It is partly through setting personal goals that people organize, guide, and sustain their own behavior, even in the absence of external rewards or under less-than-supportive conditions.

According to the SCCT interest and choice models, persons with strong self-efficacy beliefs and positive outcome expectations in a performance domain will not only develop interests in that area, they are also likely to develop goals for further activity involvement. Goals then facilitate activity involvement. Goals are important in the other SCCT models as well. Setting challenging work or educational goals (as a result of self-efficacy beliefs, outcome expectations, and abilities) can facilitate performance. Persons are also more likely to engage in career self-management tasks, such as retirement planning, to the extent that they possess favorable self-efficacy beliefs and outcome expectations and set specific goals relevant to these tasks.

Although self-efficacy beliefs, outcome expectations, and personal goals form the basic building blocks of SCCT, they do not operate in a vacuum. Rather, they interact with other types of person inputs (e.g., gender, race, traits) and contextual variables (e.g., family socioeconomic status, quality of education, experiences of discrimination) to influence educational and career development. SCCT integrates these additional person and contextual variables with self-efficacy beliefs, outcome expectations, and personal goals to predict the (a) types of interests people develop and the choices they make, (b) the levels of performance and satisfaction that they attain in various educational and occupational domains, and (c) how they manage their own educational and career development.

SCCT Interest and Choice Models

Figure 7.1 integrates SCCT's interest and choice models into a single schematic. Home, educational, and community environments in which

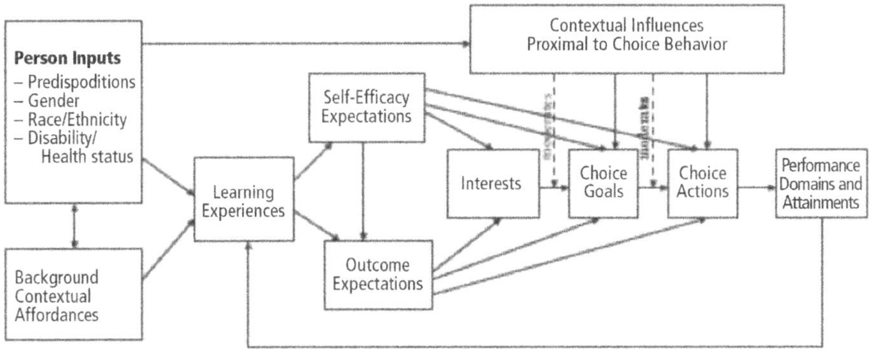

Figure 7.1 Model of person, contextual, and experiential factors affecting career-related choice behavior. *Note:* Direct relations between variables are indicated with solid lines; moderator effects (where a given variable strengthens or weakens the relations between two other variables) are shown with dashed lines. Copyright 1993 by R. W. Lent, S. D. Brown, and G. Hackett. Reprinted with permission.

children and adolescents live expose them to a variety of different activities. Young people are selectively encouraged or discouraged by parents, teachers, peers, and other socialization agents to pursue and do well in certain activities that are available to them. Some of the activities to which they are exposed are linked to "social address" factors, such as gender and socioeconomic conditions. By approaching (e.g., setting goals) and practicing different activities and by receiving ongoing positive and negative feedback, children and adolescents refine their skills, develop performance standards, and develop self-efficacy beliefs and outcome expectations regarding different tasks and domains of behavior.

According to SCCT's interest model, self-efficacy and outcome expectations regarding different activity domains (e.g., math, science, baseball, music) are primary predictors of educational and career interests (patterns of likes, dislikes, and indifferences to career-relevant tasks). Thus, interest in an activity domain is likely to blossom when people view themselves as competent (self-efficacious) in the domain and anticipate that entering and performing in that domain will produce positive outcomes (outcome expectations). On the other hand, people are likely to develop disinterest in, or even an aversion to, a domain in which they doubt their efficacy and expect to receive negative outcomes.

Direct and vicarious experiences affect self-efficacy beliefs, outcome expectation, and therefore interests over the course of childhood and adolescence in an ongoing feedback loop. Interests become increasingly stabilized (Low, Yoon, Roberts, & Rounds, 2005) through adolescence and are used prior to work entry to identify subsequent educational and career paths to pursue. SCCT assumes that interest stability is largely a function of crystallizing self-efficacy beliefs and outcome expectations, yet interests are not perfectly stable. SCCT, thus, further assumes that when interest shifts occur, they are due to changing self-efficacy beliefs or outcome expectations occasioned by compelling new educational, work, volunteer, or leisure experiences.

In summary, the SCCT interest and choice models hypothesize that interests derive from self-efficacy beliefs and outcome expectations and that people often attempt to select occupations on the basis of their interests. However, the interests they develop and the choices they make are influenced by additional person and contextual influences. For example, as mentioned earlier, one important person input is ability, but SCCT hypothesizes that ability influences interests only indirectly via its influence on self-efficacy beliefs and outcome expectations. In other words, substantial ability in an educational or work domain will not translate into interests in that domain in the absence of efficacy beliefs and positive outcome expectations.

Self-efficacy beliefs, outcome expectations, interests, and choices are also influenced by the context in which they develop (or fail to develop). These contextual influences are distal and proximal to the enactment of an educational or occupational choice. Distally, positive (e.g., having opportunities for activity involvement, supportive others) and negative contextual influences (e.g., limited opportunities or nonsupportive others) shape the learning experiences that are critical for self-efficacy belief and outcome expectation development. Thus, a math-talented woman will be less likely to develop an interest in math-related activities if she lives in an environment where opportunities (and supports) for math involvement are limited than if her environment provides rich opportunities for curricular and extracurricular math involvement. Similarly, she will be less likely to develop an interest in math if her environment (at home, school, or in the larger society) downplays women's abilities to succeed at math. In both cases, her failure to develop math interests is a function of the influence of the contextual variables that undergird self-efficacy beliefs and outcome expectations.

Proximally, positive and negative contextual influences affect persons' abilities to translate interests into goals and goals into actions (choices). That is, they can function as moderators of the relations between interests and goals and between goals and actions. These relationships will be stronger when people have sufficient material and social contextual resources than if their resources are more meager or they experience other barriers (e.g., family disapproval) that limit their abilities to turn interests into real choices. In the latter case, self-efficacy and outcome expectations will override interests in occupational or educational choices (e.g., people will enter occupations which they think they can do and that will bring a modicum of what they need, even if the options they select are not at all interesting to them).

Race and ethnicity, gender, socioeconomic status, sexual orientation, and other person variables (e.g., ability and personality) are hypothesized in the SCCT interest and choice models to influence interests and choices via the types of learning experiences to which people of different races, genders, socioeconomic statuses, sexual orientations, abilities, and personalities are exposed. For example, living in poverty may limit the types of efficacy- and outcome-expectation-building experiences to which children and adolescents are exposed. Children and adolescents living in depressed economic conditions may then not develop interests in educational and occupational endeavors at which they might otherwise succeed and find satisfaction. Poverty, as a proximal decision-making condition, also limits people's abilities to turn their interests into real choices.

SCCT Performance and Satisfaction Models

Performance Model

SCCT's performance model focuses on the performance and persistence predictions derived from Bandura's (1986, 1997) social cognitive theory of motivation and self-regulation (the interest and choice models are derived primarily from the hypothesized behavioral initiation aspects of the theory). As shown in Figure 7.2, SCCT hypothesizes that educational and vocational performance and persistence involve an interplay among people's abilities, self-efficacy beliefs, outcome expectations, and performance goals. Specifically, ability, as assessed by indicators of aptitude, achievement, and past performance, affects performance attainments and persistence in two ways: directly via the task knowledge and performance strategies that people develop, and indirectly by informing self-efficacy and outcome expectations.

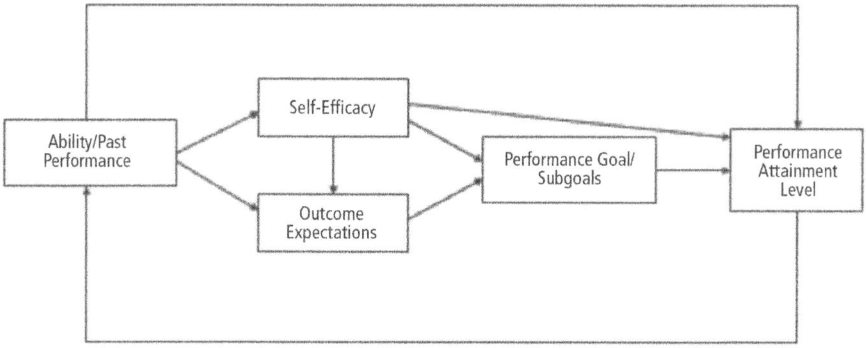

Figure 7.2 Model of task performance. Copyright 1993 by R. W. Lent, S. D. Brown, and G. Hackett. Reprinted with permission.

In other words, people base their self-efficacy and outcome expectations in part on perceptions of the skills that they currently possess as well as on how they have performed in the past in domain-relevant situations. Self-efficacy and outcome expectations then influence the levels of goals that people set for their educational and occupational performance in relevant domains. Together, abilities, self-efficacy beliefs, outcome expectations, and goals predict performance.

Using STEM-major performance again as an example, SCCT predicts that the STEM-related abilities that people possess and that were cultivated via earlier experiences both help them learn what is required to perform adequately in their chosen STEM major *and* inform their self-efficacy beliefs and outcome expectations. Strong self-efficacy beliefs and positive outcome expectations lead to more challenging personal performance goals. Performance (e.g., grades) in a STEM major is then the result of cultivated talents, self-efficacy beliefs, outcome expectations, and challenging goals. Self-efficacy influences (has a direct effect on) this process in several ways in addition to promoting more challenging performance goals. First, self-efficacy beliefs are associated with effort and persistence in the face of difficulties. Thus, STEM majors with higher versus lower self-efficacy beliefs will work harder to succeed and persist longer (hence the persistence prediction of SCCT) in the face of obstacles. Second, self-efficacy helps workers and students to organize, orchestrate, and make the greatest use of their talents.

We want to reemphasize that SCCT's performance model does not ignore the important role that abilities play in promoting work and academic performance. To the contrary, self-efficacy is seen as complementing, not substituting for, objectively measured ability. Complex performances draw on requisite abilities yet are also aided by an optimistic sense of self-efficacy. The interplay among abilities, self-efficacy beliefs, outcome expectations, and goals helps explain why individuals with similar levels of objective abilities often display achievements that vary widely in quality. Capable individuals who doubt their capabilities may, for example, be less likely to use their skills effectively or to remain focused when problems occur.

Although it may be tempting to conclude that higher self-efficacy is always a good thing, the effects of self-efficacy seem to be maximized when self-efficacy is somewhat higher than, but reasonably congruent with, current measured capabilities. Such slight overconfidence serves to promote optimum skill use and motivation for further skill development. On the other hand, self-efficacy that greatly exceeds current capabilities may motivate people to engage in work and educational activities for which they are ill-prepared, risking failure and discouragement. Underestimating what one is capable of accomplishing may also interfere with performance by promoting less persistence, lower performance goals, and avoidance of realistic challenges.

Satisfaction Model

As shown in Figure 7.3, work and educational satisfaction (i.e., the degree to which one is happy with one's work or school environment) is influenced by the same core SCCT variables that appear in the other models (Lent & Brown, 2006, 2008). Specifically, SCCT hypothesizes that people are likely to be satisfied with their work and school environments to the extent that they are involved in activities that they value (outcome expectations), see themselves as making progress at personally relevant goals (goal progress), possess confidence at performing necessary tasks and achieving goals (self-efficacy), and have access to resources and supports in their environments for promoting self-efficacy and aiding in their goal pursuits.

In addition, satisfaction can be influenced by people's personalities and the conditions in which they work. Certain personality dispositions (e.g., positive and negative affect) have been found to be consistently, but modestly, related to job satisfaction (e.g., Bowling, Eschleman, & Wang, 2010). Certain working conditions (e.g., work overload, supervisor and organizational support, interpersonal harassment, workplace incivility) have also been found to be reliably related to work satisfaction (e.g., Lim & Cortina, 2005; Rhoades & Eisenberger, 2002). As we will discuss later, although personality traits and dispositions are clearly linked to workers and students' satisfaction, SCCT emphasizes potentially malleable features of the person (e.g., self-efficacy beliefs) and environment (e.g., supervisor support) that can be used to design counseling and preventive interventions.

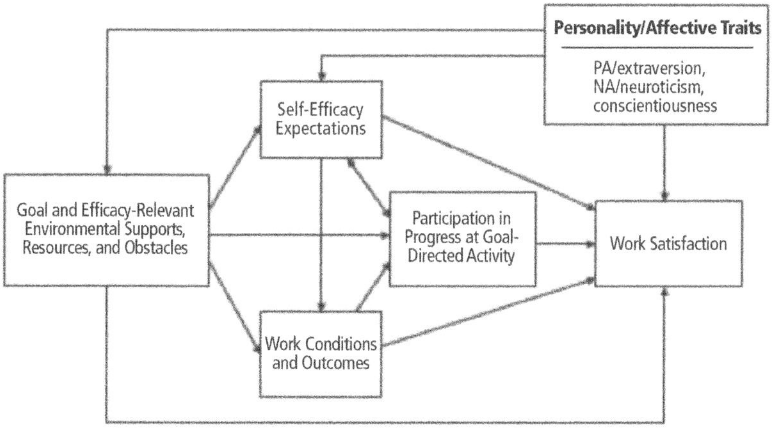

Figure 7.3 A social cognitive model of work satisfaction. From Lent and Brown (2008, p. 10). Adapted with permission.

SCCT Self-Management Model

The newest SCCT model (Lent & Brown, 2013) focuses on explaining and predicting the processes by which people can manage their own educational and career development in normal as well as in trying times. It is also intended, like all SCCT models, to provide a template for counseling and preventive interventions. It focuses on the types of tasks that seem central to optimum career and educational development and to managing career and educational transitions and crises. Lent and Brown (2013) presented a taxonomy of potentially important career and educational development tasks (see p. 560, Table 1). Examples include developing decision-making and employability skills, making relevant educational and career decisions, searching for employment, managing multiple roles and work-family-life conflict, managing school-to-work and work-to-retirement transitions, and dealing with negative school and work events such as job layoff or harassment.

The self-management model relies on the core SCCT person and contextual variables to explain and predict the conditions under which people will engage in these (and other) career self-management tasks. For example, it is predicted that job-search behavior will be facilitated when people have (or can be helped to develop) strong job-search self-efficacy beliefs, goals for job-search engagement, supports from others for their job-search efforts (as well as few job-search barriers), and beliefs that their efforts will be worth it or lead to positive outcomes (job-search outcome expectations). Certain personality dispositions also facilitate task initiation and effort, depending on the career self-management task. For example, both conscientiousness and extraversion are implicated in the job-search process, while openness to experience may be important to managing job or career changes (see Brown & Hirschi, 2013).

As in all SCCT models, the core person (as well as personality) variables do not operate in a vacuum. Rather, they function in a social context that, distally, shapes the types of self-efficacy beliefs and outcome expectations that people develop and, proximally, facilitates (or deters) their abilities to execute self-management behaviors. Students living in poverty may not have the same resources in their schools as do students residing in more affluent areas, nor may they have ready access to the same types of models of successful career development. They may therefore not develop the same levels of self-efficacy for earlier career-development tasks (e.g., making career decisions) nor be as likely to see the benefit (positive outcome expectations) of engaging in assertive career self-management as do their peers living in families and communities with more resources and models.

Viewed as proximal to career exploration and decision-making, contextual influences may facilitate or hinder persons' abilities to translate their self-efficacy beliefs and outcome expectations into career self-management goals or actions. Students living in poverty may, for example, feel that they have the skills to make good career decisions, see the benefits of working in a career that they like, and establish goals to learn more about careers. However, their abilities to turn these goals into actions may be hindered if their school and community lack resources that would facilitate career exploration and decision-making. Thus, contextual supports and barriers may influence the types of career self-management-efficacy beliefs and outcome expectations that persons develop as well as their ability to pursue their self-management goals. We next turn to a discussion of research (primarily meta-analytic) on the SCCT models. We finish by discussing counseling and preventive interventions.

RESEARCH ON SCCT

SCCT's original interest, choice, and performance models (Lent et al., 1994) have attracted a good deal of research over the past 20 years. This research has generally focused on testing various model hypotheses and on exploring the models' validity in diverse populations. In this section, we will first discuss meta-analytic evidence on the empirical viability of the interest, choice, and performance models. We will then discuss research exploring the cross-cultural validity of the models and their hypotheses. We will finish by briefly summarizing research on the newer satisfaction and self-management models.

Meta-Analytic Findings

Sufficient research had accrued on the interest, choice, and performance models (or variables within the models) by the mid-2000s to yield studies exploring the fit of the models to meta-analytically derived data. For example, Sheu et al. (2010) found substantial fit for the interest and choice models. Results revealed that self-efficacy and outcome expectations related to interests across each of the six Holland (1997) RIASEC themes, and interests along with self-efficacy and outcome expectations were substantially related to choice goals. The standardized parameter estimates of all paths in the models were lower than the bivariate relations found in prior meta-analyses. These however provide more-accurate estimates of the unique predictive contribution of each SCCT core variable in that the variance they share with other variables in the model has been removed. For example, standardized path estimates were .43, .33, and .35 for the relations, respectively, between self-efficacy and interest, outcome expectations and interest, and interest and choice goals within the Investigative occupational theme. Findings from this meta-analysis also suggested that rather than producing direct paths to choice goals, the primary role of contextual supports and barriers was to strengthen or weaken self-efficacy beliefs and outcome expectations that in turn promote interest and choices.

Two meta-analytic tests of the performance model in educational (Brown et al., 2008) and work (Brown et al., 2011) contexts have largely supported performance-model predictions, although performance goals explained unique variance beyond ability and self-efficacy only in predicting educational persistence. Consistent with SCCT performance hypotheses, indicators of ability and past performance success were linked to academic and work performance both directly and indirectly via self-efficacy beliefs. However, ability and past performance indicators were linked to educational persistence only indirectly through self-efficacy.

Collectively, these meta-analyses are consistent with theoretical hypotheses derived from the SCCT interest and choice models that (a) self-efficacy and outcome expectations, when measured in a domain-specific manner, are good predictors of interests; (b) self-efficacy and outcome expectations predict career-related choices both directly and indirectly via their influences on interests; and (c) contextual supports and barriers promote (supports) or hinder (barriers) choices via their linkages to self-efficacy beliefs and outcome expectations. Meta-analyses of performance-model predictions suggest that educational and work success (performance and persistence) are enabled both by abilities and self-efficacy, which can help people organize their skills and persist despite setbacks. The unique role of goals relative to performance and persistence is unclear from these meta-analyses, but other research has suggested that goal challenge does consistently relate to performance, especially in work contexts (e.g., Locke & Latham, 2002).

Research With Diverse Populations

SCCT was designed to aid in the understanding of career and educational development of a diverse array of students and workers, taking into account such factors as race/ethnicity, sexual orientation, gender, socioeconomic status, age, and disability status. Much research has examined SCCT variables in relation to gender and race/ethnicity. Recent attention has also focused on the potential applicability of SCCT models to understanding the career and educational behavior of LGBTQ workers and to exploring the role of socioeconomic status in interest development and choice-making.

Beginning with Betz and Hackett's (1981) study of the role of self-efficacy beliefs in explaining women's underrepresentation in traditionally male occupations, research has clearly shown the applicability of SCCT to explaining the interest and choice processes of both men and women. For example, Williams and Subich (2006) explored how learning experiences inform self-efficacy belief development. They found that men and women reported having differential exposure to efficacy-building information in gender-typed domains (e.g., women reported more social-type and men reported more investigative-type learning experiences). Such findings suggest, as hypothesized by SCCT's interest and choice models, that gender differences in occupational membership may be partly due to gender-based learning experiences that give rise to self-efficacy, outcome expectations, and ultimately interests and choices.

The SCCT interest, choice, and performance models have also been examined in relation to the underrepresentation of women and people of color in STEM fields (Byars-Winston, Estrada, Howard, Davis, & Zalapa, 2010; Byars-Winston & Fouad, 2008: Hackett, Betz, Casas, & Rocha-Singh, 1992). Other studies have used SCCT to explain the interests and choices of student groups that are quite diverse in terms of race/ethnicity, social class, and geographical region (Lent & Sheu, 2010). SCCT has also been extended to the study of persons with disabilities (Lent, Morrison, & Ezeofor, 2014), lesbian and gay workers (Morrow, Gore, & Campbell, 1996; Prince, 2013), and survivors of domestic violence (Chronister & McWhirter, 2006). Finally, SCCT hypotheses and models have been found to be viable in emerging cross-cultural and cross-national tests (Lent & Sheu, 2010; Lindley, 2006).

Research on the Satisfaction and Self-Management Models

The new SCCT self-management model is just beginning to generate research directly relevant to its predictions, while the satisfaction model has stimulated a good deal of recent research, both in the United States (Duffy & Lent, 2009; Lent et al., 2005; Lent, Singley, Sheu, Schmidt, & Schmidt, 2007) and internationally (Lent et al., 2011; Lent, Taveria, Sheu, & Singley, 2009; Verbruggen & Sels, 2010). Although the model has generally been shown to fit the data well in all samples, support has not been found consistently for all hypothesized paths in the model. For example, the predicted relationships of outcome expectations to goal progress and satisfaction were not supported in some studies (e.g., Lent et al., 2005). The most consistent findings across studies seems to be the role of self-efficacy beliefs, positive affectivity, and environmental supports in predicting domain satisfaction, either directly or indirectly via goal progress. The findings concerning the roles of positive affectivity and environmental (e.g., organizational) support on job satisfaction echo findings from the industrial/organizational literatures (e.g., Bowling et al., 2010; Rhoades & Eisenberger, 2002). The fact that perceptions of self-efficacy for work tasks and goal progress also seem to be related to satisfaction outcomes in a replicable manner is consistent with SCCT predictions and also suggests other avenues through which academic and job satisfaction might be promoted.

APPLICATIONS OF SCCT

In an ideal world, people would arrive at late adolescence with (a) an understanding of the broad array of occupations available in contemporary society; (b) a clear idea of their interests, values, and talents, and of vocational options that would fit these self-attributes; (c) goals to implement some of their preferred options; (d) adequate skills to make decisions, set goals, and manage goal pursuit; (e) ample supports and resources in relation to their goals; and (f) minimal goal-related barriers. Unfortunately, most of us do not grow up or live in such an ideal world. Rather, our experiences may cause problems in any or all of these areas, which may hamper our abilities at occupational-choice making and implementation. SCCT was designed to aid in the development of interventions to promote more satisfying choices for all people, regardless of their current circumstances—in effect, to promote people's abilities to take at least some control over their educational and occupational development. Although a full-scale discussion of SCCT's applied implications is beyond the scope of this chapter, we highlight a few targets for SCCT-developed interventions designed to promote greater agency in the choice-making process. We then discuss the intervention implications of the performance, satisfaction, and self-management models.

Promoting Educational and Occupational Choices

In terms of its general goals, SCCT-based counseling has much in common with approaches developed from other perspectives (e.g., Dawis & Lofquist, 1984; Holland, 1997). That is, SCCT aims to help persons identify and then select from an array of occupations that correspond reasonably well with important aspects of their work personalities (e.g., interests, values, abilities). However, many people are blocked in these efforts because their work personalities are not well developed (e.g., they have low flat interest profiles) or because they feel stifled by a restricted range of career options. Counselors working from an SCCT perspective would explore the contextual influences and social cognitive processes that may underlie such choice problems in order to expand clients' career options. There are several possibilities, including increasing knowledge of the occupational world, expanding choice options, coping with barriers and building supports, and developing goal setting and self-regulations skills.

Increasing Knowledge of the Occupational World

Many people, especially those living in poverty, have limited direct exposure to the occupational world. They may have access to a limited range of work role models in their immediate environments, few opportunities to experience different types of work, and be exposed to the occupational world primarily via stereotypical media depictions of work. Such people may feel their occupational possibilities are constricted simply because they do not know enough about the variety of occupational options that might be available to them. Thus, it is important to help people gain a better understanding of available work options and how they may fit with their interests, values, and talents. Ironically, we have found standardized interest inventories (e.g., Strong Interest Inventory) to be quite useful for many persons (e.g., the poor and underresourced) whom certain writers view as poor candidates for traditional methods of counseling (e.g., Blustein, 2006). We have found such inventories to be useful because they generate occupational possibilities that people may not even know exist.

Expanding Choice Options

In addition to having a limited exposure to the occupational world, many people may have prematurely ruled out potentially viable occupational options because of inaccurate self-efficacy beliefs or outcome expectations (e.g., they may believe, erroneously, that they do not have the skills to perform effectively in a given occupation or that the occupation does not offer the working conditions or other outcomes that they value). In such cases, SCCT suggests the value of revisiting previously discarded possibilities and considering the reasons they have been discarded. Brown and Lent (1996, 2005) describe some strategies that can be used to facilitate the reconsideration of such discarded occupations.

Coping with Barriers and Building Supports

A key assumption of SCCT's choice model is that people are more likely to implement a choice (i.e., to translate their goals into actions) if they perceive that their preferred options will be accompanied by minimal barriers and ample supports. Conversely, people who expect, for example, that significant others will discourage their choice or that they will not be able to access sufficient financial support to pursue their choice, may be less willing and able to follow through with their goals. Brown and Lent (1996, 2005) also discuss strategies that can be used to help people identify, cope with, and overcome barriers as well as to build support for their plans.

Learning Goal-Setting and Self-Regulation Skills

In addition to the presence of barriers and a lack of support, another important factor that might impede people's ability to translate their interests into actions is how they frame their goals. For example, larger, ultimate goals are more likely to be enacted if they are clear, specific, divided into manageable subgoals (e.g., taking preparatory courses, applying to educational programs), stated publically, and held with strong commitment (Bandura, 1986). A meta-analysis of career intervention research (Brown & Ryan Krane, 2000) suggested that putting goals in writing may also be particularly important in pursuing career goals. People can therefore be encouraged to articulate goals, frame them in facilitative (e.g., clear, specific, and proximal) ways, outline specific steps and resources needed to implement their goals, and develop backup plans in order to remain flexible and prepared for unforeseen circumstances (Lent, 2013a).

Facilitating Work Performance

SCCT offers several implications for promoting academic and work performance. The basic hypotheses of SCCT's performance model suggest that self-efficacy beliefs can facilitate performance in a given career domain as long as the individual possesses at least minimally adequate levels of skills required in that domain. Thus, an individual can display less-than-adequate performance because his or her skills and abilities do not match the skill or ability requirements of the job or because of unrealistically low or high self-efficacy beliefs. Those with adequate abilities who underestimate their self-efficacy will likely set low goals for their performance, avoid challenging work or school tasks, and give up quickly when confronted with difficulties. On the other hand, those with unrealistically high self-efficacy beliefs will likely set goals and engage in work or educational tasks that are beyond their current capabilities.

Efforts to improve work or educational performance then depend on whether there is a discrepancy between self-efficacy beliefs and more objective indicators of ability. When self-efficacy is underestimated, efforts can be directed at building self-efficacy via modeling, providing social persuasion and support, setting manageable performance goals, or where relevant, managing debilitative performance anxiety. When self-efficacy is overestimated or when skills are lacking, intervention can focus on skill-building activities. If the skill deficit is very large, the work or educational environment is unwilling to support remediation, or the individual is unwilling to engage in skill-building efforts, then educational or career-change counseling can be offered.

Promoting Work Satisfaction

The central variables of SCCT's satisfaction model could be used to fashion interventions to promote worker or student satisfaction. SCCT-based strategies would focus on the relatively malleable aspects of the person and his or her work or school environment. Examples include helping persons access desired working conditions, activities, or reinforcers (e.g., via job redesign or skill updating); setting and making progress toward valued goals; marshalling needed supports and resources for goal pursuit; enhancing task and goal-related self-efficacy; engaging in self-advocacy (e.g., dealing with uncivil or harassing working conditions); and refining skills (e.g., time management) required for work or educational success. Research on the SCCT satisfaction model as well as research from organizational psychology has clearly implicated the lack of supervisor or organizational support as a primary source of dissatisfaction for many workers. Thus, efforts to create more caring and cohesive work environments may be a useful pathway for promoting greater satisfaction among workers. Such efforts might focus on supervisory support, fair company policies, and equal distributions of organizational rewards (Rhoades & Eisenberger, 2002).

Although focusing on the relatively modifiable aspects of work and educational satisfaction, SCCT also acknowledges that person and environment factors may limit gains in satisfaction (e.g., dispositional tendencies toward negative affectivity, nonsupportive organizational policies that are unchangeable). Where work satisfaction cannot be promoted in other ways, job or career change should be considered. Where work changes are constrained, coping and compensatory strategies might be considered, such as pursuing goal-directed activity in other domains (e.g., leisure, family, community) that offer alternative outlets for satisfaction.

Promoting Career Self-Management

The new SCCT model of career self-management (Lent & Brown, 2013) has not yet received sustained research attentions. Thus, we only tentatively offer the following strategies for promoting greater agency in career and educational development. First, the model implies that enactment of any type of career self-management behavior (e.g., career exploration, job finding, multiple-role management, retirement planning) is optimized when people possess requisite knowledge and skills for performing the behavior, along with relatively robust self-efficacy beliefs, positive outcome expectations, manageable goals, and adequate supports and minimal barriers. Interventions to facilitate self-management behaviors would begin by assessing which of these conditions may need to be addressed in order to initiate and sustain particular agentic behaviors.

Despite its remedial possibilities, we think the model's main practical value may lie in informing developmental and preventive interventions (e.g., school career education, workshops and coaching in work organizations) that can help students and workers anticipate and prepare for predictable career-development tasks by developing necessary skills and self-efficacy beliefs; promoting positive outcome expectations; setting goals; and overcoming barriers to, and building supports for, adaptive career behaviors associated with these tasks. The model might also be used to raise consciousness about events that, although less predictable, have a chance of occurring at some point during the life course (e.g., job loss, work plateauing, work-family conflict). SCCT could then be used to develop psychoeducational interventions to help students or workers prepare for these events (see Lent, 2013a).

CONCLUSION

SCCT is not a one-factor theory of self-efficacy. Rather, it is an evolving theory that places self-efficacy in the context of other cognitive-person (e.g., outcome expectations, goals) and contextual (gender, culture, supports, barriers) variables that jointly shape people's academic and occupational lives. It assumes that people can exercise (or be helped to exercise) some degree of agency in their career and educational lives despite prevailing social and economic conditions. The theory currently features four interlocking content models of career and educational interest, choice, performance, and satisfaction. The fifth and newest model (self-management) focuses on more generic, process aspects of educational and career development. While the content models have generated a great deal of research, including promising demonstrations of cross-cultural validity, the process model requires further inquiry to establish its viability and to form an empirical base for relevant interventions.

REFERENCES

Bandura, A. (1977). Self-efficacy: Toward a unifying theory of behavioral change. *Psychological Review, 84,* 191–215.

Bandura, A. (1986). *Social foundations of thought and action: A social cognitive theory.* Englewood Cliffs, NJ: Prentice-Hall.

Bandura, A. (1997). *Self-efficacy: The exercise of control.* New York, NY: Freeman.

Betz, N. E., & Hackett, G. (1981). The relationship of career-related self-efficacy expectations to perceived options in college women and men. *Journal of Counseling Psychology, 28,* 399–410.

Betz, N. E., & Hackett, G. (1986). Applications of self-efficacy theory to understanding career choice behavior. *Journal of Social and Clinical Psychology, 4,* 279–289.

Betz, N. A., & Klein, K. L. (1996). Relationships among measures of career self-efficacy, generalized self-efficacy, and global self-esteem. *Journal of Career Assessment, 4,* 285–298.

Blustein, D. L. (2006). *The psychology of working: A new perspective for career development, counseling, and public policy.* Mahwah, NJ: Erlbaum.

Bong, M., Cho, C., Ahn, H. S., & Kim, H. J. (2012). Comparison of self-beliefs for predicting student motivation and achievement. *Journal of Educational Research, 105,* 336–352.

Bong, M., & Skaalvik, E. M. (2003). Academic self-concept and self-efficacy: How different are they really? *Educational Psychology Review, 15,* 1–40.

Bowling, N. A., Eschleman, K. J., & Wang, Q. (2010). A meta-analytic examination of the relation between job satisfaction and subjective well-being. *Journal of Occupational and Organizational Psychology, 83,* 915–934.

Brown, S. D., & Hirschi, A. (2013). Personality, career development, and occupational attainment. In S. D. Brown & R. W. Lent (Eds.), *Career development and counseling: Putting theory and research to work* (2nd ed., pp. 299–328). Hoboken, NJ: Wiley.

Brown, S. D., & Lent, R. W. (1996). A social cognitive framework for career choice counseling. *Career Development Quarterly, 44,* 354–366.

Brown, S. D., & Lent, R. W. (2005). Preparing adolescents to make career decisions: A social cognitive perspective. In F. Pajares & T. Urdan (Eds.), *Self-efficacy beliefs of adolescents* (pp. 201–223). Greenwich, CT: Information Age.

Brown, S. D., Lent, R. W., & Gore, P. A., Jr. (2000). Self-rated abilities and self-efficacy beliefs: Are they empirically distinct? *Journal of Career Assessment, 8,* 223–235.

Brown, S. D., Lent, R. W., Telander, K., & Tramayne, S. (2011). Social cognitive career theory, conscientiousness, and work performance. *Journal of Vocational Behavior, 79,* 81–90.

Brown, S. D., & Ryan Krane, N. E. (2000). Four (or five) sessions and a cloud of dust: Old assumptions and new observations about career counseling. In S. D. Brown & R. W. Lent (Eds.), *Handbook of counseling psychology* (3rd ed., pp. 740–766). Hoboken, NJ: Wiley.

Brown, S. D., Tramayne, S., Hoxha, D., Telander, K., Fan, X., & Lent, R. W. (2008). Social cognitive predictors of college students' academic performance and persistence: A meta-analytic path analysis. *Journal of Vocational Behavior, 72,* 298–308.

Byars-Winston, A., Estrada, Y., Howard, C., Davis, D., & Zalapa, J. (2010). Influence of social cognitive and ethnic variables on academic goals of underrepresented students in science and engineering: A multiple groups analysis. *Journal of Counseling Psychology, 57,* 205–218.

Byars-Winston, A. M., & Fouad, N. A. (2008). Math and science social cognitive variables in college students: Contributions of contextual factors in predicting goals. *Journal of Career Assessment, 16,* 425–440.

Choi, B. Y., Park, H., Yang, E., Lee, S. K., Lee, Y., & Lee, S. M. (2012). Understanding career decision self-efficacy: A meta-analytic approach. *Journal of Career Development, 39,* 443–460.

Chronister, K. M., & McWhirter, E. H. (2006). An experimental examination of two career interventions for battered women. *Journal of Counseling Psychology, 53,* 151–164.

Dawis, R. V., & Lofquist, L. H. (1984). *A psychological theory of work adjustment.* Minneapolis: University of Minnesota Press.

Duffy, R. D., & Lent, R. W. (2009). Test of a social cognitive model of work satisfaction in teachers. *Journal of Vocational Behavior, 75,* 212–223.

Eccles, J. (2009). Who am I and what am I going to do with my life? Personal and collective identities as motivators of action. *Educational Psychologist, 44,* 78–89.

Gottfredson, L. S. (2005). Applying Gottfredson's theory of circumscription and compromise in career guidance and counseling. In S. D. Brown & R. W. Lent (Eds.), *Career development and counseling: Putting theory and research to work* (pp. 71–100.). Hoboken, NJ: Wiley.

Hackett, G., & Betz, N. E. (1981). A self-efficacy approach to career development of women. *Journal of Vocational Behavior, 18,* 326–336.

Hackett, G., Betz, N. E., Casas, J. M., & Rocha-Singh, I. A. (1992). Gender, ethnicity, and social cognitive factors predicting academic achievement of students in engineering. *Journal of Counseling Psychology, 39,* 527–538.

Heggestad, E. D., & Kanfer, R. (2005). The predictive validity of self-efficacy in training performance: Little more than past-performance. *Journal of Experimental Psychology: Applied, 11,* 84–97.

Holland, J. L. (1997). *Making vocational choices: A theory of vocational personalities and work environments* (3rd ed.). Odessa, FL: Psychological Assessment Resources.

Kanfer, R. Wanberg, C. R., & Kantrowitz, T. M. (2001). Job search and employment: A personality-motivational analysis and meta-analytic review. *Journal of Applied Psychology, 86,* 837–855.

Lent, R. W. (2013a). Career-life preparedness: Revisiting career planning and adjustment in the new workplace. *Career Development Quarterly, 61,* 2–14.

Lent, R. W. (2013b). Social cognitive career theory. In S. D. Brown & R. W. Lent (Eds.), *Career development and counseling: Putting theory and research to work* (2nd ed., pp. 115–146). Hoboken, NJ: Wiley.

Lent, R. W., & Brown, S. D. (2006). Integrating person and situation perspectives on work satisfaction: A social-cognitive view. *Journal of Vocational Behavior, 69,* 236–247.

Lent, R. W., & Brown, S. D. (2008). Social cognitive career theory and subjective well-being in the context of work. *Journal of Career Assessment, 16,* 6–21.

Lent, R. W., & Brown, S. D. (2013). Social cognitive model of self-management: Toward a unifying theory of adaptive career behavior across the life span. *Journal of Counseling Psychology, 60,* 557–568.

Lent, R. W., Brown, S. D., & Hackett, G. (1994). Toward a unifying social cognitive theory of career and academic interest, choice, and performance [Monograph]. *Journal of Vocational Behavior, 45,* 79–122.

Lent, R. W., Morrison, M. A., & Ezeofor, I. (2014). The career development of people with disabilities: A social cognitive perspective. In D. R. Strauser (Ed.),

Career development, employment, and disability in rehabilitation: From theory to practice (pp. 113–124). New York, NY: Springer.

Lent, R. W., Nota, L., Soresi, S., Ginevra, M. C., Duffy, R. D., & Brown, S. D. (2011). Predicting the job and life satisfaction of Italian teachers: Test of a social cognitive model. *Journal of Vocational Behavior, 79,* 91–97.

Lent, R. W., & Sheu, H. (2010). Applying social cognitive career theory across cultures. In J. G. Ponterotto, J. M. Casas, L. A. Suzuki, & C. M. Alexander (Eds.), *Handbook of multicultural counseling* (3rd ed., pp. 691–701). Thousand Oaks, CA: Sage.

Lent, R. W., Singley, D., Sheu, H., Gainor, K. A., Brenner, B. R., Treistman, D., & Ades, L. (2005). Social-cognitive predictors of domain and life satisfaction: Exploring the theoretical precursors of subjective well-being. *Journal of Counseling Psychology, 52,* 429–442.

Lent, R. W., Singley, D. Sheu, H., Schmidt, J. A., & Schmidt, L. C. (2007). Relation of social-cognitive factors to academic satisfaction in engineering students. *Journal of Career Assessment, 15,* 87–97.

Lent, R. W., Taveira, M., Sheu, H., & Singley, D. (2009). Social cognitive predictors of academic adjustment and life satisfaction in Portuguese college students: A longitudinal analysis. *Journal of Vocational Behavior, 74,* 190–198.

Lim, S., & Cortina, L. M. (2005). Interpersonal mistreatment in the workplace: The interface and impact of general incivility and sexual harassment. *Journal of Applied Psychology, 90,* 483–496.

Lindley, L. D. (2006). The paradox of self-efficacy: Research with diverse populations. *Journal of Career Assessment, 14,* 143–160.

Locke, E. A., & Latham, G. P. (2002). Building a practically useful theory of goal setting and task motivation. *American Psychologist, 57,* 705–717.

Low, K. S. D., Yoon, M., Roberts, B. W., & Rounds, J. (2005). The stability of vocational interests from early adolescence to middle adulthood: A quantitative review of longitudinal studies. *Psychological Bulletin, 131,* 713–737.

Lubinski, D. (2010). Neglected aspects and truncated appraisals in vocational counseling: Interpretations of the interest-efficacy association from a broader perspective. *Journal of Counseling Psychology, 57,* 226–238.

Marsh, H. W., Walker, R. & Debus, R. (1991). Subject-specific components of academic self-concept and self-efficacy. *Contemporary Educational Psychology, 16,* 331–345.

Morrow, S. L., Gore, P. A., & Campbell, B. W. (1996). The application of a sociocognitive framework to the career development of lesbian women and gay men. *Journal of Vocational Behavior, 48,* 136–148.

Multon, K. D., Brown, S. D., & Lent, R. W. (1991). Relation of self-efficacy beliefs to academic outcomes: A meta-analysis. *Journal of Counseling Psychology, 38,* 30–38.

Pajares, F., & Miller, M. D. (1994). Role of self-efficacy and self-concept beliefs in mathematics problem solving: A path analysis. *Journal of Educational Psychology, 86,* 193–203.

Pajares, F., & Schunk, D. H. (2002). Self and self-belief in psychology and education: A historical perspective. In J. Aronson & D. Cordova (Eds.), *Improving academic achievement: Impact of psychological factors on education* (pp. 3–21). New York, NY: Academic.

Pearlin, L. I., & Schooler, C. (1978). The structure of coping. *Journal of Health and Social Behavior, 19,* 2–21.

Pietsch, J., Walker, R., & Chapman, E. (2003). The relationship among self-concept, self-efficacy, and performance in mathematics during secondary school. *Journal of Educational Psychology, 95,* 589–603.

Prince, J. P. (2013). Career development of lesbian, gay, bisexual, and transgendered individuals. In S. D. Brown & R. W. Lent (Eds.), *Career development and counseling: Putting theory and research to work* (2nd ed., 275–298). Hoboken, NJ: Wiley.

Rhoades, L., & Eisenberger, R. (2002). Perceived organizational support: A review of the literature. *Journal of Applied Psychology, 87,* 698–714.

Rottinghaus, P. J., Larsen, L. M., & Borgen, F. H. (2003). The relation of self-efficacy and interests: A meta-analysis of 60 samples. *Journal of Vocational Behavior, 62,* 221–236.

Sardi, G., & Robertson, I. T. (1993). Self-efficacy and work-related behavior: A review and meta-analysis. *Applied Psychology: An International Review, 42,* 139–152.

Sherer, M., Maddux, J., Mercandante, B, Prentice-Dunn, S., Jacobs, B., & Rogers, R. W. (1982). The Self-Efficacy scale: Construction and validation. *Psychological Reports, 51,* 663–671.

Sheu, H., Lent, R. W., Brown, S. D., Miller, M. J., Hennessy, K. D., & Duffy, R. D. (2010). Testing the choice model of social cognitive career theory across Holland themes: A meta-analytic path analysis. *Journal of Vocational Behavior, 76,* 252–264.

Stajkovic, A. D., & Luthans, F. (1998). Self-efficacy and work-related performance: A meta-analysis. *Psychological Bulletin, 124,* 240–261.

Verbruggen, M., & Sels, L. (2010). Social-cognitive factors affecting clients' career and life satisfaction after counseling. *Journal of Career Assessment, 18,* 3–15.

White, R. W. (1959). Motivation reconsidered: The concept of competence. *Psychological Review, 66,* 297–333.

Williams, C. M., & Subich, L. M. (2006). The gendered nature of career related learning experiences: A social cognitive perspective. *Journal of Vocational Behavior, 69,* 262–275.

CHAPTER 8

SELF-BELIEFS AND SELF-REGULATION IN HEALTH BEHAVIOR CHANGE

Ralf Schwarzer
Australian Catholic University

Aleksandra Luszczynska
University of Social Sciences and Humanities

SELF-REGULATION: PROCESS AND DISPOSITION

Self-regulation refers to all human contexts where goal setting and goal striving are at stake. It is related to self-control, self-discipline, or willpower and applies to various domains of human functioning. In a general sense, self-regulation is a process that includes setting goals for oneself, what courses of action one chooses to pursue, how much effort one invests in given endeavors, and how long one perseveres in the face of barriers and setbacks (Bandura, 1997; Baumeister, Heatherton, & Tice, 1994; Carver & Scheier, 1998; Kuhl, 2001; Mischel, Cantor, & Feldman, 1996). It encompasses reflective as well as nonconscious processes that guide goal-directed thoughts and behaviors in a more or less adaptive way.

Self-Concept, Motivation, and Identity, pages 201–223

Social-emotional-cognitive process models often distinguish phases of self-regulation and allocate persons in terms of their individual position within these phases. A useful distinction is the one between motivation and volition (Heckhausen & Gollwitzer, 1987). In the motivation phase, individuals are in a deliberative mindset while setting a goal (intention), whereas in the volitional phase, they are in an implementation mindset while pursuing their goal. Some health self-regulation theories are in line which this process perspective (e.g., health action process approach; Schwarzer, 1992, 2008). In such models, self-regulation is viewed as a multiphase process that involves a set of beliefs, expectancies, emotions, or actions.

As an alternative approach to this process view of self-regulation, some authors have focused on specific constructs that may help to investigate how people engage in goal-directed actions, how they bring about desirable outcomes, or how they disengage from goals that appear unattainable. Whereas the social-cognitive self-regulation models are process based, perceived self-efficacy is a capacity-based belief, and self-control is a capacity-based volitional strategy. Such constructs are seen as personal resources that facilitate resisting temptations, modifying habits, and overriding impulses. With this capacity, individuals exert a conscious effort to alter their dominant responses to internal or environmental challenges.

The strength model of self-control (Baumeister et al., 1994) regards self-control as a finite resource that can be exhausted if expended or overused. According to this view, self-regulation requires strength that can be equated with what is commonly called willpower. This self-control energy allows people to resist temptations, persist at tasks, cope with adverse emotions, make choices, or overcome undesired impulses. However, when they do so, they deplete their reservoir of limited resources. When this happens, failure on a subsequent, unrelated task requiring self-control is more likely. This drop in willpower is regarded as a state of ego depletion. Self-control is seen as analogous to a muscle that also requires energy to exert force over a period of time (Muraven & Baumeister, 2000). Effortfully inhibiting tempting impulses depletes cognitive and motivational resources. Once depleted, subsequent efforts to resist temptation are less successful because self-control is seen as a global, limited resource that relates to different domains of human functioning. Depletion is not just a matter of fatigue but various beliefs, moods, and attitudes might affect one's ability to resist temptation and control one's desired path of action. Experimental research has attempted to identify factors that manage to prevent ego depletion, including manipulating levels of fatigue, changing expectancies for task performance, forming action plans, or stimulating the organism by glucose supplementation. A meta-analysis of 83 studies examined the effects of ego depletion on various kinds of outcomes, investigated moderators of such effects as well as alternative explanations, providing limited support for the strength model of self-control (Hagger, Wood, Stiff, & Chatzisarantis, 2010).

Self-regulation of attention and emotion might also be seen as a stable personal disposition, an individual's characteristic that enables habitual control over recurrent actions. Psychometric tools were developed that tap the trait dimension of self-control. For example, the Self-Control Scale (Tangney, Baumeister, & Boone, 2004) assesses people's ability to override or change inner responses (e.g., "I get carried away by my feelings."; reversed) and to interrupt undesired behavioral tendencies and refrain from acting on them (e.g., "I am good at resisting temptations."). The Self-Regulation Scale by Schwarzer, Diehl, and Schmitz (1999) refers to postintentional self-regulation when individuals are in the phase of goal pursuit and face difficulties in maintaining their action. In such a maintenance situation, it is required to focus attention on the task at hand and to keep a favorable emotional balance. Thus, attention-regulation and emotion-regulation are reflected in these scale items ("I stay focused on my goal and don't allow anything to distract me from my plan of action," "If an activity arouses my feelings too much, I can calm myself down so that I can continue with the activity soon" (Luszczynska, Diehl, Gutiérrez Doña, Kuusinen, & Schwarzer, 2004). In the following, we will concentrate on one single factor in the self-regulation process, namely, self-efficacy, which has been found to be very influential in various domains of human functioning.

PERCEIVED SELF-EFFICACY: THE CONSTRUCT

According to Social Cognitive Theory (Bandura, 1997), human motivation and action are regulated by forethought. The core construct in this theory is perceived self-efficacy. Perceived self-efficacy is concerned with individuals' beliefs in their capability to exercise control over challenging demands and their own functioning. Expectations of self-efficacy are self-regulatory cognitions that determine whether instrumental actions will be initiated, how much effort will be expended, and how long it will be sustained in the face of obstacles and failures. Self-efficacy has an influence on preparing for action because self-related cognitions are a major ingredient in the motivation process. Self-efficacy levels can enhance or impede motivation. Persons with low self-efficacy harbor pessimistic thoughts about their likely accomplishments and personal development. Self-efficacy can also be directly related to behavior. Perceived self-efficacy represents the confidence that one can employ the skills necessary to resist temptation, cope with stress, and mobilize one's resources required to meet the situational demands. Self-efficacy beliefs affect the amount of effort to change risk behaviors and the persistence to continue striving in the face of barriers and setbacks that may undermine motivation.

Self-efficacy is based on different sources (Bandura, 1997; Warner et al., 2014). First, self-efficacy beliefs can be enhanced through personal accomplishment or mastery, as far as success is attributed internally and can be repeated. A second source is vicarious experience. When a role model who is similar to the individual successfully masters a difficult situation, social comparison processes can enhance self-efficacy beliefs. Third, self-efficacy beliefs can also be changed through verbal persuasion by others (e.g., a health educator reassures a patient that she will certainly adhere to a demanding dietary regimen due to her competence). The last source of influence is emotional arousal, that is, the person may experience no apprehension in a threatening situation and, as a result, may feel capable of mastering the situation. These four informational sources vary in strength and importance in the order presented here, with personal mastery being the strongest source of self-efficacy.

A meta-analysis has compared the effects of various intervention techniques upon changes in self-efficacy for physical activity (Ashford, Edmunds, & French, 2010). They identified 27 physical activity intervention studies and found a small relationship between the interventions and changes in self-efficacy. Mastery of the behavior during intervention sessions, vicarious experience with role models, but also feedback provision, tailoring the intervention to the audience, as well as goal setting by the interventionist were associated with higher levels of self-efficacy.

Compared to related constructs such as self-esteem, self-concept, perceived behavioral control, or locus of control, the distinct nature of self-efficacy lies in three aspects: (a) self-efficacy implies an internal attribution (one's capability is the cause of the action); (b) it is prospective, referring to future actions; and (c) it is an operative construct, which means that this cognition is proximal to the critical behavior to be executed. This implies that one has to obey the correspondence rule in item construction: items should be formulated at a level of specificity that corresponds with the specificity level of the behavioral criterion. A rich resource on self-efficacy is available at http://www.uky.edu/~eushe2/Pajares/self-efficacy.html

MEASUREMENT OF SELF-EFFICACY

Self-efficacy is typically not measured with standardized inventories but rather with brief sets of items that are matched to the particular research context. There are good reasons for such a less formal approach, and this first requires general comments on validity.

Authors are often asked whether they have used "validated" scales, making the impression that something has been found valid forever. However, the past tense, "validated," may reflect a misunderstanding of the validity concept. Validity is not to be understood as a job that has been done once, with results that can be imported in all kinds of future research. Instead, validation is a never ending process. A scale that is "valid" in one study need not be empirically valid in the next one, due to differences in samples, procedures, context, and such. Validity is not a lasting internal property of a scale that can be carried unharmed from one research context to the next one. Thus, the main components that establish some level of construct validity are replication and content validity. If expert judges all agree on the content validity of an item, then this is more trustworthy than any correlation coefficient with external criteria. Of course, the more psychometric information is available, the better it is. A cumulative body of evidence supporting convergent and discriminant validity is always desirable, but over-reliance on one validity coefficient from a previous study reflects a biased understanding of the validity concept.

To measure self-efficacy, one can apply a semantic rule: "I am confident that I can... (perform an action), even if... (a barrier)." An example of a self-efficacy item is "I am confident that I can skip desserts even if my family continues to consume them in my presence." This semantic rule need not be applied rigidly but might serve as a useful heuristic. The barrier need not be explicitly mentioned. For example, in the sentence "I am confident that I can swim across the river," the barrier is inherent in the high difficulty level, given that the nature of the task challenges the competence of this particular person. Compared to self-concept of ability ("I am good at X"), self-efficacy targets a future behavior ("I can do X"). A comprehensive book chapter with detailed guidelines on the construction of various kinds of self-efficacy measures has been provided by Bandura (2006). In the following, we give examples of how perceived self-efficacy has been assessed in various studies.

Measurement Example: Dietary Behaviors

Measures of self-efficacy for dietary behaviors address beliefs about the ability to perform a lifestyle change. These behaviors may be defined broadly (i.e., healthy food consumption) or in a more narrow way (i.e., fruit intake, salt avoidance, or consumption of high-fiber food). The measurement of dietary self-efficacy aims at statements that include control over the temptation to eat too much or to choose the wrong foods. Items may include particular foods, such as "I am certain that I can eat five portions of fruits and vegetables per day," or they may refer to self-regulatory efforts such as "I am confident that I can resist my craving for chocolate." Some instruments target very specific components of nutrition, such as fat intake in specific populations.

Measurement Example: Physical Activity

The measurement of exercise self-efficacy may relate to a specific task, such as "I am certain that I can run for half an hour without pausing, even uphill." Or the target behavior is not directly specified in favor of explicit barriers, such as "I am confident that I can stick to a demanding exercise regimen." Perceived motivational and volitional self-efficacy can be composed of items such as the following: Motivational self-efficacy (task self-efficacy) refers to the goal-setting phase and can be measured with the stem "I am certain..." followed by items such as "...that I can be physically active on a regular basis, even if I have to mobilize myself," or "...that I can be physically active on a regular basis, even if it is difficult" (Lippke, Fleig, Pomp, & Schwarzer, 2010). Volitional self-efficacy refers to the goal-pursuit phase. It can be subdivided into maintenance self-efficacy and recovery self-efficacy. Maintenance self-efficacy has been measured with the stem "I am capable of strenuous physical exercise on a regular basis..." followed by barriers such as "...even if it takes some time until it becomes routine," or "...even if I need several attempts until I will be successful" (Lippke et al., 2010). Items on recovery self-efficacy can be worded "I am confident that I can resume a physically active lifestyle, even if I have relapsed several times," "I am confident that I am able to resume my regular exercises after failures to pull myself together," or "I am confident that I can resume my physical activity, even when feeling weak after an illness" (Parschau et al., 2013).

Measurement Example: Oral Self-Care

When it comes to self-efficacy, the barrier here is not the technical difficulty but rather the regular performance that is not easy for some people. In the following examples, the first items refer to task self-efficacy before acting, whereas the next items pertain to maintenance self-efficacy while flossing. (i) "Please think about the few days before adopting your new flossing habit: I am confident that I can frequently floss my teeth, (a)...even if it is time consuming; (b)...even if others do not floss their teeth." (ii) "Please think about the few days after adopting your new flossing habit: I am confident that I can frequently floss my teeth regularly on a long term basis... (a)...even when I cannot see any positive changes immediately; (b)...even when I am in a hurry; (c)...even when it takes a long time to become part of my daily routine." Examples are from Gholami (2014) and Schwarzer, Antoniuk, and Gholami (2014).

SELF-EFFICACY AS A PREDICTOR OR MEDIATOR

Perceived self-efficacy is an essential factor in various domains of human functioning, and therefore it has been found to predict a large number of different outcomes (Bandura, 1997). Self-efficacy has turned out to be a highly important variable in health behavior change intervention. However, it does not always operate as a single predictor exerting a main effect on the behavioral outcome. Instead, it has been found to operate in different ways, in particular as a mediator or as a moderator, depending on the research context. To illustrate approaches where self-efficacy operates as a predictor or mediator, we present several research examples.

In the health action process approach (HAPA; Schwarzer, 2008), self-efficacy is specified as a predictor of intentions, planning, and behavior. Action self-efficacy is expected to predict intentions and planning, whereas coping self-efficacy should predict planning and behavior directly. In addition, indirect effects should emerge (see Figure 8.1).

HAPA can be briefly characterized by the following main principles:

- *Principle 1: Motivation and volition.* The health behavior change process is divided into two phases. There is a switch of mindsets when people move from deliberation to action. First comes the motiva-

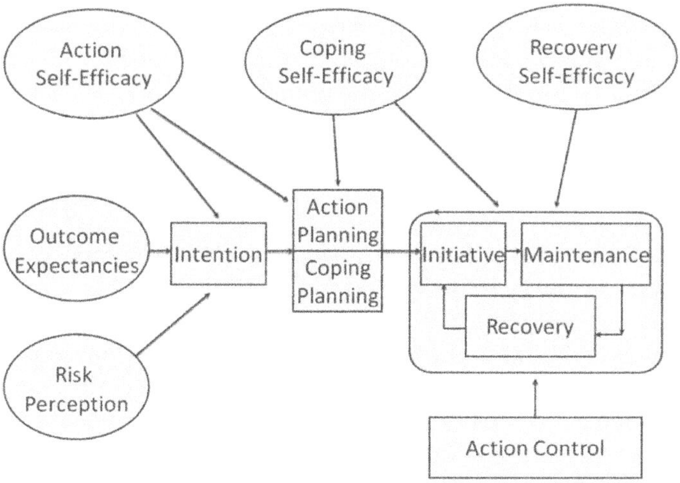

Figure 8.1 Health action process approach (Schwarzer, 2008).

tion phase in which people develop their intentions. Afterwards, they enter the volition phase.

- *Principle 2: Two volitional phases.* In the volition phase, there are two groups of people: those who have not yet translated their intentions into action and those who have. Thus, there are inactive as well as active persons in this phase. In other words, in the volitional phase one finds intenders as well as actors, who are characterized by different psychological states. Thus, in addition to viewing health behavior change as a continuous process, one can also create three categories of people with different mindsets, depending on their current location within the course of behavior change: preintenders, intenders, and actors. This segmentation serves to develop matching treatments.
- *Principle 3: Postintentional planning.* Intenders who are in the volitional preactional stage are motivated to change, but they do not act because they might lack the correct skills to translate their intention into action. Planning is a key strategy at this point. It serves as an operative mediator between intentions and behavior.
- *Principle 4: Two kinds of mental simulation.* Planning can be divided into action planning and coping planning. Action planning pertains to the when, where, and how of intended action. Coping planning includes the anticipation of barriers and the design of alternative actions that help to attain one's goal in spite of impediments.
- *Principle 5: Phase-specific self-efficacy.* Perceived self-efficacy is required throughout the entire process. However, the nature of self-efficacy differs from phase to phase. This is because there are different challenges as people progress from one phase to the next one. Goal setting, planning, initiation, action, and maintenance all pose challenges that are not of the same nature. Therefore, one can distinguish between action self-efficacy, maintenance self-efficacy, and recovery self-efficacy.

Research Example: A Meta-Analysis in the Context of Physical Activity Prediction

Gholami (2014) has conducted a meta-analysis on the application of HAPA to physical activity, including 11 studies. In this set of studies were six longitudinal, two cross-sectional, and three intervention designs. Total sample size was N = 2,677, age range was 12–93 years, the majority were women, and one third were patients. Of the 21 paths that were included in the HAPA model, four direct paths are of interest here.

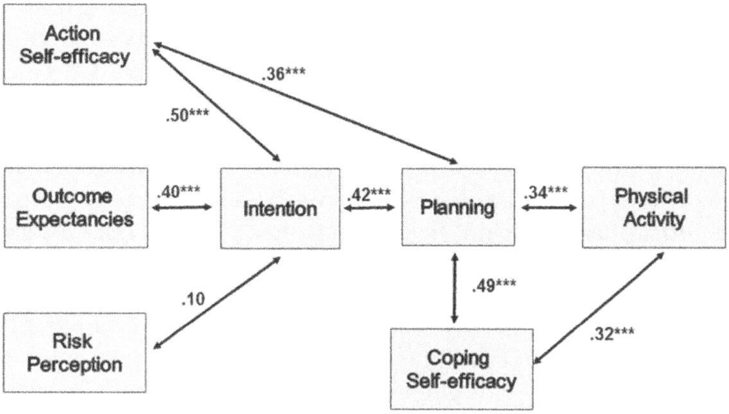

Figure 8.2 Meta-analytic population effect sizes based on correlations from 11 studies (Gholami, 2014).

Figure 8.2 depicts zero-order associations among all variables under study. Tests of heterogeneity revealed significant variations in the individual effect sizes indicating lack of homogeneity. Search for moderators did not yield satisfactory results. As can be seen, planning for physical activity was directly associated with action self-efficacy (.36) and with coping self-efficacy (.49). An indirect effect (.21) from action self-efficacy via intentions has to be added. Physical activity is associated with coping self-efficacy directly (.32), and indirectly via planning (.17). These effect sizes seem to characterize the current state of affairs in the domain of physical activity, until more studies become available. It is, however, also of note that this meta-analysis does not consider all possible causal relationships between self-constructs and behavior. A skill-development view regards changes in the self as a consequence of skillful behavior (mastery experience), whereas a self-enhancement view considers changes in behavior as a result of improved self constructs. Both ways exist at some time, and therefore reciprocal effects between self-related constructs and behavior are generally assumed, for example explicitly in social-cognitive theory (Bandura, 1997), and there is evidence for the empirical modeling of such reciprocity (e.g., Marsh, Papaioannou, & Theodorakis, 2006).

Research Example: Sunscreen Use to Prevent Skin Cancer

Sunscreen use is less frequent and less regular than desired to prevent skin cancer, and therefore research investigates psychological predictors. As sunscreen use also depends partly on self-beliefs and appearance norms, it is worthwhile to examine their interplay. In a longitudinal online study with 154 individuals in several countries, we have, among others, looked at the way how self-efficacy predicted sunscreen use (Craciun, Schüz, Lippke, & Schwarzer, 2012). Self-efficacy toward using sunscreen was measured at Time 1, with four items that asked about people's confidence that they can continue to apply sunscreen even if they face different barriers such as desiring a tan, friends not using sunscreen, having forgotten to bring sunscreen along, and the cost of sunscreen. The item content pertained to the volitional phase of health behavior change ("coping self-efficacy") and followed a semantic rule that assures content validity: "I am certain that I can do... (behavior), even if... (barrier) occurs."

Appearance norms were assessed at Time 1 by one item stating, "The tanner I am, the more attractive I feel." Sunscreen use was measured at Time 2, fourteen weeks later, with one item asking participants if they repeatedly applied sunscreen with a sufficient sun protection factor (SPF 15+) during the sunny days when being outside.

Figure 8.3 demonstrates that there is a main effect of self-efficacy: the higher it is, the more likely will sunscreen be used later on at Time 2. It also illustrates the joint effects of self-efficacy and appearance norms on sunscreen use. The slopes are depicted for three levels of values of the

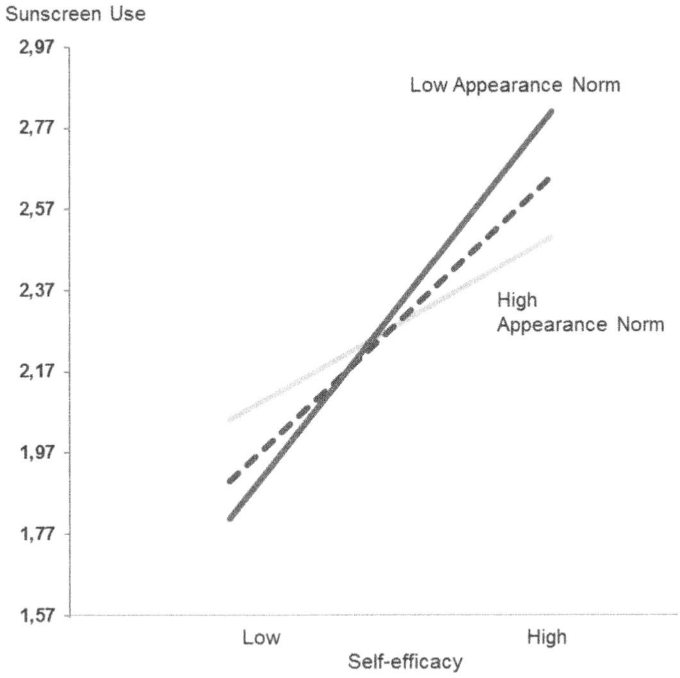

Figure 8.3 Self-efficacy at Time 1 predicts sunscreen use at Time 2 , moderated by appearance norms at Time 1 (Craciun et al., 2012).

moderator variable appearance norm. The figure indicates that for individuals with lower appearance norms (i.e., having a tan is less valued), the relation between self-efficacy and sunscreen use is higher than for those with high appearance norms. For individuals who believe that they would look more attractive with a tan, self-efficacy did not have as strong an effect on behavior. Thus, for skin-protection motivation to become effective, self-efficacy is beneficial in conjunction with less-positive appearance norms.

Research Example: Self-Efficacy as a Mediator Predicts Dietary Changes

An example of a mediator effect is found in the experimental study by Kreausukon, Gellert, Lippke, and Schwarzer (2012), in which Thai students received a self-regulatory intervention to increase their fruit and vegetable consumption. As shown in Figure 8.4, two simultaneous mediators were responsible for the treatment effect, in particular the baseline level of dietary self-efficacy. This means that the self-regulatory intervention has increased participants' levels of self-efficacy and planning, which in turn has facilitated the later surge in fruit and vegetable consumption.

Research Example: Three Kinds of Self-Efficacy Predict Sports Performance

This research investigates the role of beliefs about the ability to deal with specific social barriers and its relationships to mindfulness, football performance, and satisfaction with one's own and team performance (Blecharz et al., 2014). The study tested whether self-efficacy referring to social barriers would predict performance over and above task-related self-efficacy and collective efficacy, and the mediating role of self-efficacy to overcome social barriers in the relationship between mindfulness and performance. Collective

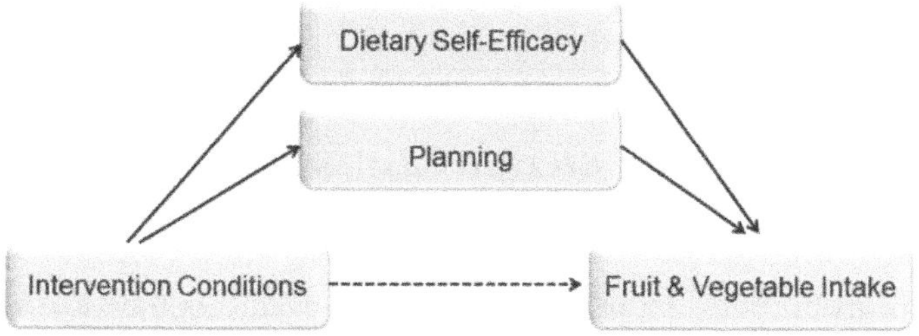

Figure 8.4 Dietary self-efficacy mediates between self-regulatory treatment and fruit and vegetable intake (Kreausukon et al., 2012).

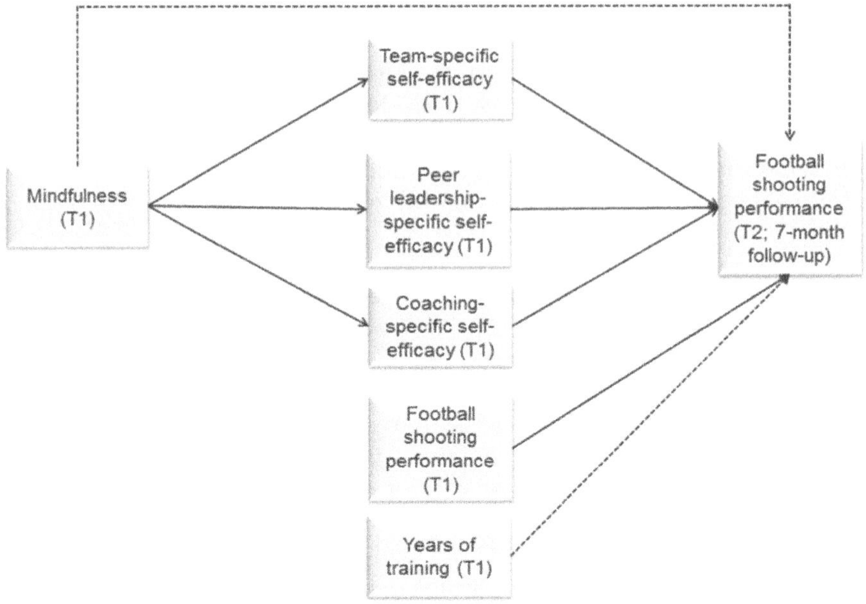

Figure 8.5 Three types of self-efficacy mediate between mindfulness and sports performance (Blecharz et al., 2014).

efficacy refers to the team's shared beliefs in their perceived allied competence to organize and execute the demanded actions (Bandura, 1997). Participants were 88 football (soccer) players aged 16–21 years. Results showed that task-related self-efficacy and collective efficacy explained performance satisfaction at 7-month follow-up, whereas self-efficacy referring to social barriers explained shooting performance at 7-month follow-up. Indirect associations between mindfulness and performance were found with three types of self-efficacy referring to social barriers, operating as parallel mediators (Figure 8.5). Results provide evidence for the role of beliefs about the ability to cope with social barriers and show a complex interplay between different types of self-efficacy and collective efficacy in predicting team sport performance.

SELF-EFFICACY AS AN OUTCOME: HOW SELF-EFFICACY CAN BE IMPROVED

The relationship between perceived self-efficacy and behavior is reciprocal (Bandura, 1997). Self-efficacy predicts behavior, and behavior predicts self-efficacy (see also Marsh et al., 2006). When conducting research on this topic, one has to specify which causal window is being addressed. This also pertains to the question of how self-efficacy can be improved. There are typically three sources of self-efficacy change (Warner et al., 2014). First, mastery experience is the best source. Second, vicarious experience (imitating a role model) is useful. Third, if there is no better way, then also verbal persuasion can be applied to improve one's level of self-efficacy ("You can do it."). Obviously, wherever possible, one should use the first approach. Self-regulatory interventions can be applied where participants learn to cope with small steps toward mastery to build up confidence in being able to master the task (graded approximation).

Research Example: Oral Self-Care by the Use of Dental Floss

Regular dental flossing as a part of oral self-care is improved with a combination of self-efficacy and self-monitoring. This is the finding of a study that investigated the combined roles of dental self-efficacy and self-monitoring when predicting the frequency of dental flossing as part of one's dental routine (Schwarzer et al., 2015). The study of 287 university students, aged from 19 to 26 years, examined whether a self-regulatory intervention would make a difference to flossing behaviors by comparing an intervention group with controls. Each group was given a questionnaire at two assessment points in time, requesting demographic information and social cognitive variables, as well as being asked how regularly they flossed their teeth.

In the intervention group, participants received with their pretest questionnaire information about the benefits of dental flossing: what it is, why it is done, and how it is done. They were then encouraged to create action plans for three occasions. After each of the three situations, a question relating to self-efficacy was posed on a four-point scale. Participants were then asked to produce three coping plans to overcome barriers to flossing and solutions. At the end, participants received a calendar that served as a self-monitoring tool.

The study found that the intervention led to an increase in dental flossing regardless of experimental conditions, which means that the self-regulatory treatment itself had no direct effect on the outcome. Both groups improved, the control group as well as the experimental group. However, differential effects were visible for self-efficacy and self -monitoring, confirming that the mindset of the participants had changed due to the self-regulatory treatment, and moreover, that both played a mediating role in facilitating flossing (see below). As Figure 8.6 shows, the intervention led to increased levels of self-efficacy, which was a secondary outcome variable. Completing self-regulatory tasks has strengthened individuals' self-beliefs of being capable to adhere to regular oral self-care. This way, the experiment

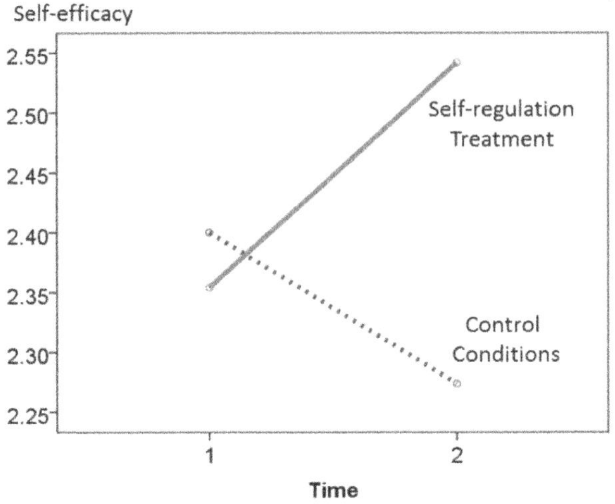

Figure 8.6 A brief self-regulatory intervention improves levels of dental self-efficacy (Schwarzer et al., 2015).

was successful, although the primary outcome variable, dental flossing, was not directly affected.

However, a sequential mediator model showed that the increase in self-efficacy also improved self-monitoring (Figure 8.7). Participants who optimistically believed that they could adhere to oral self-care were also more compliant with using their flossing calendar. As a result, their level of daily flossing was further improved. This finding shows that the health behavior process can be specified as a chain of constructs, with self-beliefs not only as an immediate outcome of interventions but also as a predictor of subsequent behaviors. In

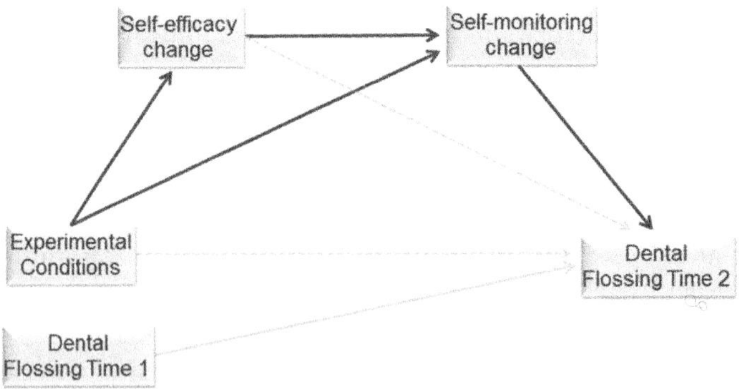

Figure 8.7 Dental self-efficacy change as part of a sequential mediator chain toward improved dental flossing (Schwarzer et al., 2015).

other words, although no direct treatment effect emerged, the analysis demonstrates a mechanism upon self-constructs that is due to a brief self-regulatory intervention. Those who have become more self-efficacious and who have self-monitored their behavior yielded higher frequencies of dental flossing. In health promotion research, it is generally important to search not only for a behavioral target outcome (that often is not improved) but to look also for secondary outcomes which can be proximal antecedents of the target. This way, an intervention may have been successful in moving participants one step further toward behavioral change, without having accomplished already the final step, the targeted action. Identifying sequential mediation chains helps to gain insight into putative mechanisms of behavior change.

SELF-EFFICACY AS A MODERATOR

Self-efficacy can serve as an independent (X) or dependent variable (Y), and it can operate as a mediator or as a moderator (M). In the latter case, there is an interaction between X and M, and the relationship between X and Y depends on the levels of self-efficacy. To probe an interaction, the slopes of X and Y are depicted separately for each level of M. For example, in high self-efficacious persons, the slope can be much steeper than for low self-efficacious persons.

Research Example: Social Support and Self-Efficacy Predict Physical Activity in Older Adults

The purpose of the study (Warner, Ziegelmann, Schüz, Wurm, & Schwarzer, 2011) was to examine whether the effects of social support on physical exercise in older adults depend on individual perceptions of self-efficacy. Some 309 older German adults (age 65–85) were assessed at three points in time (3 months apart). In hierarchical regression analyses, support received from friends and exercise self-efficacy were specified as predictors of exercise frequency, while baseline exercise, sex, age, and physical functioning were controlled for. Besides main effects of self-efficacy and social support, an interaction between social support and self-efficacy emerged (Figure 8.8). People with low self-efficacy were less likely to be active in spite of receiving social support. People with low support were less likely to be active even if they were high in self-efficacy. This points to the importance of both social support and self-efficacy and implies that these resources could be targets of interventions to increase older adults' exercise.

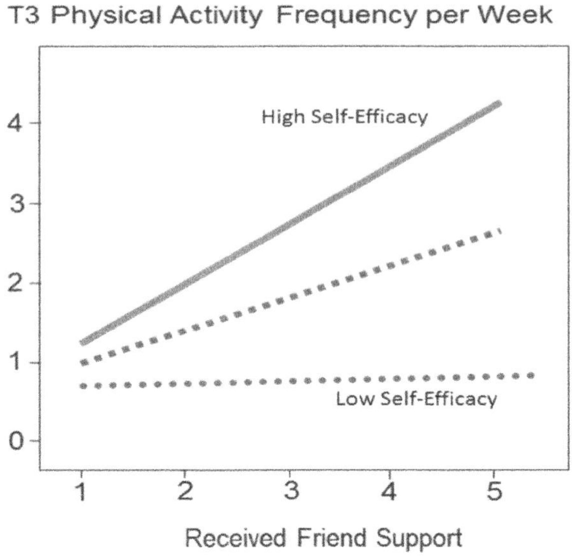

Figure 8.8 Interaction between self-efficacy and social support (Warner et al., 2011).

Research Example: Planning Interventions to Improve Physical Activity in Patients With Diabetes

In the second example, the independent variable is intervention conditions. (Luszczynska, Schwarzer, Lippke, & Mazurkiewicz, 2011). The study included 58 patients with diabetes who received a face-to-face action-planning intervention to improve their physical activity levels. The question was whether subgroups with different levels of self-efficacy responded in the same manner to the planning intervention in terms of the outcome, which here was the number of physically active sessions per week. Exercise self-efficacy turned out to moderate the relationship between experimental conditions and weekly activity frequency (Figure 8.9). This means that those participants have benefitted most from the planning intervention who were initially quite optimistic about their capability to change their physical activity levels.

SELF-EFFICACY AS A MODERATOR WITHIN MORE COMPLEX BEHAVIOR CHANGE MODELS

Research Example: Planning Interventions to Improve Physical Activity in Chinese Adolescents

A longitudinal study has been designed in China to examine the putative moderating role of self-efficacy in the planning-behavior relationship

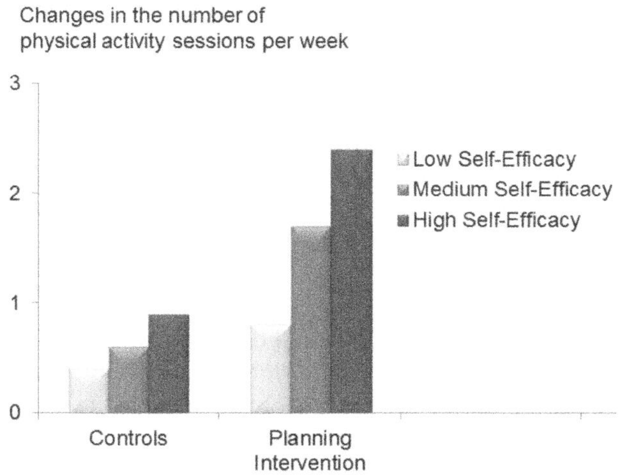

Figure 8.9 Planning intervention increases physical-activity frequency in self-efficacious individuals: Self-efficacy as a moderator (Luszczynska et al., 2011).

(Luszczynska et al., 2010). High school students (N = 534) were given questionnaires at two points in time. Intentions were assessed at baseline, whereas planning, self-efficacy, and physical activity were measured 4 weeks later. A moderated mediation model was examined. Planning was specified as a mediator between intentions and behavior, whereas self-efficacy was specified as a moderator of the planning-behavior relationship. Results confirm that levels of self-efficacy moderate the mediation process (Figure 8.10). The strength of the mediated effect (intention via planning on behavior) increased along with levels of self-efficacy. These results remained valid after accounting for baseline physical activity. For planning to mediate the

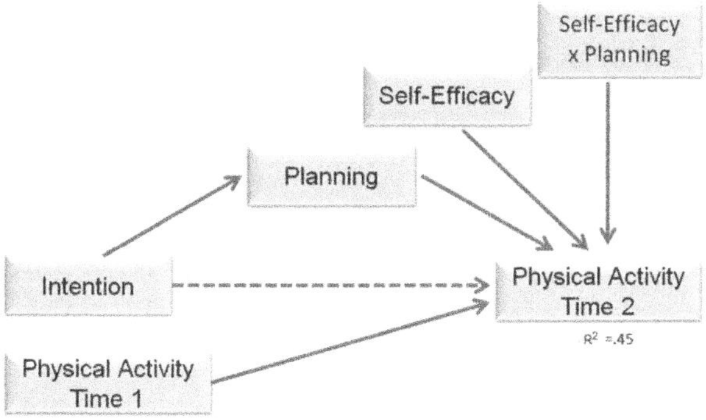

Figure 8.10 Self-efficacy moderates the planning-physical activity relationship in Chinese high school students: Self-efficacy as a moderator (Luszczynska et al., 2010).

intention-behavior relation, adolescents must have sufficiently high levels of self-efficacy, otherwise, planning might be in vain.

Research Example: Predicting Dietary Changes in an Online Study

A study surveyed German Internet users in terms of their fruit and vegetable consumption at two measurement points in time. It was advertised by press releases (magazine reports, university press), announcements on university websites, and mailing lists. Follow-up measures were taken 4 weeks after baseline assessments. The sample (N = 1,140) comprised 19% men and had a mean age of 37.3 years, SD 12.5 years, ranging from 16 to 77 years. Intentions served as predictor, planning as mediator, self-efficacy as moderator, and behaviors as outcomes. First, intentions were translated into nutrition behaviors by planning. Second, self-efficacy moderated this mediation: The strength of the mediated effect increased along with levels of self-efficacy, even when accounting for baseline behaviors (Figure 8.11).

For planning to mediate the intention-behavior relation, people must not harbor self-doubts. If they lack self-efficacy, intentions are not well translated into nutrition behavior through planning..

When adding a moderator to a mediation model, the question arises whether the moderator operates at the left or the right side of the mediator (Hayes, 2013). In the present example, it was on the left side, reflecting an interaction between intention and self-efficacy on planning. There was no moderation on the right side, where it comes to predict behavior. This

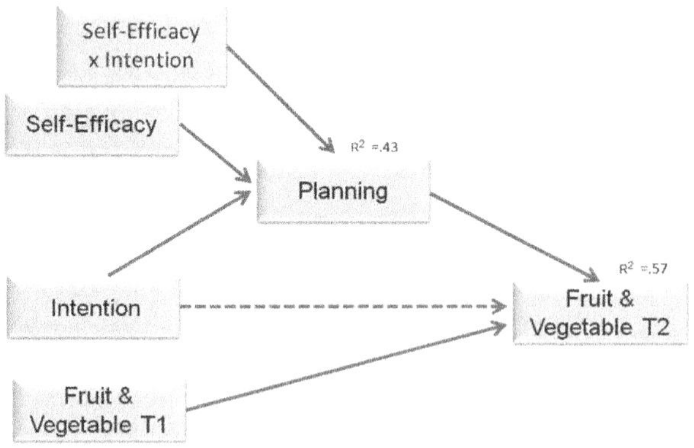

Figure 8.11 Self-efficacy moderates the intention-planning relationship in an online study on fruit and vegetable consumption: Self-efficacy as a moderator (Schwarzer et al., 2010).

contradicts the previous study in which there was an interaction between self-efficacy and planning.

Research Example: Predicting Dietary Changes in Worksite Health Promotion

Worksite health promotions to affect dietary changes often include self-regulatory strategies such as planning. Strategic planning as a mediator is expected to move people from intention to action. However, individuals who lack perceived action-specific self-efficacy might fail to apply their plans when encountering challenging situations. Thus, self-efficacy might operate as a moderator variable when it comes to studying the mediator effects of planning on behaviors. This study (Richert et al., 2010) examined the interactive role of planning and self-efficacy in the context of dietary changes. A longitudinal sample of 411 employees was surveyed twice in terms of their fruit and vegetable consumption over a 4-week interval. Intentions, planning, and fruit and vegetable consumption were specified as a mediator chain with self-efficacy as a moderator at two stages of the putative change process. Baseline behavior served as a covariate in the model. Intentions were translated into dietary behavior by planning. Self-efficacy moderated this mediation at the second stage (right side of the model), reflected by a planning-self-efficacy interaction on fruit and vegetable consumption (Figure 8.12). The strength of the mediated effect increased along with levels of self-efficacy. Individuals with very low self-efficacy did not benefit from planning. If a person lacks self-efficacy, planning does not seem to translate intentions into fruit and vegetable consumption

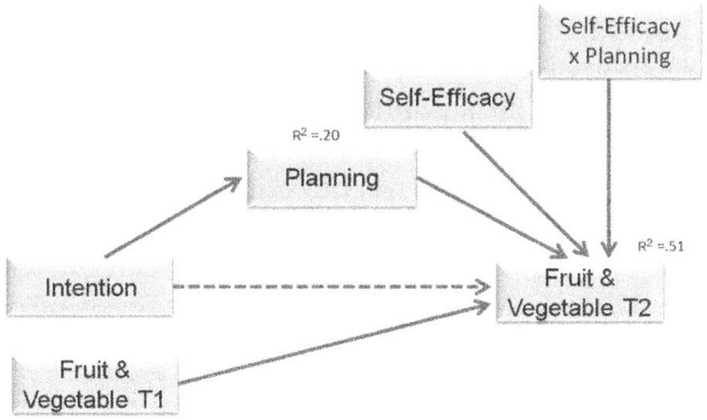

Figure 8.12 Self-efficacy moderates the planning-fruit and vegetable consumption relationship: Self-efficacy as a moderator (Richert et al., 2010).

CONCLUSIONS, LIMITATIONS, AND DIRECTIONS FOR FURTHER RESEARCH

Health behavior change is associated with changes in self-beliefs. The main reason lies in the control processes that drive the adoption and maintenance of health-enhancing behaviors as well as the liberation from addictive or health-compromising behaviors. Self-regulatory efforts require a sense of agency. Various process models and psychological constructs have been employed to shed light on the antecedents and consequences of personal attempts to make a difference in one's life. In the present chapter, we have focused on perceived self-efficacy as a dominant self-belief that has been found influential in a large number of studies.

Self-efficacy is considered to operate in various ways. It works as a predictor that forms good intentions to change, and it is associated with efforts to maintain a novel behavior and to counteract the temptations to relapse. As most research is not limited to a bivariate design, the question arisesof how self-efficacy operates in multivariate designs. Here it can be specified either as a mediator or as a moderator, depending on the context of variables and the theoretical backdrop. As a mediator, it may translate some part of an initial independent variable, such as social support, to a chosen outcome, such as well-being or proactive behavior. As a moderator, it may reflect the association between other variables at one level, but the lack of associations at the other level, for example, if dietary habits lead to weight gain in low self-efficacious but not in high self-efficacious individuals. In the mediator case, researchers ask how things happen, whereas in the moderator case, they ask for whom things happen.

The summarized research shows that there is no single universal mechanism that is valid for all domains of human functioning, all kinds of behaviors, cultures, samples, and time points. How self-beliefs operate needs to be identified uniquely within each research context. They can be predictors, mediators, moderators, or outcomes, depending on the research purpose and the specification of multivariate structural models that are supposed to reflect the data. As self-efficacy and behavior are seen as being reciprocal, the choice of time windows in a longitudinal or experimental research design may also influence the observed direction of causality.

Self-beliefs can be modified by self-regulatory interventions. For example, one can practice skills to be mastered or one can expose participants to role models. The outcome would be increased levels of perceived self-efficacy. If this outcome operates then also as a precursor of health behavior, then self-efficacy becomes predictor and mediator at the same time. Further research should address the behavior-change techniques that are most suitable for modifying self-beliefs (Ashford et al., 2010) under various conditions and for individuals who reside at different stages of behavior change. For example, a smoker may hold different self-beliefs before quitting, while quitting, and after a relapse.

In sum, the research examples in this chapter shall serve to underscore the various functional roles that self-beliefs may take within different contexts and research agendas. In any case, self-beliefs can be seen as powerful cognitions that make a difference when it comes to behavior change.

REFERENCES

Ashford, S., Edmunds, J., & French, D. P. (2010). What is the best way to change self-efficacy to promote lifestyle and recreational physical activity? A systematic review with meta-analysis. *British Journal of Health Psychology, 15*(2), 265–288. doi:10.1348/135910709X461752

Bandura, A. (1997). *Self-efficacy: The exercise of control.* New York, NY: Freeman.

Bandura, A. (2006). Guide for creating self-efficacy scales. In F. Pajares & T. Urdan (Eds.), *Self-efficacy beliefs of adolescents* (pp. 307–338). Greenwich, CT: Information Age.

Baumeister, R. F., Heatherton, T. F., & Tice, D. M. (1994). *Losing control: How and why people fail at self-regulation.* San Diego, CA: Academic.

Blecharz, J., Luszczynska, A., Scholz, U., Schwarzer, R., Siekanska, M., & Cieslak, R. (2014). Predicting performance and performance satisfaction: The role of mindfulness and beliefs about the ability to deal with social barriers in sport. *Anxiety, Stress, & Coping, 27*(3), 270–287. doi:10.1080/10615806.2013.839989

Carver, C. S., & Scheier, M. F. (1998). *On the self-regulation of behavior.* New York, NY: Cambridge University Press.

Craciun, C., Schüz, N., Lippke, S., & Schwarzer, R. (2012). Translating intentions into sunscreen use: An interaction of self-efficacy and appearance norms. *Psychology, Health & Medicine, 17,* 447–456. doi:10.1080/13548506.2011.613941

Gholami, M. (2014, March). Self-regulation and health behavior across the life span. (Doctoral dissertation). FUDISS_derivate_000000015447 Retrieved from http://www.diss.fu-berlin.de/diss/servlets/MCRFileNodeServlet/FUDISS_derivate_000000015447/Dissertation_Maryam_Gholami_online_submission.pdf;jsessionid=B7C992882B27C8A262FCC10DD0AAAED2?hosts=

Hagger, M. S., Wood, C., Stiff, C., & Chatzisarantis, N. L. D. (2010). Ego depletion and the strength model of self-control: A meta-analysis. *Psychological Bulletin, 136,* 495–525.

Hayes, A. F. (2013). *Introduction to mediation, moderation, and conditional process analysis: A regression-based approach.* New York, NY: Guilford.

Heckhausen, H., & Gollwitzer, P. M. (1987). Thought contents and cognitive functioning in motivational vs. volitional states of mind. *Motivation and Emotion 11,* 101–120.

Kreausukon, P., Gellert, P., Lippke, S., & Schwarzer, R. (2012). Planning and self-efficacy can increase fruit and vegetable consumption: A randomized controlled trial. *Journal of Behavioral Medicine, 35,* 443–451. doi:10.1007/s10865-011-9373-1

Kuhl, J. (2001). *Motivation und persönlichkeit. Interaktionen psychischer systeme* [Motivation and personality: Interactions of mental systems]. Göttingen, Germany: Hogrefe.

Lippke, S., Fleig, L., Pomp, S., & Schwarzer, R. (2010). Validity of a stage algorithm for physical activity in participants recruited from orthopedic and cardiac rehabilitation clinics. *Rehabilitation Psychology, 55,* 398–408. doi:10.1037/a0021563

Luszczynska, A., Cao, D. S., Mallach, N., Pietron, K., Mazurkiewicz, M., & Schwarzer, R. (2010). Intentions, planning, and self-efficacy predict physical activity in Chinese and Polish adolescents: Two moderated mediation analyses. *International Journal of Clinical and Health Psychology, 10*(2), 265–278.

Luszczynska, A., Diehl, M., Gutiérrez-Doña, B., Kuusinen, P., & Schwarzer, R. (2004). Measuring one component of dispositional self-regulation: Attention control in goal pursuit. *Personality and Individual Differences 37,* 555–566.

Luszczynska, A., Schwarzer, R., Lippke, S., & Mazurkiewicz, M. (2011). Self-efficacy as a moderator of the planning-behaviour relationship in interventions designed to promote physical activity. *Psychology and Health, 26*(2), 151–166. doi:10.1080/08870446.2011.531571

Marsh, H. W., Papaioannou, A., & Theodorakis, Y. (2006). Causal ordering of physical self-concept and exercise behavior: Reciprocal effects model and the influence of physical education teachers. *Health Psychology, 25,* 316–328.

Mischel, W., Cantor, N., & Feldman, S. (1996). Principles of self-regulation: The nature of willpower and self-control. In E. T. Higgins & A. Kruglanski (Eds.), *Social psychology: Handbook of basic principles* (pp. 329–360). New York, NY: Guilford.

Muraven, M., & Baumeister, R. F. (2000). Self-regulation and depletion of limited resources: Does self-control resemble a muscle? *Psychological Bulletin 126,* 247–259.

Parschau, L., Fleig, L., Koring, M., Lange, D., Knoll, N., Schwarzer, R., & Lippke, S. (2013). Positive experience, self-efficacy, and action control predict physical activity changes: A moderated mediation analysis. *British Journal of Health Psychology, 18*(2), 395–406.

Richert, J., Reuter, T., Wiedemann, A. U., Lippke, S., Ziegelmann, J., & Schwarzer, R. (2010). Differential effects of planning and self-efficacy on fruit and vegetable consumption. *Appetite, 54,* 611–614. doi:10.1016/j.appet.2010.03.006

Schwarzer, R. (1992). Self-efficacy in the adoption and maintenance of health behaviors: Theoretical approaches and a new model. In R. Schwarzer (Ed.), *Self-efficacy: Thought control of action* (pp. 217-`–243). Washington, DC: Hemisphere.

Schwarzer, R. (2008). Modeling health behavior change: How to predict and modify the adoption and maintenance of health behaviors. *Applied Psychology, 57,* 1–29. doi:10.1111/j.1464-0597.2007.00325.x

Schwarzer, R., Antoniuk, A., & Gholami, M. (2015). A brief intervention changing oral self-care, self-efficacy, and self-monitoring. *British Journal of Health Psychology, 20*(1), 56–67. doi:10.1111/bjhp.12091

Schwarzer, R., Diehl, M., & Schmitz, G. (1999). *Self-regulation.* Retrieved from http://userpage.fu-berlin.de/~health/selfreg_e.htm

Schwarzer, R., Richert, J., Kreausukon, P., Remme, L., Wiedemann, A. U., & Reuter, T. (2010). Translating intentions into nutrition behaviors via planning requires self-efficacy: Evidence from Thailand and Germany. *International Journal of Psychology, 45,* 260–268. doi:10.1080/00207591003674479

Tangney, J., Baumeister, R. F., & Boone, A. L. (2004). High self-control predicts good adjustment, less pathology, better grades, and interpersonal success. *Journal of Personality, 72,* 271–324.

Warner, L. M., Schüz, B., Wolff, J. K., Parschau, L., Wurm, S., & Schwarzer, R. (2014, April 7). Sources of self-efficacy for physical activity. *Health Psychology.* Advance online publication.

Warner, L. M., Ziegelmann, J. P., Schüz, B., Wurm, S., & Schwarzer, R. (2011). Synergistic effect of social support and self-efficacy on physical exercise in older adults. *Journal of Aging and Physical Activity, 19,* 249–261. PMid: 21727305

CHAPTER 9

CONFIDENCE

Is It Different From Self-Efficacy and Is It Important?

Lazar Stankov
Australian Catholic University

Jihyun Lee
University of NSW

Over the past two decades self-beliefs have been among the most extensively studied constructs in psychology and education. Two self-beliefs constructs—self-efficacy and confidence—have raised the question among practitioners and researchers alike whether they are in fact conceptually and methodologically the same but labeled differently. Both constructs are seen as tapping into the areas in-between cognitive and non-cognitive attributes (Bandura, 1997; Stankov, 2000a) and they are interpreted as one's structure of knowledge about oneself and about the task being evaluated. Thus, both constructs incorporate the cognitive processes of self-reflection and evaluation of the difficulty of the task being asked. However, their differences can also be readily conceptualized. While self-efficacy can be suf-

Self-Concept, Motivation, and Identity, pages 225–248

ficiently expressed as "I can do this" (Bandura, 2012, p.16), confidence has another layer of self-belief and can be expressed as "I am *sure* I have done this correctly." Confidence, as used in studies of ours, taps into the mindset of "done well." When these two constructs are applied in the context of learning, students with high self-efficacy would think, "Although this task looks hard, I can do this. Therefore, I should push myself to successfully complete this task no matter how hard it may seem to me now." On the other hand, students with high confidence may think, "I am sure I have done this correctly. Therefore I do not have to work hard on this nor do I have to reflect on my decision, because I already know I have done the right thing." Students with high self-concept—another self-beliefs construct that has also been studied extensively—would think along the lines of "I am good at this and this is part of who I am. Therefore I can do this."

As can be seen, self-efficacy operates when there is a task at hand to solve or overcome. It operates within the context of "the goals they set for themselves... and effort they devoted" to the tasks (Bandura, 2012, p. 26). Its functional properties become even stronger when there is a subjectively perceived challenge or difficulty that one wishes to overcome. Thus, self-efficacy can be defined as a person's belief that s/he can complete a task when it is perceived as challenging or difficult; that is, self-efficacy is concerned with people's beliefs in their capabilities to produce the target attainments. The effect of self-efficacy on a student's achievement is often described as "the stronger their self-efficacy the more effort they enlist and the higher their performance attainments" (Bandura, 2012, p. 27). As such, mediating variables of effort, persistence, and confidence are part of the make-up of one's self-knowledge that may be referred to as self-efficacy disposition. For example, if a man decides to run four miles in an hour, knowing he has never done it before but wanting to push himself, then self-efficacy (thinking of "I can do this") is said to operate. When the knowledge about his ability to run four miles in an hour becomes a part of who he is (i.e., "I am a type of a person who can run four miles and I know I can do it in that time"), that is his/her self-concept. When he finishes his run, without having a look at his watch, he may think to himself, "I am sure I have run four miles in one hour." That is confidence.

While one can place confidence in their estimation that an event will take place in the future, Bandura (2012, p. 16) states that "it is meaningless to ask individuals to judge their efficacy in guessing, for example, randomly changing color patterns." Such guessing games cannot have the self-efficacy component. Confidence, on the other hand, can operate when one is asked to guess about some future events. For instance, Kleitman and Stankov (2007) showed that there is a reliable tendency to be confident even in the predictions of some events that cannot be confirmed at the time of testing, that is, there will be World War III or it will rain tomorrow. Indeed, confidence is deemed to be an important component of forecasting, risk-taking behaviors, and in the studies of eyewitness testimonies.

Theoretical foundations for both constructs are quite separate, with studies on self-efficacy originating in education, while studies in confidence originated in psychophysics and cognitive psychology, including decision-making. In addition to its applications in business, sport, and health settings, self-efficacy is seen as being of particular relevance to academic achievement, course selection, academic continuance and aspirations, teacher education, vocational interests and choice of college majors and careers (cf. Caprara, Vecchione, Alessandri, Gerbino, & Barbaranelli, 2011). Confidence has been linked to more traditional psychological constructs, such as memory and attention, psychomotor tasks, sensory and perceptual processes from all five sensory modalities, metacognition, decision-making, eyewitness testimonies, and many primary abilities identified within the theory of fluid and crystallized intelligence (Horn & Blankson, 2005). Cognitive performance has been linked to both self-efficacy and confidence. However, self-efficacy is extensively studied in the context of learning and school-based achievement and thus has been related to school grades or achievement scores in the 3Rs: reading, writing, arithmetic/mathematics among school-aged students (cf. Caprara et al., 2011). The types of cognitive performance that have been examined in studies of confidence are much broader, including various IQ-type tests in populations of ages varying from young adults through to the elderly.

In terms of the sources affecting self-beliefs, the most frequently cited are the four sources of self-efficacy proposed by Bandura (1997): mastery experiences (personal experience with success or failure), vicarious experiences (most often learned by observing experiences of others), verbal persuasion (receiving direct, verbal encouragement), and physiological state (experiences of physiological symptoms such as anxiety, depression, helplessness, nervousness). However, these types of "causes" that have been linked to self-efficacy have not been applied to confidence. Researchers on confidence tend to believe that confidence is less affected by the kinds of reflection that influence self-efficacy. Instead, confidence is more affected by the tasks performance at hand. Kahneman (2011) suggests that the accuracy of confidence judgments depends on two conditions: the regularity of the phenomena under consideration, and the extensive practice that leads to expertise in the area. Thus, an improvement in one's realism of confidence judgments is possible should extensive ongoing practice be provided to the students.

It is necessary to clarify three points at the outset. First, it is important to keep in mind that the term *confidence* as used in the present chapter differs from the colloquial and broader psychological meanings of this term. Stankov, Kleitman, and Jackson (2014) make a distinction between personality-like measures of confidence, that is, "My self-confidence is greatly affected by the outcome of competition," and "online" measures that assess confidence in the way described below. In this chapter, our focus will be on the latter, that is, the answer to the question "How confident are you that your answer is correct?" Second, even though self-efficacy questions may use the word confidence to assess one's "can do" feelings, the trait of confidence is limited to the postdecision or postaction "done well" measurement (Stankov, Kleitman et al., 2014). Examples are students giving an answer to a test item (e.g., How sure are you that your answer to a test item is correct?), a doctor diagnosing a patient with an illness, a meteorologist reporting on a likely percentage of rain falling at a particular locality, a political supporter believing in the win of a party's candidate, an investor making a financial decision, and a gambler making their next bet. In other words, it has been recognized that confidence plays a major role in one's decision-making process across diverse fields, such as education, business leadership, stock-market investment, and legal practice. However, the basic notion of confidence is the same. It has to do with self-assuredness of one's feeling and evaluation of his/her own cognitive act of thinking or decision-making. Clearly, this type of confidence has little relevance to what a layperson associates with the term, that is, "charisma" or extraversion or even "a loud voice" or "big gestures"; confidence is not flamboyance. Although one may think that these characteristics are related to confidence (especially facets of extraversion), empirical evidence indicates that this is not the case.

On a final note, we also wish to add (although this is a minor issue) that our preference is to use the label "confidence" instead of "self-confidence." This is because if one were to consult thesaurus on "confidence," "self-confidence" is immediately suggested as a synonym. Hence, there is no need to insert self when describing confidence. In contrast, neither "efficacy" nor "concept" summons the "self-" prefix.

The goal of this review is to capitalize on recent advances in theory, measurement, methodology and studies of nomological networks, to document empirical evidence and to illustrate conceptual differences between these two related constructs. We must admit that the authors of this review have done work on both constructs, but have done more work on confidence. The second part of the review will therefore focus on the main findings in studies of confidence. Specifically, we shall address the following aspects: contexts for understanding conceptual differences between self-efficacy and confidence and their place within the self-beliefs system; measurement issues; empirical evidence for a general factor of confidence; predictive validity; correlations between confidence, personality, and other constructs; overconfidence and self-enhancement; and developmental trajectories of one's self-belief system.

1. Broader Context: Self-Efficacy and Confidence as Self-Beliefs and Metacognitive Processes

Self-Beliefs

Among a host of student variables listed by Hattie (2009) as good predictors of academic achievement, there is a strong presence of the variables reflecting students' self-beliefs. Self-beliefs include self-perceptions of one's own competency to carry out particular cognitive activities. Lee and Stankov (2013) also showed that measures of the constructs popular among educational researchers, such as motivation, attitudes toward school, and learning strategies, have zero or even small negative correlations with cognitive achievement in large-scale data (e.g., Programme for International Student Assessment [PISA] 2003). On the other hand, the three self-belief measures in the PISA 2003—self-efficacy, self-concept, and anxiety (one's physio-emotional reactions when she/he thinks about or performs a task)—presented a different picture. These three constructs are often studied together as they are seen as closely related but yet separate constructs (Lee, 2009; Stankov, Lee, Luo, & Hogan, 2012). Theoretical accounts of conceptual separation between self-efficacy and self-concept have been documented (Bong & Skaalvik, 2003). The conceptual and measurement separation among the self-constructs was also empirically supported by Lee's (2009) study, where self-concept, self-efficacy, and anxiety were revealed as independent constructs in more than 40 countries, even when stringent invariance principles were applied (i.e., invariant factor loadings, factor residuals, factor correlations, and factor variances). In a later study (Lee & Stankov, 2013), it was also found that the correlations among these three self-constructs are sufficiently high (ranging from $r = 0.45$ to $r = 0.67$ across 41 countries) to implicate a self-belief factor that encompasses all three at a higher order of analysis. The general conclusion was that there is sufficient empirical evidence to support their separation into distinct entities, and each of these constructs shows good predictive validity of achievement scores (Lee, 2009; Lee & Stankov, 2013). Although PISA surveys do not include measures of confidence, we believe that confidence is also a self-belief construct. Empirical evidence in support of this claim will be reviewed below.

Metacognition

Metacognition was the term originally proposed by Flavell (1979) and subsequently it became a part of Sternberg's (1985) Triarchic Theory of Intelligence. Of particular importance for Flavell (1979) was the monitoring aspect of cognitive performance. In Sternberg's (1985) theory, there are three components of metacognition: planning, monitoring, and evaluation. Self-efficacy asks whether the task is achievable, thus relating to future events (i.e., the event that one thinks of has not yet occurred) and the process is in the "planning" stage of metacognitive awareness.

In cognitive psychology, metacognitive processing is typically assessed in a more objective way by linking cognitive test performance to subjective assessments of one's quality of performance. Confidence is most closely related to the monitoring component of metacognition. Contemporary research of confidence was initiated by an inquiry, "Do those who know more also know more about how much they know?" (Lichtenstein & Fischoff, 1977). Confidence is defined as a subjective feeling and judgment about the correctness of one's decision. This kind of decision-making is manifested in one's opinion, beliefs, behaviors, answers, tasks, or diagnosis, and ways of doing and thinking, all of which fall under the broad category of one's cognitive act (see Keren, 1991). In short, confidence is made up of one's subjective judgment ingrained in his/her own thinking process and behaviors.

Metacognition is seen as closely linked to the area of self-regulated learning (Pintrich & De Groot, 1990). One way to assess metacognitive processing is with questionnaires such as Schraw and Denison's (1994) Metacognitive Awareness Questionnaire (MAQ). However, we may note that the relationship of MAQ and measures of confidence is low to moderate, with correlations ranging from .15 to .40 (Kleitman, 2008), showing that confidence taps somewhat different aspects of human cognition than questionnaire measures of metacognitive processing. In education, questionnaire-based measures of metacognition tend to be linked to the choice of learning strategies.

Stankov (2000b) reports findings from a study in which both components of metacognition—monitoring and evaluation—were incorporated within the typical tests of fluid intelligence. Monitoring was assessed by asking participants to provide confidence ratings after submitting the answer to every test item. Thus, confidence is an essential part of monitoring which in turn is a critical aspect of metacognition.

2. Measurement Issues

Self-Efficacy

Measurement of self-efficacy has been typically done by presenting statements or questions followed by Likert-type ratings. Measures have been developed aiming to assess self-efficacy at different levels: general-trait level, domain level, or specific-task level. The general-trait level self-efficacy is still being considered and employed in some studies (e.g., Chen, Gully, & Eden, 2001; Yeo & Neal, 2006), although it is criticized by Bandura (2012), who states that "an all-purpose scale with a small set of items proclaiming that one is uniformly self-efficacious" (p. 30) cannot have predictive power for a specific outcome. He elaborates that "trait measures mask existing variability in people's beliefs in their capabilities for different types of activities under different levels of challenge. Therefore, in personality assessment, one size cannot fit all without sacrificing explanatory and predictive power." (pp. 30–31).

In recent years, the PISA has adopted an approach to measuring self-efficacy (in mathematics) by focusing on specific (mathematics) tasks, that is, asking whether the respondents can solve a particular mathematics problem. Examples of such questions are as follows: "How confident do you feel about being able to solve (a) using a train timetable to work out how long it would take to get from one place to another; (b) calculating how much cheaper a TV would be after a 30% discount; (c) calculating how many square meters of tiles you need to cover a floor; (d) understanding graphs presented in newspapers; (e) solving an equation like $3x + 5 = 17$; (f) finding the actual distance between two places on a map with a 1:10,000 scale; (g) solving an equation like $2(x + 3) = (x + 3)(x - 3)$; and (h) calculating the petrol consumption rate of a car." Each item is accompanied by a 4-point rating scale. The 2003 scale was used again in the PISA 2012 assessment. With eight items, the reliabilities are shown to be in the .80s range ($\alpha = 0.83$ and $\alpha = 0.84$ in the PISA 2003 and 2012, respectively). This PISA self-efficacy assessment differs from the traditional confidence measurement (see below) in that the participants are not asked to solve the problems. Hence, responses indicate "true" representation of "can do" attitudes of self-efficacy. Although education research has not outwardly proposed the optimal level of self-efficacy, the literature hints that the more self-efficacy, the better you are in overcoming difficult and challenging situations.

Confidence

Traditional measurement of confidence, in particular the method used by cognitive psychologists, is also item based. Participants are asked to solve a cognitive item first. An exemplary cognitive item would be "A TV set costs $300 and the store offers 30% discount. How much would you have to pay?" After providing an answer, the participants are told to rate their confidence level on a scale from 0% to 100% in 10% intervals (0%, 10%, 20%, . . . 80%, 90%, 100%.). This measurement approach rests on the idea that confidence, often labeled as "subjective probability," tends to differ from the objective accuracy of knowledge expressed in the participants' answers. Thus, the aim is to capture the difference between one's confidence and actual accuracy (i.e., knowledge) and to be able to indicate the gap between confidence and accuracy, often called the "realism" of confidence ratings.

Since the 1960s, a lot of effort has been devoted to the development of statistical procedures that link accuracy and confidence scores. The best known are the following four: (a) Partial scoring (De Finetti, 1965); (b) Calibration curves (Keren, 1991; Stankov, 1998; Yates, 1982); (c) Calibration plots (e.g., Crawford & Stankov, 1996; Kleitman & Stankov, 2007; Stankov, 1998; Stankov & Crawford, 1996b; Stankov & Lee, 2008); and (d) Item-level and test-level discrepancy index utilizing the item response theory (Paek, Lee, Stankov, & Wilson, 2013; Stankov, Lee, & Paek, 2009).

Partial scoring method replaced the dichotomously scored accuracy scores with the confidence rating scores, often between 1 and 5. For example, before completing a problem, a participant first rates his confidence on a scale between 1 and 5. After completing the problem, his answer is assessed. If it is correct, his score becomes the previously stated confidence level. If his answer is incorrect, no confidence score is attached to the overall scoring and he simply gets a score of zero. Thus, in this scoring scheme, the person's inaccurate answer will be punished and his accurate score will represent both his accuracy and confidence scores. This partial scoring, compared to the traditional scoring based on the accuracy information only, tends to be more reliable but has shown weaker validity (cf. Hakstian & Kansup, 1975). For that reason, the use of partial scoring has declined over the past 30 years.

In the methods based on calibration curves, the two-dimensional coordinate system is formed with accuracy scores on the Y-axis and confidence scores on the X-axis (see Stankov, 1998). A diagonal line in such a plot represents the perfect calibration line. Empirically obtained calibration curves can be compared to the perfect calibration line in order to assess the amount of confidence-accuracy bias. However, this method utilizes only the group-summary information (i.e., averages across individuals and across all the items in the test), and thus calibration curves do not provide information about individuals' or items' characteristics that are of interest to psychologists working in the area of individual differences.

The next method that has been developed and frequently used over the past decade is based on the item-calibration plot. It is designed to overcome a limitation of the calibration-curves method and provide information about the item characteristics. The group means of the individual items are displayed in a two-dimensional plot with accuracy scores on the Y-axis and confidence scores on the X-axis (i.e., like in the calibration curves described above). The items can be compared in terms of their distances from the perfect calibration line (see Stankov, 1998; Stankov, Lee et al., 2012).

Thus, one's optimal level of confidence is not overconfidence or underconfidence but perfect calibration (i.e., matching of one's confidence to accuracy). It can be seen that both measures of calibration, either using curves or plots, are important tools for assessing metacognitive monitoring. Item information such as miscalibration indicates the presence of the inefficiency or error in the item construction and thus can be of use to item developers.

Confidence scores can be calculated for each individual, just like test scores, as the averages of confidence ratings over all items in the test. One's confidence score can be compared to his or her accuracy score expressed as the percentage of correctly solved items in the same test. Then, the difference between confidence score and accuracy score—termed the Bias score—represents a single measure of (over)confidence bias for each individual.

The latest development is the confidence-accuracy discrepancy index, which was developed using the Item Response Theory (IRT) methodology (cf. Paek et al., 2013; Stankov et al., 2009). In this method, confidence and accuracy and an additional person-parameter of ability are placed on the same metrics. By using multivariate IRT, the strength of the relationship between confidence and accuracy can be estimated, and confidence-accuracy discrepancy indices can be calculated at both local person-ability level and at the item and test level.

3. The g-Factor of Confidence?

A considerable amount of evidence shows that confidence is a general trait or disposition (cf. Crawford & Stankov, 1996; Kleitman & Stankov, 2001, 2007; Pallier et al., 2002; Stankov, 1998, 1999, 2000b; Stankov & Crawford, 1996a, 1996b, 1997; Stankov & Kleitman, 2008; Stankov & Lee, 2008; Stankov et al., 2009; Stankov, Pallier, Danthiir, & Morony, 2012; Stankov & Schweizer, 2007). A broad confidence factor did emerge even though the composition of the batteries of cognitive tests from which confidence ratings were derived varied considerably. The test batteries included, in various combinations, psychomotor tasks, tests of memory and attention, measures of sensory and perceptual processes from all five sensory modalities, and many primary abilities identified within the theory of fluid and crystallized intelligence (see Horn & Blankson, 2005). Some studies also included atypical tasks such as the Sureness scale of Kleitman and Stankov (2007) described above. Despite this diversity of tasks, whether involving solving a problem, predicting future events, or simply stating one's political views, a confidence factor tends to appear. This factor signifies individuals' habitual nature and their consistency in possessing and expressing confidence. The confidence factor has been equally pronounced among children aged 9 to 12 years (Kleitman & Gibson, 2011; Kleitman Stankov, Allwood, Young, & Mak, 2013), adolescents (Morony, Kleitman, Lee, & Stankov, 2013; Stankov, Lee et al., 2012) and adults (e.g., Kleitman, 2008; Pallier et al., 2002; Stankov, 2000b; Stankov & Crawford, 1996a, 1997; Stankov & Lee, 2008). Furthermore, recent theoretical accounts of confidence and empirical evidence cited in support of the proposed theory are in agreement with the general factor of individual differences in confidence (see Koriat, 2012).

The existence of a general factor of confidence is particularly important. Apart from the "g" factor identified among the cognitive tasks, and the still-contested general factor of personality (see Musek, 2007), there are no other constructs in psychology that are of comparable broadness. A general factor of confidence has theoretical and practical implications that are parallel to those of the cognitive g factor. From the theoretical point of view, confidence is domain-independent, like g factor itself, but unlike other achievement-related self-beliefs (e.g., self-efficacy, self-concept). This means that the nature of the cognitive act (e.g., solving verbal, spatial, or mathematical problems) is irrelevant, and confidence can be manifested regardless of the type of medium used to elicit the answer/decision. One of its powerful practical implications in education is that individuals' confidence ratings obtained with one test (say, mathematics) will be able to predict their confidence, as well as academic performance, on another test (say, English). Thus, while researchers of self-efficacy or self-concept have emphasized domain-specificity (with reading self-concept predicting reading achievement but not predicting mathematics achievement), researchers on confidence proclaim the "superiority" of confidence as it is not domain-specific but "omnipresent" in one's cognitive behaviors and thus can predict cross-domain competency whether it relates to reading, mathematics, or science.

4. Empirical Evidence for a Separate Confidence Construct

Confidence and Accuracy Factors

When confidence and accuracy are measured within the same battery of tests and linked to the same question (i.e., asking about his/her confidence and accuracy of the same tasks/event), some researchers start to question whether both confidence and accuracy measured in this way are in fact tapping the same construct. Studies conducted to answer this question have provided strong empirical evidence for the constructs' separation. That is, correlations between accuracy and confidence scores from the same test typically range from $r = 0.20$ to around $r = 0.65$, with the majority being in between $r = 0.40$ and $r = 0.60$. These are moderate correlations indicating that, although related, confidence and accuracy scores do not measure exactly the same underlying process. But can it be shown that accuracy and confidence define separate factors?

Stankov (2000b) provides evidence that the confidence factor is separate from other factors that can be derived from various cognitive tests. In that study, five tests of fluid intelligence (Gf)—Counting Letters, Letter Series, Raven's Progressive Matrices, Swaps, and Triplets—were used and four different scores were calculated from each test (i.e., in total, 20 scores). All five Gf tests were scored in a way that produced four measures:

accuracy (percentage of correctly solved items), average speed of answering an item, confidence (average of confidence ratings over all items in the test), and evaluation (estimate of correctly solved items in the test). Confirmatory Factor Analyses (CFA) produced four factors corresponding to the types of each of the scores (i.e., accuracy, speed, confidence, and evaluation). Confidence was clearly defined as a separate factor that had loadings from all five tests. It also had a moderately strong correlation with the evaluation factor, suggesting a possible metacognitive factor at the second order of analysis. Stankov (2000b) also concludes that confidence ratings function in a similar way as accuracy and speed measures. All three measures can be easily derived from any cognitive test performance. In fact, traditional psychophysicists used to employ these three measures in their studies of sensory thresholds to draw unique information about examinees' cognitive ability.

The establishment of a confidence factor in the way described above coupled with the trend towards the item-based self-efficacy measurement suggests future studies investigating whether self-efficacy can also show (like confidence) a broad (or perhaps general) factor, especially if the scales are constructed similar to those on the PISA tests. A whole test battery including self-efficacy items in cognitive domains other than mathematics, for example, science and reading, can be compiled and evaluated in order to find out if such self-efficacy items define a self-efficacy factor. Needless to say, this factor can then be compared to the analogous confidence factor.

A Higher-Order Self-Beliefs Factor: Confidence, Self-Efficacy, Self-Concept, and Anxiety

Over the past several years, we have explored the relationship between confidence and measures that have been of interest to educational psychologists and in particular measures of self-beliefs. First of all, Lee and Stankov (2013) used the PISA 2003 data to show that self-efficacy, self-concept, and anxiety do define a common self-belief factor at the second-order. PISA surveys do not assess confidence, but the emergence of the self-belief factor readily leads to questions about its links to confidence.

We have also examined the relationship between confidence and the other three self-belief measures in studies carried out with samples of 14–15-year-old adolescents from Singapore and several Confucian Asian and European countries (Morony et al., 2013). This study examined the structure and cross-cultural invariance of mathematical self-beliefs in nine countries (N = 7,167): Singapore, South Korea, Hong Kong, Taiwan, Denmark, The Netherlands, Finland, Serbia, and Latvia. The cross-cultural invariance tests (i.e., whether the same factorial structure will emerge across different countries) were carried out. Six self-beliefs scales were used in the study: mathematics self-efficacy, mathematics self-concept, memory and reasoning self-concept, mathematics anxiety, and confidence/estimate. The six scales produced two broader, correlated factors: one is a self-beliefs factor consisting of math self-concept, math anxiety, and memory self-concept, and the other is a self-assessment factor consisting of confidence, accuracy, and estimate (see Figure 9.1). Interestingly but yet understandably, math self-efficacy loads on both factors. This also means that when confidence and self-efficacy are put together in the context of other self-beliefs constructs, they can actually be closer to each other than they are to the other factors, such as self-concept.

Similar results were reported in Stankov, Morony and Lee (2014). This study was based on 600 middle-school students from Singapore. They were given several questionnaires regarding psychological maladjustments (depression and anxiety), mathematics self-efficacy, mathematics self-concept, mathematics anxiety and enjoyment of mathematics, confidence in mathematics, and broadly defined self-concept (memory, reasoning, and academic self-concepts). Results showed that measures of confidence on mathematics tasks define a single factor together with the scales assessing mathematics self-efficacy, mathematics self-concept, mathematics anxiety,

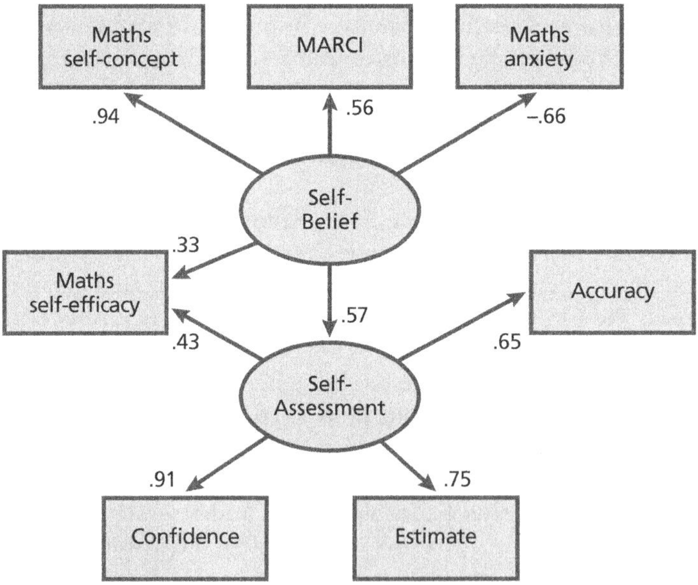

Figure 9.1 Structural equation model (SEM) outcome—standardized path coefficients for predicting accuracy from measures of self-beliefs and self-assessment (adopted from Morony et al., 2013). *Note:* MARCI is an acronym for the Memory and Reasoning Self-Concept Inventory. Fit indices for this model are as follows: SRMR: .058, CFI: .967, TLI: .942, RMSEA: .087.

and enjoyment of mathematics. This is clearly a self-belief factor—a proof that confidence is related to the other self-beliefs constructs.

Another related study is Stankov, Lee, et al. (2012). In this study, a distinct confidence factor was identified based on student performance in the domains of mathematics (N = 1,940) and English (N = 1,786). Table 9.1 was constructed on the basis of the Stankov, Lee, et al. (2012) report. As can be seen in that table, a battery of seven self-beliefs measures that are identical to those listed above was administered to the participants. (We hasten to add that self-efficacy in this study was not assessed at the item level, although it is domain specific, that is, "I can do almost all the work in English/mathematics class if I do not give up."). Each group of students was also given a test of English and/or mathematics. It is remarkable how similar the findings are with English and mathematics displayed in Table 9.1.

The first column in Table 9.1, entitled "1st Principal Component," is an estimate of the first latent dimension that was extracted from the correlation matrix. The matrix for this analysis does not include the accuracy scores since the intention was to form a single factor of self-beliefs and thus include only

TABLE 9.1 The Structure of Self-Beliefs and Accuracy in English and Mathematics and Predictions of Achievements

	1st Principal Component	Two-Factors Solution		Standardized Beta Coefficients
		F1	F2	
a) English (N = 1,786)				
English accuracy	Not included		.80	Criterion
English confidence	.51		.80	.56**
English self-efficacy	.71	.62		.00
English anxiety	–.48		–.45	–.19**
English self-concept	.69	.61		–.10*
Academic self-concept	.63	.69		.01
Memory self-concept	.63	.77		–.10*
Reasoning self-concept	.76	.78		.01
b) Mathematics (N = 1,940)				
Math accuracy	Not included		.95	Criterion
Math confidence	.54		.88	.65**
Math self-efficacy	.75	.62		.05
Math anxiety	–.60	–.40	–.33	–.11**
Math self-concept	.77	.62		–.03
Academic self-concept	.74	.78		–.05
Memory self-concept	.65	.81		–.02
Reasoning self-concept	.76	.85		–.04

Source: Adapted from Stankov, Lee, et al., 2012.

seven self-belief measures. It is easy to see that a common factor exists and all loadings are substantial for both English and mathematics. For our purposes here, it is important to notice the loadings of the confidence measures on the first principal component. For mathematics, even though the loading of the confidence variable is reasonable in size (.54), it is still the smallest loading in that column. For English, only anxiety has a loading lower than that for confidence. This means that even though confidence shares common variance with other self-beliefs, a sizable amount of unique variance in confidence remains in the separate analyses of English and mathematics.

The next two columns in Table 9.1 show two-factor solutions for both English and mathematics. This time the matrix being analyzed contains not only the seven noncognitive self-beliefs measures, but also a measure from a different domain—cognitive accuracy. The first factor, F1, in both solutions is the self-beliefs factor; it has loadings from self-efficacy, self-concept, academic self-concept, memory self-concept and reasoning self-concept. Note that in both solutions (i.e., English and mathematics), neither accuracy nor confidence load on the first factor. Mathematics anxiety loads on the first factor, but English anxiety is not salient on it. The second factor, F2, has only three salient loadings in both solutions: accuracy scores, confidence scores, and (negative) anxiety. Clearly, the factor is defined primarily by confidence and accuracy, and the presence of anxiety makes it broader in scope.

Overall, the single-factor solution, without accuracy present, together with the two-factors solution with accuracy scores included, indicate that confidence shares its variance with both self-beliefs measures and with the accuracy measures. On the other hand, self-efficacy remains as a self-belief and does not tap accuracy since it shares little variance with accuracy. Our results clearly show that confidence is a robust individual-differences construct in both English and mathematics.

6. Predictive Validity of Self-Efficacy

The ultimate value of educational-psychological constructs is often evaluated by their predictive validity of academic achievement. Self-efficacy has been studied, not exclusively but certainly extensively, in the areas of mathematics and writing. The PISA item-based measures of mathematics self-efficacy show a moderately strong correlation between self-efficacy and achievement in mathematics, up to $r = 0.46$ in the most recent 2012 assessment. Lee (2009) also reported that all three self-beliefs had moderate to moderately strong correlations with the PISA 2003 mathematics scores ($r = 0.23$ with mathematics self-concept; $r = 0.43$ with mathematics self-efficacy; and $r = -0.39$ with mathematics anxiety). The study also shows that the self-belief measures of self-efficacy and anxiety were the best predictors of mathematics achievement in the PISA 2003 when they were considered together with variables of intrinsic and extrinsic motivation, attitudes toward school, and learning strategies. Lee (2009) concluded that self-beliefs appear to be a dynamic and critical driver of achievement for the 15-year-old students from around the world.

When students' self-efficacy and academic achievement were examined longitudinally (e.g., Caprara et al., 2008, 2011), and self-efficacy was not assessed at the item level, the association tends to be lower. For example, Caprara et al. (2011) report that students' perceived efficacy for self-regulated learning measured at 13 was significantly correlated with their achievement scores one year later, with $r = 0.30$.

7. Confidence: The Best Non-Cognitive Predictor of Achievement

There have been a number of studies conducted by Stankov and his associates that lead to the same conclusion: although all self-beliefs have good predictive validity for academic achievement, confidence does a better job. For instance, Morony et al. (2013) included confidence in addition to a host of noncognitive variables and demonstrated that confidence explains most of the variance in the achievement scores captured by the other self-constructs combined; and confidence accounts for 46% of total variance in achievement while the combined measures of other noncognitive variables, plus the previous cognitive performance, account for only 41% of the total variance in achievement. This is quite remarkable since it is well known that one's previous cognitive performance is typically the best predictor of his/her current achievement.

The same general conclusion about the predictive properties of confidence arises from the studies of Morony et al. (2013) and Stankov, Lee, et al. (2012). Inspection of the diagram in Figure 9.1 from Morony et al. (2013) shows that accuracy scores in mathematics are predicted only from the self-assessment factor (circle) which has the highest (.91) loading from confidence. Self-beliefs factor does not have a direct link to accuracy in that figure, implying that all other noncognitive measures have indirect paths that pass through the self-assessment node.

Standardized beta coefficients from the Stankov, Lee, et al. (2012) study, which are presented in the last column of Table 9.1, tell the same story. In the top part of Table 9.1, English accuracy scores were used as a criterion. English confidence was the best predictor of achievement among all examined self-constructs. The same is repeated with mathematics accuracy scores, which is shown in the bottom part of Table 9.1. The next-best predictor was anxiety, which was the case in both domains. It is also noteworthy that self-efficacy, which was not measured by the item-based assessment, had a predictive validity of zero for both English and mathematics achievement. If we combine the findings about the factorial structure of self-beliefs presented in the first three columns of Table 9.1, and elaborated on in the previous section with the results of regression analysis, it is reasonable to conclude that confidence captures all predictive power of self-efficacy, self-concept and, with the exception of anxiety, all other self-beliefs employed in the Stankov, Lee, et al. (2012) study. This is a powerful statement that justifies the use of confidence ratings in education and lends support to the claim that the trait of confidence is important in decision-making and behavior.

In addition, Stankov, Lee, et al. (2012, cf. Table 6) shows that confidence and anxiety remain significant predictors of school grades in mathematics even when the accuracy score that was obtained together with confidence 3 months earlier was partialled out from the prediction equation. Again, given that achievement accuracy and ability scores are the best predictors of performance. It is remarkable that confidence and anxiety showed incremental predictive validity after partialling out of accuracy scores. A similar size of incremental validity of confidence was also reported by Stankov and Lee (2008). Thus, predictive validity of confidence ratings extends beyond close temporal proximity of accuracy and confidence assessments and generalizes to different measures of the same domain after a longer time period (i.e., test of mathematics and end-of-year grade in mathematics) and because of the presence of general factor, even to different domains (i.e., confidence in mathematics to confidence in English).

8. Correlations Between Confidence, Personality, and Other Psychological Constructs

Much of our earlier work with measures of confidence was focused on establishing its relationship to personality traits, thinking dispositions, and metacognition (e.g., Kleitman & Stankov, 2007). Conclusions from that work include the following two points: confidence is not an aspect of personality, such as extraversion or anxiety, nor a thinking disposition such as rigidity, dogmatism, or the need for structure emphasized by Stanovich (2011). Also, confidence does not have substantial (or even moderate) correlations with the Big Five measures of personality (except for about $r = 0.30$s or lower correlations with the Openness to Experience). Stankov (2013) also concludes that neither confidence nor self-efficacy correlate with personality factors. Furthermore, he reports that these two constructs do not have noteworthy correlations with measures of depression and well-being.

9. Overconfidence and Self-Enhancement

One of the typical findings in confidence research has been a ubiquitous phenomenon of overconfidence—people think that they know more than what they really know, especially when they are faced with moderately difficult tasks. It is well known that those at a lower ability level tend to show more overconfidence bias than people at higher ability levels. It is generally believed that this overconfidence phenomenon is largely due to high confidence levels among comparatively lower-ability individuals.

A recent study by Stankov and Lee (2014) has extended this individual-level finding on overconfidence to cross-cultural comparisons. Nine world regions (33 countries) participated in this study. The main finding was that the countries whose average scores on the measure of fluid intelligence (i.e., Letter Series test) were lower (e.g., countries from Africa and Southeast Asia) show more overconfidence bias than the countries at the high end on this cognitive measure (e.g., Confucian Asian countries). Thus, this cross-national level finding mirrors the findings at the individual level. It is also interesting to note a consistent pattern in that the profile of the means of confidence scores is relatively flat across the countries and world regions. This pattern is occasionally also observed at the individual level. In other words, people in African countries have the same average confidence score as do people in Confucian countries. The authors interpreted this pronounced confidence as an indication of an "innate" human propensity for self-enhancement. It is plausible that the expression of higher confidence at the lower levels of cognitive performance can act as a cushion against feelings of failure, softening the blows people may receive in life, which helps preserve self-esteem and allows them to keep on living as effective members of the society. As pointed out by H. Marsh (personal communication, March 2014), this is also the prediction one would get from the frame-of-reference effect in which confidence is determined by comparative evaluations with others in the same context.

In order to arrive at an understanding of the overconfidence phenomenon, Stankov, and Lee (2014) suggest that it may be useful to consider the distinction between typical and maximal cognitive performance (Goff & Ackerman, 1992). In cognitive testing, the scores are believed to assess persons' maximal performance levels. These scores are often used in, and are perceived to be, the "high-stakes" assessments. This type of performance (where the maximum ability of a person is believed to be demonstrated) differs from the concept of intelligence called for in typical performance/behaviors which do not require a maximum level of a person's cognitive engagement (i.e., how a person routinely behaves when performing intellectual tasks such as reading or figuring out the change at a grocery shop). The suggestion is that people may use different criteria when they are solving the test items versus when they are asked about subjective feelings about what has just happened. While they try to produce their own maximal performance on the ability test, their judgment of the accuracy of their performance (confidence) may have been based on their own worldview, which tends to be more stable and influenced by general feelings of being able to overcome and successfully navigate through daily tasks (i.e., their typical behaviors/performance in life) and social comparison in relation to others in that context.

10. Developmental Trajectories of Confidence and Self-Efficacy

Psychologists' important goal is to be able to map out developmental trajectories of the constructs they study. While researchers in confidence are more interested in its starting point and when it is stabilized as an individual's trait, researchers interested in self-efficacy have explored more about when it begins to decline and the influences on its decline. It is believed to be a worldwide trend that students' self-beliefs in academic abilities and interest decline continually during adolescent years. The empirical evidence is abundant in studies with secondary school students (e.g., Denissen, Zarrett, & Eccles, 2007; Haussler & Hoffmann, 2002; Nagy et al., 2010; Otis, Grouzet, & Pelletier, 2005) and from grades 1 to 8 in subject areas of reading, mathematics, social science, science, physical education, art, and music (Haladyna & Thomas, 1979). In studies by Caprara et al. (2008, 2011), student's self-efficacy for self-regulated learning tended to fluctuate over time. For instance, in Caprara et al. (2008), the self-efficacy correlations decreased from $r = 0.67$ (at age 13), $r = 0.63$ (at age 14), $r = 0.50$ (at age 16) to $r = 0.27$ (at age 18) with self-efficacy measured at age 12 (among male students). These data clearly show that students' self-efficacy is open to change, probably due to their school experience.

It is currently unknown the age at which confidence develops into a general, stable trait. However, contemporary cognitive development theories of self-belief constructs and metacognition allow limited but plausible predictions regarding potential developmental trajectories of confidence. For instance, metacognitive awareness tends to start to increase around age 5 (Veenman & Spaans, 2005). Metacognitive skills are not formulated until age 11 (Veenman & Spaans, 2005). This view stems from the notion that children around age 11 start to think about self as a motivator that influences their own task performance. Given that confidence is related to self-monitoring capacity, we can expect that the early stages of confidence development may emerge (therefore we can measure it) at age 11 or 12. There has been some initial, at least partial, support for such a prediction in the study by Kleitman and Moscrop (2010), where confidence was a recognizable metacognitive trait among children aged 9 to 11.

11. Understudied Aspects of Confidence

In this section, we shall briefly consider some of the areas that have been neglected in previous research on confidence and can benefit from additional research. Some suggestions are of practical use and others are of theoretical importance. First, there is a paucity of research concerning the cultivation of confidence. As such, it remains unknown whether confidence can be manipulated, either during childhood and adolescence or at the adult level. Stankov and Crawford (1997) indicate that providing feedback after each test item does not improve confidence in university students, suggesting that confidence is an individual trait and thus hard to be manipulated by an intervention carried out in a relatively short period of time. On the other hand, if the feedback practice sessions were longer and more extensive in scope, there might be some "successful" intervention on people's confidence. Of particular interest, of course, would be the improvement in calibration (i.e., match between accuracy and confidence) and metacognitive skill of self-monitoring.

Second, expansion of self-beliefs studies to childrearing practice is another area to develop. There has been some evidence that parental practices during childhood may be related to person's confidence later on in life. For example, the impostor phenomenon (i.e., feelings of overachievement when the achievement is compared with one's perception of what he or she really deserves), which is related to confidence, is affected by parental upbringing practices (Want & Kleitman, 2006). The role of parental childrearing practices in confidence development was subsequently confirmed in studies with children (Kleitman & Gibson, 2011; Kleitman & Moscrop, 2010).

Third, a new exciting development is happening in medical research. This profession has become particularly concerned about the role of overconfidence in surgeons' misdiagnosis (Berner & Graber, 2008; Norman, 2008). Undoubtedly, other professions such as financial decision-making or economic forecasting may also be adversely affected by overconfidence. Thus, it will be particularly important to investigate overconfidence manifested in the profession-specific ways to improve calibration and reduce errors.

Fourth, little is known about the relationship between confidence and cognitive biases that have emerged from the studies of rationality (Stanovich, 2011). Indeed, overconfidence is usually treated as another example of cognitive bias. Our own recent work in this area indicates that cognitive biases do not have high correlations among themselves and do not define a single factor; they each have a sizeable amount of unique variance

(Teovanović, Knežević, & Stankov, 2014). Cognitive biases also do not correlate with measures of fluid and crystallized intelligence or personality. Overconfidence is the exception—it is the only cognitive bias that has a significant correlation with fluid intelligence. As the work on rationality is one of the most important developments in studies of individual differences, it will be necessary to examine the relationship of confidence and rationality measures in more detail in the future.

Finally, in addition to self-enhancement, which was mentioned earlier, there are at least two other conceptually related measures that may be linked in an interesting way to confidence. One of these is the measurement of overclaiming, which was developed by Paulhus and his associates (see Paulhus & Harms, 2004). This is an unobtrusive measure of both intelligence and self-enhancement biases. Participants rate their familiarity with persons, events, and things on a 5-point scale. Some of these items do not exist; responses greater than 1 for such items suggest overclaiming of their knowledge. The relationship between overconfidence and overclaiming is not known at present. One's expression of familiarity with nonexisting concepts is likely to be linked to confidence. A closely related area is self-assessment of ability. Furnham and Chamorro-Premuzic (2004) report low to moderate correlations between the objectively determined IQ scores and one's estimate of IQ. At present, it is not known to what extent this correlation can be accounted for by one's confidence.

CONCLUSIONS

Psychological constructs of self-efficacy and confidence are clearly distinct conceptually, in terms of measurement and in terms of the nomological nets they encompass. Self-efficacy refers to "can do" whereas confidence captures a "done well" attitude. Self-efficacy is typically measured prior to one's acting. Confidence relates to postaction. Self-efficacy measures seem to be conceptually closer to self-concept than they are to confidence. Confidence, on the other hand, is a self-beliefs construct but also captures one's cognitive ability and achievement to a larger extent than self-efficacy does. Both are good predictors of cognitive achievement, but confidence does a better job in that prediction. Nevertheless, there can be no doubt that they are useful constructs for both psychological and educational inquiries.

A fairly recent development has been the identification of the 21st Century Skills. Confidence has been included in various frameworks such as in the 2010 Assessment and Teaching of 21st Century Skills (called ATC 21 set by a consortium consisting of the University of Melbourne and Microsoft, Intel and Cisco, the 2009 Partnership for 21st Century Skills, the 2011 National Research Council of the United States, and the 2012 National Council on Measurement in Education of the United States). Apart from being the best-known noncognitive predictor of achievement, confidence has other features that recommend it for use in the social sciences. The most important is the existence of a general factor of confidence, suggesting that confidence is a trait akin to general ability that is not domain specific. Confidence scores are also comparable to the performance measures from objective tests, allowing for the assessment of calibration. Substantive findings of a pervasive overconfidence at both individual and country levels, along with a lack of pronounced differences between countries on the overall level of confidence, indicate that confidence may be a part of our survival mechanism. Fostering confidence-related self-monitoring skills can be a critical aspect of the development of self-regulated learning. Failure to master these skills can have major long-term influences on persons' educational and life outcomes.

REFERENCES

Bandura, A. (1997). *Self-efficacy: The exercise of control.* New York, NY: Freeman.

Bandura, A. (2012). On the functional properties of perceived self-efficacy revisited. *Journal of Management, 38,* 9–44. doi:10.1177/0149206311410606

Berner, E. S., & Graber, M. L. (2008). Overconfidence as a cause of diagnostic error in medicine. *The American Journal of Medicine, 121,* S2–S23.

Bong, M., & Skaalvik, E. M. (2003). Academic self-concept and self-efficacy: How different are they really? *Educational Psychology Review, 15,* 1–40.

Caprara, G. V., Fida, R., Vecchione, M., Del Bove, G., Vecchio, G. M., Barbaranelli, C., & Bandura, A. (2008). Longitudinal analysis of the role of perceived self-efficacy for self-regulated learning in academic continuance and achievement. *Journal of Educational Psychology, 100,* 525–534.

Caprara, G. V., Vecchione, M., Alessandri, G., Gerbino, M., & Barbaranelli, C. (2011). The contribution of personality traits and self-efficacy beliefs to academic achievement: A longitudinal study. *British Journal of Educational Psychology, 81,* 78–96.

Chen, G., Gully, S. M., & Eden, D. (2001). Validation of a new general self-efficacy scale. *Organizational Research Methods, 4,* 62–83.

Crawford, J., & Stankov, L. (1996). Age differences in the realism of confidence judgments: A calibration study using tests of fluid and crystallized intelligence. *Learning and Individual Differences, 6,* 84–103.

De Finetti, B. (1965). Methods of discriminating levels of partial knowledge concerning a test item. *British Journal of Mathematical and Statistical Psychology, 18,* 87–123.

Denissen, J. J. A., Zarrett, N. R., & Eccles, J. S. (2007). I like to do it, I'm able, and I know I am. *Child Development, 78,* 430–447.

Flavell, J. H. (1979). Metacognition and cognitive monitoring: A new area of cognitive-developmental inquiry. *American Psychologist, 34,* 906–911.

Furnham A., & Chamorro-Premuzic, T. (2004). Estimating one's own personality and intelligence scores. *British Journal Psychology, 95,* 145–160.

Goff, M., & Ackerman, P. L. (1992). Personality-intelligence relations: Assessment of typical intellectual engagement. *Journal of Educational Psychology, 84,* 537–552.

Hakstian, A. R., & Kansup, W. (1975). A comparison of several methods of assessing partial knowledge in multiple-choice tests: II. Testing procedures. *Journal of Educational Measurement, 12,* 231–239.

Haladyna, T., & Thomas, G. (1979). The attitudes of elementary school children toward school and subject matters. *Journal of Experimental Education, 48,* 18–23.

Hattie, J. (2009). *Visible learning: A synthesis of over 800 meta-analyses related to achievement.* London, UK: Routledge/Taylor & Francis.

Haussler, P., & Hoffmann, L. (2002). An intervention study to enhance girls' interest. *Journal of Research in Science Teaching, 39,* 870–888.

Horn, J. L., & Blankson, N. (2005). Foundations for better understanding of cognitive abilities. In D. P. Flanagan & P. L. Harrison (Eds.), *Contemporary intellectual assessment: Theories, tests, and issues* (pp. 41–68). New York, NY: Guilford.

Kahneman, D. (2011). *Thinking, fast and slow.* New York, NY: Farrar, Straus and Giroux.

Keren, G. (1991) Calibration and probability judgments: Conceptual and methodological issues. *Acta Psychologia, 77,* 217–273.

Kleitman, S. (2008). *Metacognition in the rationality debate: Self-confidence and its calibration.* Saarbücken, Germany: VDM Verlag Dr. Müller.

Kleitman, S., & Gibson, J. (2011). Metacognitive beliefs, self-confidence and primary learning environment of sixth grade students. *Learning and Individual Differences, 21,* 728–735.

Kleitman, S., & Moscrop, T. (2010). Self-confidence and academic achievements in primary-school children: Their relationships and links to parental bonds, intelligence, age, and gender. In A. Efklides & P. Misailidi (Eds.), *Trends and prospects in metacognition research* (pp. 293–326). New York, NY: Springer.

Kleitman, S., & Stankov, L. (2001). Ecological and person-driven aspects of metacognitive processes in test-taking. *Applied Cognitive Psychology, 15,* 321–341.

Kleitman, S., & Stankov, L. (2007). Self-confidence and metacognitive processes. *Learning and Individual Differences, 17,* 161–173.

Kleitman, S., Stankov, L., Allwood, C. M., Young, S., & Mak, K. (2013). Metacognitive self-confidence in school-aged children. In M. M. Mok (Ed.), *Self-directed learning oriented assessments in the Asia-Pacific* (pp. 139–153). New York, NY: Springer.

Koriat, A. (2012). The self-efficacy model of subjective confidence. *Psychological Review, 119,* 80–113.

Lee, J. (2009). Universals and specifics of math self-concept, math self-efficacy, and math anxiety across 41 PISA 2003 participating countries. *Learning and Individual Differences, 19,* 355–365.

Lee, J., & Stankov, L. (2013). Higher-order structure of motivation, self-beliefs, learning strategies, and attitudes toward school and its prediction of PISA 2003 mathematics scores. *Learning and Individual Differences, 26,* 119–130.

Lichtenstein, S., & Fischhoff, B. (1977). Do those who know more also know more about how much they know? *Organizational Behavior and Human Performance, 20*(2), 159–183.

Morony, S., Kleitman, S., Lee, Y.-P., & Stankov, L. (2013). Self-efficacy, anxiety, self-concept and confidence as predictors of achievement in Confucian and European countries. *International Journal of Educational Research, 58,* 79–96.

Musek, J. (2007). A general factor of personality: Evidence for the big one in the five-factor model. *Journal of Research in Personality, 41,* 1213–1233.

Nagy, G., Watt, H. M. G., Eccles, J. S., Trautwein, U., Lüdtke, O., & Baumert, J. (2010). The development of students' mathematics self-concept in relation to gender: Different countries, different trajectories? *Journal of Research on Adolescence, 20,* 482–506

Norman, G. (2008). The bias in researching cognitive bias. *Advances in Health Science Education, 19,* 291–295. doi:10.1007/s10459-014-9517-5

Otis, N., Grouzet, F. M. E., & Pelletier, L. G. (2005). Latent motivational change in an academic setting. *Journal of Educational Psychology, 97,* 170–183.

Paek, I., Lee, J., Stankov, L., & Wilson, M. (2013). Rasch modeling of accuracy and confidence measures from cognitive tests. *Journal of Applied Measurement, 14,* 232–248.

Pallier, G., Wilkinson, R., Danthiir, V., Kleitman, S., Knezevic, G., Stankov, L., & Roberts, R. (2002). The role of individual differences in the realism of confidence judgments. *Journal of General Psychology, 129,* 257–300.

Paulhus, D. L., & Harms, P. D. (2004). Measuring cognitive ability with the over-claiming technique. *Intelligence, 32,* 297–314.

Pintrich, P. R., & De Groot, E. V. (1990). Motivational and self-regulated learning components of classroom academic performance. *Journal of Educational Psychology, 82,* 33–40. doi:10.1037/0022-0663.82.1.33

Schraw, G., & Denison, R. (1994). Assessing metacognitive awareness. *Contemporary Educational Psychology, 19,* 460–475.

Stankov, L. (1998). Calibration curves, scatterplots and the distinction between general knowledge and perceptual tests. Learning *and Individual Differences, 8,* 28–51.

Stankov, L. (1999). Mining on the "no man's land" between intelligence and personality. In P. L. Ackerman, P. C. Kyllonen, & R. D. Roberts (Eds.), *Learning and individual differences: process, trait, and content determinants* (pp. 315–338). Washington, DC: American Psychological Association.

Stankov, L. (2000a). Structural extension of a hierarchical view on human cognitive abilities. *Learning and Individual Differences, 12,* 35–51.

Stankov, L. (2000b). Complexity, metacognition, and fluid intelligence. *Intelligence, 28,* 121–143.

Stankov, L. (2013). Noncognitive predictors of intelligence and academic achievement: An important role of confidence. *Personality and Individual Differences, 55,* 727–732.

Stankov, L., & Crawford, J. D. (1996a). Confidence judgments in studies of individual differences support the 'Confidence/frequency effect.' In C. Latimer & J. Michell (Eds.), *At once scientific and philosophic: A festschrift in honour of J. P. Sutcliffe* (pp. 215–239). Sydney, Australia: University of Sydney Press.

Stankov, L., & Crawford, J. D. (1996b). Confidence judgments in studies of individual differences. *Personality and Individual Differences, 21*(6), 971–986.

Stankov, L., & Crawford, J. D. (1997). Self-confidence and performance on cognitive tests. *Intelligence, 25,* 93–109.

Stankov, L., & Kleitman, S. (2008). Processes on the borderline between cognitive abilities and personality: Confidence and its realism. In G. J. Boyle, G. Matthews, & D. Saklofske (Eds.), *The handbook of personality theory and testing* (pp. 545–559). London, UK: Sage.

Stankov, L., Kleitman, S., & Jackson, S. (2014). Measures of trait confidence. In G. J. Boyle, G. Matthews, & D. H. Saklofske, (Eds.), *Measures of personality and social psychological constructs* (pp. 158–189). New York, NY: Academic.

Stankov, L., & Lee, J. (2008). Confidence and cognitive test performance. *Journal of Educational Psychology, 100,* 961–976.

Stankov, L., & Lee, J. (2014). Overconfidence across world regions. *Journal of Cross-cultural Psychology, 45,* 821–837.

Stankov, L., Lee, J., Luo, W., & Hogan, D. (2012). Confidence: A better predictor of academic achievement than self-efficacy, self-concept and anxiety? *Learning and Individual Differences, 22,* 747–758.

Stankov, L., Lee, J., & Paek, I. (2009). Realism of confidence judgements. *European Journal of Psychological Assessment, 25,* 123–130.

Stankov, L., Morony, S., & Lee, Y. P. (2014). Confidence: The best non-cognitive predictor of academic achievement? *Educational Psychology, 34*(1), 9–28.

Stankov, L., Pallier, G., Danthiir, V., & Morony, S. (2012). Perceptual underconfidence: A conceptual illusion? *European Journal of Psychological Assessment, 28,* 190–200.

Stankov, L., & Schweizer, K. (2007) Raven's Progressive Matrices, manipulations of complexity and measures of accuracy, speed and confidence. *Psychology Science, 49,* 326–342.

Stanovich, K. E. (2011). *Rationality and the reflective mind.* New York, NY: Oxford University Press.

Sternberg, R. J. (1985). *Beyond IQ: A triarchic theory of human intelligence.* New York, NY: Cambridge University Press.

Teovanović, P., Knežević, G. & Stankov, L. (2015). Individual differences in cognitive biases. *Intelligence. 50,* 75–86.

Veenman, M. V. J., & Spaans, M. A. (2005). Relation between intellectual and metacognitive skills: Age and task differences. *Learning and Individual Differences, 15,* 159–176.

Want, J., & Kleitman, S. (2006). Imposter phenomenon and self-handicapping: Links with parenting styles and self-confidence. *Personality and Individual Differences, 40,* 961–971.

Yates, J. F. (1982). External correspondence: Decompositions of the mean probability score. *Organizational Behaviour and Human Decision Processes, 30,* 132–156.

Yeo, G. B., & Neal, A. (2006). An examination of dynamic relationship between self-efficacy and performance across levels of analysis and levels of specificity. *Journal of Applied Psychology, 91,* 1088–1101.

CHAPTER 10

ACHIEVEMENT AND THE SELF

Approach and Avoidance as Self-Growth and Self-Protection

Emily J. Greenwood
University of Rochester

Rachel M. Korn
University of Rochester

Andrew J. Elliot
University of Rochester

Achievement motivation and achievement goal pursuit are invariably tied to the self. According to the hierarchical model of achievement motivation, achievement goals arise out of, and are distinct from, motive dispositions (Elliot & Church, 1997). The distinction between motives and goals is important to maintain in the conceptual analysis of motivation. Motivation consists of two parts: the energization of behavior and the direction of behavior (Elliot & Covington, 2001). Motives supply the energy of behavior through anticipation of the affect that will be experienced during or after

Self-Concept, Motivation, and Identity, pages 249–271

an achievement situation (Elliot, 1997; McClelland, 1951; Murray, 1938), whereas goals provide the specific direction for the motive-derived energy. In other words, motives supply a reason and energy source for behavior (Elliot & Thrash, 2001), while goals supply concrete and specific aims for behavior. Consequently, goals are the proximal influence on behavior (compared to the distal influence of motives).

To illustrate, in self-regulated learning, students engage in proactive behavior by using knowledge and strategic oversight to adjust their affect, cognition, and behavior in education-relevant settings (Zimmerman, 1989). Achievement goal pursuit is analogous to strategic planning processes in the self-regulation literature because goals represent situation-specific strategies that students plan to use, as well as outcomes students seek to attain or avoid (Dweck, 1986; Elliot, 1997; Nicholls, 1984). As specific and proximal predictors of behavior, achievement goals afford improved predictive power compared to the predictions supplied by further distanced motives. However, goals by themselves do not fully account for achievement outcomes; instead, goals combine and interact with underlying motives to form "goal complexes" that predict behavior (Elliot & Thrash, 2001).

Furthermore, achievement motives overlap with the self in the form of dispositions or personality traits. In personality psychology, need for achievement is a personality dimension that contains some overlap with mastery motivation and is concerned with self-growth. Need for achievement refers to an individual's desire to do things as quickly and as well as possible, to accomplish something difficult, and to master or manipulate physical objects, people, or ideas (Murray, 1938). Conversely, other achievement motives, such as fear of failure, are not focused on self-expansion but instead are concerned with defense or protection of the self (Birney, Burdick, & Teevan, 1969). In addition to achievement motives driving concerns for self-growth and self-defense, achievement goals guide self-growth or self-protecting behaviors.

The only dimension shared across both achievement motives and achievement goals is the approach-avoidance dimension. Importantly, the approach-avoidance dimension parallels the two directions of self-regulation mentioned previously: approach is concentrated on self-growth and avoidance is concentrated on self-defense. As such, this chapter will explicate how the approach-avoidance distinction is critical to a deep understanding of motivation and its link with the self. We will begin this chapter with an overview of the history and conceptualization of the approach-avoidance dimension as it applies to achievement motives. We will then carefully define goals and describe the development of the 2 × 2 achievement goal framework, giving particular attention to how the inclusion of the approach-avoidance dimension contributed to the achievement goal literature. We end with a brief description of the unique outcome profiles of each achievement goal and explain those profiles by noting the approach and avoidance aspects of underlying motives. Lastly, the self-esteem literature is referenced as support for the ties between approach and avoidance with self-growth and self-protection.

APPROACH AND AVOIDANCE

As noted above, motivation represents the energization and direction of behavior. The energization segment of this definition refers to the initial activation of a response that leads to a behavior (Elliot, 1997), while the direction element describes the way that the behavior is enacted in response to the stimulus (Elliot & Thrash, 2001). Approach motivation, then, is the energization and/or direction of behavior toward a positive stimulus, whereas avoidance motivation is the energization and/or direction of a behavior away from a negative stimulus (Elliot, 2006).

History of Approach and Avoidance Motivation

The distinction between approach and avoidance has roots in the field of philosophy and has been used in a number of different ways by various scholars over the past 2000 years. Initially, Democritus (460–370 BCE), a Greek philosopher, posited that individuals ought to be motivated by the pursuit of pleasure and the avoidance of pain, and as such follow what he called "ethical hedonism" (Elliot & Covington, 2001). Jeremy Bentham (1779/1879) proposed a similar concept termed "psychological hedonism" to suggest that human beings are motivated to pursue pleasure and to avoid pain. Bentham's work moves beyond Democritus' proposition of how individuals ought to strive to behave, and instead provides an actual explanation of observable behavior.

In the field of scientific psychology, the approach-avoidance distinction has been of great interest to scholars for well over a century. Wilhelm Wundt (1887), one of the founding figures in psychology, suggested that through the processes of sensation and cognition, the psychological experiences of pleasure and pain come into conscious awareness. William James (1890) posited that the experiences of pain and pleasure serve as "springs of action" that energize behavior: specifically, that pleasure serves as a reinforcer and pain as an inhibitor of action. In his psychodynamic theory, Freud (1957/1915) theorized that individuals are motivated to seek pleasure and to avoid pain, and that these tendencies are regulated, in part, by the superego (Freud, 1947/1923). The work of these early scholars served to move the research focus from the pain-pleasure distinction per se to ensuing approach and avoidance behaviors (Elliot, 2008).

After this early work on approach and avoidance motivation paved the way, a large number of scholars in the field of psychology began adapting this conceptualization to fit their own theories. For example, Jung (1921) posited that extroverts would be more likely to move toward (approach) social objects, while introverts would be more likely to move away from (avoid) social objects. In his work on classical conditioning, Pavlov (1927) differentiated between an "orienting" response toward stimuli and a "defensive" response away from stimuli. Lewin (1935) suggested that goal objects repulse or attract organisms with their positive and negative valences. Skinner (1938, 1953) distinguished between reinforcement, which strengthens responses, and punishment, which weakens responses.

Murray (1938) continued and extended this early work on the approach-avoidance distinction by suggesting that organisms have two types of needs: "adient" needs, which draw them toward objects, and "abient" needs, which lead them away from objects. Hull (1943) described conditioned appetitive and aversive drives, which lead organisms toward or away from a stimulus as a result of positive or negative associations with the stimulus. Maslow (1955) posited that humans have two basic needs: growth needs, which lead them to seek out more of a positive stimulus, and deficit needs, which lead them to seek to avoid a negative stimulus. Cattell (1957) similarly proposed that humans have two innate motives: exploration and escape to security. Rogers (1961) theorized that individuals hold personal goals which represent the desire to move toward or away from a positive or negative stimulus. Lastly, Eysenck (1967), building on earlier work, suggested that extroverts are "stimulus hungry" and tend to move toward stimuli, while introverts are "stimulus shy" and tend to move away from stimuli.

This brief overview of the roots of the approach-avoidance distinction (for more extensive coverage, see Elliot, 1999; Elliot & Covington, 2001,) highlights this basic idea as important and generative for the scientific study of motivation in the field of psychology. Researchers from many different backgrounds have applied this idea to their own theories in a variety of different ways (Elliot, 2008).

Conceptualization of Approach and Avoidance Motivation

Approach and avoidance motivational processes are present across all levels of species and have been observed in a wide variety of situations. Approach motivation serves to enable organisms to thrive, while avoidance motivation has generally been linked to the facilitation of behaviors that are linked to survival. Nevertheless, both approach and avoidance motivation are important adaptive mechanisms that are integral to the physical and psychological well-being of organisms (Elliot, 2006).

Approach and avoidance motivation have been observed in a variety of life forms, ranging from simple single-celled organisms to complex human beings. The amoeba, at the most basic end of the spectrum, has been observed exhibiting approach and avoidance behavior: specifically, when a weak light stimulus is introduced, there is a movement of protoplasm toward the light, which represents an approach behavior. An intense light stimulus results in a movement away from the light, a prototypical example of an avoidance behavior (Schneirla, 1959). This type of basic adaptive mechanism has the potential to facilitate adaptation by helping organisms find food and shelter and also avoid harm; it has been found at all evolutionary levels. While the complexity of these need-satisfying behaviors may vary considerably across different species, the underlying approach and avoidance mechanisms are constant across different life forms (Schneirla, 1959). These behaviors have been documented in a number of different species (for a review, see Elliot & Covington, 2001). For example, by implementing factor analysis, Budaev (1997) found two temporally stable factors underlying behavioral patterns in guppies: approach and fear avoidance. In addition, factor analysis conducted with behavioral data from other species has further supported the separation of approach and avoidance behaviors (Elliot & Covington, 2001). Overall, the approach and avoidance tendencies that are present across species have adaptive benefits, because they tend to facilitate need satisfaction (Schneirla, 1959).

The evidence for an inherent approach-avoidance motivational distinction is also supported by the instantaneous nature of many approach and avoidance behavioral responses (Elliot & Covington, 2001); in fact, even low-level organisms are capable of immediate, reflexive responses to stimuli. To return to the previous example of a single-celled organism, the amoeba instantly withdraws in response to a bright light stimulus. As such, it is important to note that the immediacy of the response is a part of its adaptive significance (Berntson, Boysen, & Cacioppo, 1993; Orians & Heerwagen, 1992). Human beings also display a variety of instantaneous approach and avoidance behaviors as reflexive responses to stimuli; indeed, many of the most basic survival mechanisms can be classified as orienting (approach) or defensive (avoidance) (Dickinson & Dearing, 1979; Sokolov, 1963). For example, the blink reflex is an immediate physiological response that occurs automatically after a startling stimulus, such as a bright light or puff of air (Bradley & Vrana, 1993). This type of adaptive avoidance response serves to protect the eye from injury and also to prepare the body for potential threats in the environment (Lang, 1995; Öhman, 1997). Immediate behavioral responses such as the blink reflex may vary along with the motivational state of the individual: the reflex will be triggered more quickly and in greater strength when the individual is in an avoidance motivational state, rather than a neutral or approach motivational state (Lang, Bradley, & Cuthbert, 1990).

Human beings have a tendency to make evaluative judgments of the stimuli they encounter almost immediately (Osgood, Suci, & Tannenbaum, 1957) and sometimes without conscious awareness (Bargh, 1997; Zajonc, 1998). In one study, individuals who were subliminally primed with positively valenced words were able to pronounce other positively valenced words more quickly; since the primes were subliminal, it was clear that the valence of the words was automatically processed (Bargh, Chaiken, Raymond, & Hymes, 1996). It is possible that this type of evaluation represents automatic cognitive processing (Fiske, 1982), or that it represents a reflexive reaction to a stimulus independent of cognitive processes (Kuhl, 1986; LeDoux, 1987; Zajonc, 1980). The automatic evaluation process is also applicable to the immediate behavioral response tendencies toward (approach) or away from (avoidance) a stimulus that has been observed in various situations (Elliot & Covington, 2001). For instance, participants who are asked to complete an approach or avoidance behavior (pulling a lever toward oneself or pushing a lever away, respectively) after reading a valenced word react more quickly when the valence of the word matches the valence of the response (Chen & Bargh, 1999). Research of this nature supports the idea that the automatic evaluation process leads almost instantaneously to corresponding approach and avoidance behaviors (Bargh & Chartrand, 1999).

The concept of movement may seem integral to the definition of approach and avoidance motivation; however, the automatic evaluation process does not necessarily create an explicit behavioral response. Rather, it may simply evoke a predisposition toward certain behaviors (Elliot & Covington, 2001). A stimulus may elicit a positively or negatively valenced evaluation and therefore induce preparedness for approach or avoidance behaviors (Arnold, 1960). The behavior that is produced, though, does not have to be linked to the initial evaluative responses (Lang, Bradley, & Cuthbert, 1997). In simple organisms, automatic evaluations of stimuli may reliably lead to predictable behavioral responses; however, in humans, individuals sometimes hold goals that guide behaviors that are not linked to the initial approach or avoidance behavioral predisposition (Elliot & Covington, 2001). Therefore, when predicting the behavior of humans, it is necessary to take into account the different goals an individual may hold, along with the automatic evaluative responses a stimulus may evoke.

Evidence for the fundamental importance of the approach-avoidance distinction also takes the form of neuropsychological data. Numerous studies have sought to determine the localization of approach and avoidance motivation in the left and right cerebral hemispheres (for a review, see Davidson,

1995). Greater resting activity in the left prefrontal cortex has been linked to approach motivation, while greater resting activity in the right prefrontal cortex has been linked to avoidance motivation using electroencephalograph (EEG) recordings. In addition, further neuropsychological research using PET and fMRI data has found that approach motivation is associated with activation of the left hemisphere, while avoidance motivation is associated with activation of the right hemisphere (Murphy, Nimmo-Smith, & Lawrence, 2003). Other scholars have explored the possibility that different areas of the brain may be associated with the approach and avoidance constructs: for instance, historical work using electrical stimulation of the brain linked the septal area of the limbic system with pleasure and the hypothalamic area of the limbic system with pain (Delgado, Roberts, & Miller, 1954; Olds & Milner, 1954). More recently, scholars have continued this line of research to link the medial prefrontal cortex and nucleus accumbens to approach motivation and the amygdala and anterior cingulate cortex to avoidance motivation (Wager, Phan, Liberzon, & Taylor, 2003).

Additional research has examined approach and avoidance motivation at the neocortical level. Using behavioral measures of hemispheric activation, Friedman and Forster (2005) determined that anticipatory approach states were linked to greater right hemispheric activation, while anticipatory avoidance states were associated with greater left hemispheric activation; however these results were reversed when approach- and avoidance-related arousal (in comparison to anticipation) was examined. Further research determined that when participants were under time constraints, inducing approach motivational states led to right-oriented behavioral biases, which are indicative of left hemispheric activation (Roskes, Sligte, Shalvi, & De Dreu, 2011).

Clearly, approach and avoidance motivation are both vital mechanisms of our physical and psychological functioning. However, they frequently lead to very different outcomes. Approach motivation is generally linked to thriving and positive outcomes (Elliot, 2006). In contrast, avoidance motivation tends to facilitate survival, which leads to a focus on negative stimuli and potential detrimental outcomes such as stress, anxiety, and lowered well-being (Elliot & Sheldon, 1997, 1998). When approach motivation is successful, the consequences are positive; however, when avoidance motivation is successful, there is only the absence of negative outcomes. As such, avoidance motivation can lead individuals to miss opportunities for growth and development (Elliot, 2006).

To conclude, the approach-avoidance distinction is an integral part of studying the energization and direction of behavior across all types of living organisms. Whereas motives capture the energization of behavior, we must turn to the goal construct to understand how the approach and avoidance dimension directs behavior.

THE GOAL CONSTRUCT

Before delving into the achievement goal literature, it is critical to understand how the goal construct is defined. For science to proceed smoothly, researchers need to reach consensus on the definition of central constructs. This is particularly important in the social sciences where the object of study is often an unobservable phenomenon, in contrast to directly observable, concrete entities. A "goal" is one such object of study. The goal construct, unfortunately, has neither been well defined nor well conceptualized in the motivational literature (Heckhausen & Kuhl, 1985).

Defining the Goal Construct

Given the lack of a consensus on a clear definition and conceptualization of "goal" in the contemporary psychological literature, and the importance of obtaining such clarity, we explicitly utilize the definition of goal construct offered by Elliot and Fryer (2007). This definition and conceptualization of the goal construct is narrower than that offered by many others in the literature. We think that a more precise, restricted goal construct is important, because it affords clarity regarding both the nature and function of goals, along with clarity of how goals relate to and interact with underlying achievement motives.

The definition of "goal" provided in Elliot and Fryer (2007) was formed through a linguistic analysis of the word, as well as an extensive historical analysis of the way that the term has been used by scholars over the centuries. The definition is as follows: A goal is a cognitive representation of a future object that an organism is committed to approach or avoid. There are five basic features of the goal construct contained within this definition: (a) It is a cognitive representation, (b) it is focused on the future, (c) it is focused on an object, (d) it is a commitment, and (e) it entails approach or avoidance (for additional details beyond the present overview, see Elliot & Fryer, 2007).

Cognitive Representation

A goal is a cognitive representation, suggesting that goals are limited to only those animate organisms with mental apparatuses used in the process of regulation. Previous researchers have defined "goal" in terms of any internal process, rather than a cognitive representation (e.g., Austin & Vancouver, 1996). However, this overly inclusive definition allows the goal construct to be applied to mechanical devices. Although there exist similarities between discrepancy reduction in a mechanical context and cognitive goal striving in animate organisms, there are critical differences between these two forms of regulation (see Bandura, 1986; Locke & Latham, 1990; Nuttin, 1984). For example, because mechanical devices rely on an externally supplied energy source for operation, they have less flexible regulatory processes compared to internally and dynamically energized animate organisms (see Nuttin, 1984). For this reason, we think terms such as "standard" and "reference value" instead of "goal" should be applied to mechanical models.

In addition to defining goals as cognitive representations, another important issue in the goal literature focuses on the precise way in which goals are represented in the cognitive system (Bargh 1990; Kruglanski, 1996; Shah & Kruglanski, 2003). Goals differ from simpler cognitive representations because they contain additional features such as a commitment with regard to an object (Ach, 1935). However, little is currently known about the nature of commitment representation and the unique cognitive principles by which it might operate (for speculation, see Herbart, 1850; Lewin, 1926; Wyer & Srull, 1986; for empirical work, see Bargh, Gollwitzer, Lee-Chai, Barndollar, & Trotchel, 2001; Förster, Liberman, & Higgins, 2005; Shah, Friedman, & Kruglanski, 2002).

Future

A goal is a cognitive representation of something that is possible in the future. Thus, goal-directed behavior is inherently proactive rather than reactive. With a goal, present behaviors are guided by a future image (goal-directed behaviors) instead of being immediate, unmediated responses to a present stimulus (reflex-directed behaviors). With the mental image of a future possibility directing present behaviors, goals are assumed to have a *causal* influence.

Unlike the goal definitions from earlier theorists (Austin & Vancouver, 1996; Binswanger, 1986; Klinger, 1977; Locke, 1969), this definition of a goal does not include reflex-driven actions of plant life (e.g., a sunflower turning to face the sun) or actions of simple organisms (e.g., amoeba moving away from light). These actions are excluded from goal-directed behavior, because the organism is simply reacting reflexively to an encountered stimulus, it is not responding with regard to an envisioned possibility. Furthermore, also in contrast to previously mentioned theorists, autonomic physiological functions (e.g., digestion or blood circulation) are not considered goal directed because these functions occur in the absence of any prevision or cognitive imaging of the future. Overall, plants, simple organisms, and internal organs may carry out actions that mimic goal-directed behavior, but because they are not guided by cognitive representations of the future, they are excluded from our goal definition.

Object

The hub or focal point of regulation is known as the object of a goal (i.e., goal-object). The object of the goal is, for example, a future outcome that the person is committed to approach or avoid. The term "object" can refer to an entity, event, experience, characteristic, and so on that is the centerpiece of the goal. Objects are unconstrained by content; they may be concrete or abstract, observable or unobservable, psychological or physical. Additionally, objects may be valenced—some entities, events, experiences, characteristics, and such have a positive valence, whereas other objects have a negative valence.

We should stress that the object of a goal is not the goal itself. A goal consists of both an object and an approach or avoidance commitment in relation to the object. For example, in the goal "develop greater patience with my children," "greater patience with my children" is the object and "develop" is the appetitive, or approach-oriented commitment. Similarly, in the goal "avoid failing my biology class," "failing my biology class" is the object and "avoid" is the aversive, or avoidance-oriented commitment. Both an object and commitment (to approach or avoid that object) are essential and conceptually distinct parts of a goal.

Committed To

Without active commitment, a cognitive representation of a future object that an organism would like to approach or avoid is merely a wish or a fantasy (Gollwitzer, 1990; cf. Ford, 1992) or a goal candidate (Elliot & Friedman, 2005), but not an actual goal. In other words, goals differ from desires or wishes, because a person holding a goal is deliberately and actively pursuing (or avoiding) a future outcome. An organism is said to adopt a goal the moment that organism commits to some directional action with respect to the cognitively represented future object. Of course, strength of commitment may vary considerably across goals, time, and individuals. This variability has important implications for effort and persistence in the goal pursuit process.

Commitment to approach or avoid a future object must be done consciously. The term "goal" is restricted to commitments that at the very least *originate* in conscious acts of volition. However, after its conscious development, a goal may be activated and may operate automatically, under the level of consciousness, as demonstrated by Bargh and colleagues (see Bargh & Ferguson, 2000; Chartrand & Bargh, 2002) and others. Conscious development is an aspect unique to goals, differentiating goals from needs and motives, for needs and motive originate from inherent tendencies or nonconscious affective learning processes (McClelland, 1951; Murray, 1938). The terminal point of a need or a motive is sometimes referred to as a "goal," but to avoid confusion, this construct should instead be labeled as a "need- or motive-object," "satisfier," or "end state." Critically, by carefully separating goals from needs and motives, we can examine how these constructs interact with each other in a hierarchical fashion. To illustrate, needs, and motives function as energizers of behavior; goals then direct this energization in a way that flexibly (and idiographically) serves those needs and motives (Elliot & Church, 1997). Accordingly, the same need or motive can be satisfied through different goals, and different needs or motives can be satisfied by the same goal. This raises questions as to how certain needs and motives are best addressed by congruent, or matching goals—some pairings of needs and motives with goals are adaptive whereas others may be maladaptive for performance. Also, needs and motives may at times affect behavior over and above the influence of goals (McClelland, Koestner, & Weinberger, 1989). It should be noted that there are many antecedents of goal adoption besides needs and motives (e.g., self-beliefs and perceptions, relational histories, specific environmental affordances), some of which may derive from or be associated with needs and motives, and others of which may be completely independent of them (see Elliot, 1999; Kuhl, 2000; Shah, 2003).

Approach or Avoid

As previously discussed, approach-avoidance is a basic psychological distinction that is applicable to motivational constructs in general, goals included (Elliot & Covington, 2001). In this context, by "approach" we mean move toward or maintain a positively valenced object, and by "avoid" we mean move or stay away from a negatively valenced object. Approach and avoidance "movement" may entail actual physical activity (e.g., "reaching for a cookie") or psychological activity (e.g., "seeking to develop a positive relationship with a co-worker").

Approach and avoidance actions are manifested differently depending on the current presence or absence of the goal object. If a positively valenced object is absent, then approach entails moving toward the object, whereas if a positively valenced object is present, then approach entails maintaining closeness with the object. Avoidance is manifested in the opposite pattern: if a negatively valenced object is currently absent, avoidance entails maintaining a distance from the object, whereas if a negatively valenced object is currently present, avoidance entails trying to get away from the object (see Lewin, 1938; Mowrer, 1960). In addition to these broad patterns, there are myriad idiographic manifestations of approach and avoidance.

Achievement Goals: History and Development

Achievement goals are a subset of goals affiliated with achievement and concerned with competence. The achievement goal construct emerged in the late 1970s and early 1980s, and its initial development can be credited to the independent and, in some instances, collaborative work of Carol Ames, Carol Dweck, Marty Maehr, and John Nicholls (Ames 1984; Dweck &

Leggett, 1988; Maehr, 1983; Nicholls, 1989). Dweck's achievement goal research developed from her studies on helplessness demonstrated by school-aged children in achievement settings. Dweck and colleagues found that students reacted differently to failure on achievement tasks, even across children with equal abilities (Diener & Dweck, 1978, 1980; Dweck, 1975; Dweck & Reppucci, 1973). Some children responded adaptively to failure, taking a "mastery" stance by attributing failure to inadequate effort, persisting in subsequent tasks, and pursuing future challenges. In contrast, other children responded maladaptively to failure, displaying defeat and a "helpless" response pattern characterized by attributing failure to inadequate ability, less persistence in subsequent tasks, and avoidance of future challenges. To explain these opposing response patterns, Dweck suggested that these children held different achievement goals. Achievement goals were defined as a person's purpose for engaging in behavior in an achievement situation (Dweck & Leggett, 1988).

The initial achievement goal conceptalization was split into two types of goals: performance (or ego) goals and mastery (or learning) goals. Performance goals focused on demonstrating competence relative to others, and mastery goals focused on developing competence and task mastery. Elliot, McGregor, and Gable (1999) posited that this performance-mastery distinction was rooted in the way competence is defined (defined by the standard used in competence evaluation).

In the early to mid-1990s, several reviews of achievement goal research were conducted. Nearly all of these reviews portrayed mastery goals as leading to positive processes and outcomes and portrayed performance goals as leading to negative processes and outcomes. However, this portrait of mastery goals as being exclusively positive and performance goals as being exclusively negative seemed overstated by some researchers (Butler, 1992; Harackiewicz & Elliot, 1993). Close examination of available research showed that mastery goals did indeed tend to lead to a host of positive processes, but that these goals many times did not lead to positive performance outcomes. Close examination of research on performance goals revealed that although performance goals sometimes resulted in negative consequences, these goals sometimes had null effects or even positive effects in certain achievement contexts (see Koestner, Zuckerman, & Koestner, 1987; Miller & Hom, 1990; Sansone, Sachau, & Weir, 1989) and for individuals with certain personality dispositions (see Elliot & Harackiewicz, 1994; Harackiwicz & Elliot, 1993).

These mixed results for performance goals were addressed by applying the approach-avoidance distinction. In the trichotomous achievement goal framework, Elliot (1994) bifurcated performance goals by introducing the approach-avoidance dimension. He noted that in past literature, some performance goal manipulations drew participants' attention to the possibility of a positive outcome (encouraging approach motivation) while other performance goal manipulations drew participants' attention to the possibility of a negative outcome (encouraging avoidance motivation). In a meta-analysis, Rawsthorne and Elliot (1999) found that manipulations classified as approach tended to produce a positive set of processes and outcomes while manipulations classified as avoidance tended to produce a negative set of processes and outcomes. Eventually, the approach-avoidance dimension was also applied to mastery goals resulting in the 2 × 2 achievement goal framework (Elliot, 1999; Elliot & McGregor, 2001).

The 2 × 2 Achievement Goal Framework

In the 2 × 2 framework, achievement goals are organized by two aspects of competence, definition, and valence (Elliot, 1999; Elliot & McGregor, 2001; see Elliot, 1999, and Elliot, Murayama, & Pekrun, 2011 on considerations regarding a 3 × 2 achievement goal framework). Definition refers to how competence is evaluated, by absolute/intrapersonal standards or by normative standards. Valence refers to the positive or negative focus of the goal, which instantiates an approach or avoidance aim. Crossing these aspects of competence gives way to four different achievement goals: mastery-approach (focused on a positive absolute or intrapersonal standard), performance-approach (focused on a positive normative standard), mastery-avoidance (focused on a negative absolute or intrapersonal standard), and performance-avoidance (focused on a negative normative standard).

Each of the four achievement goals has a unique profile and set of predictions with regard to outcomes (Moller & Elliot, 2006). Mastery-approach goals consistently lead to the most positive outcomes. These goals usually predict deep processing of material (Elliot, et al., 1999), challenge appraisals (McGregor & Elliot, 2002), decreased procrastination (Wolters, 2004), increased self-regulation (Pajares & Valiante, 2001), adaptive help-seeking (Linnenbrink, 2005), less disruptive behavior (Kaplan, Gheen, & Midgley, 2002), long-term retention of material (Elliot & McGregor, 1999), persistence (Elliot et al., 1999), enjoyment of the learning process (Pekrun, Elliot, & Maier, 2006), and intrinsic motivation (Harackiewicz, Barron, & Elliot, 1998).

In contrast, performance-avoidance goals most consistently lead to maladaptive processes and negative outcomes. These goals are strongly associated with fear of failure (Elliot & Church, 1997) and emerge from avoidance temperament (Elliot & Thrash, 2002), insecure attachment (Elliot & Reis, 2003), an entity theory of ability (Cury, Elliot, Da Fonseca, & Moller, 2006), and a perception of the achievement environment as harshly evaluative (Church, Elliot, & Gable, 2001). Performance-avoidance goals lead to the surface processing of material (Elliot et al., 1999), evaluation anxiety

(Elliot & McGregor, 1999), self-handicapping (Urdan, 2004), the avoidance of help-seeking (Middleton & Midgley, 1997), depression (Sideridis, 2005), disengagement (Wolters, 2004), and decreased performance attainment (Elliot, Shell, Bouas Henry, & Maier, 2005). In general, theorists agree that adoption of performance-avoidance goals should be discouraged.

Performance-approach and mastery-avoidance goals have more complex profiles and mixed outcomes than the more straightforward effects of mastery-approach and performance-avoidance goals. Mastery-avoidance goals are the least understood because as relatively recent additions to the achievement goal framework, these goals have been the least studied. Sharing the negative antecedents of performance-avoidance goals, mastery-avoidance goals are often driven by fear of failure (Elliot & McGregor, 2001), emerge from an entity theory of ability (Cury et al., 2006), and from parental worrying about mistakes and failures (Elliot & McGregor, 2001). Likely due to these negative antecedents, it is not surprising that mastery-avoidance goals lead to some negative consequences, such as the avoidance of help-seeking (Karabenick, 2003) and reduced intrinsic motivation (Cury et al., 2006). However, further study is needed to confidently connect mastery-avoidance goals to a clear nomological network.

Performance-approach goals have been more extensively studied than mastery-avoidance goals, yet their effects are neither strictly positive nor strictly negative. For example, although performance-approach goals sometimes result in positive processes, such as persistence, effort, and challenge appraisals (Elliot et al., 1999; Lopez, 1999; McGregor & Elliot, 2002), performance-approach goals can also encourage superficial processing of material (Elliot et al., 1999), threat appraisals (McGregor & Elliot, 2002), and decreased help-seeking behaviors (Karabenick, 2003). As for outcomes, we find a similar pattern of both positive and negative consequences; performance-approach goals can be beneficial by facilitating performance (Elliot et al., 2005) and yet at other times can be disadvantageous by lowering well-being and intrinsic motivation (Elliot & Moller, 2003; Midgley, Kaplan, & Middleton, 2001).

Performance-approach goals may lead to a complexity of outcomes because these goals are driven by both approach and avoidance forms of energization. Although the goals themselves are approach oriented, performance-approach goals are predicted by both need for achievement and fear of failure (Elliot & Church, 1997), and by both approach and avoidance temperament (Elliot & Thrash, 2002). This complex pairing of motives and goals further highlights the need for evaluating achievement motivation through a hierarchal model. By separating motives and goals we can conduct a more detailed examination of how approach and avoidance motivation functions and interacts across the motive and goal levels. Perhaps outcomes vary depending on whether approach and avoidance dimensions are congruent or incongruent across motives and goals. Further empirical examination is necessary to draw any conclusions on how approach and avoidance dimensions interact across hierarchical levels.

Self-Esteem and Achievement From an Approach and Avoidance Perspective

The effects of approach and avoidance on achievement and self-regulation is further supported by the self-esteem literature. Research indicates that low self-esteem, in comparison to high self-esteem, leads to negative effects on motivation, performance, and well-being (for reviews, see Leary & MacDonald, 2003; Tice, 1993). Individuals with high self-esteem and individuals with low self-esteem have been shown to exhibit different motivational tendencies (Baumeister & Tice, 1985; Baumeister, Tice, & Hutton, 1989; Tice, 1993). Specifically, individuals with low self-esteem experience a loss of motivation and performance decrements after a failure, while individuals with high self-esteem experience a bolstering of motivation and better performance following a setback (Baumeister & Tice, 1985; Brockner, 1979; McFarlin, Baumeister, & Blascovich, 1984). Furthermore, Baumeister and colleagues suggest that individuals with low self-esteem experience self-protective motives that drive them to avoid situations that could threaten their self-esteem. On the other hand, individuals with high self-esteem experience self-enhancement motives that allow them to present themselves in a positive way, exhibit their strengths, and feel better about themselves (Baumeister & Tice, 1985; Baumeister et al., 1989; Tice, 1991; Wood, Giordano-Beech, Taylor, Michela, & Gaus, 1994).

Heimpel, Elliot, and Wood (2006) included the approach and avoidance distinction when linking self-esteem to achievement goals. Specifically, these researchers documented that the self-protective motivation that low self-esteem individuals experience leads them to adopt avoidance goals, and the self-enhancing motivation that high self-esteem individuals experience leads them to adopt approach goals. This evidence, coupled with the negative outcomes of avoidance goals, suggests that it is possible that self-esteem exerts its negative impact on processes and outcomes through the mechanism of approach and avoidance goals (Heimpel et al., 2006)

CONCLUSION

In sum, this chapter has attempted to clarify the nature of achievement motives, achievement goals, and self-regulation more generally through application of the approach-avoidance distinction. We have focused extensively on the conceptual nature of approach and avoidance motivation and communicated its foundational nature and utility in the study of motivation. The purpose of this chapter has been to highlight the relevance of the approach-avoidance distinction in research on the self, specifically in motivational and self-regulation contexts. This framework for the study of motivation is applicable across the self literature, and researchers would do well to attend to approach-avoidance considerations in their conceptual and empirical work on the self.

ACKNOWLEDGMENT

This chapter draws on material from the following publications: Elliot, A. J. & Fryer, J. W. (2007). The goal construct in psychology. In J. Shaw and W. Garder (Eds.), *Handbook of motivational science.* New York, NY: Guilford Press; Elliot, A. J. & Mapes,R. R. (2004). Approach-avoidance motivation and self-concept evaluation. In A. Tesser, J. Wood, & D. Stapel (Eds), *The psychology of the self: On the edge of understanding.* Washington, C: Psychological Press.; and Fryer, J. W., & Elliot, A. J. (2007). Self-regulation of achievement goal pursuit. In D. Schunk & B. Zimmerman (Eds.), *Motivation and Self-Regulated Learning: Theory, Research, and Applications.* Hillsdale, NJ: Lawrence Erlbaum Associates.

REFERENCES

Ach, N. (1935). *Analyse des Willens* [The analysis of willing]. Berlin: Urban & Schwarzenberg.

Ames, C. (1984). Achievement attributions and self-instructions under competitive and individualistic goal structures. *Journals of Educational Psychology, 76,* 478–487.

Arnold, M. (1960). *Emotion and personality.* New York, NY: Columbia University Press.

Austin, J., & Vancouver, J. (1996). Goal constructs in psychology: Structure, process, and content. *Psychological Bulletin, 120,* 338–375.

Bandura, A. (1986). *Social foundations of thought and action.* Englewood Cliffs, NJ: Prentice-Hall.

Bargh, J. A. (1990). Auto-motives: Preconscious determinants of social interaction. In E. T. Higgins & R. M. Sorrentino (Eds.), *Handbook of motivation and cognition: Foundations of social behavior* (Vol. 2, pp. 93–130). New York, NY: Guilford.

Bargh, J. A. (1997). Bargh, J. A. (1997). The automaticity of everyday life. In R. S. Wyer, (Ed.), *Advances in social cognition, Vol. 10* (pp. 1–62). Mahwah, NJ: Erlbaum.

Bargh, J., Chaiken, S., Raymond, P., & Hymes, C. (1996). The automatic evaluation effect: Unconditional automatic attitude activation with a pronunciation task. *Journal of Experimental Social Psychology, 32,* 104–128.

Bargh, J., & Chartrand, T. (1999). The unbearable automaticity of being. *American Psychologist, 54,* 462–479.

Bargh, J. A., & Ferguson, M. J. (2000). Beyond behaviorism: On the automaticity of higher mental processes. *Psychological Bulletin, 126,* 925–945.

Bargh, J. A., Gollwitzer, P., Lee-Chai, A., Barndollar, K., & Trotchel, R. (2001). The automated will: Nonconscious activation and pursuit of behavioral goals. *Journal of Personality and Social Psychology, 81,* 1014–1027.

Baumeister, R. F., & Tice, D. (1985). Self-esteem and responses to success and failure. Subsequent performance and intrinsic motivation. *Journal of Personality, 53,* 450–467.

Baumeister, R. F., Tice, D. M., & Hutton, D. G. (1989). Self-presentational motivations and personality differences in self-esteem. *Journal of Personality, 57,* 547–579.

Bentham, J. (1779/1879). *Introduction to the principles of morals and legislation.* Oxford, UK: Clarendon.

Berntson, G., Boysen, S., & Cacioppo, J. (1993). Neurobehavioral organization and the cardinal principle of evaluative bivalence. *Annals New York Academy of Science, 702,* 75–102.

Binswanger, H. (1986). The goal-directedness of living action. *The Objectivist Forum, 7,* 1–10.

Birney, R., Burdick, H., & Teevan, R. (1969). *Fear of failure.* New York, NY: Van Nostrand Reinhold.

Bradley, M., & Vrana, S. (1993). The startle probe in the study of emotion and emotional disorders. In N. Birbaumer & A. Ohman (Eds.), *The structure of emotion* (pp. 270–287). Seattle, WA: Hogrefe & Huber.

Brockner, J. (1979). The effects of self-esteem, success-failure, and self-consciousness on task performance. *Journal of Personality and Social Psychology, 37,* 1732–1741.

Budaev, S. (1997). "Personality" in the guppy (Poecilia reticulata). *Journal of Comparative Psychology, 111,* 399–411.

Butler, R. (1992). What young people want to know when: Effects of mastery and ability goals on interest in different kinds of social comparisons. *Journal of Personality and Social Psychology, 62,* 934–943.

Cattell, R. (1957). *Personality and motivation: Structure and measurement.* Yonkers, NY: World Book.

Chartrand, T. L., & Bargh, J. A. (2002). Nonconscious motivations: Their activation, operation, and consequences. In A. Tesser & D. A. Stipek (Eds.), *Self and motivation: Emerging psychological perspectives* (pp. 13–41). Washington, DC: American Psychological Association.

Chen, M., & Bargh, J. (1999). Consequences of automatic evaluation: Immediate behavioral predispositions to approach or avoid the stimulus. *Personality and Social Psychology Bulletin, 25,* 215–223.

Church, M. A., Elliot, A. J., & Gable, S. L. (2001). Perceptions of classroom environment, achievement goals, and achievement outcomes. *Journal of Educational Psychology, 93,* 43–54.

Cury, F., Elliot, A. J., Da Fonseca, D., & Moller, A. C. (2006). The social-cognitive model of achievement motivation and the 2 × 2 achievement goal framework. *Journal of Personality and Social Psychology, 90,* 666–679.

Davidson, R. (1995). Cerebral asymmetry, emotion, and affective style. In R. Davidson & K. Hugdahl (Eds.), *Brain asymmetry* (pp. 362–87). Cambridge, MA: MIT Press.

Delgado, J. M. R., Roberts, W. W., & Miller, N. E. (1954). Learning motivated by electrical stimulation of the brain. *American Journal of Physiology, 179,* 587–593.

Dickinson, A., & Dearing, M. (1979). Appetitive-aversive interactions and inhibitory processes. In A. Dickinson & R. Boakes (Eds.), *Mechanisms of learning and motivation* (pp. 203–231). Hillsdale, NJ: Erlbaum.

Diener, C. I., & Dweck, C. S. (1978). An analysis of learned helplessness: Continuous changes in performance, strategy, and achievement cognitions following failure. *Journal of Personality and Social Psychology, 36,* 51–462.

Diener, C. I., & Dweck, C. S. (1980). An anlaysis of learned helplessness: II. The processing of success. *Journal of Personality and Social Psychology, 39,* 940–952.

Dweck, C. S. (1975). The role of expectations and attributions in the alleviation of learned helplessness. *Journal of Personality and Social Psychology, 31,* 674–685.

Dweck, C. (1986). Motivational processes affecting learning. *American Psychologist, 41,* 1040–1048.

Dweck, C. S., & Leggett, E. (1988). A social-cognitive approach to motivation and personality. *Psychological Review, 95,* 256–273.

Dweck, C. S., & Reppucci, N. D. (1973). Learned helplessness and reinforcement responsibility in children. *Journal of Personality and Social Psychology, 25,* 109–116.

Elliot, A. J. (1994). *Approach and avoidance achievement goals: An intrinsic motivation analysis.* Unpublished doctoral dissertation. University of Wisconsin, Madison.

Elliot, A. J. (1997). Integrating the "classic" and "contemporary" approaches to achievement motivation: A hierarchical model of approach and avoidance achievement motivation. In P. Pintrich & M. Maehr (Eds.), *Advances in motivation and achievement* (Vol. 10, pp. 143–179). Greenwich, CT: JAI.

Elliot, A. J. (1999). Approach and avoidance motivation and goals. *Educational Psychologist, 34,* 169–189.

Elliot, A. J. (2006). The hierarchical model of approach and avoidance motivation. *Motivation and Emotion, 30,* 111–116.

Elliot, A. J. (2008). Approach and avoidance motivation. In A. J. Elliot (Ed.), Handbook of approach and avoidance motivation (pp. 3–14). New York, NY: Psychology.

Elliot, A. J., & Church, M. A. (1997). A hierarchical model of approach and avoidance achievement motivation. *Journal of Personality and Social Psychology, 72,* 218–232.

Elliot, A. J., & Covington, M. V. (2001). Approach and avoidance motivation. *Educational Psychology Review, 13,* 73–92.

Elliot, A. J., & Friedman, R. (2005). Approach and avoidance personal goals. In B. Little, K. Salmela-Aro, J. Nurmi, & S. Phillips (Eds.), *Personal project pursuit: Goals, action, and human flourishing.* Hillsdale, NJ: Erlbaum.

Elliot, A. J., & Fryer, J. W. (2007). The goal construct in psychology. In J. Shaw & W. Gardner (Eds.), *Handbook of motivational science.* New York, NY: Guilford.

Elliot, A. J., & Harackiewicz, J. M. (1994). Goal setting, achievement orientation, and intrinsic motivation: A meditational analysis. *Journal of Personality and Social Psychology, 66,* 968–980.

Elliot, A. J., & McGregor, H. A. (1999). Test anxiety and the hierarchical model of approach and avoidance achievement motivation. *Journal of Personality and Social Psychology, 76,* 628–644. doi:10.1037/0022- 3514.76.4.628

Elliot, A. J., & McGregor, H. A. (2001). A 2 × 2 achievement goal framework. *Journal of Personality and Social Psychology, 80,* 501–519.

Elliot, A. J., McGregor, H. A., & Gable, S. (1999). Achievement goals, study strategies, and exam performance: A meditational analysis. *Journal of Educational Psychology, 91,* 549–563.

Elliot, A. J., & Moller, A. (2003). Performance-approach goals: Good or bad forms of regulation? *International Journal of Educational Research, 39,* 339–356.

Elliot, A. J., Murayama, K., & Pekrun, R. (2011). A 3 × 2 achievement goal model. *Journal of Educational Psychology, 103*(3), 632–648.

Elliot, A. J., & Reis, H. T. (2003). Attachment and exploration in adulthood. *Journal of Personality and Social Psychology, 85,* 317–331.

Elliot, A. J., & Sheldon, K. M. (1997). Avoidance achievement motivation: A personal goals analysis. *Journal of Personality and Social Psychology, 73,* 171–185.

Elliot, A. J., & Sheldon, K. M. (1998). Avoidance personal goals and the personality-illness relationship. *Journal of Personality and Social Psychology, 75,* 1282–1299.

Elliot, A. J., Shell, M. M., Bouas Henry, K., & Maier, M. A. (2005). Achievement goals, performance contingencies, and performance attainment: An experimental test. *Journal of Educational Psychology, 97,* 630–640.

Elliot, A. J., & Thrash, T. M. (2001). Achievement goals and the hierarchical model of achievement motivation. *Educational Psychology Review, 12,* 139–156.

Elliot, A. J., & Thrash, T. M. (2002). Approach-avoidance motivation in personality: Approach and avoidance temperaments and goals. *Journal of Personality and Social Psychology, 82,* 804–818.

Eysenck, H. (1967). *The biological basis of personality.* Springfield, IL: Thomas.

Fiske, S. (1982). Schema-triggered affect. In M. Clark & S. Fiske (Eds.), *Affect and cognition.* Hillsdale, NJ: Erlbaum.

Ford, M. E. (1992). *Motivating humans: Goals, emotions, and personal agency beliefs.* Thousand Oaks, CA: Sage.

Forster, J. Liberman, N., & Higgins, E. T. (2005). Accessibility from active and fulfilled goals. *Journal of Experimental Social Psychology, 41,* 220–239.

Freud, S. (1947). The ego and the id. In the standard edition of *Complete psychological works of Sigmund Freud, Vol. XIX.* London, UK: Hogarth. (Original work published 1923)

Freud, S. (1957). Repression. In the standard edition of *Complete Psychological Works of Sigmund Freud, Vol. XIV.* London, UK: Hogarth. (Original work published 1915)

Friedman, R. S., & Forster, J. (2005). Effects of motivational cues on perceptual asymmetry: Implications for creativity and analytical problem solving. *Journal of Personality and Social Psychology, 88,* 263–275.

Gollwitzer, P. M. (1990). Action phases and mind-sets. In E. T. Higgins & R. M. Sorrentino (Eds.), *Handbook of motivation and cognition: Foundations of social behavior* (Vol. 2, pp. 53–92). New York, NY: Guilford.

Harackiewicz, J. M., Barron, K. E., & Elliot, A. J. (1998). Rethinking achievement goals: When are they adaptive for college students and why? *Educational Psychologist, 33,* 1–21.

Harackiewicz, J. M., & Elliot, A. J. (1993). Achievement goals and intrinsic motivation. *Journal of Personality and Social Psychology, 65,* 904–915.

Heckhausen, H., & Kuhl, J. (1985). From wishes to action: The dead ends and short cuts on the long way to action. In M. Frese & J. Sabini (Eds.), *Goal directed behavior: The concept of action in psychology* (pp. 134–159). Hillsdale, NJ: Erlbaum.

Heimpel, S., Elliot, A. J., & Wood, J. V. (2006). Basic personality dispositions, self-esteem, and personal goals: An approach-avoidance analysis. *Journal of Personality, 74*(5), 1293–320. doi:10.1111/j.1467-6494.2006.00410.x

Herbart, J. F. (1850). Psychologie als wissenschaft. In G. Hartenstein (Ed.), *Sämmtliche Werke* (Vol. 5, pp. 191–514; Vol. 6). Leipzig, Germany: Voss. (Original work published 1824/25)

Hull, C. (1943). *Principles of behavior.* New York, NY: Appleton-Century-Crofts.

James, W. (1890). *The principles of psychology* (Vol. II). New York, NY: Holt.

Jung, C. (1921). Psychological types. In *The Collected Works of C. G. Jung, Vol. 6.* Princeton, NJ: Princeton University Press.

Kaplan, A., Gheen, M., & Midgley, C. (2002). Classroom goal structure and student disruptive behaviour. *British Journal of Educational Psychology, 72,* 191–212.

Karabenick, S. A. (2003). Seeking help in large college classes: A person-centered approach. *Contemporary Educational Psychology, 28,* 37–58.

Klinger, E. (1977). *Meaning and void: Inner experience and the incentives in people's lives.* Minneapolis: University of Minnesota Press.

Koesnter, R., Zuckerman, M., & Koestner, J. (1987). Praise, involvement, and intrinsic motivation. *Journal of Personality and Social Psychology, 53,* 383–390.

Kruglanski, A. W. (1996). Goals as knowledge structures. In P. M. Gollwitzer & J. A. Bargh (Eds.), *The psychology of action: Linking cognition and motivation to behavior* (pp. 599–618). New York, NY: Guilford.

Kuhl, J. (1986). Motivation and information processing. In R. Sorrentino & E. Higgins (Eds.), *Handbook of motivation and cognition, Vol. 1* (pp. 404–434). New York, NY: Guilford.

Kuhl, J. (2000). A functional-design approach to motivation and self-regulation: The dynamics of personality systems and interactions. In M. Boekaerts & P. R. Pintrich (Eds.), *Handbook of self-regulation* (pp. 111–169). San Diego, CA: Academic.

Lang, P. (1995). Studies of motivation and attention. *American Psychologist, 50,* 372–385.

Lang, P., Bradley, M., & Cuthbert, B. (1990). Emotion, attention, and the startle reflex. *Psychological Review, 97,* 377–395.

Lang, P., Bradley, M., & Cuthbert, B. (1997). Motivated attention: Affect, activation, and action. In P. Lang, R. Simmons, & M. Balaban (Eds.), *Attention and orienting: Sensory and motivational processes* (pp. 87–135). Hillsdale, NJ: Erlbaum.

Leary, M. R., & MacDonald, G. (2003). Individual differences in self-esteem: A review and theoretical integration. In M. Leary & J. Tangney (Eds.), *Handbook of self and identity* (pp. 401–418). New York, NY: Guilford.

LeDoux, J. (1987). Emotion. In F. Plum (Ed.), *Handbook of physiology* (Vol. 5, pp. 419–454. Bethesda, MD: American Physiological Society.

Lewin, K. (1926). Vorsatz, wille und bedürfnis [Intention, will, and need]. *Psychologische Forschung, 7*, 330–385.

Lewin, K. (1935). *A dynamic theory of personality.* New York, NY: McGraw-Hill.

Lewin, K. (1938). *The conceptual representation and the measurement of psychological forces.* Durham, NC: Duke University Press.

Linnenbrink, E. A. (2005). The dilemma of performance-approach goals: The use of multiple goal contexts to promote students' motivation and learning. *Journal of Educational Psychology, 97*, 197–213.

Locke, E. A. (1969). Purpose without consciousness: A contradiction. *Psychological Reports, 25*, 991–1009.

Locke, E. A., & Latham, G. P. (1990). *A theory of goal setting and task performance.* Engelwood Cliffs, NJ: Prentice Hall.

Lopez, D. F. (1999). Social cognitive influences on self-regulated learning: The impact of action-control beliefs and academic goals on achievement-related outcomes. *Learning and Individual Differences, 11*, 301–319.

Maehr, M. L. (1983). On doing well in science: Why Johnny no longer excels, why Sarah never did. In S. Paris, G. Olseon, & H. Stevenson (Eds.), *Learning and motivation in the classroom* (pp. 179–210). Hillsdale, NJ; Erlbaum.

Maslow, A. (1955). Deficiency motivation and growth motivation. In M. Jones (Ed.), *Nebraska symposium on motivation.* Lincoln: University of Nebraska Press.

McClelland, D. C. (1951). *Personality.* Oxford, UK: Sloane.

McClelland, D. C., Koestner, R., & Weinberger, J. (1989). How do self-attributed and implicit motives differ? *Psychological Review, 96*, 690–702.

McFarlin, D. B., Baumeister, R. F., & Blascovich, J. (1984). On knowing when to quit: Task failure, self-esteem, advice, and nonproductive persistence. *Journal of Personality, 52*, 138–155.

McGregor, H. A., & Elliot, A. J. (2002). Achievement goals as predictors of achievement-relevant processes prior to task engagement. *Journal of Educational Psychology, 94*, 381–395.

Middleton, M. J., & Midgley, C. (1997). Avoiding the demonstration of lack of ability: An underexplored aspect of goal theory. *Journal of Educational Psychology, 89*, 710–718.

Midgley, C., Kaplan, A., & Middleton, M. (2001). Performance-approach goals: Good for what, for whom, under what circumstances, and at what cost? *Journal of Educational Psychology, 93*, 77–86. doi:10.1037/0022-0663.93.1.77

Miller, A., & Hom, H. L. (1990). Influence of extrinsic and ego incentive value on persistence after failure and continuing motivation. *Journal of Educational Psychology, 82*, 539–545.

Moller, A. C., & Elliot, A. J. (2006). The 2 × 2 achievement goal framework: An overview of empirical research. In A. V. Mitel (Ed.), *Focus on educational psychology research* (pp. 307–326). New York, NY: Nova Science.

Mowrer, O. H. (1960). *Learning theory and the symbolic processes.* New York, NY: Wiley.

Murphy, F. C., Nimmo-Smith, I., & Lawrence, A. D. (2003). Functional neuroanatomy of emotions: A meta-analysis. *Cognitive, Affective & Behavioral Neuroscience, 3,* 207–233.

Murray, H. (1938). *Explorations in personality.* New York, NY: Oxford University Press.

Nicholls, J. (1984). Achievement motivation: Conceptions of ability, subjective experience, task choice, and performance. *Psychological Review, 91,* 328–346.

Nicholls, J. G. (1989). *The competitive ethos and democratic education.* Cambridge, MA: Harvard University Press.

Nuttin, J. (1984). *Motivation, planning, and action: A relational theory of behavior dynamics* (R. P. Lorion & J. E. Dumas, Trans.). Hillsdale, NJ: Erlbaum.

Öhman, A. (1997). As fast as the blink of an eye: Evolutionary preparedness for preattentive processing of threat. In P. Lang, R. Simmons, & M. Balaban (Eds.), *Attention and orienting: Sensory and motivational processes* (pp. 87–135). Hilldale, NJ: Erlbaum.

Olds, J., & Milner, P. (1954). Positive reinforcement produced by electrical stimulation of septal area and other regions. *Journal of Comparative and Physiological Psychology, 47,* 419–427.

Orians, G., & Heerwagen, J. (1992). Evolved responses to landscapes. In J. Barkow, L. Cosmides, & J. Tooby (Eds.), *The adapted mind* (pp. 555–579). New York, NY: Oxford University Press.

Osgood, C. E., Suci, G., & Tannenbaum, P. (1957). *The measurement of meaning.* Urbana: University of Illinois Press.

Pajares, F., & Valiante, G. (2001). Gender differences in writing motivation and achievement of middle school students: A function of gender orientation? *Contemporary Educational Psychology, 26,* 366–381.

Pavlov, I. (1927). *Conditioned reflexes: An investigation into the physiological activity of the cortex* (G. Anrep, Trans.). New York, NY: Dover.

Pekrun, R., Elliot, A. J., & Maier, M. A. (2006). Achievement goals and discrete achievement emotions: A theoretical model and prospective test. *Journal of Educational Psychology, 98,* 583–597.

Rawsthorne, L. J., & Elliot, A. J. (1999). Achievement goals and intrinsic motivation: A meta-analytic review. *Personality and Social Psychology Review, 3,* 326–344.

Rogers, C. (1961). *On becoming a person: A therapist's view of psychotherapy.* Boston, MA: Houghton Mifflin.

Roskes, M., Sligte, D., Shalvi, S., & De Dreu, C. K. W. (2011). The right side? Under time pressure, approach motivation leads to right-oriented bias. *Psychological Science, 22,* 1403–1407.

Sansone, C., Sachau, D. A., & Weir, C. (1989). Effects of instruction on intrinsic interest: The importance of context. *Jouranl of Personality and Social Psychology, 57,* 819–829.

Schneirla, T. (1959). An evolutionary and developmental theory of biphasic processes underlying approach and withdrawal. In *Nebraska symposium on motivation* (pp. 1–42). Lincoln: University of Nebraska Press.

Shah, J. Y. (2003). Automatic for the people: How representations of significant others implicitly affect goal pursuit. *Journal of Personality and Social Psychology, 84,* 661–681.

Shah, J. Y., Friedman, R., & Kruglanski, A. W. (2002). Forgetting all else: On the antecedents and consequences of goal shielding. *Journal of Personality and Social Psychology, 83,* 1261–1280.

Shah, J. Y., & Kruglanski, A. W. (2003). When opportunity knocks: Bottom-up priming of goals by means and its effects on self-regulation. *Journal of Personality and Social Psychology, 84,* 1109–1122.

Sideridis, G. D. (2005). Goal orientation, academic achievement, and depression: Evidence in favor of a revised goal theory framework. *Journal of Educational Psychology, 97,* 366–375.

Skinner, B. F. (1938). *The behavior of organisms: An experimental analysis.* Englewood Cliffs, NJ: Prentice-Hall.

Skinner, B. F. (1953). *Science and human behavior.* New York, NY: Macmillan.

Sokolov, E. (1963). *Perception and the conditioned reflex.* Oxford, UK: Pergamon.

Tice, D. M. (1991). Esteem protection or enhancement? Self-handicapping motives and attributions differ by trait self-esteem. *Journal of Personality & Social Psychology, 60,* 711–725.

Tice, D. M. (1993). The social motivations of people with low self-esteem. In R. Baumeister (Ed.), *Self-esteem: The puzzle of low self-regard* (pp. 37–53). New York, NY: Plenum.

Urdan, T. (2004). Predictors of academic self-handicapping and achievement: Examining achievement goals, classroom goal structures, and culture. *Journal of Educational Psychology, 96,* 251–264.

Wager, T. D., Phan, K. L., Liberzon, I., & Taylor, S. F. (2003). Valence, gender, and lateralization of functional brain anatomy in emotion: A meta-analysis of findings from neuroimaging. *NeuroImage, 19,* 513–531.

Wolters, C. A. (2004). Advancing achievement goal theory: Using goal structures and goal orientations to predict students' motivation, cognition, and achievement. *Journal of Educational Psychology, 96,* 236–250.

Wood, J. V., Giordano-Beech, M., Taylor, K. L., Michela, J. L., & Gaus, V. (1994). Strategies of social comparison among people with low self-esteem: Self-protection and self-enhancement. *Journal of Personality and Social Psychology, 67,* 713–731.

Wundt, W. (1887). *Grundzüge der physiologishen psychologie* (3rd ed.). Leipzig, Germany: Engelmann.

Wyer, R. S., & Srull, T. K. (1986). Human cognition in its social context. *Psychological Review, 93,* 322–359.

Zajonc, R. B. (1980). Feeling and thinking: Preferences need no inferences. *American Psychologist, 35,* 151–175.

Zajonc, R. B. (1998). Emotion. In D. Gilbert, S. Fiske, & G. Lindzey (Eds.), *The handbook of social psychology* (4th ed., pp. 591–632). New York, NY: McGraw-Hill.

Zimmerman, B. J. (1989). A social-cognitive view of self-regulated academic learning. *Journal of Educational Psychology, 81,* 329–339.

CHAPTER 11

MOTIVATION

A Philosophical and Psychological Synthesis

Laurance J. Splitter and Dennis M. McInerney
The Hong Kong Institute of Education

Reflecting on what a satisfactory conceptual account of motivation amounts to is an important ingredient in the practical task of motivating someone to act. In this chapter, we specifically examine the role of agency, goals, and reasoned persuasion and will argue that these components are central to both our commonsense ideas about, and a range of theoretical perspectives on motivation. More specifically, we clarify the conceptual frameworks governing ordinary descriptions of motivation. In our description, persons are seen both in causal, physical, and extensional terms as agents of change; and in semantic and intensional terms as goal setters, believers, and reasoners who are open to being reasoned with. We resolve some apparent tensions between these frameworks, maintaining that an integrated account of motivation involves the activity of reasoned persuasion with those we seek to motivate, notably students, about their own causal powers. In this account, the concept of goals is crucial, but the precise nature and point of

Self-Concept, Motivation, and Identity, pages 273–297

goals require clarification, since the intuitive notion that goals function as causes of behavior is seen to be incoherent. We also clarify the dualities of cognition/affect and motivating reason/normative (justifying) reason in accounting for agency and motivation. In doing so we confront the familiar difficulty that arises when the key ingredients for motivated behavior appear to be in place, yet the agents in question are not moved to act.

In most motivational contexts, we can identify chains of actions and events—both mental (springing from within the person) and physical (belonging to the external world)—linking long-term goals with more proximal ones. In addition to clarifying the precise nature of such chains, we propose bringing to the forefront the affective components of motivation, most notably, our desires, and suggest a simple alternative to the so-called problem of motivating students intrinsically rather than extrinsically.[1] With a view to providing further support for the motivational framework proposed, we discuss and resolve several challenges that will be familiar to educators and/or researchers in the field.

In the final sections of the chapter, we turn our attention more directly to the semantic and linguistic components of agency and particularly the practical task of engaging students in reasoned conversations—dialogue—about what it is that we want them to learn, know, and understand. In this context, we endorse the transformation of teaching and learning environments into inquiring communities. We conclude with reference to the semantic and ontological theories of causality and agency articulated by the philosopher, Donald Davidson (1963, 1993, 2001). Davidson's influential views challenge the notion that psychology alone can provide a scientific account of human behavior in general, and motivation in particular.

MOTIVATION THEORY, PHILOSOPHY, AND TERMINOLOGY

Motivation is one of those core psychological constructs which has been the subject of enormous amounts of literature, particularly in the domain of educational psychology. Beginning with the very practical challenge of how to motivate students to act in ways which are desirable, the literature has responded with a broad range of theories, all of which, in one form or another, attempt to explain and/or predict what is in fact going on when motivation is optimized. Early cognitive theories of motivation, such as Need Achievement Theory (McClelland, Atkinson, Clark, & Lowell, 1953), dealt with unconscious motives tapped through projective tests. But the "black box" of motives and motivation still appears to be inaccessible.

The theoretical and research motivation literature is replete with terms such as being moved, motives, causes, reasons, intention, persuasion, the self (self-efficacy, self determination, self-concept), affect, explanation, choice, volition, will(ing), interest, voluntary, freedom, agency, action, event, wanting, desire, belief, goal, incentive, inclination, and inspiration—all ripe for interrogation to ascertain whether there is an underlying construct, psychological process, or other mechanism(s) that draws the theoretical literature together and that might be of value to educators trying to make sense of what seems a set of disparate theories on motivation.

Philosophers, too, have weighed in on the topic of motivation, but with an important shift of focus. The philosophical challenge may be viewed in conceptual terms, as a demand to analyze—to understand—what we really mean when we describe certain scenarios in terms of motivation. Our aim in this chapter is to undertake such an analysis, focusing particularly on key semantic and epistemological considerations, within the frameworks offered by relevant psychological literature. In the absence of some kind of analytical consensus, we may ask with what degree of confidence can we even use the term "motivation" in a coherent or unified way?

As mentioned, the terms listed above are ripe for psychological reflection (e.g., see Murphy & Alexander, 2000). That philosophers and psychologists typically produce distinct (albeit overlapping) lists in such cases is not altogether surprising, given their respective disciplinary foci (philosophers being inclined to look for unifying and clarifying conceptual accounts; psychologists being more interested in indicating different but related fields of theorizing and research). If the former strategy risks ignoring important differences, the latter tends to confuse definitions with exemplars.[2] If psychologists have not taken proper account of the philosophical dimensions of motivation, the converse is also true; we know of nowhere in the recent literature where philosophers have taken up the conceptual issue of motivation in the context of students and classrooms.

SETTING THE CONCEPTUAL SCENE

Motivation moves us to act, that is, to behave intentionally. While behavior is something public and observable, intentionality is neither. What we are calling the practical challenge of motivation must confront this dichotomy, if only because the challenge itself is not really about getting people to behave as we want them to act, so much as moving them to do so intentionally and freely. Centrally, it would appear that the ideas of agency and persons as agents are important. According to Bandura (1986, 1997, 2008), "agency" is an inherent capacity that distinguishes the human species and is at the root of motivated behavior, but further, as we shall discuss, ideas of causality, reasoning, and the interplay of cognition and affect are important.

Motivation, causality, reasoning, and personhood are relational concepts, the first three of which are naturally regarded as playing a role in explaining why people do what they do. By "relational," we simply mean that we understand these concepts primarily in terms of how they relate to other things. Introduce persons into the picture and this relatively simple scenario is much more complex. In particular, while causality is always at work whenever persons engage in behavior, whether intentionally or not, their intentionality is normally explained by reasons rather than causes per se. Likewise, motivated behavior is behavior accounted for by reasons. More fine-grained and philosophically underpinned analysis of the forces that underpin motivated action may provide a better explanation and prediction of learning processes and outcomes. We examine the forces that underpin motivated action in the next section.

REASONS AND CAUSES

While trying to understand the dynamics of motivation in the classroom, we are confronted by the necessity to distinguish between a motivating reason (which is a kind of psychological state) and a normative or justifying reason (which is a kind of moral principle) for two reasons. First, it helps to explain the frustration felt by teachers who believe that they have good (normative) reasons for compelling students to do their homework, but are nonetheless unable to motivate them so to do. Secondly, as Smith (1987) and others have pointed out, a coherent account of motivation and its associated reasons cannot ignore the normative or moral domain because that domain helps to determine what counts as rational or sensible behavior, and guiding students in the direction of rationality (or, more broadly, of reasonableness) is an important educational norm.

Students may be persuaded, for example, that there are good normative reasons for doing their homework, in that they understand the connection between homework completion and meeting course requirements, earning a good grade, and so on. Further, they may naturally desire to do well in this broader sense (whether they see this desire in instrumental terms—doing well will lead to acceptance into a good college, a good job—that is, a type of future time perspective, or intrinsically—they simply want to do well for its own sake—that is, a type of mastery goal orientation). Still, they may not wish to do their homework (may even hate the idea of doing it) and so may simply not do it. Even allowing that teachers can see that such students are not acting in their own best interests and so, are behaving irrationally, at least in one sense, there remains the motivational challenge: the students accept and desire the appropriate long-term goals and, further, accept the causal connection between certain present actions and these goals, and yet are not motivated to act.

While this scenario contains both affective and cognitive elements which are salient in contemporary theories of motivation, notably, desires, beliefs, and understandings, the breakdown or gap which blocks the motivation to act in the present is essentially an affective one: these students simply do not want to do what they need to do and accept that they need to do in order to achieve their own long-term goals. This view of things reflects a broadly Humean conception (after the Scottish philosopher David Hume, 1969/1739) of human action generally and motivated behavior specifically: viz., that at the end of the day, we are moved to act in accordance with our desires, supported by cognitive elements such as beliefs, rather than the cognitive elements alone (see Smith, 1987, 1998). Hume's view has been contested in the literature, most notably by philosophers in the Kantian tradition in which one's sense of duty or moral principle always trumps one's desires and inclinations (e.g., see Guevara, 2000). Needless to say, this is a huge and ongoing issue in moral philosophy, and while we do not intend to contribute to it directly here, it does warrant acknowledgement.

Intensional and Extensional Relationships

Returning to the distinction between reasoning and causality, and the role each plays in accounting for action, the distinction between them is quite fundamental, in that they operate in quite different conceptual frames or contexts. Where causality is an extensional relationship that links entities in the "real" ultimately physical world of objects and events, reasoning is an intentional, semantic relationship of inference among sentences, statements, propositions, thoughts, and such. How is this difference represented in a general conceptual account of motivation? Motivated behavior is not just caused behavior, it is reasoned or rational behavior, and while a plausible theory of action does posit that reasons for action function as causes (otherwise there would be no action), the challenge and success of motivation in practice depends upon such logicolinguistic activities as rational persuasion, which cannot be accounted for in purely causal terms.

Such an account may be framed by the commonplace notion that to be motivated to act is to be moved by some goal. I may be motivated by a stirring lecture by the prospect of becoming fabulously rich or by the goal of being a good public speaker. In the particular context of the classroom, students might be motivated by such goals, incentives, prospects, and threats (negative incentives) as getting good grades; earning a gold star; being acknowledged in a positive way by teachers, parents, and classmates; or conversely, facing a reprimand or a poor grade.

In each of these scenarios, there is a real or projected sequence of events, causally linked, that includes the (intentional) actions of those involved and their outcomes, culminating in an event which is constitutive of the desired goal. To see intentional action as part of this sequence is to position it as both cause and effect. It is a cause in the sense that human agency posits individuals as being able intentionally to bring about certain events (e.g., doing homework as part of earning a good grade; alternatively, not doing homework and perhaps not earning a good grade). And it is an effect because it is directly brought about by such mental events as desires and beliefs (e.g., my desire to get a good grade and my belief that I need to do my homework in order to satisfy this desire). The example offered may be expanded upon as follows: My goal of achieving a good grade translates into a desire to do my homework now, given the abovementioned belief (where "translation" here is a process of reasoning). Accordingly, I do my homework and continue to fulfill the course requirements, until finally, I earn an A. Notwithstanding the mixing of mental and physical events in this sequence, it may still be seen as a sequence of causes and effects.

The combination of mental and physical events involved is likely to be part of a longer causal chain, stretching both forward and back in time. This chain consists of those "token" events[3] constituting a pathway toward actually attaining my goals, which are situated around that of achieving a good result at the end of the semester. We say "situated around" because some events precede this achievement: choosing to attend and then actually attending every class; choosing to listen to the teacher (which might come down to choosing not to be distracted by the kids at the back of the classroom), and then listening; choosing to complete each assignment and then doing so, and so on; advancing to the next level; completing my degree; getting a good job; and being financially secure in order to enjoy the material pleasures that life has to offer. This chain is one of causes and their effects, whose links consist of both ordinary physical (real world) events—attending class every day of the week, handing in an assignment, attaining a specific grade, being told that I may advance to the next level, and so on—and specific mental events—choosing to get up in time each morning and believing that I need to finish this assignment by tomorrow.

RATIONAL PERSUASION

While identifying such causal sequences may be part of the motivational story, it is both incomplete and unsatisfying. As we asked earlier, What causes the "choosing" to occur? Motivated behavior is not just caused behavior, it is reasoned or rational behavior, and while a plausible theory of action does posit that reasons for action function as causes (otherwise there would be no action), the challenge and success of motivation in practice depends upon such logicolinguistic activities as rational persuasion, which cannot be accounted for in purely causal terms.

To see that the concept of causality is inadequate to ground motivation, let us reflect further on our example. It appears that attaining a good grade is the object of my motivation—the event that causes me to do my homework, where the latter event is the effect. However, this familiar way of talking masks a deeper and more complex truth. In a causal theory of action, it is hard to see how entities like goals can be causal motivators, since they are not (specific) events and certainly not psychological events. Granted, goals are, at least in part, affective: they are defined by our desires (and perhaps by our beliefs as well, e.g., that our goals are attainable), but while grammatically, verbs expressing such attitudes nearly always have objects—if I believe or desire, then I believe or desire something. However, the logic, which makes sense of these entities, tells us otherwise. I can believe in ghosts, that the tooth fairy came last night, and that if I work hard enough, I can become a billionaire, in the complete absence of any such entities as ghosts, tooth fairies, and actual connections between hard work and becoming a billionaire. Similarly, I can desire first prize in a spelling competition, yearn for a good night's sleep, and hope that the class bully will leave me alone where again the prize, the sleep and the state of being left alone are either not yet existent or never will be. Language and grammatical usage are often misleading with respect to their ontological commitments.

This kind of consideration has led many philosophers to conclude that neither the attitudes of belief and desire nor their supposed objects exist independently of the language we use to describe them. Such a conclusion finds further support in the semantic point that a generic description such as "My desire to achieve a good grade" cannot have as its object the event which happens to make "I achieved a good grade" true. This is because, in addition to the point just noted, that desired objects are not really objects at all in any independent sense and so cannot be causes of anything. There is also a commonsense point that whereas the actual event of my achieving a good grade must be specific in terms of its time, context, and such, my desire to achieve a good grade, even in that particular subject, can be satisfied by an indefinite number of possible actions or events (Davidson, 2001).

It follows that if I am motivated to work hard in class by the prospect of getting a good grade (i.e., my goal, or one of them, is to get a good grade), then it is not the motivation or goal itself (nor the intention to achieve it) which actually causes me to work hard in class, on specific occasions. This is just as well since causes, we may assume, always precede their effects. Regardless of how far we choose to break down the various component actions involved (on October 4, I get up in time for class, I listen attentively, I carry out the teacher's instructions, I cooperate with my fellow students, etc.), we can be reasonably confident that all such actions, qua specific, datable actions which begin and end, are caused by (perhaps among things) my specific, datable desires and beliefs. As Davidson remarks when discussing a different but similar example, all these individual actions are the sorts of things we do when we have such goals (Davidson, 1963, also Miller, 2008).

Motivation and the Language of Reasoning

These and other considerations lead naturally to the view that the language of motivation, like that of belief and desire, but unlike that of causality, does not include direct references to events related as causes and effects. As suggested earlier, motivation is a matter of rational persuasion (i.e., reasoning) whose major players are persons who reason with one another within the frameworks of logic and language. Accordingly, if we want to explore the practical challenge of motivation in the classroom, we need to examine how these frameworks operate rather than attempt to delve deeper into the causal dimensions of behavior. As noted above, it is not enough (though it is important) for students to realize their power as intentional agents who are capable of putting certain causal chains into play whereby their mental states and actions have real-world consequences. Motivation also involves persuading/encouraging students that certain goals are both worthwhile and achievable via certain types of actions. Hence, our goals (help to) rationalize or explain our actions. We may assume that there is an underlying causal sequence at work in any specific case, but we do not need to know the details.[4]

The idea that motivation is essentially tied to reasoning (specifically, to reasons about beliefs and desires) has been defended by several philosophers in the Humean tradition (e.g., Smith, 1987). The key ingredients here which, taken together, constitute a reason for performing some action, are certain desires and beliefs held by the person who performs the action. More specifically, the person desires an outcome which represents a goal for her; further, she believes that were she to do a particular action, she would achieve the goal. While this chain of reasoning corresponds to some existing or projected state of affairs in the world, its effectiveness depends crucially on the language employed and the concurrence of the individual (i.e., her mental states).

We are primarily interested here in describing motivation from a third person perspective, that is, what it is that motivates another, notably a student, to act accordingly. It is that person's desires, goals, and beliefs that matter, along with acceptance of the motivating reason that results. As we noted above, it is not enough for me (as a teacher) to have goals, desires, and beliefs on behalf of the student; in short, my motivation is not necessarily hers. Still, teachers play an important motivational role by inviting their students to acknowledge and accept the chain of reasoning described here. We can help students to identify and "own" goals that they desire, value, and believe are attainable.

SOME CHALLENGES

If we are serious about operating within a motivational framework based on chains of reasoning involving desires, goals, and beliefs, we need to see how well this account can respond to several potential challenges which will be familiar to educators and/or researchers. We will consider four challenges, as follows:

1. The motivational chain may not get started because students may have no long-term desires or goals at all or at least none which are appropriately relevant to the curriculum or subject matter at hand.
2. The motivational chain may not get started because (some) students may lack the appropriate beliefs; for example, they do not believe that the goals they (or others) have set are attainable or realistic for them, or that they do not value the goals.[5]
3. There is no motivational chain with respect to specific students; notably, young children, because they are incapable of reasoning.
4. The motivational (reasoning) chain exists and is accepted by students, but the actual (causal) chain of events does not begin because although they desire the goal and believe that in completing particular behavior they would achieve the goal, they nevertheless do not desire to do the behavior and so do not do it.

We will consider these points in turn, but begin with a general constraint which needs to be borne in mind. Notwithstanding our concern with third-person motivation (where, typically, the "third person" is the student), and with finding practical ways to promote and strengthen it, there is something conceptually problematic about the very idea that one person can motivate another. If we accept that motivated behavior, like intentional action generally, is grounded in what agents desire, believe, and value and thereby in what they choose freely to do; then as with such pedagogic goals as making things meaningful (providing understanding) for students, we should simply concede that one person just cannot perform such tasks for another. Still, good teachers do what they can to maximize the prospects of meaningful learning occurring with respect to their students, which is why the challenges posed here are worthy of consideration. We now discuss each of the proposed challenges

Challenge 1: Setting Goals

The motivational chain may not get started because students may have no long-term desires or goals at all, or at least none which are appropriately relevant to the curriculum or subject matter at hand.

Goals, by definition, are both desired and valued by those who have them (Locke & Latham, 1984, 2002). Goal setting involves establishing quantitative and qualitative standards or objectives to serve as the aim of one's actions. Setting appropriately challenging levels of goals, according to different phases of attainment, is crucial in motivating students to engage in learning (Bandura, 1997; Locke & Latham, 2002) and make them self-regulated learners (Locke & Latham, 1990; Schunk, 1990). Goals help give structure to student learning and a set of benchmarks by which students and teachers can evaluate progression.

Goals are also, again by definition, long term, at least in the sense that they can be distinguished from more immediate desires. But the "term" in question is relative: my goal to do well at school triggers a desire to finish my homework tonight; in turn, my (instrumental) goal to finish my homework tonight triggers a desire to finish my dinner quickly. Conversely, in the absence of the long(er)-term goal or desire, I may well lack the short(er)-term ones. To take the challenge of third-person motivation seriously is to assist and encourage students in the formation of medium and longer-term goals in order to enable them to reason their way to action in the short term.

For this reason, teachers should help students to set personal long-term, medium-term, and short-term goals that relate explicitly to the purpose for them doing the activity or course. Schunk (1990; Schunk & Pajares, 2004; see also McInerney & Liem, 2008) suggested a number of useful strategies to assist teachers help students set goals effectively: determine what subproximal goals must be accomplished to attain their long-term goals, view the goals as reasonably attainable and commit themselves to attaining them, provide verbal encouragement (persuasion) ("I am sure you can do this") to enhance motivation to accomplish their goals, teach students how to self-monitor their own progress, and provide feedback on tasks where it is difficult for students to gauge their progress. In summary, helping students set goals with appropriate levels of proximity, specificity, and difficulty is critical for their continued motivation and engaged learning.

Students are likely to experience somewhat different, less satisfying scenarios as they proceed from one grade level to the next. It is commonplace that young children, on account of their natural sense of curiosity and wonderment, require little by way of motivation. Subject to such constraints as short attention span, they care less for goal-directed behavior than for doing things that are enjoyable and interesting or that please the teacher (Anderman, Maehr, & Midgley, 1999; Wigfield, Eccles, & Rodriguez, 1998).

However, the downside is that as they advance to higher grades and more difficult subject matter, they will likely become increasingly dissatisfied with following the teacher's instructions in the absence of at least a partial understanding of longer-term goals, particularly if the tasks in question are not enjoyable in their own right. To repeat, the teacher may be clear about her own goals and that of the syllabus she is teaching, but such goals are not automatically embraced by students as theirs.

The problem here is easy to state and equally, easy to resolve, at least in principle. Instead of merely accepting the transition from "no goals" to "someone else's goals," teachers can work with children from the earliest years to help them understand and appreciate the role that goals play in our lives.

Challenge 2: Expectations and Values

The motivational chain may not get started because (some) students may lack the appropriate beliefs; for example, they do not believe that the goals they (or others) have set are attainable or realistic for them or that they do not value the goals.

Students need to have a strong expectation that they will achieve the desired outcome; that it is attainable and realistic. If they believe success is beyond their capacity, they will be demoralized and thus less motivated. However, even if students possess a strong expectation of success but don't value an activity/outcome, they will not be motivated (Wigfield & Eccles, 2000, 2002).

Wigfield and Eccles (2000, 2002) postulate that expectancies and values are influenced by task-specific beliefs, such as ability beliefs (i.e., the individuals' perceptions of their current competence for a given activity); perceived difficulty of the task; and the individual's goals for schooling, sense of self, and affective memories for similar tasks. These social cognitive variables are influenced by an individual's perceptions of their previous experiences and socialisation (Wigfield & Eccles, 2000, 2002; Wigfield et al., 1998; Wigfield, Tonks, & Eccles, 2004). They also contend that students' expectancy and task values directly predict their achievement outcomes, including performance, persistence, and choices of which activities to do (McInerney & Liem, 2008). In this context, teachers play a fundamental role in encouraging (persuading) students to believe in their capacity to achieve specified and valued goals. In order to enhance students' expectancy for success, teachers should help students identify the behaviors associated with successful learning, for example, by asking questions, searching for answers from knowledgeable sources, and reflecting on learning progress (i.e., understanding) as well as teach strategies for learning and metacognition which aim to bolster expectation of success as a result of students' own personal actions.

Challenge 3: Rational Persuasion and Reasoning

There is no motivational chain with respect to specific students, notably, young children, because they are incapable of reasoning.

The third challenge to effective motivation refers specifically to young children who, it may be claimed, are not able to reason effectively and accordingly, are not open to rational persuasion. However, it is not clear that this point adds anything substantial to what has already been considered in Challenges 1 and 2 above. For example, it may be that part, at least, of the inability to reason is an inability to formulate goals in the first place. Granted, young children have and express many desires, but the more sophisticated idea that fulfilling certain desires is a necessary and/or sufficient condition of fulfilling others (the latter being goals) may be beyond their grasp.

However, as a general point, adults are often guilty of underestimating the reasoning and conceptual abilities of young children. Piagetian theory and methodology, to take one influential example, may not have allowed the full capacities of children to be explored (McInerney, 2014). More-advanced research techniques (such as video cameras and digital audio recorders) are now available for observing infants and children, although the most sophisticated observations reveal, at best, what they do, not what they can or might do under appropriate circumstances (Flavell, 1985). In general, research using alternative methodologies and new techniques has established that Piaget underestimated the cognitive capacity of children (e.g., Gelman, & Baillargeon, 1983; Halford, 1989; Siegler, 1991). Such discrepancies between the theory and what we now know children are really capable of doing (because we observe them doing it) call into question what was once thought to be the limits of children's capacities to reason (Van Horn & Ramey, 2003). In the formulation of motivated behavior suggested above, all that is required is a relatively straightforward inference of the form, "I have a goal G; I believe that were I to do A, I would attain G, therefore I will/should do A." What evidence is there to suggest that young children are incapable of making this most basic of conditional inferences? Indeed, subject to the proviso that children may require assistance in order to improve their reasoning capacities (as with most other skills), there is plenty of evidence to the contrary.[6]

Challenge 4: Self-Regulation and Self-Determination

The motivational (reasoning) chain exists and is accepted by students but the actual (causal) chain of events does not begin because, although they desire the goal and believe that in completing particular behavior they would achieve the goal, they nevertheless do not desire to do the behaviour and so do not do it.

This final challenge is arguably the most difficult in conceptual as well as practical terms, because it strikes at the very heart of what we mean by such concepts as desire and (intentional) action, and the crucial role desires play as both causes of and reasons for action. Given the dual role played by desires in the account of motivation we are advocating, that is, desires as long-term goals and as triggers for action, the problem becomes even more pressing.

We begin with a restatement of the problem as formulated earlier: Students may be persuaded that there are good normative reasons for doing their homework, in that they understand the connection, which is, at least partly, a causal one, between homework completion and meeting course requirements, earning a good grade, and so on. Further, they may naturally desire to do well in this broader sense (whether they see this desire in instrumental terms—doing well will lead to acceptance into a good college, a good job, etc.—or intrinsically—they simply want to do well). Still, they may not wish to do their homework (may even hate the idea of doing it) and so may simply not do it.

The problem here is the existence of an affective "gap" between or among different desires. While our concern here is with motivation specifically, we note that the underlying issue is much broader: what philosophers have called "weakness of will" (I should do X, at some level I may even want to do X, I realize that doing Y negates X, but I do Y anyway, perhaps because I just want to do Y more than I want to do X).

At one level, this problem may be met by the simple requirement that students act consistently and reasonably; after all, having agreed that they desire and value a particular goal, and that a particular action leads to the goal, hence, the goal provides a motive for doing the action, they ought now be motivated to actually do it! Even supposing that students are open to being so persuaded, they might still simply refuse. Such a strategy of persuasion appears to be at odds with the intuitive idea that motivated behavior is, inter alia, behavior that is freely chosen by the agents in question (i.e., the students themselves). If our primary concern is to ensure that students do what we require of them, then the loss of student freedom may seem the lesser of two evils; but if our interest is in cultivating positive student attitudes as well as producing certain kinds of behavior, then more needs to be said here.

Can we appeal to the fact that all of us, not just children, are familiar with variations on the affective gap in our own experience? Whether it is a matter of conflicting desires or the realization that what we desire and what is desirable are all too often in conflict, we make choices for better or for worse. We develop strategies for balancing such conflicting forces in our lives, and we (parents, teachers, and society in general) should seek to encourage children to do likewise.

However, there is still a problem here, although in articulating it more clearly, we may also see a way to resolve it. The problem strikes right at the heart of the intuitive notion that our desires are the driving forces behind our actions (Smith, 1987). Consider again the student who wants to do well but does not want to do his homework, even though he accepts that there is a causal connection between the two. In reality, he may act on this negative desire or he may heave a sigh and accept what is desirable instead, thereby exercising what Smith calls self-control, regarded in the psychological literature as a form of self-regulation (Zimmerman, 1998a, 1998b). But paraphrasing Smith, in order to succeed in exercising self-control, he must have sufficient desire to perform the very action (doing his homework) that he lacks the desire to perform (Smith, 1998, pp. 33–34). This has been called "the paradox of self-control" (Mele, 1987). How can we resolve this paradox without giving up the central role of desire in causing and explaining our actions?

One answer to this question derives from reversing the usual order of disposition and action, namely, that a particular attitude such as desire induces or brings about an appropriate action. In fact, it often happens that our feelings and attitudes change, perhaps to our surprise, as a result of actions that occur in spite of our original feelings, which ordinarily would rule out those very actions. I end up liking, even loving, someone for whom my initial feelings are quite negative, as a direct result of my ongoing contact with that person; my students, while never actually enjoying doing homework, come to accept not only its relevance to their future success, but that it is not so bad after all. Indeed (and this is the important point), they come to the realization that its benefits, in terms of enabling the construction of new knowledge and understandings, are both worthwhile and satisfying. Bearing in mind that desire does not require great displays of passion and feeling, we may say that the students have developed a desire to do their homework, not just in terms of their long-term goals but also in terms of more immediate ones. Such processes described above are core to both self-regulation and self-determination theories briefly described in the next sections.

Self-Regulation

Zimmerman (1998a, 1998b, 2004, 2008) defines self-regulation as a process that involves self-generated thoughts, feelings, and actions for attaining academic goals. Self-regulated learners view learning as a systematic and controllable process and accept responsibility for their achievement outcomes. Psychological dimensions implicated in whether a student self-regulates or not (at least in Western educational settings) include the individual's degree of self-motivation for the task (involving goal setting and self-efficacy), the opportunity to choose learning approaches and manage time limits (involving task strategies, self-instruction, and time management), some control over the physical and social environment (involving environmental restructuring to make it more conducive to learning and selective help-seeking from peers, teachers, and others), level of control over selecting appropriate outcome behavior (involving self-monitoring, self-evaluation, and self-consequences), and the balance between teacher- and student-perceived control over classroom learning (Eshel & Kohavi 2003; McInerney & Liem, 2008; Perry, 1998; Zimmerman, 1998a, 1998b).

Self-Determination Theory

Deci and Ryan's (2000) self-determination theory (SDT) posits that a full understanding of goal-directed behaviors, including students' engagement in learning, requires addressing the needs that give goals their psychological potency and influence people's self-regulated activities. Three psychological needs, which are postulated to be universal, fundamental, and broad ranging in their influences on goal-oriented pursuits, are needs for *autonomy* (i.e., self-determination in deciding what to do and how to do it), *competence* (i.e., developing and exercising skills for manipulating and controlling the environment), and *relatedness* (i.e., affiliation with others through prosocial relationships). According to SDT, satisfaction of these three basic needs provides the necessary conditions that give people the freedom to engage in self-determined activities. Thus, the theory postulates that students are likely to be intrinsically motivated to be engaged in learning activities when they are placed in a learning environment that supports satisfaction of their autonomy, competence, and relatedness needs (Deci & Ryan, 2000; Perry, 1998; Reeve, Deci, & Ryan, 2004).

Nevertheless, since students are, or at least should be, free agents, there is no guarantee, irrespective of the learning environment, that they will modify their desires to suit the requirements of teachers or curriculum. Fortunately, teachers do not need to sit back in the hope that their students will eventually "come around." Smith (1987, 1998) suggests, in addition to encouraging students to acknowledge and accept the reasoning that leads (in principle but not always in practice) to motivated action ("I want to attain a particular goal; if I do a particular action, then I will attain the goal, therefore I will do the action"), teachers can help students to exercise self-control and self-regulation when their own proximal desires tempt them in other directions. Smith (1998) offers the example of someone choosing between a carrot stick and a chocolate bar; aware that he desires the latter and not the former, while realizing that the former is healthier, he is inclined to choose the latter because desire trumps his sense of what is good for him. The simple exercise of self-control here results in a paradox, as we saw above, but suppose now that he is accustomed to reflecting on his past experiences, including ones where he did indeed act on a desire to be healthy (which he used to, and still does, see as the more rational option) by joining a health club, for example, and recollects that as he became healthier, he developed a desire to continue to be healthy. Granted, somewhere along the line, he lost this desire, hence, his inclination to gobble the chocolate now, but this process of reflection and recollection which we can see now as the exercise of self-control and self-determination actually causes him to desire to be healthy once more, hence to desire and choose the carrot stick.[7]

Putting these ideas together allows us to see how self-regulation and self-determination might work in the classroom consistently with the aim of maximizing student desire and hence motivation. Extending the reasoning process we have already described, we encourage students to reflect on their past experiences where certain (freely chosen) actions akin to joining and using the health club resulted in benefits both desired and desirable. Indeed, undertaking such a reflective activity could be a regular classroom activity to which students become accustomed; an activity which is, to the maximum extent possible, led by the students themselves. Thus, we come back to the idea, outlined above, that learners modify their own desires in line with what they have already accepted as their long-term goals and beliefs about how to attain them. Our argument is that in order for students to move across the continuum of motivation to self-regulation requires skillful guidance on the part of teachers, particularly through helping students establish a sense of agency, helping them set appropriate goals, and through effective persuasion.

If this process seems rather convoluted and contrived, let us be honest about the context in which it becomes necessary. Put simply, notwithstanding the desirability of long-term goals, much of what we require of students on a day-to-day basis (in pursuit of those goals, let us presume) is boring, repetitive, and invasive of time in which they would rather be doing other things. On one hand, we might expect that teachers will take the time to engage students in the kinds of reasoning activities we have been discussing rather than simply assuming that students will fall into line because they can see and embrace the long-term benefits. On the other hand, there is a circuit breaker here, which has the effect of maximizing student desire to perform required tasks much more straightforwardly, making required tasks interesting and enjoyable for students so that they will want to do them. In the context of making tasks more interesting and enjoyable for students, we discuss intrinsic and extrinsic motivation in the next section.

INTRINSIC "VERSUS" EXTRINSIC MOTIVATION

The notion that agents will want to perform certain tasks, in contrast to having long-term goals which are intended to motivate them to perform these tasks, calls to mind the familiar distinction between intrinsic and extrinsic motivation. Since teachers are often exhorted to focus on the former, where possible, it is worth examining this issue in the context of our broader motivational framework. Deci and Ryan (2000) define intrinsically motivated behaviors as those behaviors performed out of interest and requiring no external prods, promises, or threats. These behaviors are experienced as wholly self-determined, with no external pressure, as representative of and emanating from one's sense of self. Whang and Hancock (1994) define intrinsic motivation as "a task... performed because it is rewarding within itself not because of a reward to be earned as a consequence" (p. 306). If we think of goals instead of rewards here, we may say that whereas extrinsic motivation assumes a distinction between a goal G and the task A for which G is the motivational reason, intrinsic motivation collapses G and A, so that A is its own goal (alternatively, there is no goal). We suggest that for practical pedagogic purposes, what is required is simply that P performs the task because she desires or wants to, irrespective of any perception she might have as to its causal significance in relation to a future goal.

Suppose that the teacher sees an action as merely one step in a causal chain (A... A1... A2... A3...) which does, indeed, culminate in some separate, and later, identifiable goal. Then, by some accounts (see Deci & Ryan, 2000), the task of motivating a given student involves enabling her to internalize each element of the causal chain leading to the goal, where internalization here amounts to the student performing each action along the causal chain simply because she wants to, irrespective of any further beliefs or desires about other elements in the chain, including the goal itself. We support the notion that our interests and desires ideally spring from our attraction to activities which we find meaningful and satisfying, but there is no reason to rule out the realization that what we do is actually part of a longer chain culminating (perhaps much later) in the attainment of a desired goal. Desired goals ought to generate desire all the way along the chain, but as we have noted, in reality they may not. What does enhance desire, however, is engagement in activities which are fun, challenging, connected to student life outside school, and otherwise meaningful to those students (McInerney & Liem, 2008).[8]

Good teachers are both realistic and flexible when it comes to maximizing desire, reasonableness, and hence, motivation. We do not rule out the need for such short-term incentives as rewards and penalties, but in the absence of any more substantive or meaningful motivating factors, they are a poor substitute (because either they are readily seen by students to be superficial or they habituate students into expecting immediate rewards, or penalties, for everything that they do, as John Locke [1989/1693] pointed out 300 years ago in his famous essay on education). Words of praise and encouragement (or, more cautiously, of criticism),[9] "gold stars," occasional small gifts, early release from class, and of course, grades and other marks of achievements, have their place, but they should be regarded as incentives (and, as in the case of grades, external markers as well) rather than motivators per se. In practice, effective teaching strikes a balance here: as long as the overall context (which includes long-term goals but, at least for younger students, more proximate motivators as well) provides sufficient degrees of satisfaction (both affective and cognitive) for students, then there is room for motivating students to perform other necessary but less enjoyable or interesting tasks by the use of such short-term incentives as those mentioned (e.g., see McInerney, 2014).

THE IMPORTANCE OF LANGUAGE AND "COMMUNITIES OF INQUIRY"

The importance of language in the classroom is self-evident; but less widely acknowledged, at least in practice, is the contribution that language can make to nurturing environments which are (relatively) egalitarian rather than teacher dominated. This sense of equality, of a robust but respectful "give and take," is one feature of classrooms that function as communities of inquiry or dialogue. Much has been written about the power of these concepts to transform both the "what" and the "how" of teaching and learning, but this topic is not our major concern here (Splitter, 2010, 2015) However, it is worth pointing out that the community of inquiry has several features which tie in nicely with our analysis of motivation.

A community of inquiry is an environment in which students are engaged in the process of becoming persons; a process with profound affective, cognitive, ethical, and social implications (Splitter, 2010, 2015). These implications include a recognition that through dialogue, students and teachers interact according to norms of respect, reasonableness, and reflection; all features we have highlighted as contributing to effective motivation. Conversely, both inquiry and dialogue are driven by a desire to understand or resolve something which is puzzling or intriguing. Here we have what is arguably the most familiar and powerful form of motivation, particularly for children: the urge to solve a puzzle. It is also the crux of mastery motivation in achievement goal theory (Covington, 2000).

Moreover, to pick up an earlier point, teachers do not have to wait for students to catch on to these skills and dispositions by themselves. The idea of building communities of inquiry rests on the twin claims (which may be traced to Vygotsky, C. S. Peirce, and Dewey, among others) that we should not underestimate what children might do, mentally as well as physically, when supported by others who can guide them into and beyond their respective zones of proximal development; and while teachers are exemplary guides here, we should not forget the influence of other students and of the classroom community itself (see Hickey & Granade, 2004). The "three Rs" noted above (respect, reasonableness, and reflection) have both personal and interpersonal dimensions; indeed, following Vygotsky (1978, 1986), we may hypothesize that children develop deeper understandings of these and other cognitive and affective procedures through internalization. Among the publicly observable interactions which are subject to internalization, dialogue is arguably the most powerful, because it both represents and generates the thinking of individual participants. In the context of our concerns in this chapter, the upshot is that dialogue, viewed as a process of externalized thinking about questions, topics, and concepts that are puzzling or intriguing (and therefore, at the very least, interesting), has a great deal to do with motivation. This connection warrants further exploration and analysis.[10] In the next section of the chapter, we discuss the nature and importance of dialogue with students about motivation.

TALKING WITH STUDENTS ABOUT MOTIVATION

Motivation, we have suggested, has both causal and semantic dimensions, but we have argued that it is the latter that carry more psychological weight. We see the importance of engaging students in discussions about goals, both shorter and longer term, perhaps persuading them that certain goals are more worthwhile than others. We also envisage discussions about what needs to be done in order to attain these goals. The latter may in turn involve considerations of means and ends, better and worse reasons, the importance of developing self-control (self-regulation) as a form of reasonable behavior, evaluations of alternative courses of action, the kinds of activities which resonate most strongly with students and their life experiences, and so on, several of which have strong causal resonance (but, to repeat, are part of the motivational story, not elements in any causal chain per se). Granted, such discussions neither provide motivation in and of themselves nor lay claim to substituting for the actual lessons and activities which, one might say, are the real agenda. But they are important components of both, in that they signal to students that their views and attitudes are valued (as part of the underlying processes of empowerment, developing autonomy, cultivating a democratic conception of citizenship, etc.), all of which may be summed up by referring to the process of becoming a person) (Splitter, 2015); and they contribute to a much needed metalevel perspective that is ideally part of each and every lesson and class activity. We are not saying that teachers should begin their classes or, at least, their courses and subjects with recitations on procedures, rules, good conduct, expectations, and such prior to actually engaging students in the subject matter itself. Creative teachers will often commence with something designed to intrigue, puzzle, and fascinate (with their own sense of intrigue, puzzlement, and fascination as an important source of inspiration and motivation in its own right).[11] But at some point, the motivational teacher will engage students in the meta-level issue of why they are doing certain things, where they are heading, and the potential consequences. We take the concept of engagement seriously here; it is a democratic, egalitarian process, not a "top-down" one.

CONCLUDING REMARKS

In this chapter, we have attempted to outline a conceptual framework through which some apparently disparate accounts of motivation such as self-regulation, self-determination, expectancy value, intrinsic and extrinsic motivation, might at least find sufficient common conceptual ground to engage with one another. We have proposed that the central constructs underlying a sound theory of motivation are agency, goals, and reasoned persuasion to assist students to generate self-thoughts that are conducive to effective engagement with learning. The primary underlying dynamic that gives "power" to all positive self-constructs, such as self-regulation and self-determination, is the unleashing of agency and purpose. We believe that reasoned persuasion and dialogue with students about their agency, purpose, and goal setting leads to enhanced self-regulation and self-determination, a greater expectation and valuing of success, as well as greater engagement with learning through intrinsic motives. From our perspective, all cognitive theories of motivation, including, among others, attribution theory and achievement goal theory, are nested within this broader framework of agency. While the diverse theoretical frameworks provide useful facets of information on the motivational process, the underlying dynamic that drives motivation, whatever its theoretical color, is agency.

Our aim in proposing a conceptual framework for motivation, one which accommodates both the causal and the cognitive relationships involved, especially those relationships involving persons as agents, is itself motivated by our observation that the psychological literature on motivation, particularly that fragment concerned with education, has generated "theories" whose interrelationships are unclear. It is not the theoretical multiplicity that troubles us so much as the apparent failure of these theories and their respective advocates to engage with one another. This failure may be due, at least in part, to the peculiar nature and status of the theories in question, along with the key terms of these theories, specifically, those standing for or appearing to stand for mental or psychological objects.

This being said, the prospects for wholly psychological accounts of explanation, including motivation, must be regarded as mixed at best. On the one hand, we may hope for increasingly insightful and detailed descriptive accounts of why we do what we do (and thereby how we might encourage others to do and to want to do what we want or expect them to do). But on the other hand, between the domain of physics, with its laws and theories (both macro- and microlevel), and those of language and logic, with their laws and theories (e.g., rules of logic), there seems no room for an additional psychological domain with its own laws and theories. Still, old habits die hard, and attempts at "theorizing" about motivation continue unabated. Hence, an abundance of theoretical accounts, each with its own characteristic but a limited and contentious capacity to explain and predict motivation and action. In pinpointing the essential role played by agents and their beliefs, desires, goals, and reasons for action, we hope to have, at least, dug some common ground for a more coherent, structured and, perhaps, unified dialogue on these topics.

NOTES

1. The psychological literature refers more frequently to needs, drives, interests, motives, and values than to desires *per se*, in contrast to the "folk psychology" tradition in the philosophy of mind, where the opposite is the case. This might reflect the traditional view that desires, like beliefs, *qua* subjective or intensional entities, are too murky and mysterious to be taken seriously at a theoretical level. But the conceptual framework we propose leaves room for just such concepts by distinguishing between our linguistic and our ontological commitments.
2. Evidence of conceptual confusion in the educational psychology literature on topics related to motivation is cited by Martin and McLellan (2008). Such confusion trades on persisting with a "black box" view of the mind. Kant famously struggled with the dialectic of sensibility and reason throughout his seminal writings. In fact, there are three forces at work in the case of moral action generally, and the concept of *free will* in particular: our inclinations or feelings, our susceptibility to natural (scientific) law, and our capacity to reason directly about right and wrong, duty, obligation, etc.
3. By "token events," we mean specific events that are situated in space and time and hence can only occur once. By contrast-type events (or states)—like my getting up from my computer from time to time, my desire to eat something, or even *desire per se*—are relatively abstract and are exemplified by specific tokens. Compare the concept *cat* with real-life cats.
4. In response to the concern that our ability to explain things is threatened by our ignorance of underlying causal laws, Davidson points out that we often explain why something happened, even when we do not know such laws: "I am certain the window broke because it was struck by a rock—I saw it all happen; but I am not (is anyone?) in command of laws on the basis of which I can predict what blows will break which windows" (Davidson, 1963, p. 697).
5. Notice that for purposes of motivation, it is the belief in one's ability, not the ability itself, which counts. No doubt the (repeated) failure to attain my goals will impact on my future beliefs and desires in relation to such goals, but that is about future, not present motivation.

6. For example, the many classrooms around the world in which children as young as six years old are engaged in doing philosophy. For a detailed example of young children's reasoning in philosophy, see McCall (1989)
7. As Smith explains, it is important that the exercise of self-control *not* constitute an action, otherwise we would simply have another paradox to resolve (Smith, 1998, p. 36).
8. We prefer the affective term "desire" over "interest" here since, presumably, the relevance of being interested is that it sparks a desire to act; furthermore, interests are not always self-identified: if teachers explain to students that doing A is *in their interests* because it will lead to some future G, then the students' interest in A is, at best, extrinsic.
9. The nature and role of praise and criticism in good teaching remains contentious. Many writers maintain that these affective tools should be directed at specific actions performed by students rather than the students themselves (see Hattie & Timperley, 2007 on different forms of feedback and their effectiveness). The distinction assumed here should be treated cautiously: a person's actions, like her views and opinions, are still *her* actions, not disembodied entities that can be evaluated in isolation.
10. Splitter (2010, 2015) describes a community of inquiry as an environment in which children see themselves as *one among others*: they and their views and concerns are important and valued, but not more so than those of others in the community. The aim here is to avoid the extremes of Individualism and Collectivism. See also Hickey and Granade (2004) for an example of a sociocultural approach with the educational psychology literature.
11. One writer discussing the challenge of inspiring students to "practice toward perfection" points out that good teachers can motivate, not just by convincing students that an activity or topic is interesting to the students, but by revealing that the topic is interesting to *them*, the teacher. She cites a student whose interest in science was revived by a teacher who "brought boring material to life": "Any field has something interesting about it. You [the teacher] can start by saying 'Look how interesting this is,' and ask us to think about 'Why is this? Where does this come from?" This is a nice illustration of how cognitive persuasion has an affective component (since we argue that both are involved in motivation): it is not just her *saying* that it is interesting, it is her *showing* her interest thereby, that has an impact on students (Cushman, 2010, p. 54).

REFERENCES

Anderman, E. M., Maehr, M. L., & Midgley, C. (1999). Declining motivation after the transition to middle school: Schools can make a difference. *Journal of Research and Development in Education, 32,* 131–147.

Bandura, A. (1986). *Social foundations of thought and action: A social cognitive theory.* Englewood Cliffs, NJ: Prentice-Hall.

Bandura, A. (1997). *Self-efficacy: The exercise of control.* New York, NY: Freeman.

Bandura, A. (2008). Toward and agentic theory of the self. In H. W. Marsh, R. Craven, & D. M. McInerney (Eds.), *Self-processes, learning, and enabling human potential: Dynamic new approaches*. Charlotte, NC: Information Age.

Covington, M. V. (2000). Goal theory, motivation, and school achievement: An integrated review. *Annual Review Psychology, 51*, 171–200.

Cushman, K. (2010). The strive of it. *Educational Leadership, 67*, 50–55.

Davidson, D. (1963). Actions, reasons and causes. *Journal of Philosophy, 60*, 685–700.

Davidson, D. (1993). Thinking causes. In J. Heil & A. Mele (Eds.), *Mental causation* (pp. 1–17). Oxford, UK: Clarendon University Press.

Davidson, D. (2001). *Essays on actions and events* (2nd ed.). Oxford, UK: Oxford University Press.

Deci, E. L., & Ryan, R. M. (2000). The "what" and "why" of goal pursuits: Human needs and the self-determination of behavior. *Psychological Inquiry, 11*, 227–268.

Eshel, Y., & Kohavi, R. (2003). Perceived classroom control, self-regulated learning strategies, and academic achievement. *Educational Psychology, 23*, 250–260.

Flavell, J. H. (1985). *Cognitive development* (2nd ed.). Englewood Cliffs, NJ: Prentice Hall.

Gelman, R., & Baillargeon, R. (1983). A review of some Piagetian concepts. In P. Mussen, J. H. Flavell, & E. M. Markman (Eds.), *Handbook of child psychology: Cognitive development (Vol. 3)*. New York, NY: John Wiley.

Guevara, D. (2000). *Kant's theory of moral motivation*. Boulder, CO: Westview.

Halford, G. S. (1989). Reflections on 25 years of Piagetian cognitive developmental psychology, 1963–1988. *Human Development, 32*, 325–357.

Hattie, J. A., & Timperley, H. (2007). The power of feedback. *Review of Educational Research, 77*, 81–112.

Hickey, D. T., & Granade, J. B. (2004). The influence of sociocultural theory on our theories of engagement and motivation. In D. M. McInerney & S. Van Etten (Eds.), *Research on sociocultual influences on motivation and learning (Vol. 4). Big theories revisited*. Greenwich: CT: Information Age.

Hume, D. (1969). A treatise of human nature (E. C. Mossner, Ed.). Harmondsworth, UK: Penguin. (Original work published 1739)

Locke, E., & Latham, G. P. (1984). *Goal-setting: A motivational technique that works*. Englewood Cliffs, NJ: Prentice-Hall.

Locke, E., & Latham, G. P. (2002). Building a practically useful theory of goal setting and task motivation: A 35-year odyssey. *American Psychologist, 57*, 705–717.

Locke, J. (1989). *Some thoughts concerning education* (J. S. Yolton & J. W. Yolton, Eds.). Oxford: Clarendon Press. (Original work published 1693)

Martin, J., & McLellan, A. M. (2008). The educational psychology of self-regulation: A conceptual and critical analysis. *Studies in Philosophy and Education, 27*, 433–448.

McCall, C. (1989). Young children generate philosophical ideas. *Thinking: The Journal of Philosophy for Children, 8*, 22–41.

McClelland, D.C., Atkinson, J. W., Clark, R. A., & Lowell, E. L. (1953). *The achievement motive*. New York, NY: Appleton-Century-Crofts.

McInerney, D. M. (2014). *Educational psychology: Constructing learning* (6th ed.). Sydney, Australia: Pearson.

McInerney, D. M., & Liem, A. D. (2008). Motivation theory and engaged learning. In P. A. Towndrow, C. Koh, & H. C. Tan (Eds.), *Motivation and practice for the classroom* (pp. 11–36). Rotterdam, The Netherlands: Sense.

Mele, A. (1987). *Irrationality: An essay on akrasia, self-deception and self-control.* New York, NY; Oxford, UK: Oxford University Press.

Miller, C. B. (2008). Motivation in agents. *Nous, 42,* 222–266.

Murphy, P. K., & Alexander, P. A. (2000). A motivated look at motivational terminology. *Contemporary Educational Psychology, 25,* 3–53.

Perry, K. E. (1998). Young children's self-regulated learning and contexts that support it. *Journal of Educational Psychology, 90,* 715–129.

Reeve, J., Deci, E. L., & Ryan, R. M. (2004). Self-determination theory: A dialectical framework for understanding sociocultrual influences on student motivation. In D. M. McInerney & S. Van Etten (Eds.), *Research on sociocultural influences on motivation and learning, Vol. 4. Big theories revisited.* Greenwich, CT: Information Age.

Schunk, D. H. (1990). Goal setting and self-efficacy during self-regulated learning. *Educational Psychologist, 25,* 71–86.

Schunk, D. H., & Pajares, F. (2004). Self-efficacy in education revisited: Empirical and applied evidence. In D. M. McInerney & S. Van Etten (Eds.), *Research on sociocultural influences on motivation and learning; Vol. 4. Big theories revisited.* Greenwich, CT: Information Age.

Siegler, R. S. (1991). *Children's thinking* (2nd ed.). Englewood Cliffs, NJ: Prentice Hall.

Smith, M. (1987). The humean theory of motivation. *Mind, New Series, 96,* 36–61.

Smith, M. (1998). The possibility of philosophy of action. In J. Bransen & S. E. Cuypers (Eds.), *Human action, deliberation and causation* (pp. 17–41). Dordrecht, The Netherlands: Kluwer Academic.

Splitter, L. J. (2010). Caring for 'the self as one among others.' *Thinking: The Journal of Philosophy for Children, 19,* 33–39.

Splitter, L. J. (2015). *Identity and personhood: Confusions and clarifications across disciplines.* New York, NY: Springer.

Van Horn, M. L., & Ramey, S. L. (2003). The effects of developmentally appropriate practices on academic outcomes among former head start students and classmates. *American Educational Research Journal, 40,* 961–990.

Vygotsky, L. S. (1978). *Mind in society: The development of higher psychological processes.* Cambridge, MA: Harvard University Press.

Vygotsky, L. S. (1986). *Thought and language.* Cambridge, MA: MIT Press.

Whang, P. A., & Hancock, G. R. (1994). Motivation and mathematics achievement: Comparisons between Asian American and non-Asian students. *Contemporary Educational Psychology, 19,* 302–322.

Wigfield, A., & Eccles, J. S. (2000) Expectancy-value theory of achievement motivation. *Contemporary Educational Psychology, 25,* 68–81.

Wigfield, A., & Eccles, J. S. (2002). The development of competence beliefs, expectancies for success, and achievement values from childhood through adolexcence. In A. Wigfield & J. S. Eccles (Eds.), *Development of achievement motivation.* San Diego, CA: Academic.

Wigfield, A., Eccles, J. S., & Rodriguez, D. (1998). The development of children's motivation in school contexts. *Review of Research in Education, 23,* 73–118.

Wigfield, A., Tonks, S., & Eccles, J. S. (2004). Expectancy value theory in cross-cultural perspective. In D. M. McInerney & S. Van Etten (Eds.), *Research on sociocultual influences on motivation and learning (Vol. 4) Big Theories Revisited.* Greenwich: CT: Information Age.

Zimmerman, B. J. (1998a). Academic studying and the development of personal skill: A self-regulatory perspective. *Educational Psychologist, 33,* 73–86.

Zimmerman, B. J. (1998b). Academic studying and self-regulation. *Educational Psychologist, 30,* 217–221.

Zimmerman, B. J. (2004). Sociocultural influence and students' development of academic self-regulation: A social-cultural perspective. In D. M. McInerney & S. Van Etten (Eds.), *Research on sociocultural influences on motivation and learning, Vol. 4. Big theories revisited.* Greenwich, CT: Information Age.

Zimmerman, B. J. (2008). Investigating self-regulation and motivation: Historical background, methodological developments, and future prospects. *American Educational Research Journal, 45,* 166–183.

CHAPTER 12

COMPETENCE WITHIN CONTEXT

Implications for the Development of Positive Student Identities and Motivation at School

Kathryn R. Wentzel
University of Maryland, College Park

Each day as students, children are asked to respond to a broad array of expectations and challenges presented by adults and peers. They are expected to initiate and maintain positive interpersonal relationships, engage in positive forms of behavior that promote social cohesion and refrain from antisocial forms of behavior that are disruptive or harmful, learn new skills in ways that are deemed appropriate by teachers, and perform at academic standards set by others. These expectations are designed to support the development of specific competencies that are valued within school settings and as such, define for children their ideal identities as students. In addition, day-to-day experiences and feedback provide children with information concerning the extent to which their attempts to be ideal students have been successful; over

Self-Concept, Motivation, and Identity, pages 299–337

time, these social cues and feedback provide a foundation for the self that motivates engagement (or disengagement) in the educational process.

The current chapter focuses on the development of children's identities and motivational belief systems within the context of school settings. This contextual approach is based on a perspective that children develop notions about themselves as students that are context-specific and based on personal experience. At school, these identities develop as children progress through their school-age years, and they are informed by school-based norms, standards of competence, and their own personal values and goals that have evolved as a function of their social and academic experiences at school. As such, achieving a positive identity as a student requires recognition and adoption of context-specific standards for performance and the development of motivational belief systems that promote the achievement of such standards.

Student identities reflect notions of competence derived from external demands and constraints ranging from local, state, and federal policies concerning curricular content and standards for performance, to teacher and peer expectations for classroom-specific behaviors and outcomes. At the same time, student identities also reflect personal goals; beliefs about competence, control, and social belongingness; and emotional well-being. These intrapersonal characteristics are shaped by personal interests and by school-related experiences over time. Therefore, one's identity as a student cannot be understood without first understanding how competence at school is defined and the degree to which a student is motivated to be a competent student.

The approach described above suggests that viewing one's self as a competent student, and the corresponding motivational beliefs that support this positive identity, cannot be achieved without contextual supports. In this regard, social supports that emanate from interactions with teachers and peers are believed to be essential components of identity development and motivation at school. These supports take the form of explicit communications concerning norms and expectations, help, emotional caring, and physical safety. Although the mechanisms by which these supports exert influence on student identity and motivation are not well understood, practices that include direct communication and modeling, social acceptance and rejection, reinforcements and rewards, and group contagion are common in classroom and peer group settings.

Using this "competence within context" approach, in this chapter I will first provide definitions of school-based competence, motivation, and identity, and illustrate the interconnectedness of these constructs. I will then describe interpersonal relationships with teachers and peers in terms of contextual supports that can promote the development of motivation and identity at school, followed by a discussion of specific mechanisms and processes whereby these supports exert influence. The chapter will end with a discussion of implications for school-based practices and future directions for the field.

DEFINITIONS OF COMPETENCE, MOTIVATION, AND IDENTITY

Defining Competence at School

The nature of competence has been described from a variety of perspectives, ranging from skill development to adaptation within a particular setting (e.g., Sternberg & Kolligian, 1990) and is associated with outcomes such as effective behavioral repertoires, social problem-solving skills, positive beliefs about the self, achievement of social goals, and positive interpersonal relationships (see Rose-Krasnor, 1997). In my own work, I define classroom competence as a set of context-specific outcomes, reflecting the degree to which students are able to meet the social demands of the classroom as well as pursue their own personal goals. Support for a definition of healthy classroom functioning as "competence within context" can be found in the work of several theorists (e.g., Bronfenbrenner, 1989; Eccles & Midgley, 1989; Ford, 1992).

Bronfenbrenner (1989) argued that competence can only be understood in terms of context-specific effectiveness, being a product of personal attributes such as goals, values, self-regulatory skills, and social and cognitive abilities, and of ways in which these attributes contribute to meeting situational requirements and demands. In addition, central to many definitions of social competence is the notion that contextual affordances and constraints contribute to and mold the development of these individual outcomes in ways that enable them to contribute to the social good (Bronfenbrenner, 1989). In this manner, social contexts are believed to play an integral role in providing opportunities for healthy development as well as in defining the appropriate parameters of children's accomplishments (Bronfenbrenner, 1989).

Expanding on this notion of situated competence, Ford (1992) argued that several contextual supports can promote positive engagement, including information concerning what is expected and valued; help and instruction such that attempts to achieve these valued outcomes are met; a safe, nonthreatening environment; and emotional involvement such that individuals are made to feel like a valued member of the group (see also Connell & Wellborn, 1991; Skinner, Kindermann, Connell, & Wellborn, 2009; Wentzel, 2004). Applying these dimensions of supportive contexts specifically to classroom and school settings, this perspective implies that students will engage in the pursuit of adaptive goals in part when their teachers and peers communicate expectations and standards for achieving multiple goals; provide direct assistance and help in achieving them; and create a climate of emotional support, including protection from physical threats and harm. At a general level, these dimensions of support promote allegiance to the broader social group and to engagement in group-valued activities. As a result, members of the classroom and school (i.e., teachers and peers) as well as individual students are responsible for achieving competent outcomes at school.

In essence, therefore, competent students are those who achieve goals that are personally valued and those that are sanctioned by their teachers and peers. Moreover, the goals they pursue result in social integration as well as in positive developmental outcomes for the self. Evidence supports this notion in that pursuit of socially integrative goals, such as to be prosocial and socially responsible, has been related consistently and positively to displays of prosocial and responsible behavior at school (e.g., Ryan & Shim, 2008; Salmivelli, Ojanen, Haanpaa, & Peets, 2005; Wentzel, Filisetti, & Looney, 2007), social approval and acceptance from peers and teachers (Wentzel, 1991a, 1994; Wentzel & Asher, 1995), and academic achievement (Wentzel, 2013). By definition, self-assertive goals are unique to the individual. Positive attributes that have been related to successful achievement of personal goals such as positive self-concept, a sense of efficacy and self-determination, and emotional well-being also have been related consistently and positively to various aspects of social (e.g., positive relationships with peers, displays of prosocial and responsible behavior) and academic (e.g., academic engagement, grades) competence at school (for reviews, see Wentzel & Wigfield, 2009).

Defining Motivation at School

Motivation is typically defined as a set of interrelated beliefs about the self that explain the initiation, direction, intensity, persistence, and quality of behavior. Motivational beliefs most commonly studied in school settings are personal goals, values associated with goals, beliefs about ability, and beliefs about causality and control; research typically is focused on these beliefs in relation to academic tasks and activities (see Wentzel & Wigfield, 2009). As suggested by a "competence within context" perspective, students' behavior can also be motivated by beliefs reflecting social concerns that emanate from social interactions and contextual cues (see Ford, 1992; Wentzel, 2004; Wentzel & Brophy, 2013). Beliefs about interpersonal belongingness and emotional connectedness to others are central in this regard, determining the extent to which students engage in socially valued activities (Connell & Wellborn, 1991; Wentzel, 2004). In addition, students' beliefs concerning what they are supposed to do, based on a sense of moral or social obligation, can have a powerful influence on behavior (Wentzel, 1991b).

As conceptualized by Wentzel (Wentzel & Brophy, 2013), these beliefs can be described as reflecting a set of questions relevant for motivational decision-making: (1) What do I want to do? (2) What am I supposed to do? (3) Is this important and enjoyable to do? (4) Can I do it? (5) What causes success and failure? and (6) Does anybody care if I do it? Based on intrapersonal and interpersonal cues, the answers to these questions reflect beliefs about goals (Questions 1 through 3), causality and control (Questions 4 and 5), and a sense of social belongingness (Question 6) that combine to explain why students may or may not be motivated to engage in classroom activities.

With regard to goal-related beliefs (Question 1: What do I want to do?), personal goals determine the focus and direction of behavior, that is, why students do what they do. The content of goals (e.g., Ford, 1992) directs efforts toward specific outcomes (e.g., to learn algebra), and goal standards (e.g., Bandura, 1986) define acceptable levels of accomplishment (e.g., to learn enough algebra to pass the exam). Goal orientations (Maehr & Zusho, 2009) focus on specific reasons for trying to achieve academically, such as to gain mastery or to prove ability. Personal goals reflect the core motivational foundation of student identity because they represent the outcomes that students wish to achieve and accomplish at school. Socially integrative goals reflect outcomes that promote the smooth functioning of social groups, such as to behave appropriately or to gain social approval and social acceptance, whereas self-assertive goals reflect the achievement of outcomes reflecting idiosyncratic interests, positive beliefs concerning competence and self-determination, healthy self-concept, and feelings of social and emotional well-being (Bronfenbrenner, 1989; Ford, 1992).

Decisions to pursue goals can be influenced by internally as well as eternally derived beliefs. External forces in the form of social expectations define what it is that others expect and want you to do in a given situation (Question 2: What am I supposed to do?). Understanding and acceptance of these social expectations develops through experiences with extrinsic rewards and reinforcements, and through exposure to a range of social experiences and interactions with teachers and peers that inform students about what is valued in the classroom, what they are expected to do, and standards for performance. These social experiences also convey to students the potential affective and interpersonal consequences if they do not behave or perform as expected.

Research suggests that most students understand what is expected of them at school but that low achieving students often choose not to do what is expected because it is not important to them (e.g., Wentzel, 1989). This distinction between "should" and "want" reflects the additional importance of values emanating from personal desires and internalized beliefs about the importance of achieving a goal (Question 3: Is this important and enjoyable to do?). Decisions to pursue goals can be influenced by values that reflect the perceived costs and benefits of goal accomplishment, the importance and long-term utility of goal achievement, and the intrinsic pleasure of engaging in goal-directed behavior (Wigfield & Eccles, 2000).

To the extent that goals are perceived as self-determined, goal-directed behavior is experienced as freely chosen and emanating from one's self. It can also develop naturally through experiences of intrinsic motivation (Harter, 1978), or flow experiences (Csikszentmihalyi, 1993), or by way of socialization experiences over time (Deci & Ryan, 2002).

Students' beliefs about their abilities (e.g., "I am able to learn math") also can influence what they choose to do and why they persist at certain activities and not others (Bandura, 1986; Schunk & Pajares, 2009). These beliefs focus on whether we believe we can accomplish a task successfully (Question 4: Can I do it?). Students who enter achievement situations with positive self-efficacy perceptions believe that they can accomplish what the situation calls for, whereas students who lack positive perceptions are unsure whether they can succeed or are convinced that they cannot. As with personal values, beliefs about efficacy to accomplish tasks often distinguish high from low achieving students (Schunk & Pajares, 2009; see also Wentzel, 1989).

Beliefs about causality and control (e.g., "I passed the algebra test because I studied hard.") provide students with a lens for interpreting past events and with a basis for developing expectations for the future (Question 5: What causes success and failure?). Work by Weiner (e.g., 1992; see also Graham & Williams, 2009) has focused on the reasons that students generate to explain the outcomes of their goal pursuits. For the most part, these theorists have focused on causal attributions and beliefs about the level of performance achieved (Why did I fail that math test?), and their implications concerning future performance (e.g., Will I fail the next test as well?). Hence, these beliefs reflect reasons for why we succeed or fail and therefore for engaging in or refraining from future goal pursuit (e.g., Graham & Williams, 2009). A similar perspective has been provided by Dweck (e.g., Dweck & Master, 2009), who proposed that individuals hold theories or mindsets about if and why things change. For example, entity theories reflect beliefs that characteristics such as ability and personality are relatively stable and unchangeable (e.g., "I can't improve my math ability." "I can't help it if my classmates don't like me."), whereas incremental theories reflect beliefs that ability and personality are malleable and can be changed (e.g., "My math ability can be improved with effort and learning." "I can try some different strategies to make new friends."). In both cases, these beliefs represent reasons for why individuals think they succeed or fail and therefore for decisions concerning what to do next.

Students are also motivated by concerns that reflect the nature of their relationships with others (Question 6: Does anybody care if I do it?) (see Ford, 1992; Wentzel, 2004). Indeed, few would argue that the need to belong and to experience a sense of relatedness with others is a powerful motivator of behavior (see Baumeister & Leary, 1995). When positive, these beliefs reflect feelings that one is a valued and integral member of a relationship or of a larger social group (Connell & Wellborn, 1991). In turn, motivation to engage in a socially valued activity is more likely to occur if students believe that others care about them and want them to engage in activities that reflect group goals and promote the ongoing cohesion of the group. Beliefs that "someone cares," or interpersonal relatedness, are central to understanding the role of interpersonal relationships with teachers and classmates in motivating students to engage academically and socially at school (Wentzel, 2009a, 2009b).

Finally, in addition to beliefs that guide and direct behavior, motivation also requires the energy and will to engage in goal pursuit and to stay on task until goals are accomplished. In this regard, emotions and affective arousal (e.g., pride, excitement, anger) provide energy to sustain goal pursuit over time (see Ford, 1992; Weiner, 1992). For example, negative affective responses to failure have been associated with withdrawal and disengagement from academic goal pursuits (Dweck & Leggett, 1988), and a generalized sense of emotional distress has been associated with infrequent pursuit of positive classroom goals, negative attitudes toward school, academic performance, school avoidance, and low levels of classroom participation (Buhs & Ladd, 2001; Wentzel, 1997, 1998; Wentzel, Weinberger, Ford, & Feldman, 1990). In contrast, emotional well-being has been related positively to pursuit of goals to achieve academically (e.g., Wentzel, 1997) and to behave in prosocial and socially responsible ways (e.g., Wentzel & McNamara, 1999). Therefore, students' emotional well-being and emotion regulation must be central to discussions of motivation at school (Pekrun, 2009).

The belief systems just described, in conjunction with affective functioning, are central components of a goal-directed motivational system for at least two reasons. First, social expectations, personal values, efficacy, causality and control, a sense of relatedness, and emotional functioning represent attributes of the self that are indicators of competent, healthy adjustment in their own right. Although a full review of the literature is beyond the scope of this chapter, each of these motivation constructs also has been related to a range of positive school-related outcomes (see Wentzel & Wigfield, 2009). In addition, beliefs and emotions interact as a system to promote and sustain goal-directed behavior. Researchers have consistently identified associations between goal pursuit and efficacy beliefs (Bandura, 1986; Wentzel, 1996; Wentzel, Filisetti, & Looney, 2007), beliefs about personal control and self-determination (Wentzel, 1996, 1997, 2002a), personal values (Wigfield & Eccles, 2000), social expectations for social and academic outcomes (Wentzel, Battle, Russell, & Looney, 2010), and relatedness (Wentzel, 1997). In the following section, a definition of identity is offered, and links between motivation constructs and identity-related beliefs are discussed.

Defining Identity at School

Definitions of identity are numerous and complex. However, there are several common themes throughout the literature that are especially relevant for understanding associations between motivation and identity from a competence perspective. First, identity is typically defined with respect to beliefs about "Who I am," and "Who I want to be." These beliefs reflect personal characteristics and competencies that are embedded in a psychological sense of uniqueness and individuality, that is, the "Me" self (James, 1890). They also reflect personal characteristics that are aligned with a social collective and that contribute to the development and maintenance of social ties and relationships (e.g., Ashmore, Deaux, & McLaughlin-Volpe, 2004). This "We" self not only further defines the "Me" self but also provides a definition of the self for other people (see, e.g., Oyserman & Destin, 2010). Thus, as with definitions of competence and motivation, identity can be viewed as a set of beliefs that provide definition to the self in terms of personal history and accomplishments, and with respect to social contexts, interactions, and experiences.

Second, identity is often assigned the function of initiating and directing decision making and subsequent behavior (e.g., Eccles, 2009). Indeed, one could view identity as a higher-order "goal setter" for the self, by prioritizing (or giving value) to personal goals. In this sense, context or task-specific goal pursuit can serve to validate one's personal and social identity, and to promote the emergence of future selves by focusing energy on the development of specific desired outcomes and competencies. Accordingly, students who have developed an identity as a good student would likely prioritize personal goals that are academic (e.g., to learn new skills, get good grades) and social (e.g., to be responsible, to be socially accepted) in nature.

As just illustrated, individuals are often viewed as having multiple identities that reflect membership in socially and culturally defined groups (e.g., gender, age, ethnicity), interpersonal relationships (e.g., classmate, friend, Ms. Jones' student), or institutional contexts (e.g., eighth grader, band member) (e.g., Harter, 1998; Oyserman & Destin, 2010). As a whole, these identities compose one's overall sense of self (e.g., student), while reflecting a complex, coordinated, and often hierarchical system of specific self-related beliefs. Similarly, individuals can pursue multiple related goals that serve to sustain their identity within specific contexts. At school, students can pursue goals that reflect social and academic outcomes as well as those that result in intrapersonal outcomes such as a sense of competence, self-determination, relatedness, and emotional well-being. In turn, these goals and the ability to achieve them will contribute to a motivational belief system which then will help define an identity as a student.

Finally, factors that have been described as promoting the development of identity and motivation converge on a common set of socialization experiences and supports. In particular, a range of social supports from teachers and peers has been associated with the development of motivational belief systems, including goals, values, beliefs about causality and control, a sense of social obligation and belongingness (Wentzel, 2009a, 2009b), and with identity development (Karcher, Brown, & Elliott, 2004; Sandstrom, 2011). Because social supports are by nature situation specific, they serve as contextual affordances that define the realm of possibilities for goal pursuit and identity development; affordances that are most salient and valued will ultimately determine the nature of motivational belief systems that serve as the foundation for goal pursuit and identity development.

Summary

Definitions of competence, motivation, and identity that reflect a "competence within context" perspective underscore the importance of personal as well as socially derived attributes for understanding optimal student outcomes. Beliefs concerning the self (What do I want to do? Is this important and enjoyable to do? Can I do it? and What causes success and failure?), in combination with perceived contextual cues (What am I supposed to do? Does anybody care if I do it?), provide motivational supports for the development of identities as students. In addition, this perspective recognizes the importance of social supports for promoting positive motivational beliefs and a healthy student identity.

In the following sections, perspectives on teacher–student and peer relationships are described, with a focus on how they provide contextual supports for the development of motivational beliefs and student identities at school. Next, specific mechanisms and processes by which teachers and peers exert influence by way of these supports are discussed.

LINKING INTERPERSONAL RELATIONSHIPS TO STUDENT MOTIVATION AND IDENTITY AT SCHOOL

The Nature of Interpersonal Relationships

Relationships are typically defined as enduring connections between two individuals, uniquely characterized by degrees of continuity, shared history, and interdependent interactions across settings and activities (e.g., Collins & Repinski, 1994). In addition, definitions frequently include desirable qualities of a relationship, such as levels of trust, intimacy, and sharing; the presence of closeness and positive affective tone; and the content and quality of communication (Collins & Repinski, 1994; Laible & Thompson,

2007). Relationships are also often defined with respect to their influence and what they provide the individual. In this regard, researchers have focused on the benefits of relationship provisions such as emotional well-being, a sense of cohesion and connectedness, instrumental help, a secure base, and a sense of identity for promoting positive developmental outcomes (Bukowski & Hoza, 1989).

From a developmental perspective, relationships are believed to be experienced through the lens of mental representations developed over time and with respect to specific experiences (Bowlby, 1969; Laible & Thompson, 2007). Similar to those dimensions described as instrumental in promoting competence development (Ford, 1992), mental representations believed to be optimal for the internalization of social influence are those that associate relationships with a personal sense of power and agency, predictability and safety, useful resources, and reciprocity (see Kuczynski & Parkin, 2007). Mental representations also provide stability and continuity to relationships over time. For example, young children's representations of relationships with parents are believed to provide the foundation for developing relationships outside the family context, with the quality of parent–child relationships (especially levels of warmth and security) often predicting the quality of peer and teacher relationships in early and middle childhood (see Wentzel, 2009a). How relationships with teachers and peers might provide these supports is described next.

Teacher–Student and Peer Relationships

Teacher–Student Relationships

The prevailing theoretical models that guide work on teacher–student relationships are derived from work on parent–child relationships and typically adopt a causal approach, with the affective quality of teacher–student relationships viewed as the central motivator of student adjustment (e.g., Pianta, Hamre, & Stuhlman, 2003). The basic tenets of attachment theory (Bowlby, 1969; Bretherton, 1987) reflect this notion. Other perspectives describe teacher–student relationships with respect to specific dimensions and provisions (Wentzel, 2004), as specified by models of parent–child interactions (e.g., Baumrind, 1971), which are discussed further below.

Attachment theory has provided the strongest impetus for work on teachers' relationships with young children. According to this perspective, within the context of the relationship between a child and caregiver (usually the mother), children experience varying degrees of positive affect and responsiveness to their basic needs; predictable and sensitive responses are associated with secure attachments, and more arbitrary and insensitive responses are believed to result in insecure attachments (see Bowlby, 1969).

Within the context of attachment relationships, children are believed to develop mental representations of self and others, which are then used as a basis to interpret and judge the underlying intentions, reliability, and trustworthiness of others' actions in new relationships (Bretherton, 1987). Secure relationships are believed to foster children's curiosity and exploration of the environment, positive coping skills, and a mental representation of one's self as being worthy of love and of others as being trustworthy. In contrast, insecure attachments are believed to result in either wary or inappropriately risky exploratory behavior, difficulty in regulating stress in new settings, and negative self-concepts.

Although teacher–student relationships are not typically viewed as primary attachment relationships, attachment theory principles imply that they would be fairly concordant with the quality of parent–child attachments. A positive sense of self, curiosity, willingness to explore, and trust in others that develops out of the attachment relationship can be viewed as precursors to children's positive motivation at school, as reflected in beliefs about emotional connectedness with teachers, efficacy to learn, a sense of personal control and self-determination, and intrinsic interest in classroom activities (e.g., Harter, 1978; Raider-Roth, 2005).

An additional approach has been to consider teacher–student relationships as serving a broader range of functions that contribute to students' competence at school. Although the affective tone of teacher–student interactions is a central focus of this work, these perspectives propose that teacher–student relationships should be defined with respect to multiple dimensions that combine with emotional support to motivate students to engage in the social and academic life of the classroom (Connell & Wellborn, 1991; Wentzel, 2004). Similar to those described in models of effective parenting (e.g., Baumrind, 1971; Darling & Steinberg, 1993), these dimensions reflect concern for a student's emotional and physical well-being, predictability and structure, and instrumental resources. When applied to the classroom, these dimensions are reflected in teachers' communications of rules and expectations for behavior and performance, provisions of instrumental help, and opportunities for emotional support and interpersonal connectedness.

Support for this perspective is found in students and teachers' qualitative descriptions of caring and supportive teachers, and from studies where dimensions of support have been related to a range of student outcomes (for a review, see Wentzel, 2009a). For example, the clarity of teachers' communications and consistency of classroom management practices early in the academic year tends to predict positive academic and social outcomes in elementary and secondary level classrooms (see Gettinger & Kohler, 2006). Teachers' expectations about ability and performance are related to students' beliefs about their own ability and goals to achieve academically (e.g., see Oates, 2003; Weinstein, Gregory, & Strambler, 2004). Teachers also play the central role of transmitting knowledge and training students in academic subject areas. In this role, teachers provide instrumental help by routinely providing children information and advice, modeled behavior, or specific experiences that facilitate learning.

Finally, teachers create contexts characterized by levels of emotional support and personal safety (Connell & Wellborn, 1991; Isakson, & Jarvis, 1999). Empirical evidence supports this notion in that emotionally negative relationships with teachers have been related to students' anxiety and depression (Mitchell-Copeland, Denham, & DeMulder, 1997; Murray & Greenberg, 2000; Wentzel, 1997), emotionally secure relationships to students' identification with teachers' values and positive social self-concept (Davis, 2001), and emotional well-being (Wentzel, 1997, 1998). Of relevance for understanding students' motivational identities, the affective quality of relationships with teachers also has been related to a range of self-processes including perceived autonomy, perceived control, goal orientations, values, interest, and self-efficacy (for a review, see Wentzel, 2010). Students' appraisals of teacher emotional support also have been related to students' pursuit of academic and social goals (Wentzel, 1994, 1997, 1998, 2003).

Peer Relationships and Interactions

Researchers typically have studied children's involvement with peers at school in two ways, within the context of relationships (e.g., degree of peer acceptance by the larger peer group, membership in specific peer groups, and dyadic friendships; see Juvonen, Espinoza, & Knifsend, 2012; Ladd, Herald-Brown, & Kochel, 2009; Ryan & Ladd, 2012; Wentzel, 2009b), and within structured interactions related to instruction (e.g., cooperative and collaborative learning; see Wentzel & Watkins, 2011). In contrast to work on teacher–student relationships, this work has been fairly atheoretical. However, two general perspectives have been described in the literature reflecting constructivist principles and social support approaches.

Constructivist explanations have focused on the broad notion that positive interactions with peers contribute directly to intellectual and social functioning. In general, these perspectives have guided empirical work on collaborative and cooperative learning. Within these traditions, researchers have documented that active discussion, problem solving, and elaborative feedback among peers in collaborative settings are associated with advances in a range of cognitive competencies (see Gauvain & Perez, 2007). The effects of cooperative learning (i.e., peers working in larger groups) on social and academic outcomes and motivation have also been found to be generally positive (Slavin, 2011; Slavin, Hurley, & Chamberlain, 2003).

As with work on teachers, a more recent approach has been to consider how students' relationships with each other can provide access to critical supports that facilitate competent functioning at school. These supports take the form of communications concerning expectations and values, instrumental help, emotional support, and safety from physical threats and harm (see Wentzel, Baker, & Russell, 2012). Indirect evidence supports this approach in that having positive relationships and interactions with peers is related to positive outcomes at school. For example, sociometrically popular children and those with friends tend to be academically proficient, report pursuing socially valued academic and social goals, demonstrate positive motivational beliefs about academic pursuits, and behave prosocially and responsibly when compared to sociometrically rejected children and those without friends (e.g., Asher & McDonald, 2009; Card & Little, 2006; Cillessen & van den Berg, 2012; Jones, Audley-Piotrowski, & Kiefer, 2012; Kindermann & Skinner, 2012; Wentzel, Barry, & Caldwell, 2004; Wentzel & Caldwell, 1997). Students with positive peer relationships are more likely to enjoy a relatively safe school environment and less likely to be the targets of peer-directed violence and harassment than their peers who do not have friends (e.g., Schwartz, Dodge, Pettit, Bates, & The Conduct Problems Prevention Research Group, 2000).

With respect to specific dimensions of support, peers communicate to each other expectations and values concerning social behavior and academic performance (Wentzel, 2009b), and they are important sources of instrumental help in performing academic tasks and helping with interpersonal problems (e.g., Lempers & Clark-Lempers, 1992; Newman, 2000). With respect to emotional support, children and adolescents without friends or who are socially rejected often report feeling lonely, emotionally distressed, and depressed (e.g., Azmitia, Syed, & Radmacher, 2013; Buhs & Ladd, 2001; Flook, Repetti, & Ullman, 2005; Wentzel & Caldwell, 1997). Students who have friends also are more likely to enjoy a relatively safe school environment and less likely to be the targets of peer-directed violence and harassment than their peers who do not have friends (Hodges, Boivin, Vitaro, & Bukowski, 1999; Schwartz et al., 2000). Students who perceive that their peers care about them tend to be interested and engaged in academic pursuits and positive forms of behavior, whereas students who do not perceive their relationships with peers as positive and caring tend to be at risk for motivational and academic problems and displaying antisocial behavior (Wentzel, 1994; Wentzel et al., 2010; Wentzel, Donlan, & Morrison, 2012).

Summary

A consideration of teacher–student and peer relationships as contextual affordances reflects the notion that at the core of positive interpersonal relationships are the benefits they provide in the form of social supports.

Findings relevant to these dimensions of teacher and peer support provide evidence for this notion. However, the specific mechanisms whereby these supports might result in positive motivational beliefs, emotional well-being, and student identities have not been well articulated. In the following section, direct instruction and modeling, social acceptance and rejection, reinforcements, and group contagion are described as ways that teachers and peers can exert influence on motivation and identity development.

Mechanisms of Influence

How and why might teacher and peer supports be related to student motivation and identity development? As a guide to answering this question, Figure 12.1 depicts associations between various types of relationships, processes and mechanisms, and outcomes that have implications for motivational and student-related identities. Specifically, a range of relationship types are predicted to engender processes or mechanisms of influence, to include direct communication and modeling, social acceptance and rejection, intrinsic and extrinsic reinforcements, and group contagion. In turn, these processes are predicted to influence a range of outcomes believed to contribute to motivation and identity development. Although not exhaustive, these processes reflect common ways by which social interactions and relationships can influence individual functioning. In this section, each of these processes will be described in turn.

Direct Instruction and Modeling

Direct instruction and modeling are powerful mechanisms whereby students learn what is expected of them and how to go about meeting those expectations. These mechanisms reflect ways in which teachers and peers

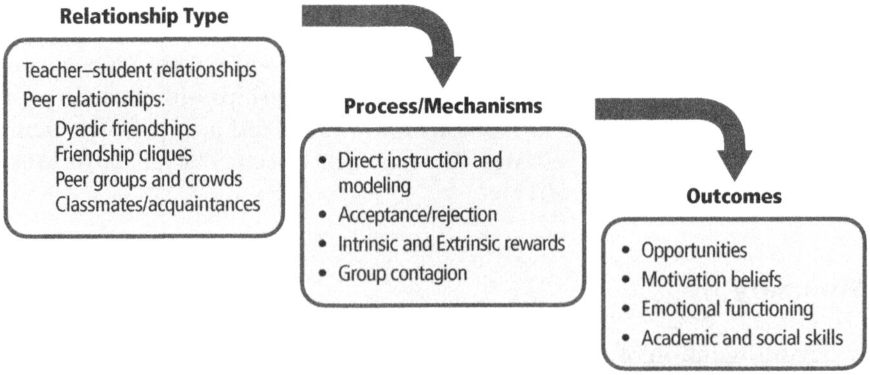

Figure 12.1 Mechanisms of teacher and peer influence at school.

communicate important information, teach valuable skills, and provide instrumental help, and in doing so provide input concerning socially valued goals and expectations for academic performance and social behavior (i.e., What am I supposed to do? Is this important and enjoyable to do?), and standards against which judgments of personal efficacy can be made (i.e., Can I do this?). Although this type of influence is probably provided most frequently by individual teachers or within dyadic or small-group peer interactions, the larger peer group also can be a source of behavioral standards, with direct instructions and modeling serving as a means whereby adherence to group standards and expectations is monitored and enforced (see Brown, Bakken, Ameringer, & Mahon, 2008).

At the simplest level, social cognitive theory (Bandura, 1986) suggests that direct communication and instruction provides students with valuable information about what is expected and how to accomplish various tasks. Therefore, teachers and peers who convey expectations that academic engagement and positive social interactions are important and enjoyable are likely to lead others to form similar values and goals related to academic performance and social behavior (Bandura, 1986). Direct instruction is also a central mechanism that allows teaching to occur, resulting in the development of skills and abilities as well as desirable social behavior.

Research has documented that teachers continuously communicate standards for academic and social outcomes directly to their students, regardless of their instructional goals, teaching styles, and ethnicity (Hargreaves, Hester, & Mellor, 1975). These communications include appropriate ways to respond to requests, appropriate contexts for different types of behavior, and expectations for impulse control, mature problem solving, and involvement in class activities (e.g., Shultz & Florio, 1979; Trenholm & Rose, 1981). Teachers also communicate expectations for students' interactions with each other (e.g., Doescher & Sugawara, 1989; Hagens, 1997; Hargreaves et al., 1975; Sieber, 1979).

In addition, researchers have focused on how teachers convey expectations about ability and performance to individual students. As part of ongoing interpersonal interactions, these communications have the potential to influence students' beliefs about their own ability and goals to achieve academically. Weinstein (2002) describes these communications as part of a process of influence whereby teachers' expectations result in their differential treatment of students. These communications most often reflect beliefs that students are able to achieve more than previously demonstrated, or negative expectations reflecting underestimations of student ability (e.g., see Oates, 2003; Weinstein et al., 2004). In turn, teachers' expectations can become self-fulfilling prophecies, with student performance changing to conform to teacher expectations (see Weinstein, 2002), especially as students get older (Valeski & Stipek, 2001).

Communications from peers are often discussed as a form of peer pressure. Peers frequently express opinions concerning appropriate behavior or desires for others to change their behavior. In fact, use of online media and text messaging has greatly increased the ability of peers to communicate opinions and expectations with ease (Ehrenreich, Underwood, & Ackerman, 2014). These communications function to define, clarify, maintain, and enforce peer norms (Brown, Bakken et al., 2008). With respect to classroom competence, middle school students report that their classmates hold expectations for them regarding social behavior and academic performance; in turn, these expectations are related to their own goals and values concerning academic and social outcomes (Wentzel et al., 2010).

Peers also provide input concerning reasons for engaging in academic tasks such that students who perceive relatively high expectations for academic learning and engagement from their peers also report that they pursue goals to learn for intrinsic or internalized reasons (e.g., because it is important or fun; Wentzel, 2004). Similarly, perceived expectations from peers for behaving prosocially are significant predictors of: internalized values for and displays of prosocial behavior (Wentzel et al., 2007); peer communications concerning antisocial behavior appear to increase levels of aggression and misconduct at school (Ehrenreich et al., 2014), and they promote "deviance training," in which peer groups undermine social conventions and promote antisocial behavior via direct communication and modeling (see Patterson, Dishion, & Yoerger, 2000).

Modeling is also a powerful process by which information is communicated. As with direct instruction, modeling can influence students' adoption of goals and values for behavior and academic performance (Bandura, 1986). Indeed, students might develop specific behavioral styles or interests because they are desirable characteristics modeled by their peers (see Barry & Wentzel, 2006; Wentzel et al., 2004). Teachers often serve as academic and social role models, demonstrating to students that long-term goals can be achieved. Experimental work also has shown that peers can serve as powerful models that influence the development of academic self-efficacy (Schunk & Pajares, 2009), especially when children observe similar peers who demonstrate successful ways to cope with failure. These modeling effects are especially likely to occur when students are friends (Crockett, Losoff, & Petersen, 1984; Ricciardelli & Mellor, 2012). Observing the behavior of others also engenders social comparison processes. High levels of social comparison tend to result in students adopting orientations toward learning that focus on performance rather than mastery of subject matter and in lowered levels of academic efficacy and aspirations for achievement especially among low-ability students (Butler, 2005).

Constructivist morals of development also reflect these processes. For example, Piaget (e.g., 1965) proposed that mutual discussion, perspective taking, and conflict resolution with peers can motivate the accommodation of new and more sophisticated cognitive approaches to problem solving, including problems in the social domain. For Piaget, development was contingent upon the relatively symmetrical nature of same-aged peer interactions that allowed conflict resolution within the context of mutual reciprocity. Conversely, Vygotsky (1978) suggested that peers can contribute directly to the development of academic and social skills when competent students teach specific strategies and standards for performance to peers who are less skilled. In this case, asymmetrical interactions were believed to contribute to competent development, primarily by way of cooperative and collaborative exchange.

Finally, help giving is perhaps the most explicit and obvious way in which peers can have a direct influence on students' academic and social competence. At least during adolescence, students report that their peers are as or more important sources of instrumental aid than their teachers (Lempers & Clark-Lempers, 1992). One reason for this growing dependence on peers is that when adolescents enter high school, the relative uncertainty and ambiguity of having multiple teachers and different sets of classmates for each class, new instructional styles, and more complex class schedules necessitates that they turn to each other for social support, ways to cope, and academic help.

Social Acceptance and Rejection

An additional mechanism of influence involves social acceptance and rejection. At the individual level, students experience varying levels of social belongingness and acceptance as a function of their relationships with teachers and peers; at the group level, students experience acceptance and rejection to the extent that peer groups are inclusive or exclusive (Bennett, 2014). Social acceptance and rejection can have a powerful impact on students' beliefs that others care about them and the opportunities they will have to interact with others to derive benefits from direct instruction and modeling. Social exclusion and exclusion within peer groups also can have important implications for identity development and motivation.

The importance of social acceptance and rejection for understanding motivation is articulated in theoretical perspectives that suggest that strong affective bonds and perceived support from others serve as buffers from stress and anxiety and contribute to a positive sense of emotional well-being (Sarason, Sarason, & Pierce, 1990). In turn, feelings of emotional security and being socially connected are believed to facilitate the adoption of goals and interests valued by others, including goals to contribute in positive ways to the overall functioning of the social group (e.g., Deci & Ryan, 2002). An extensive literature supports this notion (Baumeister & Leary, 1995).

In addition, socially accepted students have greater access to direct instruction and modeling of skills that support competence development. Although few studies have been conducted to document this process, Brophy and Good (1974) illustrated the relevance of teachers' preferences for students for gaining access to academic resources. The teachers observed in their research reported that they responded with help and encouragement to students about whom they were concerned when these students sought them out for help. In contrast, students toward whom they felt rejection were treated most often with criticism and typically were refused help. Similarly, models of peer influence also have posited that students who are rejected by their peers suffer from a lack of opportunities and supports afforded to children with accepted peers, such as positive and effective role models, direct instruction concerning normative behavior and skill development, and sources of positive reinforcements for social and academic behavior (see Parker & Asher, 1987; Patterson & Bank, 1989).

Finally, theorists have argued that goals to sustain positive group identity and cohesion can result in exclusionary practices within and between groups (e.g., Abrams & Rutland, 2008; Bennett, 2014), including the formation of stereotypes and discriminatory practices (e.g., Dovidio, Gaertner, Hodson, Houlette, & Johnson, 2005; Tajfel & Turner, 1979). As with social acceptance and rejection, these group-level processes can have a profound effect on students' emotional well-being (Brown, Bakken et al., 2008), their access to opportunities and supports (Haslam, Reicher, & Levine, 2012), and motivational beliefs, including a sense of group efficacy (Bandura, 1986).

Intrinsic and Extrinsic Reinforcement

Teachers and peers can also exert influence by way of reinforcements and reward systems. These reinforcements and rewards are important sources of information concerning social expectations, perceptions of control, and values. In general, "exchange of reinforcements" is a central mechanism that serves to define the normative expectations, costs, and benefits of a relationship (see Pittman, Boggiano, & Main, 1992). These reinforcements can be intrinsic or extrinsic and can be conveyed through tangible benefits (e.g., help, social inclusion, or exclusion), feedback and instruction (e.g., praise or criticism), and coercive strategies (e.g., bullying, persuasion). Intrinsic rewards are those associated with engaging in a task or activity; students might engage in behavior valued by teachers and peers because they experience the behavior and the social interactions as enjoyable and of personal value (Boggiano, Klinger, & Main, 1986; Ojanon, Stratman, Card, & Little, 2013; Wentzel et al., 2007). Extrinsic rewards are outcomes associated with a task that are externally imposed or viewed as an endpoint, such that the task is viewed as a means to an end. In this case, engaging in positive social interactions and conforming to social expectations is a way to achieve other goals, such as social acceptance or a better grade.

An extensive literature has documented ways in which teachers administer rewards to students through instruction, feedback, and behavioral management strategies (see Wentzel & Brophy, 2013). For example, instructional strategies that involve competition, salient rewards (e.g., food, stickers, free time), or public feedback reflect extrinsically motivating strategies that can lead to perceptions by students that engaging in the activity is controlling and a threat to autonomy and choice (Deci & Ryan, 1985). Extrinsic rewards can also be detrimental to students' intrinsic motivation to learn, especially when students perceive themselves to be engaged in academic tasks in order to please an authority figure, obtain a reward, or escape punishment (Deci & Ryan, 1985; Flink, Boggiano, Main, Barrett, & Katz, 1992; Lepper, 1983; Sweet, Guthrie, & Ng, 1998). However, extrinsic rewards can also be valuable because they send a message concerning what students are supposed to do in order to achieve success in school, whether or not they find activities interesting or enjoyable.

Peer influence has also been studied with respect to reinforcements and reward systems, although to a lesser extent. In this literature, use of intimidation, power assertion, and negative reinforcement has been the primary focus of interest as a way to understand the negative outcomes of peer pressure and how peer groups function to establish normative standards and power hierarchies (e.g., Cairns, Neckerman, & Cairns, 1989). For example, popular children appear to exert power over others by using social acceptance and status as a reward for compliance and conformity (Cillessen & Rose, 2005; Sandstrom, 2011). Use of prosocial (positive rewards) as well as coercive and aggressive (negative reinforcement) tactics appears to be a particularly effective strategy to gain social control and power among peers (e.g., Hawley, Little, & Pasupathi, 2002) and to solidify and maintain group norms and practices (Cairns et al., 1989). An extensive literature has also demonstrated how negative reinforcement in the form of physical and relational aggression results in a broad range of outcomes related to motivation, emotional functioning, and social behavior, for perpetrators as well as victims (e.g., Crick, Murray-Close, Marks, & Mohajeri-Nelson, 2009).

Peer groups also appear to reinforce communication of specific values and norms associated with desirable behavior. With respect to academics, evidence suggests that students can experience negative reinforcement for doing well academically through labeling and stigmatization (Boehnke, 2008; Fordham & Ogbu, 1986). In contrast, in the area of sports, students often create task-oriented group climates that are intrinsically motivating and that influence beliefs about autonomy and relatedness in positive ways (Joesaar, Hein, Vello, & Hagger, 2011).

Group Contagion

Group contagion is a process of influence that has been studied as a unique aspect of peer-group functioning. As defined by Dishion and Piehler (2009), peer contagion "describes a mutual influence process that is not intentional, purposeful, or planned, but is initiated and maintained by social dynamics" (p. 589). In essence, it is influence that occurs as a function of being a member of a peer group or social network and of patterns of reinforcement that occur as a product of group functioning (Dishion, 2013; Hayes et al., 2001). Peer contagion is associated most often with disinhibition of behavior and the disruption of normative behavior. It has also been associated with a range of problem behaviors (e.g., substance abuse, antisocial behavior, delinquency (e.g., Boxer, Guerra, Huesman, & Morales, 2005; Ehrenreich et al., 2014; Lee & Thompson, 2009), deviance training among peers (Dishion & Piehler, 2009), and with mood regulation and depressive symptoms (Connell & Dishion, 2006; Hogue & Steinberg, 1995). Although studied less often, peer-group dynamics have also been associated with positive aspects of motivation, such as pursuit of intrinsic goals (Duriez, Giletta, Kuppens, & Vansteenkiste, 2013) and emotional well-being (Hogue & Steinberg, 1995; Prinstein, 2007; Van Workham, Scholte, Cillessen, Lodder, & Giletta, 2013).

Of particular interest for the current discussion is that membership in peer groups appears to play a unique role in the formation of students' identity and self-concept (Brown & Dietz, 2009). Although rarely discussed with reference to contagion effects, research on adolescent peer crowds provides examples of how this occurs with respect to identity development. In essence, peer crowds provide prototypical examples of various identities for those who wish to "try out" different lifestyles, and in doing so, can affirm an adolescent's sense of self. Typical crowds include "Populars," students who engage in positive forms of academic as well as social behavior but also in some delinquent activities; "Jocks," students characterized by athletic accomplishments but also relatively frequent alcohol use; more alienated groups (e.g., "Druggies"), characterized by poor academic performance and engagement in delinquent and other illicit activities; and "Normals," who tend to be fairly average students who do not engage in delinquent activities (Brown, 1989).

Research on peer-group membership has been mostly descriptive, identifying the central norms and values that uniquely characterize adolescent crowds. However, the power of crowd influence on the adoption of attitudes toward school and academic identity is reflected in findings that adolescent peer groups differ in the degree to which they pressure members to become involved in academic activities. Although the reasons for why these pressures differ as a function of group membership, "Jocks" and "Popular" groups tend to provide significantly more pressure for academic involvement than other groups (see Brown, 1989, 2011; Brown & Dietz, 2009).

Researchers who identify friendship-based peer groups using statistical procedures also have found relations between group membership and changes in motivation (e.g., pursuit of intrinsic vs. extrinsic goals, academic engagement) and academic performance (e.g., test scores) over time (Duriez et al., 2013; Kindermann & Skinner, 2012).

Summary

Direct instruction and modeling, social acceptance and rejection, reinforcements, and group contagion are illustrative mechanisms whereby social supports from teachers and peers can influence outcomes related to students' motivation and identity. Outcomes take the form of information to support the development of motivation beliefs (i.e., What do I want to do? What am I supposed to do? Is this important and enjoyable to do? Can I do it? What causes success and failure? and Does anybody care if I do it?), emotional functioning, opportunities to gain information, and for skill development.

However, research on teacher and peer influence on student motivation and identity is in its infancy. Studies that can establish causal directions of influence, requiring sophisticated experimental or longitudinal designs, are rare (see Ladd et al., 2009). In addition, a range of confounding factors must be taken into account. For example, teachers and their relationships with students appear to exert influence, depending on a broad range of factors. To illustrate, some studies have documented differential teacher treatment of students as a function of student gender, race (Jussim, Robustelli, & Cain, 2009), and behavioral styles (Chang, 2003), with these differences sometimes attributed in part, to teachers' own race and gender (Saft & Pianta, 2001). Teachers' reports of close and warm relationships with students tend to differ for boys and girls (e.g., Birch & Ladd, 1998; Hamre & Pianta, 2001; Silver, Measelle, Armstrong, & Essex, 2005) and for minority and majority children (Ladd & Burgess, 2001), with teachers reporting closer and less conflictual relationships with girls and majority (Caucasian) children. Similarly, students' positive perceptions of teacher support are typically stronger for girls than for boys (Blankemeyer, Flannery, & Vazsonyi, 2002; Wentzel, 2002a) and for Caucasian than for ethnic minority students (Wentzel, 2002a). Finally, relatedness with teachers appears to differ as a function of students' age, with more elementary grade students reporting optimal or adequate relationships than middle school students (Lynch & Cicchetti, 1997).

In addition, relations between perceived emotional support from teachers and student outcomes appear to be moderated by SES and race such that students from lower SES backgrounds (Dornbusch, Erickson, Laird, & Wong, 2001) and members of minority groups (Certo, Cauley, & Chafin,

2003; Crosnoe, Johnson, & Elder, 2004) tend to benefit more from close relationships with teachers than do other students. Relatedness with teachers also tends to influence student outcomes more strongly for special education students than for regular students (Little & Kobak, 2003), and more strongly for boys than for girls (Furrer & Skinner, 2003). Contextual factors also appear to moderate the effects of teacher influence on student outcomes and determine the quality of teacher–student relationships. For example, class size has been related significantly and negatively to teachers' provisions of emotional support (Mashburn, Hamre, Downer, & Pianta, 2006; Pianta et al., 2003). School-level factors such as safety, racial homogeneity, SES of the student body (Crosnoe et al., 2004), and composition of instructional teams (Murdock & Miller, 2003) appear to moderate relations between perceived teacher support and student outcomes.

Peer influence also appears to be effective depending on individual differences, such as the extent to which a student feels connected to and affiliates with the peer group (Kiesner et al., 2002), ability to resist overt pressures (Brown & Lohr, 1987; Brown, Von Bank & Steinberg, 2008; Wright, Nichols, Graber, Brooks-Gunn, & Botvin, 2004), ability to self-monitor (Perrine & Aloise-Young, 2004), age (Clasen & Brown, 1985), gender (Boehnke, 2008; Brown, 1982; Brown, Lohr & McClenahan, 1986), and SES (Santo et al., 2013). As with teachers, contextual factors can also determine the mode and effectiveness of peer influence processes, including the social status and salience of the person exerting influence, power differentials between individuals, the type of situation and setting, and cultural status (Brown, Von Bank et al., 2008; Sandstrom, 2011; Santo et al., 2013).

Finally, it is important to note that processes of influence are not mutually exclusive and most likely operate in tandem with each other and at various and multiple levels (e.g., dyadic, group; friends, acquaintances) (Karcher et al., 2004; Sandstrom, 2011). Of particular interest in this regard is that the affective climate of teacher–student and peer relationships appears to serve as a moderator between other forms of support and student outcomes. For example, Wentzel and colleagues (see Wentzel, 2012) found that teachers and peers' communications of specific expectations for social and academic outcomes was more predictive of adolescents' academic motivation and engagement if they were communicated within the context of an emotionally caring relationship. Processes of influence can also be contradictory and work against each other, such as when individuals communicate one set of values yet behave in opposite fashion or use prosocial and coercive strategies at the same time (Sandstrom, 2011).

Despite these many caveats, there are clear implications for school-based practices. In the following section, these implications are discussed, along with recommendations for future research in this area.

IMPLICATIONS FOR PRACTICE AND FUTURE DIRECTIONS

Teachers and Implications for Practice

If teachers have influence by way of the relationships and interactions they have with students, it also becomes essential to understand those factors that contribute to teachers' ability and willingness to engage in these positive forms of social interaction. Research that examines factors that foster supportive and caring behavior on the part of teachers is relatively rare. However, teacher stress appears to contribute to the number of negative relationships that elementary school teachers report having with their students (Yoon, 2002), depression has been related to the sensitivity and responsiveness of preschool teachers (Hamre & Pianta, 2004), and a secure attachment style has been related to positive as opposed to conflictual interactions of elementary school teachers with their students (Morris-Rothschild & Brassard, 2006). Teachers' years of experience and sense of efficacy with regard to classroom management also has been related to positive relationships and interactions with preschool and elementary-aged students (Mashburn et al., 2006; Morris-Rothschild & Brassard, 2006; Yoon, 2002).

School-level factors also are likely to influence teachers' ability to create supportive classroom environments for their students. For example, job satisfaction, over and above gender, teacher education, and classroom management skills, has been related to high school teachers' provisions of instrumental help and challenge, especially with low-ability students (Opdenakker & Van Damme, 2006). Other factors, such as the quality of feedback given to teachers from administrators, teacher autonomy and participation in school decision making, opportunities for collaboration and development of positive relationships with peers, and instructional help and resources, are likely to contribute to teachers' ability and willingness to provide similar kinds of supports for their students (see Firestone & Pennell, 1993). Indeed, if provisions of positive supports contribute to students' successful functioning at school, provisions of similar supports to teachers are likely to improve their practice as well.

Given these findings, it is clear that teacher characteristics and school-level factors have the potential to influence teachers' motivation and ability to develop positive relationships with students. These factors need to become a more central focus of research and of school administrators' efforts to improve the impact of instruction on students. In addition, interventions that are focused on promoting positive teacher–student interactions are needed. In this regard, school-based interventions are beginning to shed light on the efficacy of training teachers and students to interact with each other in supportive ways to facilitate the development of social and academic skills (Durlak, Weissberg, Dymnicki, Taylor, & Schellinger, 2011; Vazsonyi, Belliston,

& Flannery, 2004). Training teachers to develop positive relationships with individual students through individualized coaching (e.g., MyTeachingPartner, Hamre et al., 2010) and to create positive emotional climates in classrooms by teaching teachers emotional management and perspective-taking skills (RULER Curriculum, Brackett, Rivers, Reyes, & Salovey, 2012) also has shown promising results. Professional development efforts to improve teachers' classroom management strategies (Evertson & Weinstein, 2006) and disciplinary strategies (Developmental Studies Center [n.d.] www.devstu.org) also have shown promise for improving teachers' relationships with students and their ability to promote positive outcomes in students.

Interventions, however, also need to be sensitive to student characteristics that can influence the development of teacher–student relationships. Individual characteristics such as racial identity, perceived discrimination, and the extent to which students are oriented toward gaining social approval are also likely to influence the degree to which students are open to forming relationships with teachers and being influenced by them. Student ability also appears to influence characterizations of supportive teachers. For example, students from high-ability tracks value teachers who challenge them, encourage class participation, and who express educational goals that are similar to those of students, whereas students from low-ability tracks tend to value teachers who treat them with kindness, who are fair, explain subject matter clearly, and maintain control in the classroom (Daniels & Arapostathis, 2005). Academically successful inner-city ethnic minority adolescents report valuing instrumental help from teachers but also warmth and acceptance coupled with high academic expectations (Smokowski, Reynolds, & Bezrucko, 2000).

Peers and Implications for Practice

In contrast to work on teacher–student relationships, much is known concerning ways in which instructional practices can influence the nature and quality of peer relationships and their impact on school-related outcomes (Epstein, 1983; Farmer, Irvin, Sgammato, Dadisman, & Thompson, 2009). For example, students enjoy more positive relationships with classmates (and therefore more positive peer influence) when teachers use learner-centered practices (e.g., involving students in decision making) as opposed to teacher-centered practices (e.g., focusing on rote learning, norm-referenced evaluation; Donohue, Perry, & Weinstein, 2003), use heterogeneous grouping practices, and encourage students to interact and work with each other in the classroom (Epstein, 1983; Gest & Rodkin, 2011; Luckner & Pianta, 2011).

Use of competitive instructional practices can also have a direct influence on student motivation and identity formation (Mikami, Griggs, Reuland, & Gregory, 2012), especially when individuals or teams lose competitions. Individuals who lose may suffer at least temporary embarrassment, and those who lose consistently may suffer more permanent losses in confidence, self-esteem, and enjoyment of school (Chan & Lam, 2008; Epstein & Harackiewicz, 1992; Moriarty, Douglas, Punch, & Hattie, 1995). As predicted by the work on social exclusion, losing in competitions can also lead team members to devalue one another and scapegoat those they hold responsible for the team's loss (Ames, 1984; Johnson & Johnson, 1985).

The quality of students' relationships with teachers also can have an impact on peers' ability to influence each other. For example, research indicates that preschool children who enjoy emotionally secure relationships with their teachers are more likely to model prosocial, gregarious, and complex play with peers and less likely to show hostile aggression and withdrawn behavior toward their peers (e.g., Howes & Hamilton, 1993). The affective quality of individual teacher–student relationships predicts students' peer relationships and experiences up to 8 years later (Hamre & Pianta, 2001), as well as the relation between students externalizing behavior and peer social acceptance across the school year (Mikami et al., 2012).

Evidence of school-level influence on peer interactions and relationships has been less forthcoming. However, school-level norms can have a negative impact on ways in which students interact with each other, especially when they reflect competitive academic standards and norm-referenced criteria for evaluating achievements that heighten social comparison among students. High levels of social comparison tend to result in students adopting orientations toward learning that focus on performance rather than mastery of subject matter, and in lowered levels of academic efficacy and aspirations for achievement especially among low-ability students (Butler, 2005). Competitive standards can also promote formation of stereotypes about students with varying levels of ability.

On a positive note, schoolwide policies and programs that accentuate the importance of students' prosocial development can facilitate the development of positive peer relationships (Durlak et al., 2011; Gresham, Van, & Cook, 2006). Social skills training programs can increase the prevalence of prosocial behaviors (e.g., sharing, cooperating) by teaching students how to recognize emotions more effectively, negotiate conflict resolutions, and control impulsive behaviors (Gresham et al., 2006). These programs also facilitate a reduction in the use of maladaptive social skills, thus enabling the formation of more functional relationships with peers (Lavallee, Bierman, & Nix, 2005; Wilson & Lipsey, 2007). Teachers and school administrators also can play a critical role in creating schools that are free of peer harassment and in alleviating the negative effects of harassment once it has occurred (Olweus & Limber, 2009). Schools that stress intergenerational bonding (i.e., between students and teachers) support the development of teacher–student relationships that can act as buffers against the negative effects of aggressive peers on behavior (Crosnoe & Needhan, 2004).

Finally, systematic efforts to enhance prosocial behavior and positive peer interactions that target classroom, school, and family processes are exemplified by the Caring School Community program (CSC, formerly known as the Child Development Project, Developmental Studies Center). The CSC curriculum provides cooperative learning and class activities designed to reinforce positive behavioral and social norms of the classroom, foster cognitive and social problem-solving, and to build classroom unity and a sense of community (e.g., Battistich, Solomon, Kim, Watson, & Schaps, 1995; Schaps, 2005). The effectiveness of the program on student behavior has been acknowledged by the What Works Clearinghouse (2007).

Summary and Conclusion

The literature offers a range of practices that can facilitate the formation and maintenance of positive teacher–student and peer relationships at school. Administrative practices that support teacher efficacy, autonomy, and emotional well-being are likely to enhance teachers' ability to develop positive relationships with students. Heterogeneous classrooms and learner-centered instruction can facilitate positive peer interactions and friendship formation. Efforts to deter negative peer interactions such as bullying and harassment should include clear messages from administrators and teachers that such behavior is not condoned, consistent enforcement of rules when antisocial behavior occurs, and ongoing discussions that focus on the negative consequences of these interactions and how to combat them. Simultaneously, schools can implement strategies to promote the development of positive peer interactions, such as frequent communication of prosocial values, use of inductive discipline to promote empathy and interpersonal understanding, use of collaborative and cooperative activities for instruction, and encouragement of students to help each other.

All of these practices are likely to have a direct impact on children's goals, beliefs about themselves, their emotional well-being, their overall sense of competence, and their identities as students that will allow them to thrive in school contexts. Understanding ways in which teachers, peers, classroom climates, school-level policies, and students themselves contribute to these positive outcomes remains an important objective for future studies in this area.

REFERENCES

Abrams, D., & Rutland, A. (2008). The development of subjective group dynamics. In. S. Levy & M. Killen (Eds.), *Intergroup attitudes and relations in childhood through adulthood* (pp. 47–65). Oxford, England: Oxford University Press.

Ames, C. (1984). Competitive, cooperative, and individualistic goal structures: A cognitive-motivational analysis. In R. Ames & C. Ames (Eds.), *Research on motivation in education. Vol. 1: Student motivation* (pp. 177–208). New York, NY: Academic.

Asher, S. R., & McDonald, K. L. (2009). The behavioral basis of acceptance, rejection, and perceived popularity. In K. Rubin, W. Bukowski, & B. Laursen (Eds.), *Handbook on peer relationships* (pp. 232–248). New York, NY: Guilford.

Ashmore, R. D., Deaux, K., & McLaughlin-Volpe, T. (2004). An organizing framework for collective identity: Articulation and significance of multidimensionality. *Psychological Bulletin, 30,* 80–114.

Azmitia, M., Syed, M., & Radmacher, K. (2013). Finding your niche: Identity and emotional support in emerging adults' adjustment to the transition to college. *Journal of Research on Adolescence, 23,* 744–761.

Bandura, A. (1986). *Social foundations of thought and action: A social cognitive theory.* Englewood Cliffs, NJ: Prentice-Hall.

Barry, C., & Wentzel, K. R. (2006). The influence of middle school friendships on prosocial behavior: A longitudinal study. *Developmental Psychology, 42,* 153–163.

Battistich, V., Solomon, D., Kim, D., Watson, M., & Schaps, E. (1995). Schools as communities, poverty levels of student populations, and students' attitudes, motives, and performance: A multilevel analysis. *American Educational Research Journal, 32,* 627–658.

Baumeister, R. F., & Leary, M. R. (1995). The need to belong—Desire for interpersonal attachments as a fundamental human motivation. *Psychological Bulletin, 117,* 497–529.

Baumrind, D. (1971). Current patterns of parental authority. *Developmental Psychology Monograph, 4,* (1, pt. 2), 101–103.

Bennett, M. (2014). Intergroup social exclusion in childhood: Forms, norms, context, and social identity. *Journal of Social Issues, 70,* 183–195.

Birch, S. H., & Ladd, G. W. (1998). The teacher-child relationship and children's early school adjustment. *Journal of School Psychology, 35,* 61–79.

Blankemeyer, M., Flannery, D. J., & Vazsonyi, A. T. (2002). The role of aggression and social competence in children's perceptions of the child-teacher relationship. *Psychology in the Schools, 39,* 293–304.

Boehnke, K. (2008). Peer pressure: A cause of scholastic underachievement? A cross-cultural study of mathematical achievement among German, Canadian, and Israeli middle school students. *Social Psychology of Education, 11,* 149–160.

Boggiano, A., Klinger, C., & Main, D. (1986). Enhancing interest in peer interaction: A developmental analysis. *Child Development, 57,* 852–861.

Bowlby, J. (1969). *Attachment and loss. Vol. 1, Attachment.* New York, NY: Basic.

Boxer, P., Guerra, N., Huesmann, L., & Morales, J. (2005). Proximal peer-level effects of a small-group selected prevention on aggression in elementary school children: An investigation of the peer contagion hypothesis. *Journal of Abnormal Child Psychology, 33,* 325–338.

Brackett, M. A., Rivers, S. E., Reyes, M. R., & Salovey, P. (2012). Enhancing academic performance and social and emotional competence with the RULER feeling words curriculum. *Learning and Individual Differences, 22,* 218–224.

Bretherton, I. (1987). New perspectives on attachment relations: Security, communication and internal working models. In J. Osofsky (Ed.), *Handbook of infant development* (pp. 1061–1100). New York, NY: Wiley.

Bronfenbrenner, U. (1989). Ecological systems theory. In R. Vasta (Ed.), *Annals of child development* (Vol. 6, pp.187–250). Greenwich, CT: JAI.

Brophy, J. E., & Good, T. L. (1974). *Teacher–student relationships: Causes and consequences.* New York, NY: Holt, Rinehart & Winston.

Brown, B. (1982).The extent and effects of peer pressure among high school students: A retrospective analysis. *Journal of Youth and Adolescence, 11,* 121–133.

Brown, B. B. (1989). The role of peer groups in adolescents' adjustment to secondary school. In T. J. Berndt & G. W. Ladd (Eds.), *Peer relationships in child development* (pp. 188–215). New York, NY: Wiley.

Brown, B. B. (2011). Popularity in peer group perspective: The role of status in adolescent peer systems. In A. Cillessen, D. Schwartz, & L. Mayeux (Eds.), *Popularity in the peer system* (pp. 165–192). New York, NY: Guilford.

Brown, B. B., Bakken, J. P., Ameringer, S. W., & Mahon, S. D. (2008). A comprehensive conceptualization of the peer influence process in adolescence. In M. Prinstein & K. Dodge (Eds.), *Understanding peer influence in children and adolescents* (pp. 17–44). New York, NY: Guilford.

Brown, B. B., & Dietz, E. L. (2009). Informal peer groups in middle childhood and adolescence. In K. H. Rubin, W. M. Bukowski & B. Laursen (Eds.), *Handbook of peer interactions, relationships and groups* (pp. 361–376). New York, NY: Guilford Press.

Brown, B. B., & Lohr, M. J. (1987). Peer-group affiliation and adolescent self-esteem: an integration of ego-identity and symbolic-interaction theories. *Journal of Personality and Social Psychology, 52,* 47–55.

Brown, B., Lohr, M., & McClenahan, E. (1986). Early adolescents' perceptions of peer pressure. *The Journal of Early Adolescence, 6,* 139–154.

Brown, B. B., Von Bank, H., & Steinberg, L. (2008). Smoke in the looking glass: Effects of discordance between self- and peer-rated crowd affiliation on adolescent anxiety, depression and self-feelings. *Journal of Youth and Adolescence, 37,* 1163–1177.

Buhs, E. S., & Ladd, G. W. (2001). Peer rejection as an antecedent of young children's school adjustment: An examination of mediating processes. *Developmental Psychology, 37,* 550–560.

Bukowski, W. M., & Hoza, B. (1989). Popularity and friendship: Issues in theory, measurement, and outcome. In T. J. Berndt & G. W. Ladd (Eds.), *Peer relationships in child development* (pp. 15–45). New York, NY: Wiley.

Butler, R. (2005). Competence assessment, competence, and motivation between early and middle childhood. In A. Elliot & C. Dweck (Eds.), *Handbook of competence and motivation* (pp. 202–221). New York, NY: Guilford.

Cairns, R. B., Neckerman, H. J., & Cairns, B. D. (1989). Social networks and shadows of synchrony. In G. R. Adams, T. P. Gullota, & R. Montemayor (Eds.), *Advances in adolescent development.* Beverly Hills, CA: Sage.

Card, N. A., & Little, R. D. (2006). Proactive and reactive aggression in childhood and adolescence: A meta-analysis of differential relations with psychosocial adjustment. *International Journal of Behavioral Development, 30,* 466–480.

Certo, J. L., Cauley, K. M., & Chafin, C. (2003). Students' perspectives on their high school experience. *Adolescence, 38,* 705–724.

Chan, J., & Lam, S. (2008). Effects of competition on students' self-efficacy in vicarious learning. *British Journal of Educational Psychology, 78,* 95–108.

Chang, L. (2003). Variable effects of children's aggression, social withdrawal, and prosocial leadership as functions of teacher beliefs and behaviors. *Child Development, 74,* 535–548.

Cillessen, A., & Rose, A. (2005). Understanding popularity in the peer system. *Current Directions in Psychological Science, 14,* 102–105.

Cillessen, A., & van den Berg, Y. (2012). Popularity and school adjustment. In A. Ryan & G. Ladd (Eds.), *Peer relationships and adjustment at school* (pp. 135–164). Charlotte, NC: Information Age.

Clasen, D. R., & Brown, B. B. (1985). The multidimensionality of peer pressure in adolescence. *Journal of Youth and Adolescence, 14,* 451–468.

Collins, W. A., & Repinski, D. J. (1994). Relationships during adolescence: Continuity and change in interpersonal perspective. In R. Montemayor, G. Adams, & T. Gullotta (Eds.), *Personal relationships during adolescence* (pp. 7–36). Thousand Oaks, CA: Sage.

Connell, J. P., & Wellborn, J. G. (1991). Competence, autonomy, and relatedness: A motivational analysis of self-system processes. In M. R. Gunnar & L. A. Sroufe (Eds.), *Self processes and development: The Minnesota symposia on child development* (Vol. 23, pp. 43–78). Hillsdale, NJ: Erlbaum.

Connell, A. M., & Dishion, T. J. (2006). The contribution of peers to monthly variation in adolescent depressed mood: A short-term longitudinal study with time-varying predictors. *Development and Psychopathology, 18,* 139–154.

Crick, N., Murray-Close, D., Marks, P., & Moharjeri-Nelson, S. (2009). Aggression and peer relationships in school-age children: Relational and physical aggression in group and dyadic contexts. In K. Rubin, W. Bukowski, & B. Laursen (Eds.), *Handbook on peer interactions, relationships, and groups* (pp. 287–302). New York, NY: Guilford.

Crockett, L., Losoff, M., & Petersen, A. C. (1984). Perceptions of the peer group and friendship in early adolescence. *The Journal of Early Adolescence, 4,* 155–181.

Crosnoe, R., Johnson, M. K., & Elder, G. H., Jr. (2004). Intergenerational bonding in school: The behavioral and contextual correlates of student-teacher relationships. *Sociology of Education, 77,* 60–81.

Crosnoe, R., & Needham, B. (2004). Holism, contextual variability, and the study of friendships in adolescent development. *Child Development, 75,* 264–279.

Csikszentmihalyi, M. (1993). *The evolving self: A psychology for the third millennium.* New York, NY: HarperCollins.

Daniels, E., & Arapostathis, M. (2005). What do they really want? Student voices and motivation research. *Urban Education, 40,* 34–59.

Darling, N., & Steinberg, L. (1993). Parenting style as context—An integrative model, *Psychological Bulletin, 113,* 487–496.

Davis, H. A. (2001). The quality and impact of relationships between elementary school students and teachers. *Contemporary Educational Psychology, 26,* 431–453.

Deci, E., & Ryan, R. (1985). *Intrinsic motivation and self-determination in human behavior.* New York, NY: Plenum.

Deci, E., & Ryan, R. (2002). *Handbook of self-determination research.* Rochester, NY: University of Rochester Press.

Developmental Studies Center. (n.d.). *Center for the Collaborative Classroom.* Retrieved August 2, 2007, from www.devstu.org/

Dishion, T. (2013). Stochastic agent-based modeling of influence and selection in adolescence: Current status and future directions in understanding the dynamics of peer contagion. *Journal of Research on Adolescence, 23,* 596–603.

Dishion, T., & Piehler, T. (2009). Deviant by design: Peer contagion in development, interventions, and schools. In K Rubin, W. Bukowski, & B. Laursen (Eds.), *Handbook on peer interactions, relationships, and groups* (pp. 589–602). New York, NY: Guilford.

Doescher, S. M., & Sugawara, A. I. (1989). Encouraging prosocial behavior in young children. *Childhood Education, 65,* 213–216.

Donohue, K., Perry, K., & Weinstein, R. (2003). Teachers' classroom practices and children's rejection by their peers. *Journal of Applied Developmental Psychology, 24,* 91–118.

Dornbusch, S. M., Erickson, K. G., Laird, J., & Wong, C. A. (2001). The relation of family and school attachment to adolescent deviance in diverse groups and communities. *Journal of Adolescent Research, 16,* 396–422.

Dovidio, J. F., Gaertner, S. L., Hodson, G., Houlette, M. A., & Johnson, K. M. (2005). Social inclusion and exclusion: Recategorization and the perception of intergroup boundaries. In D. Abrams, M. Hogg, & J. Marques (Eds.), *The social psychology of inclusion and exclusion* (pp. 245–264). New York, NY: Psychology.

Duriez, B., Giletta, M., Kuppens, P., & Vansteenkiste, M. (2013). Extrinsic relative to intrinsic goal pursuits and peer dynamics: Selection and influence processes among adolescents. *Journal of Adolescence, 36,* 925–933.

Durlak, J. A., Weissberg, R. P., Dymnicki, A. B., Taylor, R. D., & Schellinger, K. B. (2011). The impact of enhancing students' social and emotional learning: A meta-analysis of school-based universal interventions. *Child Development, 82,* 405–432.

Dweck, C. S., & Leggett, E. L. (1988). A social-cognitive approach to motivation and personality. *Psychological Review, 95,* 256–272.

Dweck, C. S., & Master, A. (2009). Self-theories and motivation: Students' beliefs about intelligence. In K. Wentzel & A. Wigfield (Eds.), *Handbook of motivation at school* (pp. 123–140). New York, NY: Routledge.

Eccles, J. (2009). Who am I and what am I going to do with my life? Personal and Collective Identities as motivators of action. *Educational Psychologist, 44,* 78–89.

Eccles, J. S., & Midgley, C. (1989). Stage-environment fit: Developmentally appropriate classrooms for young adolescents. In C. Ames & R. Ames (Eds.), *Research on motivation in education: Vol. 3* (pp. 139–186). New York, NY: Academic.

Ehrenreich, S., Underwood, M., & Ackerman, R. (2014). Adolescents' text message communication and growth in antisocial behavior across the first year of high school. *Journal of Abnormal Child Psychology, 42,* 251–264.

Epstein, J. L. (1983). The influence of friends on achievement and affective outcomes. In J. L. Epstein & N. Karweit (Eds.), *Friends in school* (pp. 177–200). New York, NY: Academic.

Epstein, J., & Harackiewicz, J. (1992). Winning is not enough: The effects of competition and achievement orientation on intrinsic interest. *Personality and Social Psychology Bulletin, 18,* 128–138.

Evertson, C., & Weinstein, C. (2006). *Handbook of classroom management—Research, practice, and contemporary issues.* Mahwah, NJ: Erlbaum.

Farmer, T. W., Irvin, M. J., Sgammato, A. N., Dadisman, K., & Thompson, J. H. (2009). Interpersonal competence configurations in rural Appalachian fifth graders: Academic achievement and associated adjustment factors. *Elementary School Journal, 109,* 301–321.

Firestone, W. A., & Pennell, J. R. (1993). Teacher commitment, working conditions, and differential incentive policies. *Review of Educational Research, 63,* 498–525.

Flink, C., Boggiano, A., Main, D., Barrett, M., & Katz, P. (1992). Children's achievement-related behaviors: The role of extrinsic and intrinsic motivational orientations. In A. Boggiano & T. Pittman (Eds.*), Achievement and motivation: A social-developmental perspective* (pp. 189–214). New York, NY: Cambridge: Cambridge University Press.

Flook, L., Repetti, R. L., & Ullman, J. B. (2005). Classroom social experiences as predictors of academic performance. *Developmental Psychology, 41,* 319–327.

Ford, M. E. (1992). *Motivating humans: Goals, emotions, and personal agency beliefs.* Newbury Park, CA: Sage.

Fordham, S., & Ogbu, J. U. (1986). Black students' school success: Coping with "the burden of 'acting white'". *The Urban Review, 18,* 176–206.

Furrer, C., & Skinner, E. (2003). Sense of relatedness as a factor in children's academic engagement and performance. *Journal of Educational Psychology, 95,* 148–162.

Gauvain, M., & Perez, S. M. (2007). The socialization of cognition. In J. E. Grusec & P. Hastings (Eds.), *Handbook of socialization: Theory and research* (pp. 588–613). New York, NY: Guilford.

Gest, S. D., & Rodkin, P. C. (2011). Teaching practices and elementary classroom peer ecologies. *Journal of Applied Developmental Psychology, 32,* 288–296.

Gettinger, M., & Kohler, K. M. (2006). Process-outcome approaches to classroom management and effective teaching. In C. Evertson & C. Weinstein (Eds.), *Handbook of classroom management—Research, practice, and contemporary issues* (pp. 73–96). Mahwah, NJ: Erlbaum.

Graham S., & Williams, C. (2009). An attributional approach to motivation in school. In K. Wentzel & A. Wigfield (Eds.), *Handbook of motivation at school* (pp. 11–34). New York, NY: Routledge.

Gresham, F., Van, M., & Cook, C. (2006). Social-skills training for teaching replacement behaviors: Remediating acquisition in at-risk students. *Behavioral Disorders, 31,* 363–377.

Hagens, H. E. (1997). Strategies for encouraging peer interactions in infant/toddler programs. *Early Childhood Education Journal, 25,* 147–149.

Hamre, B. K., Justice, L. M., Pianta, R. C., Kilday, C., Sweeney, B., Downer, J. T., & Leach, A. (2010). Implementation fidelity of MyTeachingPartner literacy and language activities: Association with preschoolers' language and literacy growth. *Early Childhood Research Quarterly, 25,* 329–347.

Hamre, B. K., & Pianta, R. C. (2001). Early teacher-child relationships and the trajectory of children's school outcomes through eighth grade. *Child Development, 72,* 625–638.
Hamre, B. K., & Pianta, R. C. (2004). Self-reported depression in nonfamilial caregivers: Prevalence and associations with caregiver behavior in child-care settings. *Early Childhood Research Quarterly, 19,* 297–318.
Hargreaves, D. H., Hester, S. K., & Mellor, F. J. (1975). *Deviance in classrooms.* London, UK: Routledge & Kegan Paul.
Harter, S. (1978). Effectance motivation reconsidered toward a developmental model. *Human Development, 21,* 34–64.
Harter, S. (1998). The development of self-representation. In W. Damon (Series Ed.) & N. Eisenberg (Vol. Ed.), *Handbook of child psychology* (Vol. 3, 5th ed., pp. 553–617). New York, NY: Wiley.
Haslam, S., Reicher, S., & Levine, M. (2012). When other people are heaven, when other people are hell: How social identity determines the nature and impact of social support. In J. Jetten, C. Haslam, & S. Haslam (Eds.), *The social cure: Identity, health and well-being.* (pp. 157–174). New York, NY: Psychology.
Hawley, P. H., Little, T. D., & Pasupathi, M. (2002). Winning friends and influencing peers: Strategies of peer influence in late childhood. *International Journal of Behavioral Development, 26,* 466–474.
Hodges, E. V., Boivin, M., Vitaro, F., & Bukowski, W. M. (1999). The power of friendship: Protection against an escalating cycle of peer victimization. *Developmental Psychology, 35,* 94–101.
Hogue, A., & Steinberg, L. (1995). Homophily of internalized distress in adolescent peer groups. *Developmental Psychology, 31,* 897–906.
Howes, C., & Hamilton, C. E. (1993). The changing experience of child care: Changes in teachers and in teacher-child relationships and children's social competence with peers. *Early Childhood Research Quarterly, 8,* 15–32.
Isakson, K., & Jarvis, P. (1999). The adjustment of adolescents during the transition into high school: A short-term longitudinal study. *Journal of Youth and Adolescence, 28,* 1–26.
James, W. (1890). The consciousness of self. In W. James (Ed.), *The principles of psychology* (Vol. I, pp. 291–401). New York, NY: Henry Holt.
Joesaar, H., Hein, V., & Hagger, M. (2011). Peer influence on young athletes' need satisfaction, intrinsic motivation and persistence in sport: A 12-month prospective study. *Psychology of Sport and Exercise, 12,* 500–508.
Johnson, D., & Johnson, R. (1985). Motivational processes in cooperative, competitive, and individualistic learning situations. In C. Ames & R. Ames (Eds.), *Research on motivation in education. Vol. 2: The classroom milieu* (pp. 249–286). Orlando, FL: Academic.
Jones, M. H., Audley-Piotrowski, S., & Kiefer, S. M. (2012). Relationships among adolescents' perceptions of friends' behaviors, academic self-concept, and math performance. *Journal of Educational Psychology, 104,* 19–31. Retrieved from http://psycnet.apa.org/doi/10.1037/a0025596
Jussim, L., Robustelli, S., & Cain, T. (2009). Teacher expectations and self-fulfilling prophecies. In K. R.Wentzel & A. Wigfield (Eds.), *Handbook of motivation at school* (pp. 349–380). New York, NY: Taylor & Francis.

Juvonen, J., Espinoza, E., & Knifsend, C. (2012). The role of peer relationships in student academic and extracurricular engagement. In S. L. Christenson, A. L. Reschly, & C. Wylie (Eds.), *Handbook on student engagement* (pp. 387–401). New York, NY: Springer.

Karcher, M. J., Brown, B., & Elliott, D. W. (2004). Enlisting peers in developmental interventions: Principles and practices. In S. Hamilton & M. Hamilton (Eds.), *The youth development handbook: Coming of age in American communities* (pp. 193–215). Thousand Oaks, CA: Sage.

Kiesner, J., Cadinu, M., Poulin, F., & Bucci, M. (2002). Group identification in early adolescence: Its relation with peer adjustment and its moderator effect on peer influence. *Child Development, 73,* 196–208.

Kindermann, T. A., & Skinner, E. A. (2012). Will the real peer group please stand up? A "tensegrity" approach to examining the synergistic influences of peer groups and friendship networks on academic development. In A. Ryan & G. Ladd (Eds.), *Peer relationships and adjustment at school* (pp. 51–77). Charlotte, NC: Information Age.

Kuczynski, L., & Parkin, M. (2007). Agency and bidirectionality in socialization:
Interactions, transactions and relational dialectics. In J. Grusec & P. Hastings (Eds.), *Handbook of social development* (pp. 259–283). New York, NY: Guilford.

Ladd, G. W., & Burgess, K. B. (2001). Do relational risks and protective factors moderate the linkages between childhood aggression and early psychological and school adjustment? *Child Development, 72,* 1579–1601.

Ladd, G. W., Herald-Brown, S. L., & Kochel, K. P. (2009). Peers and motivation. In K. R. Wentzel & A. Wigfield (Eds.), *Handbook of motivation at school* (pp. 531–547). New York, NY: Taylor & Francis.

Laible, D., & Thompson, R. A. (2007). Early socialization: A relationship perspective. In J. Grusec & P. Hastings (Eds.), *Handbook of social development* (pp. 181–207). New York, NY: Guilford.

Lavallee, K. L., Bierman, K. L., & Nix, R. L. (2005). The impact of first-grade "friendship group" experiences on child social outcomes in the Fast Track Program. *Journal of Abnormal Child Psychology, 33,* 307–324.

Lee, B., & Thompson, R. (2009). Examining externalizing behavior trajectories of youth in group homes: Is there evidence for peer contagion? *Journal of Abnormal Child Psychology, 37,* 31–44.

Lempers, J. D., & Clark-Lempers, D. S. (1992). Young, middle, and late adolescents' comparisons of the functional importance of five significant relationships. *Journal of Youth and Adolescence, 21,* 53–96.

Lepper, M. (1983). Extrinsic reward and intrinsic motivation: Implications for the classroom. In J. Levine & M. Wang (Eds.), *Teacher and student perceptions: Implications for learning* (pp. 281–317). Hillsdale, NJ: Erlbaum.

Little, M., & Kobak, R. (2003). Emotional security with teachers and children's stress reactivity: A comparison of special-education and regular-education classrooms. *Journal of Clinical Child and Adolescent Psychology, 32,* 127–138.

Luckner, A. E., & Pianta, R. C. (2011). Teacher–student interactions in fifth-grade classrooms: Relations with children's peer behavior. *Journal of Applied Developmental Psychology, 32,* 257–266.

Lynch, M., & Cicchetti, D. (1997). Children's relationships with adults and peers: An examination of elementary and junior high school students. *Journal of School Psychology, 35,* 81–99.

Maehr, M. L., & Zusho, A. (2009). Achievement goal theory: The past, present, and future. In K. Wentzel & A. Wigfield (Eds.), *Handbook of motivation at school* (pp. 77–104). New York, NY: Routledge.

Mashburn, A. J., Hamre, B. K., Downer, J. T., & Pianta, R. C. (2006). Teacher and classroom characteristics associated with teachers' ratings of prekindergartners' relationships and behaviors. *Journal of Psychoeducational Assessment, 24,* 367–380.

Mikami, A. Y., Griggs, M. S., Reuland, M. M., & Gregory, A. (2012). Teacher practices as predictors of children's classroom social preference. *Journal of School Psychology, 50,* 95–111.

Mitchell-Copeland, J., Denham, S. A., & DeMulder, E. K. (1997). Q-sort assessment of child-teacher attachment relationships and social competence in the preschool. *Early Education and Development, 8,* 27–40.

Moriarty, B., Douglas, G., Punch, K., & Hattie, J. (1995). The importance of self-efficacy as a mediating variable between learning environments and achievement. *British Journal of Educational Psychology, 65,* 73–84.

Morris-Rothschild, B. K., & Brassard, M. R. (2006). Teachers' conflict management styles: The role of attachment styles and classroom management efficacy. *Journal of School Psychology, 44,* 105–121.

Murdock, T. B., & Miller, A. (2003). Teachers as sources of middle school students' motivational identity: Variable-centered and person-centered analytic approaches. *Elementary School Journal, 103,* 383–399.

Murray, C., & Greenberg, M. T. (2000). Children's relationships with teachers and bonds with school: An investigation of patterns and correlates in middle childhood. *Journal of School Psychology, 38,* 423–445.

Newman, R. S. (2000). Social influences on the development of children's adaptive help seeking: The role of parents, teachers, and peers. *Developmental Review, 20,* 350–404.

Oates, G. L. (2003). Teacher–student racial congruence, teacher perceptions, and test performance. *Social Science Quarterly, 84,* 508–525.

Ojanen, T., Stratman, A., Card, N. A., & Little, T. (2013). Motivation and perceived control in early adolescent friendships: Relations with self-, friend-, and peer-reported adjustment. *Journal of Early Adolescence, 33,* 552–577.

Olweus, D., & Limber, S. P. (2009). The Olweus Bullying Prevention Program: Implementation and evaluation over two decades. In S. R. Jimerson, S. M. Swearer, & D. L. Espelage (Eds.), *Handbook of bullying in schools: An international perspective* (pp. 377–402). New York, NY: Routledge.

Opdenakker, M. C., & Van Damme, J. (2006). Teacher characteristics and teaching styles as effectiveness enhancing factors or classroom practice. *Teaching and Teacher Education, 22,* 1–21.

Oyserman, D., & Destin, M. (2010). Identity-based motivation: Implications for intervention. *The Counseling Psychologist, 38,* 1001–1043.

Parker, J. G., & Asher, S. R. (1987). Peer relations and later personal adjustment: Are low-accepted children at risk? *Psychological Bulletin, 102,* 357–389.

Patterson, G. R., & Bank, C. L. (1989). Some amplifying mechanisms for pathologic processes in families. In M. R. Gunnar & E. Thelan (Eds.), *Systems and development: The Minnesota symposia on child psychology, Vol. 22* (pp. 167–210). Hillsdale, NJ: Erlbaum.

Patterson, G. R., Dishion, T. J., & Yoerger, K. (2000). Adolescent growth in new forms of problem behavior: Macro-and micro-peer dynamics. *Prevention Science, 1,* 3–13.

Pekrun, R. (2009). Emotions at school. In K. R.Wentzel & A. Wigfield (Eds.), *Handbook of motivation at school* (pp. 575–604). New York, NY: Taylor & Francis.

Perrine, N. E., & Aloise-Young, P. (2004). The role of self-monitoring in adolescents' susceptibility to passive peer pressure. *Personality and Individual Differences, 37,* 1701–1716.

Piaget, J. (1965). *The moral judgment of the child.* New York, NY: Free Press.

Pianta, R. C., Hamre, B., & Stuhlman, M. (2003). Relationships between teachers and children. In W. Reynolds & G. Miller (Eds.), *Handbook of psychology, Vol. 7: Educational psychology* (pp. 199–234). New York, NY: Wiley.

Pittman, T., Boggiano, A., & Main, D. (1992). Intrinsic and extrinsic motivational orientations in peer interactions. In A. Boggiano & T. Pittman (Eds.), *Achievement and motivation: A social-developmental perspective* (pp. 37–53). New York, NY: Cambridge University Press.

Prinstein, M. (2007). Moderators of peer contagion: A longitudinal examination of depression socialization between adolescents and their best friends. *Journal of Clinical Child and Adolescent Psychology, 36,* 159–170.

Raider-Roth, M. B. (2005). Trusting what you know: Negotiating the relational context of classroom life. *Teachers College Record, 107,* 587–628.

Ricciardelli, L. A., & Mellor, D. (2012). Influence of peers. In N. Rumsey & D. Harcourt (Eds.), *The Oxford handbook of the psychology of appearance* (pp. 253–272). New York, NY: Oxford University Press.

Rose-Krasnor, L. (1997). The nature of social competence: A theoretical review. *Social Development, 6,* 111–135.

Ryan, A., & Ladd, G. (2012). *Peer relationships and adjustment at school.* Charlotte, NC: Information Age.

Ryan, A., & Shim, S. (2008). An exploration of young adolescents' social achievement goals and social adjustment in middle school. *Journal of Educational Psychology, 100,* 672–687.

Saft, E. W., & Pianta, R. C. (2001). Teachers' perceptions of their relationships with students: Effects of child age, gender, and ethnicity of teachers and children. *School Psychology Quarterly, 16,* 125–141.

Salmivalli, C., Ojanen, T., Haanpaa, J., & Peets, K. (2005). "I'm OK but you're not" and other peer-relational schemas: Explaining individual differences in social goals. *Developmental Psychology, 41,* 363–375.

Sandstrom, M. (2011). The power of popularity: Influence processes in childhood and adolescence. In A. Cillesen, D. Schwartz, & L. Mayeux (Eds.), *Popularity in the peer system* (pp. 219–244). New York, NY: Guilford.

Santo, J. B., Bukowski, W. M., Stella-Lopez, L.,Carmago, G., Mayman, S., & Adams, R. (2013). Factors underlying contextual variations in the structure of the self: Differences related to SES, gender, culture, and "majority/nonmajority" status during early adolescence. *Journal of Research on Adolescence, 23*, 69–80.

Sarason, I. G., Sarason, B. R., & Pierce, G. R. (1990). Social support: The search for theory. *Journal of Social and Clinical Psychology, 9*, 133–147.

Schaps, E. (2005). The role of supportive school environments in promoting academic success. *Center for the Collaborative Classroom.* Retrieved from https://www.collaborativeclassroom.org/research-articles-and-papers-the-role-of-supportive-school-environments-in-promoting-academic-success

Schunk, D., & Pajares, F. (2009). Self-efficacy theory. In K. R.Wentzel & A. Wigfield (Eds.), *Handbook of motivation at school* (pp. 35–54). New York, NY: Taylor & Francis.

Schwartz, D., Dodge, K. A., Pettit, G. S., Bates, J. E., & The Conduct Problems Prevention Research Group. (2000). Friendship as a moderating factor in the pathway between early harsh home environment and later victimization in the peer group. *Developmental Psychology, 36*, 646–662.

Shultz, J., & Florio, S. (1979). Stop and freeze: The negotiation of social and physical space in a kindergarten/first grade classroom. *Anthropology and Education Quarterly, 10*, 166–181.

Sieber, R. T. (1979). Classmates as workmates: Informal peer activity in the elementary school. *Anthropology and Education Quarterly, 10*, 207–235.

Silver, R. B., Measelle, J. R., Armstrong, J. M., & Essex, M. J. (2005). Trajectories of classroom externalizing behavior: Contributions of child characteristics, family characteristics, and the teacher-child relationship during the school transition. *Journal of School Psychology, 43*, 39–60.

Skinner, E. A., Kindermann, T. A., Connell, J. P., & Wellborn, J. P. (2009). Engagement and disaffection as organizational constructs in the dynamics of motivational development. In K. R. Wentzel & A. Wigfield (Eds.), *Handbook of motivation at school* (pp. 223–246). New York, NY: Taylor & Francis.

Slavin, R. (2011). Instruction based on cooperative learning. In R. Mayer & P. Alexander (Eds.), *Handbook of research on learning and instruction* (pp.344–360). New York, NY: Routledge.

Slavin, R. E., Hurley, E. A., & Chamberlain, A. (2003). Cooperative learning and achievement: Theory and research. In W. Reynolds & G. Miller (Eds.), *Handbook of psychology, Vol. 7: Educational psychology* (pp. 177–198). New York, NY: Wiley.

Smokowski, P. R., Reynolds, A. J., & Bezrucko, N. (2000). Resilience and protective factors in adolescence: An autobiographical perspective from disadvantaged youth. *Journal of School Psychology, 37*, 425–448.

Sternberg, R. J., & Kolligian, J. (1990). *Competence considered.* New Haven, CT: Yale University Press.

Sweet, A., Guthrie, J., & Ng, M. (1998). Teacher perceptions and student reading motivation. *Journal of Educational Psychology, 90*, 210–223.

Tajfel, H., & Turner, J. C. (1979). An integrative theory of intergroup conflict. In W. G. Austin & S. Worchel (Eds.), *The social psychology of intergroup relations* (pp. 33–47). Monterey, CA: Brookes-Cole.

Trenholm, S., & Rose, T. (1981). The compliant communicator: Teacher perceptions of appropriate classroom behavior. *The Western Journal of Speech Communication, 45,* 13–26.

Valeski, T. N., & Stipek, D. J. (2001). Young children's feelings about school. *Child Development, 72,* 1198–1213.

van Workum, N., Scholte, R., Cillessen, A., Lodder, G., & Giletta, M. (2013). Selection, deselection, and socialization processes of happiness in adolescent friendship networks. *Journal of Research on Adolescence, 23,* 563–573.

Vazsonyi, A., Belliston, L., & Flannery, D. (2004). Evaluation of a school-based, universal violence prevention program: Low-, medium-, and high-risk children. *Youth Violence and Juvenile Justice, 2,* 185–206.

Vygotsky, L. S. (1978). *Mind in society: The development of higher psychological processes.* Cambridge, MA: Harvard University Press.

Weiner, B. (1992). *Human motivation: Metaphors, theories and research.* Newbury Park, CA: Sage.

Weinstein, R. S. (2002). *Reaching higher: The power of expectations in schooling.* Cambridge, MA: Harvard University Press.

Weinstein, R. S., Gregory, A., & Strambler, M. J. (2004). Intractable self-fulfilling prophecies: Brown v. Board of Education. *American Psychologist, 59,* 511–520.

Wentzel, K. R. (1989). Adolescent classroom goals, standards for performance, and academic achievement: An interactionist perspective. *Journal of Educational Psychology, 81,* 131–142.

Wentzel, K. R. (1991a). Relations between social competence and academic achievement in early adolescence. *Child Development, 62,* 1066–1078.

Wentzel, K. R. (1991b). Social and academic goals at school: Achievement motivation in context. In M. Maehr & P. Pintrich (Eds.), *Advances in motivation and achievement* (Vol. 7, pp. 185–212). Greenwich, CT: JAI.

Wentzel, K. R. (1994). Relations of social goal pursuit to social acceptance, classroom behavior, and perceived social support. *Journal of Educational Psychology, 86,* 173–182.

Wentzel, K. R. (1996). Social and academic motivation in middle school: Concurrent and long-term relations to academic effort. *Journal of Early Adolescence, 16,* 390–406.

Wentzel, K. R. (1997). Student motivation in middle school: The role of perceived pedagogical caring. *Journal of Educational Psychology, 89,* 411–419.

Wentzel, K. R. (1998). Social support and adjustment in middle school: The role of parents, teachers, and peers. *Journal of Educational Psychology, 90,* 202–209.

Wentzel, K. R. (2002a). Are effective teachers like good parents? Interpersonal predictors of school adjustment in early adolescence. *Child Development, 73,* 287–301.

Wentzel, K. R. (2002b). The contribution of social goal setting to children's school adjustment. In A. Wigfield & J. Eccles (Ed.), *Development of motivation.* New York, NY: Academic.

Wentzel, K. R. (2003). Sociometric status and academic adjustment in middle school: A longitudinal study. *Journal of Early Adolescence, 23,* 5–28.

Wentzel, K. R. (2004). Understanding classroom competence: The role of social-motivational and self-processes. In R. Kail (Ed.), *Advances in child development and behavior, Vol. 32* (pp. 213–241). New York, NY: Elsevier.

Wentzel, K. R. (2009a). Students' relationships with teachers as motivational contexts. In K. Wentzel & A. Wigfield (Eds.), *Handbook of motivation at school* (pp. 301–322). Mahwah, NJ: Erlbaum.

Wentzel, K. R. (2009b). Peer relationships and motivation at school. In K. Rubin, W. Bukowski, & B. Laursen (Eds.), *Handbook on peer relationships* (pp. 531–547). New York, NY: Guilford.

Wentzel, K. R. (2010). Teacher–student relationships. In J. Meece & J. Eccles (Eds.), *Handbook on schooling and development.* Mahwah, NJ: Erlbaum.

Wentzel, K. R. (2012). Adolescents' relationships with teachers and peers. In T. Wubbels, J. van Tartwijk, P. den Brok, & J. Levy. (Eds.), *Advances in learning environments.* Rotterdam, The Netherlands: Sense.

Wentzel, K. R. (2013). School adjustment. In W. Reynolds & G. Miller (Eds.), *Handbook of psychology, Vol. 7: Educational psychology* (pp. 235–258). New York, NY: Wiley.

Wentzel, K. R., & Asher, S. R. (1995). Academic lives of neglected, rejected, popular, and controversial children. *Child Development, 66,* 754–763.

Wentzel, K. R., Baker, S. A., & Russell, S. L. (2012). Young adolescents' perceptions of teachers' and peers' goals as predictors of social and academic goal pursuit. *Applied Psychology: An International Review, 61*(4), 605–633.

Wentzel, K. R., Barry, C., & Caldwell, K. (2004). Friendships in middle school: Influences on motivation and school adjustment. *Journal of Educational Psychology, 96,* 195–203.

Wentzel, K. R., Battle, A., Russell, S., & Looney, L. (2010). Social supports from teachers and peers as predictors of academic and social motivation. *Contemporary Educational Psychology, 35,* 193–202.

Wentzel, K. R., & Brophy, J. (2013). *Motivation to learn* (3rd ed.). New York, NY: Taylor & Francis.

Wentzel, K. R., & Caldwell, K. (1997). Friendships, peer acceptance, and group membership: Relations to academic achievement in middle school. *Child Development, 68,* 1198–1209.

Wentzel, K. R., Donlan, A., & Morrison, D. (2012). Peer relationships and motivation at school. In A. Ryan & G. Ladd (Eds.), *Peer relationships and adjustment at school* (pp. 79–108). Charlotte, NC: Information Age.

Wentzel, K. R., Filisetti, L., & Looney, L. (2007). Adolescent prosocial behavior: The role of self-processes and contextual cues. *Child Development, 78,* 895–910.

Wentzel, K. R., & McNamara, C. (1999). Interpersonal relationships, emotional distress, and prosocial behavior in middle school. *Journal of Early Adolescence, 19,* 114–125.

Wentzel, K. R., & Watkins, D. E. (2011). Peer relationships and learning: Implications for instruction. In R. Mayer & P. Alexander (Eds.), *Handbook of research on learning and instruction* (pp. 322–343). New York, NY: Routledge.

Wentzel, K. R., Weinberger, D. A., Ford, M. E., & Feldman, S. S. (1990). Academic achievement in preadolescence: The role of motivational, affective, and self-regulatory processes. *Journal of Applied Developmental Psychology, 11,* 179–193.

Wentzel, K. R., & Wigfield, A. (2009). *Handbook of motivation at school.* New York, NY: Taylor & Francis.

What Works Clearinghouse. (2007). Caring school community. *Institute of Education Sciences.* Retrieved from http://www.ies.ed.gov/ncee/wwc/

Wigfield, A., & Eccles, J. (2000). Expectancy-value theory of achievement motivation. *Contemporary Educational Psychology, 25,* 68–81.

Wilson, S., & Lipsey, M. W. (2007). School-based interventions for aggressive and disruptive behavior: Update of a meta-analysis. *American Journal of Preventive Medicine, 33*(2, Suppl.), S130–S143.

Wright, J., Nichols, T., Graber, J., Brooks-Gunn, J., & Botvin, G. (2004). It's not what you say, it's how many different ways you can say it: Links between divergent peer resistance skills and delinquency a year later. *Journal of Adolescent Health, 35,* 380–391.

Yoon, J. S. (2002). Teacher characteristics as predictors of teacher–student relationships: Stress, negative affect, and self-efficacy. *Social Behavior and Personality, 30,* 485–493.

ABOUT THE CONTRIBUTORS

Stephanie Anglin is a doctoral candidate in social psychology at Rutgers University–New Brunswick. She received her BA from Hamilton College in 2010 and MS from Rutgers in 2012. Her research examines people's beliefs about religion, politics, science, and the self, including the nature, function, and origin of these beliefs, the motivated processes that underlie and sustain them, and their influence on other beliefs, judgments, and evaluations.

Steven D. Brown is the Fr. Walter P. Krolikowski Research Professor in the School of Education at Loyola University Chicago. He holds a PhD (1977) in counseling psychology from the University of California Santa Barbara. He is co-editor (with Robert W. Lent) of four editions of the *Handbook of Counseling Psychology* and two editions of *Career Development and Counseling: Putting Theory and Research to Work*. His research has mainly focused on Social Cognitive Career Theory. Dr. Brown is a fellow of the American Psychological Association and the Association for Psychological Science. He was the 2013 recipient of the Leona Tyler Award (Society of Counseling Psychology, American Psychological Association) for lifetime contributions to counseling psychology research.

Rhonda Craven is the Director of the Institute for Positive Psychology and Education at the Australian Catholic University. She is a highly accomplished researcher, having successfully secured over $7.9 million in national and highly competitive funding for 47 large-scale research projects, including 28 Australian Research Council grants. This performance is arguably

Self-Concept, Motivation, and Identity, pages 339–348

one of the strongest for an Australian educational researcher. She is the recipient of the Meritorious Service to Public Education Award, the Betty Watts Award (Australian Association for Research in Education), the Vice Chancellor's Award for Excellence in Postgraduate Research Supervision and Training, and the Vice Chancellor's Award for Excellence in Social Justice Research. Her research interests include the structure, measurement, development, and enhancement of self-concept and key psychosocial drivers of well-being and performance; the effective teaching of Indigenous studies and Indigenous students; maximizing life potential and enabling people to not just succeed but flourish in diverse settings; and interventions that make a tangible difference in educational and industry settings.

Maria K. DiBenedetto is a science teacher at Bishop McGuinness Catholic High School in Kernersville, North Carolina. Previously she was the Director of the Office of Assessment, Accreditation and Program Learning and adjunct professor in the Zicklin School of Business, Baruch College, the City University of New York. She holds a PhD in educational psychology from the Graduate School and University Center of the City University of New York. Her research on self-regulated learning, motivation, microanalytic methodology, science education, and self-efficacy, has resulted in several publications and book chapters. She previously has published with Barry Zimmerman and Dale Schunk. She recently co-authored the book, *Self-Regulation and the Common Core: Applications to ELA Standards*, to be published in 2015. The book is targeted for K–12 teachers and focuses on applications of self-regulated learning to classroom instruction.

Michael Dufner is a Principal Investigator (Akademischer Rat a. Z.) at the Psychological Assessment and Personality Psychology work unit of the University of Leipzig, Germany. He holds a PhD in personality psychology which he obtained at Humboldt-University, Berlin, Germany, in 2012. He is an alumnus of the graduate school International Max Planck Research School on the Life Course (LIFE) and worked as a postdoctoral researcher at Humboldt-University until 2013 (at the personality psychology work unit). His research deals with the consequences of self-enhancement for well-being, academic, and social outcomes. Other research foci are on the role of affective processes in implicit motive dispositions, on the assessment of implicit motives, and on the interplay between social and self-related motives.

Andrew J. Elliot is Professor of Psychology at the University of Rochester. He received his Ph D from the University of Wisconsin-Madison in 1994. His research areas include achievement motivation, approach-avoidance motivation, subjective well-being, and the development of motivation and self-regulation. He is currently editor of *Advances in Motivation Science* and is associate editor at *Personality and Social Psychology Bulletin*and *Psychological*

Science. He has edited two handbooks: *Handbook of Competence and Motivation* (with Carol Dweck) and *Handbook of Approach and Avoidance Motivation.* He has over 175 scholarly publications and has received multiple awards for his research contributions to both educational and social-personality psychology (most recently, the Diener Award from the Social for Personality and Social Psychology for career contributions). He has given keynote or university addresses in 21 different countries, and his lab has hosted professors, postdocs, and graduate students from 7 different countries.

Barbara Flunger is a postdoctoral research fellow at the Hector Research Institute of Education Sciences and Psychology. She received her PhD in education from the University of Koblenz-Landau. Her main research interests include the reasons for interindividual differences in students' motivations and their association with students' academic outcomes as well as students' behaviors, including homework behavior.

Emily Greenwood is a Robert L. and Mary L. Sproull University Fellow and a doctoral student in social psychology working with Andrew Elliot, PhD and Jeremy Jamieson, PhD at the University of Rochester. She received her BA in psychology with honors from the University of Chicago in 2013. Her research interests focus on optimizing students' academic motivation and achievement. Specifically, she studies how people perform under social-evaluative stress, in competitive contexts, and while holding specific achievement goals. To assess performance outcomes, her research applies both traditional self-report measures along with autonomic and neuroendocrine physiological indices. Currently she is investigating how and why competition has a null overall impact on performance by examining individual differences in achievement goals and physiological stress profiles.

Vera Hoorens is a full professor of Social Psychology at the University of Leuven. She holds a PhD in psychology from the University of Leuven (1990) and a PhD in arts (history) from the University of Groningen (2011). She was a postdoctoral fellow at the University of Leuven (1990) and visiting scholar at Oxford University/Wolfson College (1990), assistant professor at the University of Groningen (1991–1993), associate professor at Tilburg University (1993–1998), and visiting professor at the University of Savoie (Chambéry; 2001–2003). Her social psychological research centers around self-other and intergroup comparisons (focusing on self-enhancement biases, comparative risk perception, and comparative approaches to stereotype research) and on verbal communications about the outcome of comparisons. She has published a variety of articles and chapters in mostly social psychological journals and books.

Sara K. Johnson is a Research Assistant Professor in the Institute for Applied Research in Youth Development at Tufts University. She earned her BS from Michigan State University in Family and Community Services, and an MA and PhD in Human Development and Family Studies (with a certificate in Quantitative Research Methods) from the University of Connecticut. Her substantive research interests concern the interplay between identity development and civic engagement during adolescence and the transition to adulthood, and she has methodological interests in mixed-methods research designs and the application of mixture modeling techniques.

Lee Jussim is a Professor of Psychology, Rutgers University, where he was Chair from 2010–2013. He is the author of *Social Perception and Social Reality: Why Accuracy Dominates Bias and Self-Fulfilling Prophecy*, which received the 2013 Publisher's Prose Award for best book in Psychology. He was a Fellow at Stanford's Center for Advanced Study in the Behavioral Sciences, 2013–14, where he headed up (with Jon Krosnick and Simine Vazire) a research group on Best Practices in Science (BPS), which will continue to be active at the Center in 2014–15 (where Lee will be a Consulting Scholar). The BPS group has three main goals: 1. To understand sources and manifestations of suboptimal practices in scientific research (irreproducible results, irreplicable studies, unobtainable data, invalid or unarticulated statistical analyses and methodological procedures, misleading or overstated conclusions, etc.), 2. to empirically evaluate the success of reform attempts currently in progress; and 3. Determine what efforts, beyond existing reform efforts, are needed to produce more optimal, valid, reproducible, and generalizable scientific research.

Rachel Korn is currently a doctoral student in social psychology working with Andrew Elliot at the University of Rochester. She completed a BS in psychology from Virginia Polytechnic Institute and State University in 2010. Her research is focused on academic motivation and achievement goals. Her early work began with attempting to clarify the nature of approach and avoidance goals. From there, she continued with the examination of motivation and competence in elementary school-aged children and their parents. More recently, she has moved on to study the motivations that underlie goals, or "goal complexes," in order to determine the antecedents and consequences of goal-motive matches and mismatches. In addition, she is interested in exploring outcomes related to mismatches between motivational orientations and context-specific goals.

Jihyun Lee is a Senior Lecturer of Educational Assessment and Measurement and Psychology at the School of Education, University of New South Wales. She holds a PhD in educational measurement and applied statistics from Columbia University in New York (2003) and was a postdoctoral fellow at the Educational Testing Service, Princeton, New Jersey (2004–2006). Her primary research program has been identifying new constructs, developing innovative measures for educational and psychological constructs, and examining structure of the human mind. This has led to publications, book chapters, and scientific communications in the educational psychology as well as methodology domains. She is currently working on the structure of human interests and how it can be used to motivate students to learn more about their "true" interests.

Robert W. Lent is a professor of counseling psychology in the Department of Counseling, Higher Education, and Special Education, University of Maryland. He holds a PhD in counseling psychology from The Ohio State University (1979). He previously served as a professor of counseling psychology at Michigan State University and as a staff psychologist at the Student Counseling Bureau, University of Minnesota. His research program focuses on applications of social cognitive theory to academic and career behavior; counselor development, training, and supervision; and psychological health and well-being. Along with S. D. Brown, he is co-developer of social cognitive career theory and co-editor of the *Handbook of Counseling Psychology* (1st through 4th editions) and *Career Development and Counseling: Putting Theory and Research to Work* (1st and 2nd editions). He currently serves as Associate Editor, *Journal of Counseling Psychology.*

Richard M. Lerner is the Bergstrom Chair in Applied Developmental Science and the Director of the Institute for Applied Research in Youth Development at Tufts University. He went from kindergarten through PhD within the New York City public schools, completing his doctorate at the City University of New York in 1971 in developmental psychology. Lerner has more than 650 scholarly publications, including more than 80 authored or edited books. He is the 2013 recipient of the American Psychological Associations (Division 7) Urie Bronfenbrenner Award for Lifetime Contribution to Developmental Psychology in the Service of Science and Society. He is also the 2014 recipient of the American Psychological Association Gold Medal for Life Achievement in the Application of Psychology. Lerner is known for his theory of relations between life-span human development and social change, and for his research about the relations between adolescents and their peers, families, schools, and communities.

Oliver Lüdtke is professor of educational and psychological research methods at the Leibniz Institute for Science and Mathematics Education and the Center for International Student Assessment. He received his PhD in psychology from the Freie Universität Berlin and worked as a research scientist at the Center for Educational Research at the Max Planck Institute for Human Development. His main research interests include the application of multilevel modeling in psychological and educational research, international student achievement studies, and personality development in adolescence.

Aleksandra Luszczynska is professor of psychology at the University of Social Sciences and Humanities, Poland, and associate research professor at the Trauma, Health, and Hazards Center, University of Colorado. Her research interests concern cognitive determinants of health behavior as well as social-cognitive resources facilitating adaptation to severe illness and trauma. She is Past-President of the Health Psychology Division of the International Association for Applied Psychology, and she is the editor of *Anxiety, Stress, and Coping: An International Journal.*

Herb Marsh is the Distinguished Professor of the Institute for Positive Psychology and Education at the Australian Catholic University. He is a world-leading researcher in educational psychology. He is the author of internationally recognized psychological texts that measure self-concept, motivation, and university students' evaluations of teaching effectiveness. He is an ISI highly cited researcher with 850+ publications, 50,000+ citations, and an H-index = 122 in Google Scholar and co-edits the International Advances in Self Research monograph series. He founded the International SELF Research Centre, which has 700 members and satellite centers at leading universities around the world. He has been recognized as the most productive educational psychologist in the world and the 11th most productive researcher across all disciplines of psychology. He coined the phrase "substantive-methodological research synergy," which underpins his substantive and methodological research interests. In 1998–2003 he was awarded the Australian Research Council Special Investigator Award to fund his entire research program. In 2008 he was awarded one of the highly competitive UK ESRC Professorial Fellowships (awarded to only 3–5 social science researchers across all of the UK) to fund his research program, similar to his Australian Research Council Special Investigator Award. In 2011 Professor Marsh returned to Australia after spending 2006–2011 as Professor of Education at Oxford University, where he holds an Emeritus Professorship. His research is regularly funded by highly competitive external grants, including a 100% success record on 26 highly competitive grants from the Australian Research Council (1986–2007). He is a fellow of both the Australian and British Academies of Social Science, as well as the American Educational Research Association, and the Society of Experimental Multivariate Psychology. Professor Marsh's scholarly interests include self-concept and motivational constructs; teaching effectiveness and its evaluation; higher education with a particular emphasis on students' evaluation of teaching; developmental psychology; quantitative analysis; sports psychology, with a particular focus on physical self-concept and motivation; the peer-review process in relation to both journals and research grants; and peer support and antibullying interventions.

Dennis M McInerney studied at Macquarie University (BA), University of New England (BEd, MEd Hons), and the University of Sydney (PhD). He is Chair Professor of Educational Psychology at the Hong Kong Institute of Education. Professor McInerney has published extensively in refereed journals and book chapters, edits two international research monographs, and has written a number of textbooks, including *Educational Psychology: Constructing Learning* (Pearson, 6th edition, 2014); *Developmental Psychology for Teachers* (Allen & Unwin, 2006); *Helping Kids Achieve Their Best: Understanding and Using Motivation in the Classroom* (Information Age Publishing, 2005), and *Publishing Your Psychology Research* (Sage and Allen & Unwin, 2001). Professor McInerney's major areas of research interest are cross-cultural studies of learning and motivation, self-processes and adaptive psychological determinants of school behavior (such as self-regulation, self-concept, metacognition, learning styles), and instrument design and validation.

Benjamin Nagengast is professor of educational psychology at the Hector Research Institute of Education Sciences and Psychology, University of Tübingen. He received his PhD in psychology from the University of Jena, Germany, and worked as a postdoctoral research fellow at the SELF Research Centre at the University of Oxford. His main research interests include the application of advanced quantitative methods (structural equation modeling, multilevel modeling, causal inference) in psychological and educational research. His substantive research interests include educational effectiveness studies, intervention studies, motivation and academic self-concept.

Philip Parker is currently an Australian Research Council DECRA-funded research fellow at the Institute for Positive Psychology and Education (IPPE) at the Australian Catholic University. Philip's research uses large longitudinal databases from Australia, the United States, UK, Switzerland, Germany, and Finland, where he focuses on career pathways, personality, and well-being issues related to youths' transition from school to work or further education. Philip studied psychology at the SELF research center at the University of Western Sydney, where he received a first-class honors degree and the Australian Psychological Society Science Prize for his thesis. He then completed his PhD at the University of Sydney on the role of motivational constructs and processes in the development of teacher burnout and subjective well-being. Philip has published in a number of international journals, including *Child Development Journal, Developmental Psychology Journal, Journal of Educational Psychology, Learning and Instruction, Journal of Personality*, and *Teacher and Teacher Education Journal.* He also published a number of book chapters and peer-reviewed papers in international conference proceedings and monographs. Philip was previously a Jacob's Foundation-funded, postdoctoral research fellow in the Pathways to Adulthood program. Philip is currently an Australian Research Council Discovery Early Career Research Award holder.

Dale H. Schunk is professor in the School of Education at the University of North Carolina at Greensboro. From 2001 to 2011 he served as Dean of the School. He received his PhD in educational psychology from Stanford University. Previously he was a faculty member at the University of Houston and the University of North Carolina at Chapel Hill, and Head of the Department of Educational Studies at Purdue University. His research investigates the effects of social and instructional factors on students' motivation and self-regulated learning. He has received research grants from the National Science Foundation, the National Institute of Mental Health, and the Spencer Foundation. He has published several articles, chapters, and books including *Learning Theories: An Educational Perspective* (6th edition) and *Motivation in Education: Theories, Research, and Applications* (4th edition).

Ralf Schwarzer is professor at the Australian Catholic University in Sydney, Australia, and professor emeritus of psychology at the Freie Universität Berlin, Germany. He specializes in research on health behaviors, stress, coping, and social support. He is a Past-President of the Health Psychology Division of the International Association for Applied Psychology, the European Health Psychology Society, and the Stress and Anxiety Research Society, and he is the editor of the journal *Applied Psychology: Health and Well-Being.*

Constantine Sedikides is full professor of Social and Personality Psychology at University of Southampton, UK. Before coming to University of Southampton, he taught at University of Wisconsin-Madison, and University of North Carolina at Chapel Hill. He holds a BA from Aristotle University of Thessaloniki, Greece, and a PhD from The Ohio State University. His research program focuses on self and identity, and their interplay with motivation, emotion, close relationships, and group processes. He is currently Director of the Center for Research on Self and Identity at University of Southampton.

Laurance Splitter studied at Monash University and the University of Oxford as a Rhodes Scholar. He is currently professor of education and philosophy at the Hong Kong Institute of Education, where he is also Director of General Education. He is a renowned scholar and educator in the field of philosophy for children, and was responsible for introducing philosophy into Australian schools and classrooms during the 1980s and 1990s. He has published widely on such topics as transforming classrooms into communities of inquiry; values and citizenship education; dialogue and issues relating to identity, citizenship, and culture; and cultivating the life of the mind. He reaches, with one hand, into the murky but intriguing depths of analytic philosophy and, with the other, to the practical reality of classrooms, teachers, and learners, in an attempt to sharpen the way students and teachers think about important issues.

Lazar Stankov earned his BA at the University of Belgrade, Serbia, and PhD in psychology at the University of Denver. He worked at the Department of Psychology, the University of Sydney, Australia, for more than 30 years, where he taught courses in assessment and individual differences. The focus of his research was on intelligence, personality, and issues related to the assessment of cognitive and noncognitive traits. He was the Principle Research Scientist at the Educational Testing Service in Princeton, New Jersey, between 2003 and 2008, where he carried out large-scale studies of cross-cultural differences in personality, social attitudes, values, and social norms. Between 2008 and 2011, he was at the National Institute of Education, Singapore, and since the beginning of 2014, he is at the Australian Catholic University.

Sean T. Stevens is a Postdoctoral Researcher at Rutgers, The State University of New Jersey–New Brunswick, where he obtained his doctoral degree in social psychology in 2013. His research examines how moral convictions may develop and lead to motivated reasoning within the political domain that can result in political intolerance and create obstacles to political compromise, both between societies and within a society. He is also a member of a research group on the Best Practices in Science (BPS) whose goals include the promotion of scientific integrity practices (open sharing of data, independent replication of analyses and results) and statistical reform (a priori power analysis, use of Bayesian statistics, non-centrality parameters) in the social sciences.

Ulrich Trautwein is professor of education sciences at the Hector Research Institute of Education Sciences and Psychology and Director of the LEAD Graduate School. He received his PhD in psychology from the Free University Berlin. Prior to coming to Tübingen, Professor Trautwein was a senior researcher at the Max Planck Institute for Human Development in Berlin. His main research interests include educational transitions; the effects of different learning environments on self-concept, interest, and personality development; and the role of self-related cognitions in students' homework behavior.

Kathryn Wentzel is professor of human development in the department of Human Development and Quantitative Methodology at the University of Maryland, College Park. She received her PhD in education from

Stanford University (1987) and held postdoctoral positions at the Center for the Study of Families, Children and Youth at Stanford University and in Developmental Psychology at the University of Illinois, Urbana-Champaign. Her research focuses on teachers, peers, and parents as motivators of adolescents' classroom behavior and academic accomplishments. She has published over 100 articles and book chapters on this work and has co-edited books on academic and social motivation. She is editor of *Educational Psychologist,* the official journal of Division 15, APA. Dr. Wentzel is past vice-president of Division E (Counseling and Human Development, AERA), and a Fellow of the American Psychological Association (Division 15) and of the American Educational Research Association.

Barry J. Zimmerman is a Distinguished Professor Emeritus of Educational Psychology and former Head of the Learning, Development, and Instruction area at the Graduate School and University Center of the City University of New York. He has written extensively on social cognitive and self-regulatory processes in the learning and performance of children, youth, and adults. His contributions include journal articles, book chapters, books, and formal addresses in academic, sport, health, and music domains. He received his PhD in educational psychology from the University of Arizona and has been a visiting professor at Stanford University and the University of Padua. He was awarded grants from the U.S. Institutes of Health for his research in childhood asthma and from the U.S. Department of Education for self-regulatory instructional interventions with at-risk students.

Lightning Source UK Ltd.
Milton Keynes UK
UKOW06f0841300715

256058UK00001B/29/P

9 781681 231679